Communications in Computer and Information Science 988

Commenced Publication in 2007
Founding and Former Series Editors:
Phoebe Chen, Alfredo Cuzzocrea, Xiaoyong Du, Orhun Kara, Ting Liu,
Dominik Ślęzak, and Xiaokang Yang

More information about this series at http://www.springer.com/series/7899

Paolo Manghi · Leonardo Candela ·
Gianmaria Silvello (Eds.)

Digital Libraries: Supporting Open Science

15th Italian Research Conference on Digital Libraries, IRCDL 2019
Pisa, Italy, January 31 – February 1, 2019
Proceedings

Editors
Paolo Manghi
Italian National Research Council
Pisa, Italy

Leonardo Candela
Italian National Research Council
Pisa, Italy

Gianmaria Silvello
University of Padua
Padua, Italy

ISSN 1865-0929 ISSN 1865-0937 (electronic)
Communications in Computer and Information Science
ISBN 978-3-030-11225-7 ISBN 978-3-030-11226-4 (eBook)
https://doi.org/10.1007/978-3-030-11226-4

Library of Congress Control Number: 2018967044

This Springer imprint is published by the registered company Springer Nature Switzerland AG
The registered company address is: Gewerbestrasse 11, 6330 Cham, Switzerland

Preface

The Italian Research Conference on Digital Libraries (IRCDL) is an annual forum for the Italian research community to discuss the research topics pertaining to digital libraries and related technical, practical, and social issues. Since 2005, it has served as a key meeting for the Italian digital library community. During these years, IRCDL has touched upon many of the facets underlying the term "digital library," adapting the solicited research topics to the evolution of the issues in this domain and to the evolution of the whole process of scholarly communication. Today, the term digital library is associated with theory and practices that go well beyond its original meaning, de facto reflecting the evolution of the role of libraries in the scholarly communication domain, and of late embracing the latest questions and desiderata posed by open science.

The theme of the 2019 edition of the conference was "Digital Libraries: On Supporting Open Science." This was motivated by several reasons. The results of research are no longer just scientific publications, of which libraries have always been the custodians. Science is increasingly and rapidly becoming digital, in the sense that more and more research is performed using data services and tools available online or on desktop computers, and the products and outcome of science are increasingly encompassing also datasets, software, and experiments. Being digital, such products can be shared and re-used together with the article, thus enabling comprehensive research assessment and various degrees of reproducibility of science. Positive consequences of this shift toward open science are: accelerating science, optimizing cost of research, fraud detection, and fully-fledged scientific reward.

Digital libraries are therefore facing new challenges of supporting the digital scientific process and becoming an important element in the evolution of research outputs. Firstly, by targeting deposition, findability, preservation, interlinking, and re-use of any kind of research product, ranging from publications, to research data, to software and others. Secondly, by becoming a pro-active and integrated component of the scholarly communication process as a whole; for example, by providing support to researchers in the preparation of datasets suitable for subsequent deposition, or by enriching and linking the deposited content with data from other sources, such as other repositories, ORCID, organization IDs, recommender systems, distributed annotations, aggregated statistics, etc. Finally, by integrating with research infrastructures and e-infrastructures to serve specific research community publishing needs or to benefit from economy-of-scale provision of storage and computing capacities.

This volume contains the revised accepted papers from among those presented at the 15th Italian Research Conference on Digital Libraries (IRCDL 2019), which was held at the Italian National Research Council, Research Area of Pisa (Italy) from January 31 to February 1, 2019. Contributions touched a rich array of topics ranging from citation, provenance, and curation of scientific datasets to interlinking of research products and novel peer review practices.

To conclude, we would like to express our gratitude to all our colleagues for submitting papers to the IRCDL and for helping to finalize this volume in due time. We would like to thank those institutions and individuals who made this conference possible: the Program Committee members and the Steering Committee members who took part in the evaluation of manuscripts and provided insights helping to shape a valuable conference program; the OpenAIRE-Advance project (European Union's Horizon 2020 research and innovation program, grant agreement No. 777541) for sponsoring the event; the Organizing Committee for professionally organizing the event.

November 2018

Paolo Manghi
Leonardo Candela
Gianmaria Silvello

Organization

Program Chairs

Paolo Manghi	Italian National Research Council - ISTI, Pisa, Italy
Leonardo Candela	Italian National Research Council - ISTI, Pisa, Italy
Gianmaria Silvello	University of Padua, Italy

IRCDL Steering Committee

Maristella Agosti	University of Padua, Italy
Tiziana Catarci	University of Rome La Sapienza, Italy
Alberto Del Bimbo	University of Florence, Italy
Floriana Esposito	University of Bari, Italy
Carlo Tasso	University of Udine, Italy
Costantino Thanos	Italian National Research Council - ISTI, Pisa, Italy

Organizing Committee

Catherine Bosio	Italian National Research Council - ISTI, Pisa, Italy
Miriam Baglioni	Italian National Research Council - ISTI, Pisa, Italy
Alessia Bardi	Italian National Research Council - ISTI, Pisa, Italy
Vittore Casarosa	Italian National Research Council - ISTI, Pisa, Italy
Emma Lazzeri	Italian National Research Council - ISTI, Pisa, Italy

Program Committee

Giovanni Adorni	University of Genoa, Italy
Miriam Baglioni	Italian National Research Council - ISTI, Pisa, Italy
Lamberto Ballan	University of Padua, Italy
Lorenzo Baraldi	University of Modena and Reggio Emilia, Italy
Alessia Bardi	Italian National Research Council - ISTI, Pisa, Italy
Valentina Bartalesi	Italian National Research Council - ISTI, Pisa, Italy
Andrea Bollini	4Science, Italy
Paolo Budroni	University of Vienna, Austria
Vittore Casarosa	Italian National Research Council - ISTI, Pisa, Italy
Michelangelo Ceci	University of Bari, Italy
Giorgio Maria Di Nunzio	University of Padua, Italy
Achille Felicetti	VASTLAB – PIN S.c.R.L., Italy
Stefano Ferilli	University of Bari, Italy
Nicola Ferro	University of Padua, Italy
Elena Giglia	University of Turin, Italy
Costantino Grana	University of Modena and Reggio Emilia, Italy

Petr Knoth	The Open University, UK
Claudio Lucchese	University of Venice, Italy
Donato Malerba	University of Bari, Italy
Stefano Mizzaro	University of Udine, Italy
Nicola Orio	University of Padua, Italy
Silvio Peroni	University of Bologna, Italy
Antonella Poggi	University of Rome La Sapienza, Italy
Eloy Rodrigues	University of Minho, Portugal
Alessandro Sarretta	Italian National Research Council - ISMAR, Venice, Italy
Marco Schaerf	University of Rome La Sapienza, Italy
Lorenzo Seidenari	University of Florence, Italy
Giuseppe Serra	University of Udine, Italy
Luigi Siciliano	Free University of Bozen-Bolzano, Italy
Annamaria Tammaro	University of Parma, Italy
Francesca Tomasi	University of Bologna, Italy
Fabio Vitali	University of Bologna, Italy

Additional Reviewers

D. Dosso
E. Fabris
D. Herrmannova
P. Mignone
G. Pio
D. Pride
M. Soprano

Contents

Data Mining

Information Retrieval

On Synergies Between Information Retrieval and Digital Libraries

Maristella Agosti(✉), Erika Fabris, and Gianmaria Silvello

Department of Information Engineering, University of Padua, Padua, Italy
{maristella.agosti,erika.fabris,gianmaria.silvello}@unipd.it

Abstract. In this paper we present the results of a longitudinal analysis of ACM SIGIR papers from 2003 to 2017. ACM SIGIR is the main venue where Information Retrieval (IR) research and innovative results are presented yearly; it is a highly competitive venue and only the best and most relevant works are accepted for publication. The analysis of ACM SIGIR papers gives us a unique opportunity to understand where the field is going and what are the most trending topics in information access and search.

In particular, we conduct this analysis with a focus on Digital Library (DL) topics to understand what is the relation between these two fields that we know to be closely linked. We see that DL provide document collections and challenging tasks to be addressed by the IR community and in turn exploit the latest advancements in IR to improve the offered services.

We also point to the role of public investments in the DL field as one of the core drivers of DL research which in turn may also have a positive effect on information accessing and searching in general.

Keywords: Trends in digital libraries (DL) · Trends in information retrieval (IR) · Emerging interrelationships between DL and IR

1 Introduction

The area of Digital Libraries (DL) is a multidisciplinary research field and Information Retrieval (IR) is a research area which, amongst other things, addresses methods and technologies for accessing digital information persistently preserved in digital libraries and archives. As a matter of fact, preservation would be useless without means and techniques of accessing stored information, to find and extract useful data. There has always been a strong interrelationship among IR and DL, and one significant example of this is the major organization which promotes IR, the Association for Computing Machinery Special Interest Group on Information Retrieval (ACM SIGIR),[1] which is also one of the co-promoters

[1] http://sigir.org/.

P. Manghi et al. (Eds.): IRCDL 2019, CCIS 988, pp. 3–17, 2019.
https://doi.org/10.1007/978-3-030-11226-4_1

of one of the major international forums focusing on digital libraries, the Joint Conference on Digital Libraries (JCDL).[2] Moreover, the programs of all conferences on DL also cover IR topics, and many methods and techniques designed and developed by the IR research community are used in the design and building of DL. Another significant example of this synergy is the ideation and development of the first "online public access catalogues" (OPACs) [2,6,11], which made broad use of state-of-the-art IR methods in a typical DL setting. Thus, as stated by Edie Rasmussen in [9], "it would appear that digital library developers have the opportunity to incorporate the best results of information retrieval research".

The goal of this work is to conduct a longitudinal analysis of relevant IR research results with the aim of understanding the influence of IR research on the theory and practice of DL; moreover, we aim to identify, if possible, the topics that seem most important among those that the two areas are going to address together in the future. We are convinced that by studying IR trends we can garner useful information about the future trends of the DL community.

Hence, this study targets two main research questions:

1. Is current IR research relevant to DL?
2. Does DL research affect IR?

In order to answer these questions, we explore the recent evolution of IR research. To do so, we created a corpus containing all papers that have been published in the proceedings of the last 15 years of the ACM SIGIR Conference, one of the most relevant conferences in IR. We extracted useful information from the main text of published papers, the bibliography, topics and keywords. Afterwards, we conduced statistical analyses to identify research trends in IR and discover if there are DL topics discussed by the IR community.

The remainder of the paper is organized as follows: in Sect. 2 we present some related work; in Sect. 3 we describe the process of creating the corpus and present some statistics on the collected data; in Sect. 4 we investigate the relationships between DL and IR; and in Sect. 5 we summarize the results of our study, make some final remarks and reveal our future directions.

2 Related Work

Bibliometrics and topic analysis of corpora of scientific conference papers are quite common especially in information science. These analyses attract the researchers attention since they can offer an interesting viewpoint on the evolution of the topics addressed in the scientific areas related to the conferences.

As an example, in 2003, for the commemoration of the 25th anniversary of ACM SIGIR Conference, Smeaton et al. [10] did a content analysis on all papers presented at the ACM SIGIR Conferences from its beginning up to 2002; Smeaton et al. investigated the evolution of topics over the selected period and provided the most central author in the co-authorship graph. Five years later,

[2] http://www.jcdl.org/.

Hiemstra et al. [5] provided further analysis on papers presented in the ACM SIGIR Conferences from 1978 to 2007 focusing on other aspects such as the contributions of countries in terms of number of papers published and common aspects, such as the analysis of the co-authorship graph.

The general results we report in this paper complement the results presented in [5,10], because we present general results for the period from 2003 to 2017 that is not fully covered in the other two works. Furthermore, in order to conduct our study and answer our two research questions, rather than rely on an already populated database, we chose to create and populate our own database so as to have all the different data and metadata needed to carry out the study. Unlike [5,10] we also analyzed the synergy between IR and DL. Some considerations of interest for this further study are contained in [3], where key trends that can have implications in DL were identified and highlighted, i.e. new emerging technologies such as big data techniques on search, the growth in importance of documents containing information other than articles such as datasets, presentations, the growth in importance of other sources of data such as media and the recent broadening of technology providers of information. Other considerations have been reported in [9] where, by studying the IR research history, the synergy between IR and DL is shown and some IR key challenges that can have an impact on DL research are highlighted, i.e. multilingual and cross-lingual search, retrieval in non-textual formats, use of relevance feedback, comprehensive retrospective research and user interactive IR systems.

3 Dataset Creation and Statistics

The steps needed to gather together and organize the corpus used for the study are:

1. data collection and database design;
2. data processing and data storage.

These two steps are outlined below.

We collected all the ACM SIGIR conference proceeding papers published between 2003 and 2017 by downloading them from the ACM digital library[3] as PDF files. The collection includes long papers, short papers/posters, workshop papers and tutorials. As a result our data set consists of 2974 distinct papers.

After having built the corpus, the next step was to design and build the database for storing all the data needed to conduct the analyses of interest for our study: the general details and affiliations of authors, the denomination and location of institutions, metadata of ACM SIGIR papers (DOI, year of publication, title, abstract, keywords, ACM Computing Classification System – CCS rev. 2012[4] – categories), and lists of references for each paper. It is worth noting that the database keeps track of every change of affiliation of the authors in the years of interest.

[3] https://dl.acm.org/.

[4] https://dl.acm.org/ccs/ccs.cfm.

Table 1. Number of papers published in ACM SIGIR proceedings from 2003 to 2017 and number of active authors per year.

Year	Number of papers	Number of active authors
2003	106	252
2004	133	293
2005	138	341
2006	152	335
2007	221	482
2008	206	461
2009	207	501
2010	217	504
2011	238	559
2012	224	562
2013	210	512
2014	229	588
2015	204	524
2016	234	647
2017	255	705

We encoded the PDF files of the corpus by obtaining structured TEI-encoded XML files.[5] This pre-processing step was performed by using the open source GROBID library [1,7].

Subsequently, we parsed the TEI-encoded files by a set of custom methods to extract the raw data about papers and authors and to store them in the database. These methods were designed to allow interactive controls in order to manually solve possible homonyms amongst different authors and to detect possible errors introduced by GROBID.

After this process, we performed a manual inspection of the stored information in order to find and fix possible inconsistencies (e.g. different denominations or abbreviations for the same institution were solved). As a result, we obtained a clean database storing all the information necessary to conduct our analyses.

Before going deeper into the content analysis and examination of synergy between Digital Library and Information Retrieval, we present relevant statistics that provide a visual insight of the information within the database that clearly demonstrates the growth in activity within the IR community over the last 15 years.

Our database stores a total of 2974 papers published in the ACM SIGIR proceedings, 1155 of those are full papers and the other 1819 are short papers, posters, demos, tutorials and workshops. Table 1 compares the evolution in the number of published papers and the number of active authors. The amount of

[5] http://www.tei-c.org/index.xml.

publications increased noticeably from 2003 to 2007, then, from 2008 to 2017 there were some minor fluctuations with a minimum of 206 and a maximum of 255 papers per year.

Moreover, the number of active authors per year has been growing considerably suggesting that IR is emerging as a primary research area and that the number of researchers that choose to work in this field is growing.

This consideration is strengthened by the inspection of the distribution of the country contributions which are reported in Fig. 1 and that highlight the worldwide expansion of IR research. The contribution of each country was computed by considering the number of papers in which there is at least one author affiliated with an organization/institution located in that country. The countries with the highest number of publications are the United States, with a percentage of presence in author affiliations of 37%, and the Republic of China, with a percentage of presence of 14%. It is worth noting that located in these two countries are (were) the most active and central organizations in the research area, such as Microsoft and some universities, such as Tsinghua University and the University of Massachusetts Amherst.

4 Data Analysis

In this section we investigate the research trends in IR and the role of DL research within the IR community. We focus on the evolution of the most used terms, keywords and topics in ACM SIGIR papers from 2003 to 2017.

4.1 Most Used Keywords and Cited Terms

We analyzed the evolution of term frequencies in the title and abstract fields and the frequencies of the keywords generated by the authors in the long papers published in the ACM SIGIR Conference between 2003 and 2017.

We used the Terrier IR Platform,[6] an open source search engine which provides indexing and retrieval functionalities [8], to process the text documents of the corpus. Paper titles and abstracts have been extracted by removing stopwords (we used the Terrier default stoplist), then they were indexed and finally word frequencies were calculated.

Table 2 shows the most used words in title and abstract fields alongside the most used keywords extracted from the text of the papers of the corpus.

We can see that the most common and consolidated topics are "Evaluation", "Learning to Rank" or "Web Search", but it is also interesting to note that some topics were preponderant for a certain period of time and then vanished – a noticeable example is "Diversity" which appeared in 2010 and lasted for 4 years – whereas other topics have appeared only in recent years, such as "Twitter" which appeared in 2009 and was the second most used keyword in 2012 although since it has not been used as much in the past (as shown in Fig. 2).

[6] http://terrier.org/.

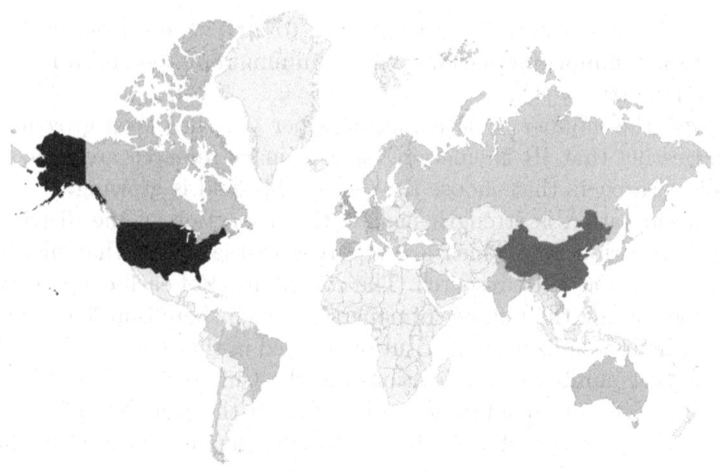

Country	Contribution Percentage
USA	37%
Republic of China	14%
United Kingdom	8%
Canada	4%
Singapore	4%
Spain	3%
The Netherlands	3%
Hong Kong	3%
Australia	3%
Italy	2%
Israel	2%
Japan	1%
Brazil	1%
Switzerland	1%
Japan	1%
India	1%
South Korea	1%
Russia	1%
Taiwan	1%
Finland	1%
France	1%
Other	4%

Fig. 1. Heat map and table showing country contributions on ACM SIGIR Conference between 2003 and 2017.

Table 2. Top 15 most used words in title and abstract and most used keywords in ACM SIGIR papers in the period 2003–2017.

	Words	Frequency	Keywords	Frequency
1	Search	4596	Information Retrieval	184
2	Retrieval	3150	Evaluation	153
3	Query	2941	Web Search	95
4	Based	2705	Learning to Rank	73
5	User	2640	Query Expansion	63
6	Results	2094	Personalization	58
7	Web	1904	Recommender Systems	53
8	Model	1889	Collaborative Filtering	52
9	Data	1754	Language Models	46
10	Users	1613	Question Answering	46
11	Document	1597	Diversity	41
12	Queries	1496	Machine Learning	41
13	Documents	1487	Ranking	41
14	Paper	1443	Twitter	38
15	Relevance	1292	Text Classification	36
...	...	...	...	...
105	...	...	Digital Libraries/Digital Library	11
...	...	...	...	...
802	Library/Libraries	71	...	...

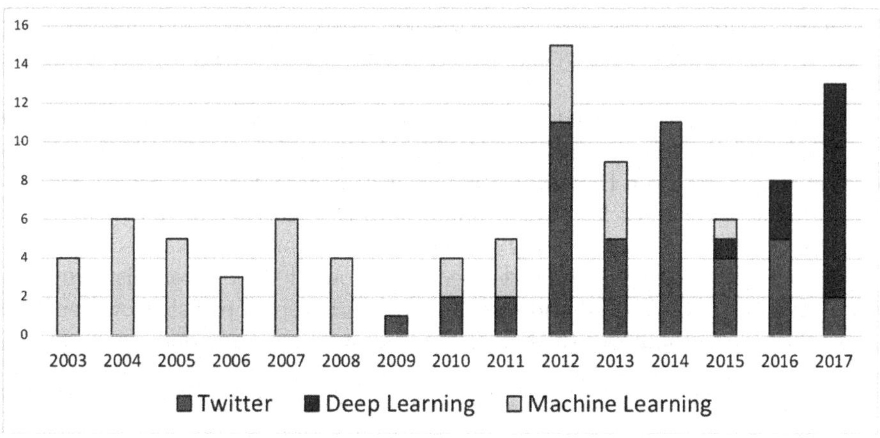

Fig. 2. Evolution of frequencies of usage of "Twitter", "Deep Learning" and "Machine Learning" keywords in the text of the ACM SIGIR papers of the period 2003–2017.

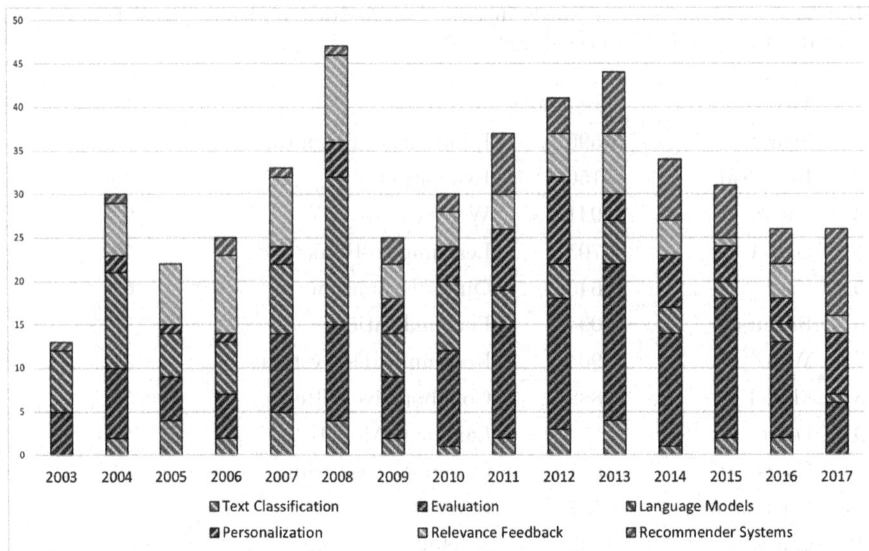

Fig. 3. Evolution of frequencies of usage of "Text Classification", "Evaluation", "Language Models", "Personalization", "Relevance Feedback" and "Recommender Systems", keywords in ACM SIGIR papers in the period 2003–2017.

Another relevant aspect is that in the initial years of the period we have analyzed, the main focus of IR research was on system-oriented topics, including data-centered and information processing aspects – keywords such as "Language Models", "Text Classification" and "Evaluation" were preponderant – whereas in later years the focus progressively shifted towards user behavior and user-system interaction – in this case the most common keywords are "Personalization", "Relevance Feedback", "Query Reformulation" and "Recommender Systems" (Fig. 3).

It is interesting to note that a crucial disruptive topic appeared in 2015: "Deep Learning" which strengthened the "Machine Learning" topic already present in the previous years, even though it was not as central as it is nowadays (Fig. 3).

The analysis of word frequencies underlines the presence of the same words appearing as the most used words in the paper title and abstract sections over all the study years; this was expected because a compiled stop-word list provided by the Terrier tool was used and not a customized stop-word list. However, this analysis is not without worth, because it supports the previous result on the transition from a data-centered to user-centered focus of the IR community that is underlined by the increasing frequency of the words "User" and "Users".

4.2 CCS Categories

It is worth noting that the results presented in Sect. 4.1 reported on the evolution of core topics by analyzing frequent words and keywords that are informally defined by authors without any specific standardization.

By contrast, good indicators of the topics that appeared and those that were left out over the last 15 years in the IR area can be derived from the analysis of the categories associated to ACM SIGIR papers. In fact all the categories associated to the papers of the ACM SIGIR collection were updated and revised in 2012 using the categories of the ACM CCS rev. 2012, which is a standard classification system. This is one of the reasons why we decided to rely on the ACM digital library, because it provides a standard updated classification system applied to all papers of all years and revised in 2012. Therefore, we analyzed the evolution of these categories, which increased the validity of our investigation, and found some particular and noticeable trends. Figures 4 and 5 show the most interesting CCS category frequencies on the ACM SIGIR Conference long papers between 2003 and 2017.

Some IR topics are consolidated and have been relatively stable in the past 15 years, such as "Document Representation", "Retrieval Model and Ranking", "Retrieval Task and Goal", "Evaluation of Retrieval Results". Other categories have been introduced in recent years such as "Query Log Analysis" and "Query Reformulation" which appeared only in the last two years, while "Search Personalization", "Search Interfaces", "Sentimental Analysis", "Retrieval on Mobile Devices", "Specialized Information Retrieval", "HCI Design and Evaluation Methods" started to play a preponderant role only in 2016. This means that IR is constantly expanding its application domain, and the expansion is driven by new and emerging technologies and changes in social lifestyle, growth both in more specific applications and in human-centered systems. Moreover, IR reacts to the effect of the dizzying growth rate of the new computer science areas: this emerges from the appearance of the use, only since 2016, of "Machine Learning Algorithms" and "Machine Learning Theory" categories.

4.3 Focused Analysis on Digital Library Topics

For the sake of our study, it is worth noting the presence of "Digital Libraries and Archives" both as a subcategory of "Applied Computing" and a subcategory of "Information Systems". Figure 4 reports that 10 long papers are classified under the "sub-tree" of the first subcategory and Fig. 5 reports that 11 long papers are classified on the other sub-tree of the classification system. Thus, we extended our analysis to all types of papers (long, short, demos, poster, ...) and we considered the presence of the "digital library" keyphrase in the abstract field. We found that the presence of "digital library" in the categories does not necessarily mean the presence of the term "digital library" in the abstract field and vice versa.

We found that a total number of 31 ACM SIGIR 2003–2017 papers are categorized with at least one "Digital Libraries and Archives" category (11 of those are long papers). Figure 6 shows the evolution of the number of papers (long papers, short papers, posters, workshops, demos) classified with "Digital Libraries and Archives" and shows a peak of 6 papers which present DL in the CCS Categories in 2007, about 3% of the total amount of ACM SIGIR papers published in that year, and a peak of 5 papers dealing with DL in the abstract field in 2013, that is about 2.5% of the total number of ACM SIGIR papers published in that year. Further investigation revealed that there were 81 authors for these papers, most of whom came from the USA and the Netherlands (as shown in Table 3). Moreover, it is worth noting that all of these authors are academic researchers, with no affiliations other than universities.

CCS Name	Level	2003	2004	2005	2006	2007	2008	2009	2010	2011	2012	2013	2014	2015	2016	2017	TOT
information systems	1	43	58	63	72	80	81	76	80	102	94	70	78	67	82	74	1100
information systems applications	2	9	12	9	8	10	16	6	8	13	10	6	7	4	4	13	135
digital libraries and archives	3	0	1	0	1	2	1	0	1	0	2	1	1	0	0	0	10
computational advertising	3	0	0	0	0	0	0	0	0	0	0	0	0	0	0	1	1
world wide web	2	1	2	2	4	1	2	4	6	3	4	2	0	3	10	16	60
web searching and information discovery	3	1	0	0	0	0	0	0	0	0	0	0	0	1	5	10	17
information retrieval	2	38	54	60	67	79	78	71	75	98	90	65	75	61	59	65	1035
information retrieval query processing	3	10	8	9	9	16	18	18	15	27	24	23	18	12	7	10	224
query log analysis	4	0	0	0	0	0	0	0	0	0	0	0	0	0	3	1	4
query suggestion	4	0	0	0	0	0	0	0	0	0	0	0	0	0	1	0	1
query reformulation	4	0	0	0	0	0	0	0	0	0	0	0	0	0	2	3	5
users and interactive retrieval	3	0	0	0	0	0	0	0	0	0	0	0	0	1	10	15	26
personalization	4	0	0	0	0	0	0	0	0	0	0	0	0	1	0	3	4
task models	4	0	0	0	0	0	0	0	0	0	0	0	0	0	1	0	1
search interfaces	4	0	0	0	0	0	0	0	0	0	0	0	0	0	5	2	7
collaborative search	4	0	0	0	0	0	0	0	0	0	0	0	0	0	0	1	1
retrieval models and ranking	3	14	15	22	17	21	23	17	22	19	23	17	12	14	25	25	286
learning to rank	4	0	0	0	0	0	0	0	0	0	0	0	0	0	10	11	21
information retrieval diversity	4	0	0	0	0	0	0	0	0	0	0	0	0	0	5	2	7
retrieval tasks and goals	3	7	15	9	9	11	17	13	11	24	19	14	12	9	16	21	207
sentiment analysis	4	0	0	0	0	0	0	0	0	0	0	0	0	0	1	1	2
search engine architectures and scalability	3	4	3	6	6	7	1	6	1	2	1	1	2	0	3	7	50
search engine indexing	4	2	3	4	5	5	1	3	0	2	1	1	1	0	2	1	31
retrieval on mobile devices	4	0	0	0	0	0	0	0	0	0	0	0	0	0	0	1	1
adversarial retrieval	4	0	0	0	0	0	0	0	0	0	0	0	0	0	0	1	1
specialized information retrieval	3	0	0	0	0	1	0	0	1	0	1	0	0	0	10	5	18

Fig. 4. CCS category frequencies on ACM SIGIR Conference long papers between 2003 and 2017 (part one).

CCS Name	Level	2003	2004	2005	2006	2007	2008	2009	2010	2011	2012	2013	2014	2015	2016	2017	TOT
human-centered computing	1	1	4	6	4	3	3	3	5	6	7	3	3	3	8	7	66
human computer interaction (hci)	2	0	4	5	3	3	3	2	3	2	4	1	2	2	5	5	44
hci design and evaluation methods	3	0	0	0	0	0	0	1	0	0	2	1	1	1	4	4	14
theory of computation	1	1	1	3	1	4	2	0	1	5	0	1	5	1	5	5	35
theory and algorithms for application domains	2	0	0	0	1	0	0	0	0	1	0	0	1	0	3	2	8
machine learning theory	3	0	0	0	0	0	0	0	0	1	0	0	0	0	3	2	6
database theory	3	0	0	0	1	0	0	0	0	0	0	0	1	0	0	0	2
semantics and reasoning	2	0	1	2	0	1	2	0	1	4	0	1	2	1	0	0	15
program reasoning	3	0	1	2	0	1	2	0	1	4	0	1	2	1	0	0	15
computing methodologies	1	13	10	14	9	8	13	13	13	18	6	3	8	3	13	16	160
machine learning	2	6	4	6	8	3	7	7	7	10	1	1	1	1	9	13	82
machine learning approaches	3	1	3	4	4	0	3	3	4	2	1	0	1	1	3	8	38
machine learning algorithms	3	0	0	0	0	0	0	0	0	0	0	0	0	0	2	1	3
applied computing	1	3	6	10	7	6	5	4	5	6	4	3	3	3	3	3	71
law, social and behavioral sciences	2	0	0	0	0	0	0	1	2	3	1	1	1	1	2	1	13
computers in other domains	2	0	1	0	1	2	1	0	1	0	2	1	1	0	1	0	11
digital libraries and archives	3	0	1	0	1	2	1	0	1	0	2	1	1	0	1	0	11
document management and text processing	2	2	4	7	5	1	3	1	1	1	0	0	0	1	0	0	26

Fig. 5. CCS category frequencies on ACM SIGIR Conference long papers between 2003 and 2017 (part two).

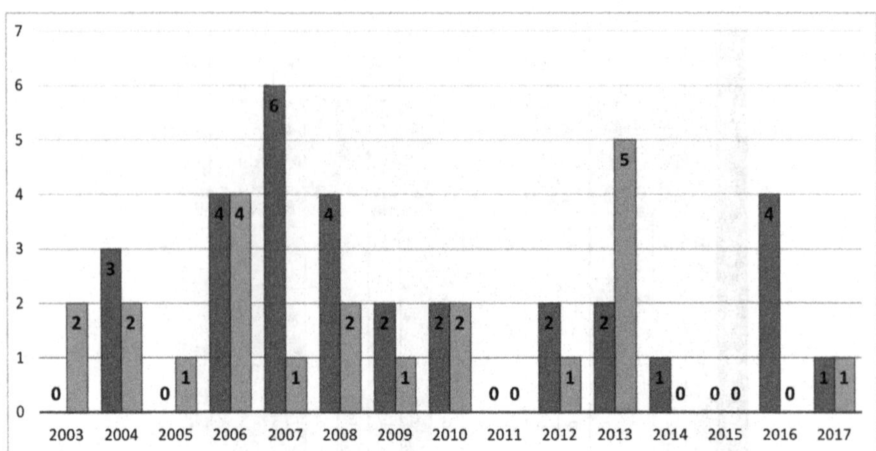

Fig. 6. Evolution of the number of papers classified with "Digital Libraries and Archives" CCS Category (left bars) and containing "digital library" keyphrase in the abstract field (right bars).

We therefore investigated what the topics of these 31 papers were and found that they mostly present, elaborate and evaluate new approaches and techniques to be applied in Digital Libraries, such as XML retrieval, natural language processing, text mining, recommendation methods, federated text retrieval, duplicate detection and methods for managing large collections.

5 Final Remarks

Discussion. In this work we analyzed the evolution of IR research topics in the last 15 years with a specific focus on DL-related aspects.

The first results we would like to emphasize are how the IR research community has been growing in recent years and how it has adapted to the most recent trends in computer science; this is clearly highlighted by the growing importance of topics such as "Deep Learning" and "Social Media" (expressed with different categories and keywords such as "Twitter" in 2012).

Another relevant aspect is the growing attention towards user-centered aspects of search, such as human-computer interaction, user studies, understanding and modeling how users search and what the most relevant tasks are nowadays. This aspect is strictly connected with the DL research field since the role of users in DL has always been preponderant, as highlighted by Rasmussen in [9]. The synergy between DL and IR foreseen in [9] can also be found in the most relevant topics addressed by ACM SIGIR papers, especially with regard to the use of relevance feedback and cross-lingual search. Digital libraries also played a relevant role within the ACM SIGIR community because they provided (and still provide) interesting search tasks and challenging collections to work with.

Table 3. Country contribution percentages on ACM SIGIR papers classified with "Digital Libraries and Archives" CCS Category.

Country	Contribution percentage
USA	23.4%
The Netherlands	20.2%
Germany	13.8%
United Kingdom	11.7%
China	8.5%
Australia	7.4%
Brazil	3.2%
Italy	3.2%
India	1.1%
Qatar	1.1%
Portugal	1.1%
Denmark	1.1%
Japan	1.1%
France	1.1%
Singapore	1.1%

Most of the ACM SIGIR papers categorized with "Digital Library" deal with: searching documents in semi-structured formats such as XML, identifying math formulas and retrieving formulas from textual documents, cooperative search done by expert users, finding translations or searching scanned book collections, federated document retrieval and using user feedback to improve search results. All these aspects are clearly related to DL since they provide wide and challenging document collections that need to be accessed and efficiently searched; in past years XML was a central format for document exchange and encoding, now RDF is growing and the use of semantics and relations between entities and documents are gaining traction. DL on the one hand provides the data and user requirements that can be addressed by IR research, while on the other hand it employs the results that the IR community produces. The relation between IR and DL constitutes a positive and factual technology transfer channel between the two disciplines.

Other aspects that relate DL to IR are user profiling and the definition of specialized search services for different user types such as general users, expert users, domain experts and so on. This is an aspect that has always been central in the DL context and that is slowly gaining traction also in IR. IR and recommendation systems are increasingly intertwined [14] as they become increasingly integrated into DL services [4, 13].

Conclusion. It is important to highlight the role of public and private investment in DL research; indeed, in the first decade of the century both the European Commission and the National Science Foundation in the USA invested conspicuously in DL-related research projects. This resulted in a growth in the interest of researchers in the DL area with positive spill-overs into other fields as shown by a growing number of DL-related papers published at ACM SIGIR in 2006–2007. In recent years, research investments have shifted to other topics, thus reducing the interest in DL topics which translated into a smaller number of researchers dedicated to this field; this is also evident when considering ACM SIGIR publications in the last three years, in fact there were almost no DL-related paper presented at the conference.

By conducting this study we realized that DL is a field which still has great potential because it has unique collections of textual and non-textual documents and a wide and heterogeneous user base with all kinds of access and search tasks. Nevertheless, in order to keep up the high level of research activity in this field it is necessary to maintain a highly multidisciplinary profile that can continue to attract researchers from other fields and that can "feed" other related research fields with challenging data and tasks to be addressed. This synergy, if constantly sustained and nurtured, has a true potential for improving DL services as well as search and access methods in general.

Future Directions. For the presented analysis we relied on a text mining approach; on the other hand, a bibliometrical approach would allow us to better investigate the interrelationships among papers and authors of the IR and DL fields, and how these two fields influence each other. This would also allow us to identify which authors are peculiar to the DL and who instead belong to both the IR and DL communities. Thus, we plan to use a bibliometric approach to undertake further analyses in the future, and we plan to extend the analysis considering in addition the impact of the public and private funding initiatives in the DL community. To this end, we could leverage on DBLP-NSF [12], that connects computer science publications extracted from DBLP to their NSF funding grants, by extending it also to European and National funding agencies.

Acknowledgments. The work was partially funded by the "Computational Data Citation" (CDC) STARS-StG project of the University of Padua. The work was also partially funded by the "DAta BenchmarK for Keyword-based Access and Retrieval" (DAKKAR) Starting Grants project sponsored by University of Padua and Fondazione Cassa di Risparmio di Padova e di Rovigo.

References

1. GROBID (2008–2018). https://github.com/kermitt2/grobid. Accessed 16 Aug 2018
2. Agosti, M., Masotti, M.: Design of an OPAC database to permit different subject searching accesses in a multi-disciplines universities library catalogue database. In: Belkin, N.J., Ingwersen, P., Pejtersen, A.M. (eds.) Proceedings of the 15th Annual International ACM SIGIR Conference on Research and Development in Information Retrieval, Copenhagen, Denmark, 21–24 June 1992, pp. 245–255. ACM (1992). https://doi.org/10.1145/133160.133207
3. Appleton, G.: Future trends in digital libraries and scientific communications. Procedia Comput. Sci. **38**, 18–21 (2014). https://doi.org/10.1016/j.procs.2014.10.004
4. Beel, J., Aizawa, A., Breitinger, C., Gipp, B.: Mr. DLib: Recommendations-as-a-Service (RaaS) for Academia. In: 2017 ACM/IEEE Joint Conference on Digital Libraries, JCDL 2017, pp. 313–314 (2017)
5. Hiemstra, D., Hauff, C., de Jong, F., Kraaij, W.: SIGIR's 30th anniversary: an analysis of trends in IR research and the topology of its community. SIGIR Forum **41**(2), 18–24 (2007). https://doi.org/10.1145/1328964.1328966
6. Hildreth, C.: The Online Catalogue: Developments and Directions. Library Association, London (1989)
7. Lopez, P.: GROBID: combining automatic bibliographic data recognition and term extraction for scholarship publications. In: Agosti, M., Borbinha, J., Kapidakis, S., Papatheodorou, C., Tsakonas, G. (eds.) ECDL 2009. LNCS, vol. 5714, pp. 473–474. Springer, Heidelberg (2009). https://doi.org/10.1007/978-3-642-04346-8_62
8. Macdonald, C., McCreadie, R., Santos, R.L., Ounis, I.: From puppy to maturity: experiences in developing Terrier. In: Proceedings of OSIR at SIGIR, pp. 60–63 (2012)
9. Rasmussen, E.: Information retrieval challenges for digital libraries. In: Chen, Z., Chen, H., Miao, Q., Fu, Y., Fox, E., Lim, E. (eds.) ICADL 2004. LNCS, vol. 3334, pp. 95–103. Springer, Heidelberg (2004). https://doi.org/10.1007/978-3-540-30544-6_10
10. Smeaton, A.F., Keogh, G., Gurrin, C., McDonald, K., Sødring, T.: Analysis of papers from twenty-five years of SIGIR conferences: what have we been doing for the last quarter of a century? SIGIR Forum **36**(2), 39–43 (2002). https://doi.org/10.1145/945546.945550
11. Walker, S.: Improving subject access painlessly: recent work on the Okapi online catalogue projects. Program **22**, 21–31 (1988)
12. Wu, Y., Alawini, A., Davidson, S.B., Silvello, G.: Data citation: giving credit where credit is due. In: Das, G., Jermaine, C.M., Bernstein, P.A. (eds.) Proceedings of the 2018 International Conference on Management of Data, SIGMOD Conference 2018, pp. 99–114. ACM Press, New York (2018). https://doi.org/10.1145/3183713.3196910
13. Yi, K., Chen, T., Cong, G.: Library personalized recommendation service method based on improved association rules. Libr. Hi Tech **36**(3), 443–457 (2018)
14. Zamani, H., Croft, W.B.: Joint modeling and optimization of search and recommendation. In: Alonso, O., Silvello, G. (eds.) Proceedings of the First Biennial Conference on Design of Experimental Search & Information Retrieval Systems (DESIRES 2018), CEUR Workshop Proceedings, Bertinoro, Italy, 28–31 August 2018, vol. 2167, pp. 36–41. CEUR-WS.org (2018). http://ceur-ws.org/Vol-2167

Making Large Collections of Handwritten Material Easily Accessible and Searchable

Anders Hast[1(✉)], Per Cullhed[2], Ekta Vats[1], and Matteo Abrate[3]

[1] Department of Information Technology, Uppsala University, Uppsala, Sweden
{anders.hast,ekta.vats}@it.uu.se

[2] University Library, Uppsala University, Uppsala, Sweden
per.cullhed@ub.uu.se

[3] Institute of Informatics and Telematics, CNR, Pisa, Italy
matteo.abrate@iit.cnr.it

Abstract. Libraries and cultural organisations contain a rich amount of digitised historical handwritten material in the form of scanned images. A vast majority of this material has not been transcribed yet, owing to technological challenges and lack of expertise. This renders the task of making these historical collections available for public access challenging, especially in performing a simple text search across the collection. Machine learning based methods for handwritten text recognition are gaining importance these days, which require huge amount of pre-transcribed texts for training the system. However, it is impractical to have access to several thousands of pre-transcribed documents due to adversities transcribers face. Therefore, this paper presents a training-free word spotting algorithm as an alternative for handwritten text transcription, where case studies on *Alvin* (Swedish repository) and *Clavius on the Web* are presented. The main focus of this work is on discussing prospects of making materials in the *Alvin* platform and *Clavius on the Web* easily searchable using a word spotting based handwritten text recognition system.

Keywords: Transcription · Handwritten text recognition · Word spotting · Alvin · Clavius on the Web

1 Introduction

Digital repositories offer a way to disseminate collections from archives, libraries and museums (ALM) on the web, where the general public can access the historical content with ease. Thus, it contributes to a world library scenario where human memory in the form of documents, books, photographs, letters, etc. is available and open to all.

The digital information is both similar and different from the original material. It is difficult to grasp a good idea of the materiality of the collections via the web, but on the other hand, completely new ways of working are available, based

P. Manghi et al. (Eds.): IRCDL 2019, CCIS 988, pp. 18–28, 2019.
https://doi.org/10.1007/978-3-030-11226-4_2

on the ability to search the digital material and process large amounts of data. These benefits widely outweigh the drawbacks and it should be a core task for everyone in the ALM sector to digitise and publish as much material as possible, as so much new knowledge for the benefits of humanity can be extracted from such collections.

This development is still in its early stages, and in this modern incunabula period of digital publications one could wish for, for example, that the handwritten material could be searched in a completely different way than is possible now. The digital repositories publish manuscripts and letters, but only as photographs of the original. Today, it is not possible to effectively translate the image of the handwritten text into a machine-readable text, in the way that can be done with printed books via Optical Character Recognition (OCR) techniques.

However, research in Handwritten Text Recognition (HTR) in advancing, and as researchers and companies work towards improvement of the HTR technology, the ALM sector must continue to publish the photographic images of the letters. This process also provides meta-data that is necessary to keep track of the material. In this regard, two popular projects *Alvin* and *Clavius on the Web* are discussed as follows.

1.1 Alvin

A Swedish repository, *Alvin* [1], consists of all groups of valuable digitised material that can be found within the ALM sector, which is unusual for digital repositories as they usually concentrate on a particular material category. *Alvin* is run by a consortium with the University libraries in Uppsala, Lund and Gothenburg at the centre, but several smaller archives and libraries also use *Alvin* for their digital publishing. In Alvin some entries contain only metadata, whereas the majority also contain digital images. At present, 163, 000 entries are published and out of those 122, 000 contain published images of the scanned books, manuscripts, drawings, maps etc. The metadata-only entries may contain unpublished images that are not visible due to, for example, copyright reasons. Among other things, *Alvin* contains tens of thousands of documents, manuscripts and letters published in digital form, but quite a few of them have been transcribed in their entirety. A war diary has been transcribed using dictation [2], and a number of documents from the Ravensbrück concentration camp have both been transcribed and translated, as in [3].

From a University library perspective, the major advantage of these documents at *Alvin* is that, due to Google indexing, their content is easily searchable on web. More people will find them and more people will use them.

There are several different repositories around the world that work with the same ambitions as *Alvin*. For example, Jeremy Bentham's archive at the University College of London has manually transcribed a large portion of Jeremy Bentham's diary pages [4]. Other archives with digitised material include, for example, the National Archives in Stockholm, which has digitised and published Court Protocols and Church Archives [5].

1.2 Clavius on the Web

Even when the main objective of a project or archive is not the publication and discoverability of the material per se, a manual transcription is often needed to enable further processing. It is the case of *Clavius on the Web* [6,7] and its sibling project *Totus Mundus*, aimed at enabling collaborative research for scholars, as well as teaching high school and undergraduate students. The Historical Archives of the Pontifical Gregorian University (APUG), upon which the initiatives are based, contain and preserve more than 5,000 manuscripts, written by Jesuits between 1551 and 1773. A portion of this wealth of material, alongside external resources such as ancient maps or computational tools, has been manually digitized and made available to the public [8,9]. Behind the scenes, scholars, technicians and students defined and developed together both the digital tools and artifacts to work with the original material, such as a domain-specific language for transcription [10] and computational lexica describing the text from a linguistic perspective [11,12]. Working within the development process and dealing with the transcription in a manual fashion was crucial for students. Nonetheless, the availability of an automatic technology for indexing and searching the digital images of the manuscript would have been of tremendous help in covering more portions of the archive and fostering understanding about its content. This is especially true for a technology that heavily relies on having a *human in the loop*, which would empower a student or researcher rather than trivialize the transcription work.

1.3 Other Projects

Several other projects work with manual transcription, often using the Omeka CMS and its Plug-in Scripto [13]. For instance, letters from the US Civil War at the Newberry Library in Chicago [14], or Moravian Lives [15], which is a collaboration between University of Göteborg and Bucknell University. However, the ALM world's way of solving the transcription issue has so far been to manually transcribe handwritten text in various ways. Manual transcription provides satisfactory results, but is rather too time consuming. Extremely few files have been made searchable through automatic transcription. The Monk system [16] is an example, but it can still be considered as a research project and not a generally useful way to automatically transcribe handwritten texts. The READ project [17] with the Transkribus software is a European project that used advanced HTR algorithms and has been used, for example, in transcribing Jeremy Bentham's archives. It has shown significant results whenever it is possible to train on a uniform material.

The amount of handwritten texts available in libraries and archives is enormous, and it will take a very long time before this material is transcribed and made searchable. However, large scale transcription can be accelerated potentially using holistic HTR techniques incorporated with expert user feedback, which is the main focus of this work.

This paper is organized as follows. Section 2 discusses related work on handwritten text transcription. Section 3 explains the proposed word spotting based HTR method in detail. Section 4 demonstrate preliminary results of using the word spotter on documents images from *Alvin* and *Clavius on the Web*. Section 5 concludes the paper.

2 Background

Transcription of historical handwritten documents is a tedious and time consuming task that requires skilled experts to manually transcribe lengthy texts. A technology driven alternative to manual transcription is to perform fully automatic transcription using HTR techniques that offer a rather cost-efficient solution. However, fully automatic transcription is often unreliable due to lack of validation of results [18], but it can be improved to deliver the desired level of accuracy by involving the user in the loop. This is often known as semi-automatic or semi-supervised transcription that is popularly used these days [18–22].

An interesting transcription technique, Computer Assisted Transcription of Text Images (CATTI), was proposed in [22] which is based on an interactive HTR technique for fast, accurate and low cost transcription. In general, it initiates an iterative interactive process between the CATTI system and the end-user for an input text line image to be transcribed. The transcription system hence generate significantly improved transcriptions by involving the end-user for providing corrective feedback.

A computer assisted handwritten text transcription approach was proposed in [20] that is based on image and language models from partially supervised data where the transcription algorithm employs Hidden Markov Models (HMMs) for text image modeling and n-gram models for language modeling. GIDOC (Gimp-based Interactive transcription of old text Documents) [23] system prototype has recently implemented this approach where a user navigates through transcription errors that are estimated using confidence measures generated using word graphs.

An active learning based line-by-line handwritten text transcription approach proposed in [21] continuously re-trains a transcription system to interact with an end-user to efficiently transcribe each line. In general, the performance of the above discussed transcription systems ([20–22]) highly depend on accurate detection and extraction of text lines in each document page. However, text line detection in old handwritten documents is a daunting task, that requires development of advanced line detection methods.

The Transcribe Bentham project [24] in collaboration with the READ project [17] is focused on generating handwritten text transcriptions using advanced HTR methods, where a significant amount of documents from Jeremy Bentham's collection have been transcribed using crowdsourcing that are used as training data for their machine learning based HTR algorithms. This innovative transcription technology is available through the Transkribus platform [25]. Similarly, the aforementioned Monk system [16] employs a HTR based word recognition system where volunteers help in labeling individual words through crowdsourcing and hence help in generating the training data. However, such systems have limited applicability in a real world scenarios where pre-transcribed documents are not available to train a machine learning algorithm.

This work presents a segmentation-free word spotting algorithm, inspired from [26], for fast, efficient and reliable transcription of handwritten documents with little human effort, and is discussed in detail in the following section.

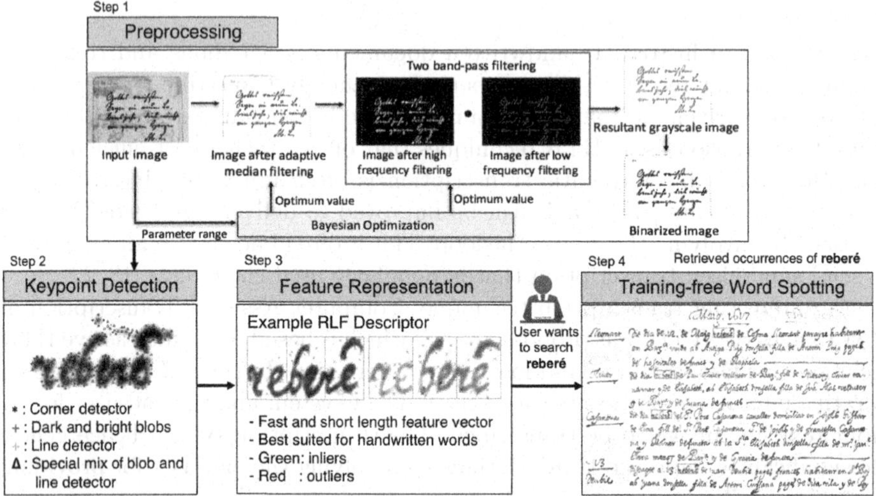

Fig. 1. General HTR pipeline involves efficient document preprocessing, keypoint detection, and feature representation before performing word spotting. If a user is interested in searching a word (say, *reberé*), all its occurrences on the document pages is retrieved as a result. (Color figure online)

3 Methodology

A training-free and segmentation-free word spotting approach towards document transcription is discussed where three important steps are formulated, as highlighted in Fig. 1. To begin with, in order to improve readability of poorly degraded manuscripts, an automatic document binarisation method was introduced in the previous work [27], which is based on two bandpass filtering approach for noise removal. With the help of Bayesian optimisation [28], best combination of hyperparameters are inferred by comparing the input image with its noise-free replica. This in turn generates an almost clean document image, free from noise such as due to bleed-through, contrast variations, wrinkles, faded ink etc. The reader is referred to *Step 1* of Fig. 1 for details on the preprocessing approach.

In general, the word spotter makes use of computer vision techniques for matching key points of the query word and a sliding window for fast recognition of words. A combination of four different types of keypoint detectors was used (similar to [26]) to capture a variety of features that represent a handwritten text, and the keypoint detectors consisted of lines, corners and blobs (refer to *Step 2* of Fig. 1).

Recently, a Radial Line Fourier (RLF) descriptor with a short feature vector of 32 dimensions for feature representation of handwritten text has been proposed by the authors in [29]. Typically, existing feature descriptors such as SIFT, SURF, etc. inhibit invariant properties that amplify noise in degraded document images [30,31], and are found to be unsuitable for representing complex handwritten words with high levels of degradations. This inspired the authors to design the RLF descriptor to capture important properties of a handwritten text, and has been presented as *Step 3* in Fig. 1.

Using the RLF descriptor, the word spotting problem is reduced to a much faster word search problem, and referring to *Step 4* of Fig. 1, word spotting is performed as follows. The proposed system generates a document page query where a user is asked to mark a query word using a drag-and-drop feature that generates a rectangle bounding box (red in color). Furthermore, the algorithm automatically finds the best fitting rectangle (green in color) to perfectly encapsulate the word, and extracts the word as a result.

The words are typically partitioned into several parts, and a part-based preconditioner matching [29] is performed to avoid confusion between similar words and reduce false positives. This is because parts of the retrieved words may be similar to some part of the query word, or a word may share several characters with other words, and hence generate false positives [30].

The partitioning step is followed by a nearest neighbor search which is performed in an optimal sliding window within the subgroups of the detected keypoints. The extent of the matching points in a word is thus computed using a simple keypoint matching algorithm, that also captures words that are partially outside the sliding window. The resultant correspondences between the query word and the retrieved word needs further refinement due to the presence of potential outliers. To do so, a deterministic preconditioner [32] is used, and the matching algorithm efficiently captures complex variations in handwriting. An advantage of the proposed method is that it is completely learning-free, which means no prior knowledge about the text is required and word searching can be performed on a non-annotated dataset as well. *Alvin* and *Clavius on the Web* are an excellent use case to test the effectiveness of the proposed word spotter, and is demonstrated in the next section.

4 Experimental Framework

This section emphasize on the overall experimental framework of the proposed word spotter, and qualitatively evaluates the proposed method. The preliminary tests are performed on the images from the *Alvin* repository and the *Clavius on the Web*.

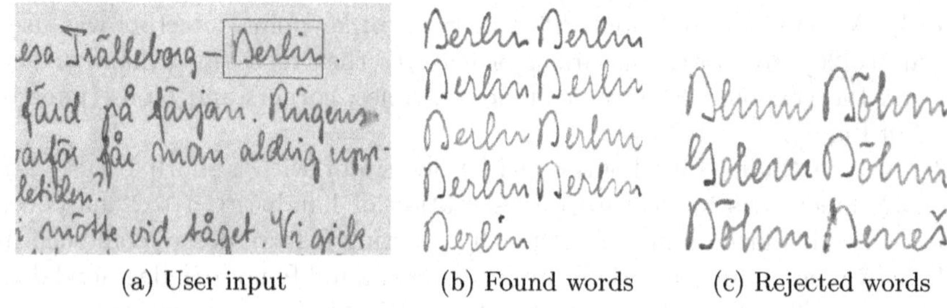

Fig. 2. Word spotting results for the query word *Berlin* for an example paper by a Swedish poet and novelist, *Karin Boye*, obtained from the *Alvin* portal [1]. Figure best viewed in colors. (Color figure online)

Figure 2 presents word spotting results on using a sample digitised image obtained from the *Alvin* portal of a travel diary by a Swedish poet and novelist, *Karin Boye*. In total, 15 pages by *Karin Boye* have been taken into account that belong to the period 1905–1943, written in Swedish language, and archived at

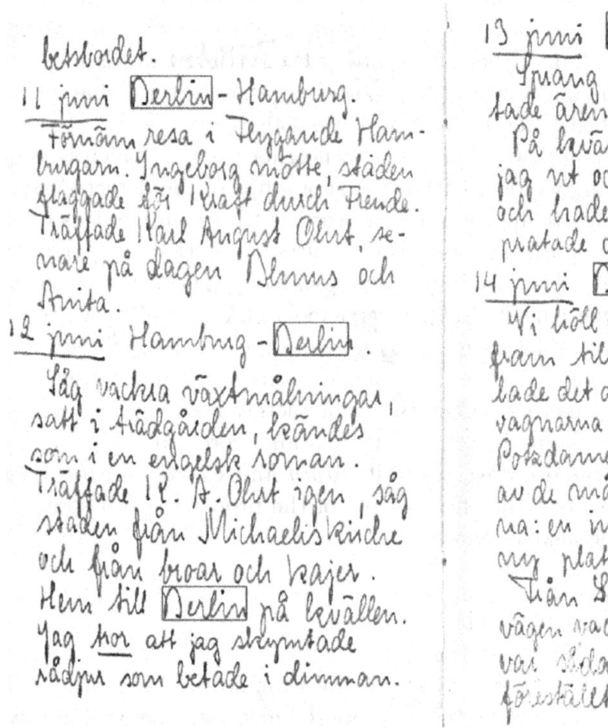

Fig. 3. Qualitative results obtained from the proposed training-free word spotter for the query word *Berlin*, for papers by *Karin Boye*, obtained from the *Alvin* portal [1]. Figure best viewed in colors. (Color figure online)

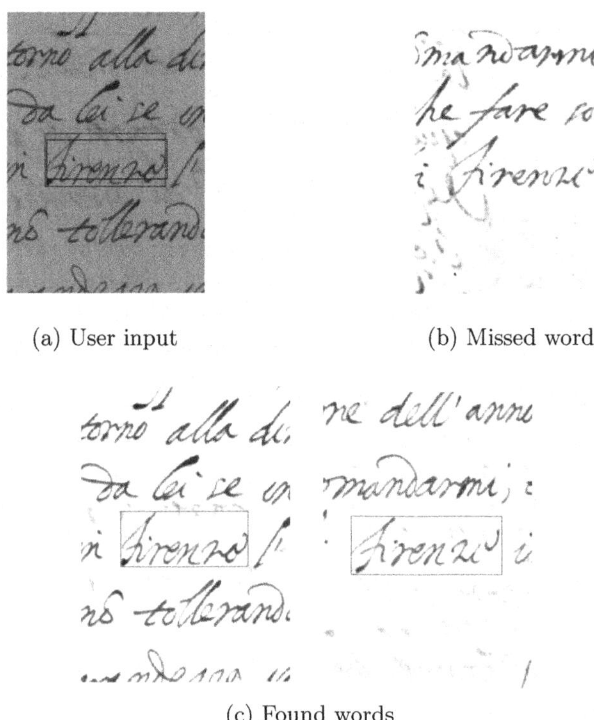

(a) User input

(b) Missed word

(c) Found words

Fig. 4. Word spotting results for the query word *Firenze*, searching two letters written by *Galileo Galilei* to *Christopher Clavius*, obtained from the *Clavius on the web* portal [8]. The marked word (a) is found along with another occurrence of the same word (c), while one word is missed (b) due to the bleed-through problem. Figure best viewed in colors. (Color figure online)

Uppsala University Library. Referring to Fig. 2a, a query word *Berlin* has been marked by a user and denoted using red bounding box. The extent of the query word *Berlin* is automatically corrected by the algorithm, so that the word is perfectly encapsulated, and is represented using green bounding box. Figure 2b highlights several instances of the word *Berlin* found in the pages by *Karin Boye*, and it can be seen that all these founds words have been accurately identified by the proposed word spotter. Figure 2c presents some sample words that are very similar in characteristic with the word *Berlin*, and have been rejected by the word spotter (as intended). Furthermore, Fig. 3 presents some qualitative results obtained from the proposed training-free word spotter, with retrieved instances of the query word *Berlin* represented in blue bounding box.

The next set of experiments are performed on the digitised images of letters from the correspondence of *Christopher Clavius*, that are preserved by the Historical Archives of the Pontifical Gregorian University (Refer to the *Clavius on the Web* project [8]). For example, Fig. 4 highlights word spotting results for letters written by *Galileo Galilei* in Florence 1588, to *Christopher Clavius* in Rome. In total, pages of two letters by *Galilei* have been taken into account. In Fig. 4a, a query word *firenze* has been marked by a user (in red bounding box), automatically corrected to perfectly fit the word in green bounding box. Figure 4c presents the retrieved instances of the query word *firenze* on 2 different letters, which have been accurately identified by the proposed word spotter. Interestingly, no word output has been rejected by the word spotter. However, there has been found an instance where the query word is missed by the word spotter due to high level of bleed-through in the document, and has been presented in Fig. 4c. This needs to be further investigated, and proposed word spotter can be further improved in future work. Usually, some amount of garbage words are found and we are currently investigating techniques to decrease the amount of such words that would only be irritating for the user. In the presented cases the algorithm was able to remove all such words, but unfortunately they are quite common, especially for shorter words. The words chosen here were names of cities as it belongs to the class of information usually interesting for historians and other users.

5 Conclusion

This paper presented a training-free word spotting method to facilitate fast, accurate and reliable transcription of historical handwritten documents available in digital repositories (such as *Alvin* and *Clavius on the Web* project). The word spotter efficiently finds multiple occurrences of a query word on-the-fly in a collection of historical document images. The preliminary experiments on sample images from *Alvin* and *Clavius on the Web* demonstrate the effectiveness of the proposed word spotter.

As future work, the aim is to develop a state-of-the-art comprehensive transcription tool to accelerate the time consuming transcription process using advanced HTR technology, incorporated with expert user feedback in the loop. The word spotting algorithm will in turn serve as a handwritten word search engine, similar to a Google for handwriting, where a user can search for a word query in historical archives in real-time.

Acknowledgment. This work was supported by the Swedish strategic research programme eSSENCE and the Riksbankens Jubileumsfond (Dnr NHS14-2068:1).

References

1. http://www.alvin-portal.org/ (2017)
2. http://urn.kb.se/resolve?urn=urn:nbn:se:alvin:portal:record-12537/
3. http://urn.kb.se/resolve?urn=urn:nbn:se:alvin:portal:record-100958
4. http://ucl.ac.uk/library/special-collections/a-z/ben-tham
5. https://sok.riksarkivet.se/digitala-forskarsalen
6. Abrate, M., et al.: Sharing cultural heritage: the clavius on the web project. In: LREC, pp. 627–634 (2014)

7. Pedretti, I., et al.: The clavius on the web project: digitization, annotation and visualization of early modern manuscripts. In: Proceedings of the Third AIUCD Annual Conference on Humanities and Their Methods in the Digital Ecosystem, p. 11. ACM (2014)
8. http://claviusontheweb.it
9. http://www.totusmundus.it
10. Valsecchi, F., Abrate, M., Bacciu, C., Piccini, S., Marchetti, A.: Text encoder and annotator: an all-in-one editor for transcribing and annotating manuscripts with RDF. In: Sack, H., Rizzo, G., Steinmetz, N., Mladenić, D., Auer, S., Lange, C. (eds.) ESWC 2016. LNCS, vol. 9989, pp. 399–407. Springer, Cham (2016). https://doi.org/10.1007/978-3-319-47602-5_52
11. Piccini, S., et al.: When traditional ontologies are not enough: modelling and visualizing dynamic ontologies in semantic-based access to texts. In: Digital Humanities 2016: Conference Abstracts, Jagiellonian University and Pedagogical University, Kraków (2016)
12. Piccini, S., Bellandi, A., Benotto, G.: Formalizing and querying a diachronic termino-ontological resource: the clavius case study. In: Digital Humanities 2016. From Digitization to Knowledge 2016: Resources and Methods for Semantic Processing of Digital Works/Texts, Proceedings of the Workshop, Krakow, Poland, 11 July 2016, pp. 38–41, no. 126. Linköping University Electronic Press (2016)
13. http://scripto.org/
14. https://publications.newberry.org/digital/mms-transcribe/index
15. http://moravian-lives.org/1
16. http://www.ai.rug.nl/~lambert/Monk-collections-english.html
17. http://read.transkribus.eu/
18. Romero, V., Bosch, V., Hernández, C., Vidal, E., Sánchez, J.A.: A historical document handwriting transcription end-to-end system. In: Alexandre, L.A., Salvador Sánchez, J., Rodrigues, J.M.F. (eds.) IbPRIA 2017. LNCS, vol. 10255, pp. 149–157. Springer, Cham (2017). https://doi.org/10.1007/978-3-319-58838-4_17
19. Terrades, O.R., Toselli, A.H., Serrano, N., Romero, V., Vidal, E., Juan, A.: Interactive layout analysis and transcription systems for historic handwritten documents. In: 10th ACM Symposium on Document Engineering, pp. 219–222 (2010)
20. Serrano, N., Pérez, D., Sanchis, A., Juan, A.: Adaptation from partially supervised handwritten text transcriptions. In: Proceedings of the 2009 International Conference on Multimodal Interfaces, ICMI-MLMI 2009, pp. 289–292. ACM, New York (2009)
21. Serrano, N., Giménez, A., Sanchis, A., Juan, A.: Active learning strategies for handwritten text transcription. In: International Conference on Multimodal Interfaces and the Workshop on Machine Learning for Multimodal Interaction, ICMI-MLMI 2010, pp. 48:1–48:4. ACM, New York (2010)
22. Romero, V., Toselli, A.H., Vidal, E.: Multimodal Interactive Handwritten Text Transcription, vol. 80. World Scientific, Singapore (2012)
23. http://prhlt.iti.es/projects/handwritten/idoc/content.php?page=gidoc.php
24. Moyle, M., Tonra, J., Wallace, V.: Manuscript transcription by crowdsourcing: transcribe Bentham. Liber Q. **20**(3–4), 347–356 (2011)
25. http://transkribus.eu/Transkribus/
26. Hast, A., Fornés, A.: A segmentation-free handwritten word spotting approach by relaxed feature matching. In: 2016 12th IAPR Workshop on Document Analysis Systems (DAS), pp. 150–155. IEEE (2016)

27. Vats, E., Hast, A., Singh, P.: Automatic document image binarization using Bayesian optimization. In: Proceedings of the 4th International Workshop on Historical Document Imaging and Processing, pp. 89–94. ACM (2017)
28. Shahriari, B., Swersky, K., Wang, Z., Adams, R.P., De Freitas, N.: Taking the human out of the loop: a review of Bayesian optimization. Proc. IEEE **104**(1), 148–175 (2016)
29. Hast, A., Vats, E.: Radial line Fourier descriptor for historical handwritten text representation. In: 26th International Conference on Computer Graphics, Visualization and Computer Vision (2018)
30. Zagoris, K., Pratikakis, I., Gatos, B.: Unsupervised word spotting in historical handwritten document images using document-oriented local features. IEEE Trans. Image Process. **26**(8), 4032–4041 (2017)
31. Leydier, Y., Ouji, A., LeBourgeois, F., Emptoz, H.: Towards an omnilingual word retrieval system for ancient manuscripts. Pattern Recognit. **42**(9), 2089–2105 (2009)
32. Hast, A., Marchetti, A.: An efficient preconditioner and a modified RANSAC for fast and robust feature matching. In: WSCG 2012 (2012)

Transparency in Keyword Faceted Search: An Investigation on Google Shopping

Vittoria Cozza[1(✉)], Van Tien Hoang[2], Marinella Petrocchi[3], and Rocco De Nicola[2]

[1] Department of Information Engineering, University of Padua, Padua, Italy
covitti@dei.unipd.it

[2] IMT School for Advanced Studies, Lucca, Italy
{vantien.hoang,rocco.denicola}@imtlucca.it

[3] IIT Institute of Informatics and Telematics, National Research Council (CNR), Pisa, Italy
marinella.petrocchi@iit.cnr.it

Abstract. The most popular e-commerce search engines allow the user to run a keyword search, to find relevant results and to narrow down the results by mean of filters. The engines can also keep track of data and activities of the users, to provide personalized content, thus filtering automatically out a part of the results. Issues occur when personalization is not transparent and interferes with the user choices. Indeed, it has been noticed that, in some cases, a different ordering of search results is shown to different users. This becomes particularly critical when search results are associated with prices. Changing the order of search results according to prices is known as price steering. This study investigates if and how price steering exists, considering queries on Google Shopping by users searching from different geographic locations, distinguishable by their values of Gross Domestic Product.

The results confirm that products belonging to specific categories (e.g., electronic devices and apparel) are shown to users according to different prices orderings, and the prices in the results list differ, on average, in a way that depends on users' location. All results are validated through statistical tests.

Keywords: Keyword faceted search · Information retrieval · Personalisation · Price steering · Automatic browser interactions · Permutation tests

1 Introduction

Popular e-commerce websites, such as *Amazon Marketplace*, *eBay* and *Google Shopping*, offer a window to thousands of merchants, providing products and services to millions of potential buyers [25,26].

Some of the most popular e-commerce websites let users search for products by simply issuing a keyword search. Then, a number of filters can be activated

P. Manghi et al. (Eds.): IRCDL 2019, CCIS 988, pp. 29–43, 2019.
https://doi.org/10.1007/978-3-030-11226-4_3

to constraint the search results. Such filters are usually defined over a number of attributes of the products, like the vendor, the brand, the size, and the price range. The filters allow to narrow the results list, and, together with characteristics of the users, such as their behavior, the location they search from, and the data on their profiles, allow to obtain a personalised set of items as the outcome of the search.

The dark side of personalization relies however in the fact that filters can be activated, or changed, without the user's awareness and consent. In this case, the search engine acts in a *not transparent* way. A recent work in [24] defines different kinds of discrimination possibly enacted by search engines, among the others the *user bias*, taking place when the values of some of the attributes that characterise the users, e.g., their race or gender, influence the results presented to them. Consequences of lack of transparency and bias are, e.g., to hide potentially interesting products [22], give relevance to some news with respect to others [7], expose different prices for the same product, depending, e.g., on the characteristics of the user making the search [18], and even reveal users' private information [4]. Recently, independent developers have started to design tools to avoid part of such consequences. As examples, there exist tools that remove users' personal information when sending an online request[1], escape from echo chambers[2], increase transparency of personalization algorithms[3].

This work considers the possible hidden actuation of a price filter by the search engines, based on the geographical location of the user that makes the research. One of the possible way in which such a filter can be actuated is to change the order of the results shown to the users according to their prices. This practice is known in the literature as *price steering* [12].

In particular, this study investigates if, and to what extent, the practice of price steering is actuated with respect to users in countries characterised by different Gross Domestic Product (GDP) values.

To minimise possible noise caused by different factors, the experiments do not consider user search behavior but only search location, based on the IP address of the users. The experiments are launched on Google Shopping US. Indeed, Google is well known for tracking users and providing them with personalised services (e.g., target advertising)[4]. Google Shopping let users perform Keyword and Facet Search to explore a large structured data collection: the retail products.

Google Shopping both associates attributes to the products and considers the information of the users' profiles to provide personalized results. Aiming at analysing if an untransparent match between products attributes and users' profiles is actually exploited, we collect the list of search results from different users in three distinct cities of three different countries. Given past literature results, highlighting the user' habits of mainly focusing on results that appear first (see, e.g., [11]), the analysis is limited to the products shown in the first

[1] http://www.debiasyourself.org/.
[2] https://www.escapeyourbubble.com/.
[3] https://facebook.tracking.exposed/.
[4] https://www.google.com/retail/shopping-campaigns/.

page of Google Shopping, corresponding to 40 items. Statistics on our results are computed by considering the top 3 and the top 10 items. Two kinds of outcome are taken into account: (i) the order in which the results are shown, in terms of prices, with respect to an ideal list where the prices are shown from the most to the least expensive ones, and (ii) the average prices shown in the results list. Both metrics lead to significant results. The main highlights of this work are as follows:

- when users search from US, Google Shopping US tends to show products ordered from the most to the least expensive, differently from searches from India and Philippines;
- considering the product category "electronic devices", and relying on an ideal list of results where the results are shown from the most to the least expensive one, the order of the electronic products shown to users searching from US is the most similar to that of the ideal list;
- the average price of the top ten electronic devices shown to users searching from US is lower than that for Philippines and India;
- considering the product category "body care", and still relying on the ideal list of results, the order of products shown to users searching from Philippines is the most similar to that of the ideal list;
- for the "body care" products category, the average price for products shown to users searching from Philippines is higher than that shown to users searching from US;

The results of the experiments are validated by means of statistical tests. To pave the way for further evaluations, even different from the ones presented in this work, the data collected during the experiments (i.e., the search results, for each product and for all the tested synthetic users) are publicly available[5].

The rest of the paper is organised as follows. Next section presents related work in the area. Section 3 describes the methodological approach, while Sect. 4 introduces the experiments and discusses their outcomes. Finally, Sect. 5 concludes the paper.

2 Related Work

The literature reports about two well-known practice of prices personalisation over the internet, i.e., "price steering" and "price discrimination", see, e.g., [12, 19]. While price steering denotes the act of changing the order of the results shown to the users according to their prices, price discrimination is the practice of offering different prices, to different users, for the very same product.

The concrete risk of price discrimination and steering was already considered more than one decade ago [21]. It was described how by relying on a large scale collection of personal information, like user behaviour and demographics, prices manipulation can be easily implemented in different scenarios. As a popular

[5] http://doi.org/10.5281/zenodo.1491557.

example, in August, 2012, the Wall Street Journal announced a real case of price steering [27]: an online travel agency, called Orbitz, was found to be steering Mac users towards more expensive hotels.

In [12], price steering and discrimination were extensively measured. With both real data collected through Amazon Mechanical Turks and synthetic data from controlled experiments using the non-GUI web browser in [13], the authors analysed the prices offered by a plethora of online vendors. The work found evidence of price differences by different merchants: their websites used to record the history of clicked products, to discriminate prices among customers.

In [18], the authors consider both price discrimination and price steering (the latter being referred as 'search discrimination). Collecting data from more than 200 online vendors, they did not find traces of price and search discrimination depending on the OSs, browsers, and their combination. Regarding price discrimination only, they discovered noticeable differences of products prices, particularly for the digital market (e.g., e-books, videogames) and depending from the kind of vendor (single e-shop *vs* aggregator of e-commerce websites). Finally, they ran experiments by synthetically varying the search history of users, thus building two kind of profiles (conscious user *vs* affluent user): the results showed a not negligible level of search discrimination.

In [19], the authors analysed real data collected from 340 internet users from 18 countries. The analysis focused on how the price of the same product, offered by a set of retailers, varied from retailer to retailer. The geographical location of users turned out to be one of the main factors affecting the prices differences, even if its constant influence over all the experiments was not assessed.

Work in [14] considered price discrimination actuated by popular accommodation websites. The authors experimented with different features: the user location and the system configuration. The study revealed that a price discrimination was indeed applied by booking providers according to locations, language and user agent (that contains information about the operating system and the browser).

According to [31], not all retailers adopt personalisation of prices. The authors monitored 25 airline websites for 3 weeks, with dozens of unique user profiles to analyze airline tickets. The experiments were automated by a headless Webkit browser (similar to that of [12,16]). The results did not reveal the use of any systematic price discrimination. Work in [6] collected price variations of search results over Google Shopping, varying the on-line behaviour of synthetic users: searched keywords, visited pages, clicked products on the visited pages; such research did not provide relevant evidence of price personalisation.

Work in [2] throws evidence on how sellers may set prices using so called dynamic pricing algorithms. While making vendors more competitive, such kind of algorithms may cause intentional agreements on prices among participants on the same side in a market, a practice known as price fixing [29], and cases exist of pricing algorithms pushing prices to unrealistic heights, like the unbelievable amount of $23.7 million for a scientific book about flies [3].

Regarding the synthesis of user profiles, work in [1,18,31] provides a useful way of constructing them based on OSs, web browsers, user behaviors and geographical locations. These investigations give useful references for further studies, including the present one.

As testified by the results in the literature, price manipulation on online markets is an actual issue. In particular, geographical areas have been already identified as an impact factor for price steering and discrimination. With respect to related work in the area, this research concentrates on price steering and it aims at identifying if, and how, such a practice is related to geo-economics features of the geographical areas from which users search on the internet. Previous work analysed the connection between online shopping habits and location and/or income of users (without however considering price steering practices). As an example, in [32], it has been shown a comparison among Chinese and Dutch people, assessing that the latter are more sensitive to advertisements proposing branded and more expensive products with respect to China.

Finally, in place of searching on specific retailers' websites, as in [12], this work focuses on Google Shopping, mainly because Google is well known to provide personalised services to the users. However, the experimental approach is general enough to be applicable to different search engine platforms.

3 Methodology

This work quantifies the differences in product prices, on search results in return to users queries on Google Shopping, US version. In particular, the considered scenario is one where users search from cities located in different countries, characterised by different values of Gross Domestic Product. All the experiments are conducted by collecting results during July, 2016. The prices are the retail ones displayed by Google Shopping in US dollars (thus, excluding shipping fees).

User Profiles. In personalization measurement studies, a very relevant aspect, often underestimated, is the quality of the user profiles [23]. This study simulates real user profiles surfing Google Shopping US from different geographic locations. The creation of a new profile corresponds to launch a new isolated web browser client instance and open the Google Shopping US web page. Also, instead of providing artificial ad hoc user profiles, the experiments consider the IP addresses of the users. Indeed, it has been shown that, in some countries (e.g., in US), the manual insertion of the user location (in the form, e.g., of a postal code) in the user profile do unfairly affects the price results [30]. Furthermore, locations and postal codes can be easily altered during the profile registration phase [17].

Emulating Users. To mimic real users, the synthetic users can browse, scroll pages, stay on a page, and click on links. A fully-fledged web browser is used to get the correct desktop version of the website under investigation. This is because websites could be designed to behave according to user agents, as witnessed by the differences between the mobile and desktop versions of the same website.

Several frameworks have been proposed for interacting with web browsers and analysing results from search engines. The interested reader can refer to [9] for a complete survey. This work considers tools able to run browser-based experiments to emulate search queries and basic interactions with the search result, and that could be easily extended with new user behaviours and new evaluation metrics. Both AdFisher[6] [8] and OpenWPM [9] meet these constraints. Past work on similar topics (see, e.g., [5–7]) experimented issues with AdFisher, mainly related to the recovery of browsers data after crashing. Thus, this research adopts OpenWPM, since it features a recovery mechanism after crashes (the experiments run, on average, 24 h). OpenWPM is automatised with Selenium[7] to efficiently create and manage different users with isolated Firefox and Chrome client instances, each of them with their own associated cookies.

In all the experiments, the software runs on our local server, but the browser's traffic is redirected to the designated remote servers (i.e., to India), via tunneling in SOCKS proxies. By operating in this way, a guarantee is that all the commands are simultaneously distributed over all the proxies. The experiments adopt the Mozilla Firefox browser (version 45.0) for the web browsing tasks and run under Ubuntu 14.04. Also, for each query, we consider the first page of results, counting 40 products. Among them, the focus of the experiments is mostly on the top 10 and top 3 results. We limit the investigation to the first results, following past studies that highlight the user's habits to concentrate only on them [11].

Metrics. To evaluate the result pages and quantify the differences in prices of the search results, this paper relies on a metric widely adopted in the information retrieval research area, namely the Normalized Discounted Cumulative Gain - NDCG - metric that measures the similarity between a given list of results and an ideal list of results. In this work, the ideal list of results is a list in which the products are listed from the most expensive to the least expensive one. This specific order is motivated by the fact that we are investigating if, and to which extent, the most expensive products are shown first to the user. In particular, the 'best' way to implement price steering would be to show products from the most expensive to the least expensive. Thus, this work will compare the results of the experiments with that ideal list.

NDCG, originally introduced in [15] in its non-normalised version DCG, has been already adopted in [12] for measuring price steering. For each search result r, there is one gain score g(r), representing its price. In a page with k results, we let $R = [(r_1), (r_2), ..(r_k)]$ and $R' = [(r'_1), (r'_2), ..(r'_k)]$, where r'_1 is the most expensive result and r'_k is the least expensive one. Thus, R' is the defined ideal list of results, obtaining:

$$DCG(R) = g(r_1) + \sum_{i=2}^{k}(g(r_i)/log_2(i))$$

$$NDCG = DCG(R)/DCG(R').$$

[6] https://github.com/tadatitam/info-flow-experiments.

[7] http://www.seleniumhq.org/.

Similar to [12], this research creates R' by first unioning the results returned for the same query to all the profiles under investigation, and then sorting such results from the most expensive to the least expensive one. For each query, this work calculates the NDCG obtained from the corresponding result page. After a profile successfully executes x queries, one NDCG vector is obtained, with x elements for it, where each element corresponds to the NDCG value of a single query. This is the *NDCG vector for a single profile.*

The *NDCG vector of a location* is instead obtained by unioning all the NDCG vectors of the profiles querying from that location. We consider more than one profile from the same location, to assure a higher confidence when evaluating the results.

As an example, with five profiles querying from the same location, there are five NDCG vectors associated to those profiles. The five vectors are then unioned into a single one (with length equal to $5 * x$ elements).

4 Experiments and Results

This section presents the experiments on different countries to measure if, and to which extent, price steering is applied in relation to the Gross Domestic Product of the location from which the user searches on Google Shopping, US version.

4.1 Cities in Different Countries

Two countries feature a significantly different Gross Domestic Product with respect to the third one:

Philippines GDP per capita 7,846.463;
India GDP per capita equal to 6,664.020;
US GDP per capita equal to 57,765.512.

All the values come from the International Monetary Fund website[8] and refer to 2016; they represent the estimated "Gross domestic product based on purchasing-power-parity (PPP) per capita GDP". For all the experiments, we use English keywords. The three countries have English speaking population. Indeed English is the official language in US, and one of the official languages in India and Philippines. Within these countries, a further selection is on three relevant cities.

Before choosing a US city, we ran experiments investigating price steering with the following targets: San Francisco, Seattle, New York, Los Angeles, Chicago and Miami. We did not unveil significant differences in terms of NDCG. Thus, we opted for choosing New York.

We acknowledge that developing countries, like India and Philippines, feature metropolitan and rural areas, which differentiate between each other for the

[8] https://www.imf.org/external/pubs/ft/weo/2014/02/weodata/index.aspx.

degree of richness[9]. Thus, we consider Manila and New Delhi, since, as metropolis, it should be more likely that people living there belong to the richest part of the population and use to shop online.

Summarizing, we emulate users searching over Google Shopping from Manila, New Delhi and New York.

For the keywords, the lists of product categories are extracted from Amazon.com (due to its richer categorisation, when compared with categories from Google Shopping). In details, 130 terms are considered, belonging to various product categories, including body care, apparel, bags, shoes, car accessories, house accessories (like lightning devices and home appliances), and electronics devices (such as personal audio devices and computer-related products). For each product category, the selection is on common nouns of products (such as luggages, telephones, books), while discarding specific brands.

The experiment settings are as follows:

- Number of locations: 3 (New York, New Delhi, Manila);
- Number of keywords: 130;
- Number of browser profiles for each location: 5;
- Web browser: Firefox 45.0;
- OS: Ubuntu 14.04.

Each browser profile contains its full web history and cookies. Moreover, each profile is kept isolated from the other profiles and it is deleted right after finishing the search. By design, all browsers work simultaneously and send the same query to Google Shopping US.

Each user visit lasts 15 s and the interval time between two searches is a random number between 15 and 30 s. For each country, this work collects the prices associated with the items in the first page of results, for all the 130 keywords, and for all the profiles searching from that country.

To measure the presence of possible price steering, this research considers the NDCG metric, as described in Sect. 3. This requires to compute an ideal list composed of all the results shown to the users, sorted from the most to the least expensive. Thus, for each country, the first 10 products shown to each of the different users are considered, and, among them, the selection is on the 10 most costly ones. The amount of 10 items has been chosen, since, through the experiments, a fact was that users searching from the same city have been shown very similar results. Being basically the difference only in the order, the list of distinct elements tends to be short. The same is done with 3 items only. In fact, statistics report that the top three results on Google account for more than 60% of the average traffic[10]. Thus, even focusing only on the first three results could provide significative outcomes. The two ideal lists are then used to compute, respectively, the measure for NDCG@10 and NDCG@3, per single profile. For each keyword search issued by the users (i.e., the profiles) from one location,

[9] https://data.worldbank.org/products/wdi-maps.
[10] https://chitika.com/google-positioning-value.

the average NDCG@3 and NDCG@10 are computed. These are the NDCG vectors per location. Table 1 reports a snapshot of the most interesting results that we have obtained.

Table 1. An excerpt of average NDCG per location, per sample product

Product	NDCG@3			NDCG@10		
	Philippines	India	US	Philippines	India	US
Boot	0.826	0.85	0.18	0.746	0.755	0.252
Ceiling fan	0.524	0.527	0.245	0.736	0.692	0.475
Desktop	0.114	0.062	0.813	0.219	0.178	0.783
Dress	0.628	0.905	0.282	0.678	0.778	0.371
Helmet	0.592	0.786	0.639	0.639	0.812	0.654
LightScribe	0.138	0.387	0.174	0.27	0.588	0.432
Moisturizer	0.775	0.524	0.48	0.755	0.549	0.523
MP3 player	0.164	0.111	0.165	0.305	0.289	0.312
Pant	0.228	0.271	0.291	0.305	0.446	0.405
Pocket video camera	0.019	0.079	0.574	0.91	0.229	0.28
Portable CD player	0.129	0.097	0.163	0.342	0.352	0.475
Portable DVD player	0.338	0.318	0.859	0.402	0.426	0.87
Television	0.222	0.282	0.542	0.422	0.461	0.592
Universal remote	0.554	0.161	0.597	0.506	0.194	0596
Wheel	0.177	0.202	0.715	0.281	0.311	0.793

Due to connection errors, one of the Philippine profiles had no associated results. Also, for Philippines, a few keywords did not lead to any results: videocassette recorders, totes, umbrellas. Similarly, for US, no results were for totes and umbrellas. This could be due to either a connection error or because Google Shopping provided no results for such items, at time of search. In the case of India, for each keyword, the list of results was never empty.

For Philippines, the top three highest NDCG@3 per location are those related to *briefcase* (0.863), *boot* (0.826) and *blankets* (0.783); For India, *dress* (0.905), *briefcase* (0.88) and *boot* (0.85). For US, *portable DVD player* get 0.859, *desktop* 0.813, and *blankets* 0.8.

Table 2. Average NDCG@10 per location, per sample product category

Category	Philippines	India	US	Category	Philippines	India	US
Apparel	0.389	**0.4**	0.31	Electronic devices	0.195	0.202	**0.4**
Body products	**0.48**	0.455	0.446	All	0.397	0.406	**0.42**

Regarding NDCG@10, per location, for Philippines we obtain *moisturizer* 0.755, *boot* 0.746 and *ceiling fan* 0.736. For India, *fuel system* 0.830, *helmet* 0.812 and *dress* 0.778. For US, *portable DVD player* 0.870, *wheel* 0.793, *desktop* 0.783. Each searched product, in each country, features average NDCG values < 1: in all cases, the search results are not ordered from the most to the least expensive one.

Figure 1 reports mean and standard deviation of the NDCG@3 values per each profile, separately. Similarly, Fig. 2 is for NDCG@10. Overall, from US we obtain the highest results in terms of mean, both for NDCG@3 and NDCG@10, while Philippines feature the lowest ones.

Since keywords can be grouped by categories, we also compute the average NDCG per location, per categories. Table 2 reports the results for the categories Apparel (29 keywords), Electronic Devices (31 keywords), and Body Products (10 keywords). The table shows that the category of products matters. Overall, the three countries have similar average values (last line in the table). Interestingly, for electronic devices US has a much higher value than the other two countries; India features a greater value, compared to US, for apparel; Philippines gets a slightly higher value for body products, *wrt* the other two countries.

Till now, we concentrate on the NDCG metric. It is worth noting that the results on NDCG show how the products prices are ordered, in the different countries, with respect to the ideal list, which, however, is different country per country. Thus, we obtain relative, and not absolute, results: the country which is subject to a higher price steering practice, without however detailing a comparison among the countries (due, in fact, to the difference of each ideal list). In order to give the flavour of the differences in prices in the various countries, we

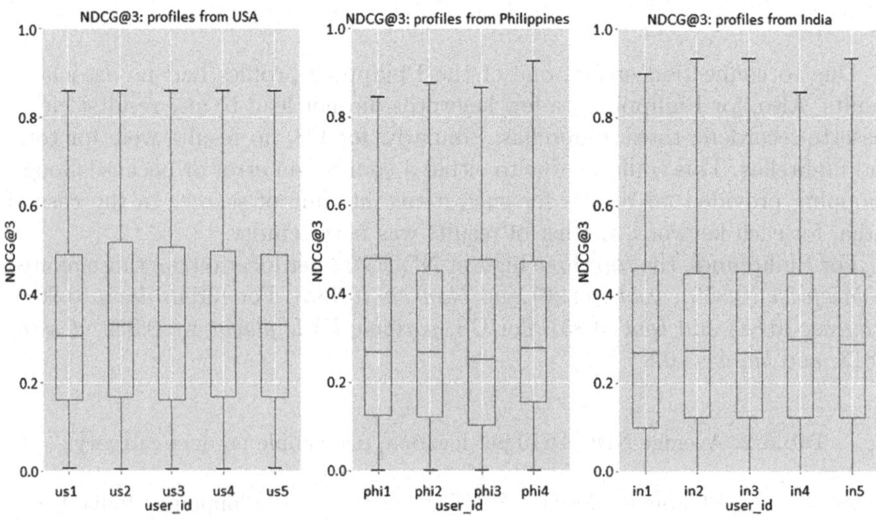

Fig. 1. NDCG@3 per single profile, per location

give some results also in terms of average prices. These are reported in Table 4, where we report average prices for all the product categories, and for sample categories (electronic devices, apparel and body products), considering, at most, the top 10 results per search, and Table 3, which gives an excerpt of the results obtained for the single keywords. Furthermore, to give the flavour of the relative difference among the prices distributions country by country, we compute the coefficient of variation, i.e., the ratio between the standard deviation and the average. This value is reported in Table 4.

Looking at a specific sample category, while Table 2 showed that the most expensive electronic products are shown first in US (with NDCG@10 (per location, per sample category) = 0.4), the average prices are lower than those for India and Philippines (see Table 4). When looking at the coefficient of variation, the relative standard deviation between the products prices is lower. Similarly,

Table 3. Average prices per country and sample products considering the top 10 results

Product	Average prices (US $)			Product	Average prices (US $)		
	Philippines	India	US	Product	Philippines	India	US
Boot	136	136	122	Pant	36	51	73
Ceiling fan	360	340	211	Pocket video camera	151	117	73
Desktop	717	887	368	Portable CD player	50	52	72
Dress	110	100	86	Portable DVD player	66	57	64
Helmet	299	378	315	Television	455	519	625
LightScribe	67	65	128	Universal remote	41	43	95
Moisturizer	22	18	14	Wheel	262	238	178

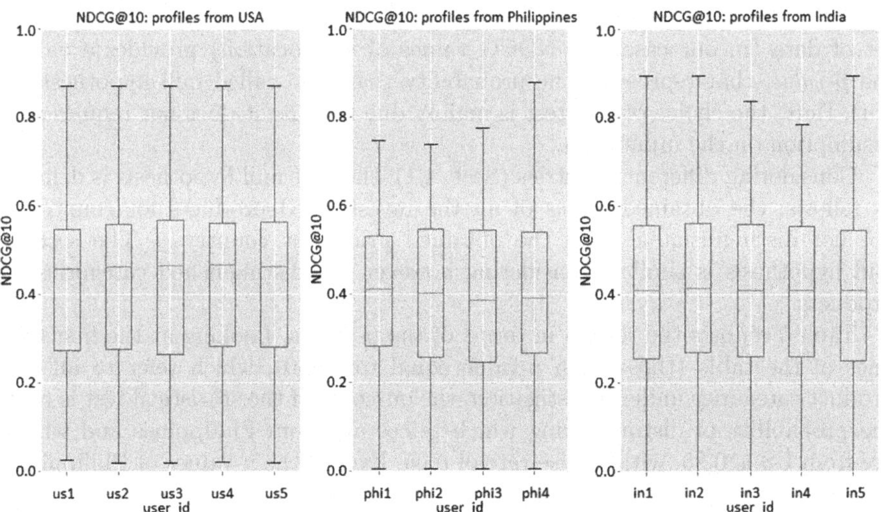

Fig. 2. NDCG@10 per single profile, per location

Table 4. Average prices and coefficient of variation per country and category considering the top 10 results

Category	Average prices (US $)			Coefficient of variation		
	Philippines	India	US	Philippines	India	US
Apparel	62	67	59	1.03	1.08	0.84
Body products	62	67	59	1.03	1.08	0.84
Electronic devices	281	289	149	1.10	1.08	0.93
All	175	173	224	1.4	1.4	5.4

for the specific products, we can notice that the average prices for 7 out of 14 sample products shown in Table 3 are lower searching from US than from the other two countries under investigation (see, e.g., the results for "desktop", with $717, $887 and $368, respectively searching from Philippines, India and US).

As a final remark, we notice that we grounded the experiments on a keyword categorization coming from the Amazon terminology. However, other kinds of choices are possible. An interesting direction is to distinguish durable and not durable goods [10]. In fact, research shows differences buying aptitudes with respect to the two category of goods, i.e., when looking for a durable good, as a laptop, users tend to listen to external recommendations, e.g., from friends. Instead, for not durable goods, they are more influenced by the first results that appear on search engines.

4.2 Statistical Significance of the Experiments

To give statistical significance to the experiments, this work runs permutation tests [20], following the approach proposed in [9,28]. A permutation test on a set of data (in our case, the NDCG values of the location) provides a value, the *p-value*, that represents the probability that a so called null hypothesis is true. Here, the choice of this test is mainly due because it does not require any assumption on the input data.

Considering different countries (Sect. 4.1), the first null hypothesis is defined as follows: the obtained prices of all the investigated products for country x are not distinguishable from the obtained prices for country y. The second null hypothesis is similar, considering however the distinguished categories of products.

Table 5 reports the results in terms of the p-values. Looking at the first two lines of the table (those with p-value equal to 0.050), which refer to all the product categories under investigation, the outcome of the statistical test is that the probability of distinguishing which prices are from Philippines and which are from US is 0.95, with a false rate of 0.05. Even if the p-values of Philippines *vs* US and India *vs* US are lower when considering all the product categories, a pretty good statistical evidence is obtained also for some specific categories (apparel, electronic devices, and "for house").

Table 5. p-values obtained from permutation tests over NDCG values.

Location	Category	p-value	Category	p-value
Philippines vs US	All	**0.050**	Electronic devices	**0.013**
India vs US	All	**0.050**	Electronic devices	**0.056**
Philippines vs India	All	0.89	Electronic devices	0.90
Philippines vs US	Accessories	0.669	For house	**0.096**
India vs US	Accessories	0.525	For house	**0.193**
Philippines vs India	Accessories	0.819	For house	0.740
Philippines vs US	Apparel	**0.136**	Others	0.449
India vs US	Apparel	**0.056**	Others	0.351
Philippines vs India	Apparel	0.629	Others	0.601
Philippines vs US	Body care	0.394		
India vs US	Body care	0.609		
Philippines vs India	Body care	0.711		

5 Conclusions

This paper investigated the impact of locations on the order of price results, searching from common products over Google Shopping US. Differently from previous work in the area, here geographical locations are combined with one of the indicators of the economic performance of the locations, i.e., the Gross Domestic Product. As locations, this work considered cities in three different countries. The analyses aimed at investigating order and averages of prices shown to users. Regarding the order, the considered metric is the difference between the list of price results, as obtained by considering the results of our queries, and an ideal list of results, defined as an ordered list, where the products with the highest prices are first shown to the user. The analysis also considers, at a glance, how the average prices for different categories of products change, location by location. While able to testify the existence of price steering and quantifying its level, country per country, the results of the investigations lead also to unexpected results: even if the experiments on the order of prices highlight the specific country that mostly adheres to the ideal list of results (from the most to the least expensive one), often the average price of the shown results for that specific country is lower than that for the other two countries under investigation. The significance of the obtained results were evaluated by running permutation tests. While satisfactory for certain product categories, they not always succeeded in proving the statistical significance of the experiments. This calls for further investigations. To the best of the authors' knowledge, this is the first work that automatically analyses price steering with respect to GDP values. This introduces a novel, and alternative, methodology, to automatically collect price results exploiting their users' searches on e-commerce search engines. Finally, this work relies on a relatively small set of synthetic accounts and investigated locations. As future work, a natural follow up is to run a wider experimental campaign, considering different e-commerce platforms, more accounts and more locations (like, e.g., different areas in the same city, and different cities in the same country). As a plus, the illustrated methodology can be easily applied on a large scale too.

Acknowledgements. Partly supported by the EU H2020 Program, grant agreement #675320 (NECS: *European Network of Excellence in Cybersecurity*); by the Starting Grants Project DAKKAR (DAta benchmarK for Keyword-based Access and Retrieval), University of Padua, Italy and Fondazione Cariparo, Padua, Italy.

References

1. Carrascosa, J.M., Mikians, J., Rumín, R.C., Erramilli, V., Laoutaris, N.: I always feel like somebody's watching me: measuring online behavioural advertising. In: Emerging Networking Experiments and Technologies (2015)
2. Chen, L., Mislove, A., Wilson, C.: An empirical analysis of algorithmic pricing on amazon marketplace. In: Proceedings of the 25th International Conference on World Wide Web WWW 2016, International World Wide Web Conferences Steering Committee, Republic and Canton of Geneva, Switzerland (2016)
3. CNN - International Edition: Amazon seller lists book at $23,698,655.93 plus shipping (2011). http://edition.cnn.com/2011/TECH/web/04/25/amazon.price.algorithm/
4. Conti, M., Cozza, V., Petrocchi, M., Spognardi, A.: TRAP: using targeted ads to unveil Google personal profiles. In: Information Forensics and Security. IEEE (2015)
5. Cozza, V., Hoang, V.T., Petrocchi, M.: Google web searches and Wikipedia results: a measurement study. In: Italian Information Retrieval. CEUR Workshop Proceedings (2016)
6. Cozza, V., Hoang, V.T., Petrocchi, M., De Nicola, R.: Online user behavioural modeling with applications to price steering. In: FINREC 2016 CEUR Workshop Proceedings (2016)
7. Cozza, V., Hoang, V.T., Petrocchi, M., Spognardi, A.: Experimental measures of news personalization in google news. In: Casteleyn, S., Dolog, P., Pautasso, C. (eds.) ICWE 2016. LNCS, vol. 9881, pp. 93–104. Springer, Cham (2016). https://doi.org/10.1007/978-3-319-46963-8_8
8. Datta, A., Tschantz, M.C., Datta, A.: Automated experiments on ad privacy settings: a tale of opacity, choice, and discrimination. In: Privacy Enhancing Technologies, vol. 1 (2015)
9. Englehardt, S., Narayanan, A.: Online tracking: a 1-million-site measurement and analysis. In: Computer and Communications Security. ACM (2016)
10. Grandinetti, R.: Concetti e strumenti di marketing. Marketing e vendite, Etas (2002)
11. Granka, L.A., Joachims, T., Gay, G.: Eye-tracking analysis of user behavior in www search. In: Proceedings of the 27th Annual International ACM SIGIR Conference on Research and Development in Information Retrieval SIGIR 2004. ACM, New York (2004)
12. Hannak, A., et al.: Measuring price discrimination and steering on e-commerce web sites. In: Internet Measurement Conference. ACM (2014)

13. Hidayat, A.: PhantomJS (2016). http://phantomjs.org
14. Hupperich, T., Tatang, D., Wilkop, N., Holz, T.: An empirical study on online price differentiation. In: Proceedings of the Eighth ACM Conference on Data and Application Security and Privacy CODASPY 2018. ACM, New York (2018)
15. Jarvelin, K., Kekalainen, J.: Cumulated gain-based evaluation of IR techniques. Trans. Inf. Syst. **20**(4), 422–446 (2002)
16. Kliman-Silver, C., Hannak, A., Lazer, D., Wilson, C., Mislove, A.: Location, location, location: the impact of geolocation on web search personalization. In: Internet Measurement Conference. ACM (2015)
17. Larson, J., Mattu, S., Angwin, J.: Unintended consequences of geographic targeting. Technology Science (2015). https://techscience.org/a/2015090103/
18. Mikians, J., Gyarmati, L., Erramilli, V., Laoutaris, N.: Detecting price and search discrimination on the Internet. In: Hot Topics in Networks. ACM (2012)
19. Mikians, J., Gyarmati, L., Erramilli, V., Laoutaris, N.: Crowd-assisted search for price discrimination in e-commerce: First results. CoNEXT (2013)
20. Nichols, T.E., Holmes, A.P.: Nonparametric permutation tests for functional neuroimaging: a primer with examples. Hum. Brain Mapp. **15**(1), 1–25 (2002)
21. Odlyzko, A.: Privacy, economics, and price discrimination on the Internet. In: Electronic Commerce. ACM (2003)
22. Pariser, E.: The Filter Bubble: What the Internet Is Hiding from You. The Penguin Group, London (2011)
23. Pasi, G., et al.: Evaluation of personalised information retrieval at CLEF 2018 (PIR-CLEF). In: Bellot, P., et al. (eds.) CLEF 2018. LNCS, vol. 11018, pp. 335–342. Springer, Cham (2018). https://doi.org/10.1007/978-3-319-98932-7_29
24. Pitoura, E., et al.: On measuring bias in online information. SIGMOD Rec. **46**(4), 16–21 (2018). https://doi.org/10.1145/3186549.3186553
25. Ross, P.: Just How Big Is the eCommerce Market? (2015). https://blog.lemonstand.com/just-how-big-is-the-ecommerce-market-youll-never-guess/
26. Statista: Statistics and facts about global e-commerce (2018). https://www.statista.com/statistics/379046/worldwide-retail-e-commerce-sales/
27. The Wall Street Journal: On Orbitz, Mac users steered to pricier hotels (2012). https://www.wsj.com/articles/SB10001424052702304458604577488822667325882
28. Tschantz, M.C., Datta, A., Datta, A., Wing, J.M.: A methodology for information flow experiments. In: Computer Security Foundations Symposium. IEEE (2015)
29. U.S. Department of Justice: Former e-commerce executive charged with price fixing in the antitrust division's first online marketplace prosecution (2015). https://www.justice.gov/opa/pr/former-e-commerce-executive-charged-price-fixing-antitrust-divisions-first-online-marketplace
30. Vafa, K., Haigh, C., Leung, A., Yonack, N.: Price discrimination in the Princeton review's online SAT tutoring service (2015). https://techscience.org/a/2015090102/
31. Vissers, T., Nikiforakis, N., Bielova, N., Joosen, W.: Crying wolf? on the price discrimination of online airline tickets. In: Hot Topics in Privacy Enhancing Technologies (2014)
32. Yu, S., Hudders, L., Cauberghe, V.: Targeting the luxury consumer: a vice or virtue? a cross-cultural comparison of the effectiveness of behaviorally targeted ads. J. Fashion Mark. Manage. Int. J. **21**(2), 187–205 (2017)

Predicting the Usability of the Dice CAPTCHA via Artificial Neural Network

Alessia Amelio[1(✉)], Radmila Janković[2], Dejan Tanikić[3], and Ivo Rumenov Draganov[4]

[1] University of Calabria, DIMES, Rende, CS, Italy
aamelio@dimes.unical.it

[2] Mathematical Institute of the S.A.S.A., Belgrade, Serbia
rjankovic@mi.sanu.ac.rs

[3] University of Belgrade, Technical Faculty in Bor, Bor, Serbia
dtanikic@tfbor.bg.ac.rs

[4] Technical University of Sofia, Department of Radio Communications and Video Technologies, Sofia, Bulgaria
idraganov@tu-sofia.bg

Abstract. This paper introduces a new study of the CAPTCHA usability which analyses the predictability of the solution time, also called response time, to solve the Dice CAPTCHA. This is accomplished by proposing a new artificial neural network model for predicting the response time from known personal and demographic features of the users who solve the CAPTCHA: (i) age, (ii) device on which the CAPTCHA is solved, and (iii) Web use in years. The experiment involves a population of 197 Internet users, who is required to solve two types of Dice CAPTCHA on laptop or tablet computer. The data collected from the experiment is subject to the artificial neural network model which is trained and tested to predict the response time. The proposed analysis provides new results of usability of the Dice CAPTCHA and important suggestions for designing new CAPTCHAs which could be closer to an "ideal" CAPTCHA.

Keywords: Prediction · CAPTCHA · Usability

1 Introduction

A digital library in its broad meaning is a collection of digital items, which can include images, videos, documents, but also multimedia interfaces. In this sense, methods for exploring, processing, and analysing a collection of digital interfaces, e.g. the CAPTCHA interface, can be important for solving specific digital libraries issues.

CAPTCHA stands for Completely Automated Public Turing test to tell Computers and Humans Apart. This is a challenging test which is required to be solved by a human user in order to understand if he/she is a human or a computer robot (also called bot). In particular, if the human user is able to correctly

P. Manghi et al. (Eds.): IRCDL 2019, CCIS 988, pp. 44–58, 2019.
https://doi.org/10.1007/978-3-030-11226-4_4

solve the test, then he/she is recognised as a human, otherwise he/she is considered as a bot [2].

The CAPTCHA test is currently used in multiple practical applications, including: (i) web systems for e-commerce, (ii) advanced authentication systems for e-mail, (iii) online pooling, (iv) different web systems, etc. [21].

The design of a CAPTCHA should follow some important requirements, such as: (i) the solution to the CAPTCHA should not depend on a given language which is known by the human user, (ii) the solution to the CAPTCHA should be independent from personal and demographic factors of the human user and should be given in no more than 30 s (postulate of "ideal" CAPTCHA [7]), (iii) the privacy of the human user should be preserved, (iv) the solution to the CAPTCHA should be easy for the human user and difficult for the bot [1].

In the last years, different types of CAPTCHA have been designed, which can be categorised as: (i) text, (ii) audio, (iii) image, (iv) video, and (v) interactive and puzzle CAPTCHA. The text and audio CAPTCHA require that a text or audio signal is recognised by the user and reported in a text field. They both proved to be insecure in different contexts since they could be solved by bots with Optical Character Recognition (OCR) and advanced speech processing algorithms. Accordingly, the CAPTCHA was equipped with image, video and interactive and puzzle tasks, for which the simulation of the human behaviour by a computer program is much more difficult. One of the last frontiers in CAPTCHA design is the interactive and puzzle area, which includes different CAPTCHA tests, e.g. FunCAPTCHA, SweetCAPTCHA as interactive ones and Dice CAPTCHA as a puzzle one [10]. In particular, in a puzzle CAPTCHA, the task is to solve a puzzle which can be equipped with images in order to discriminate a human user from a bot. Since the solution to the puzzle is quite difficult for a human subject, this CAPTCHA can take more time to be solved. Also, it is very difficult to be solved by a bot.

A CAPTCHA test can be analysed under different perspectives, which include: (i) security, (ii) practicality, and (iii) usability [4]. The security is mainly connected to the robustness of the CAPTCHA test to attacks which are made by bots. This represents the main concern of the CAPTCHA designers. The practicality includes the main aspects related to the CAPTCHA programming. Finally, the usability analyses the CAPTCHA test under a user-centric perspective. This represents the main aspect related to the use of the CAPTCHA, which includes the interaction of the user with the test.

2 Related Work

In the last decades, different works have been proposed in the literature concerning the usability of the CAPTCHA test.

Yan and El Ahmad [22] designed a framework for the exploration of the CAPTCHA usability. They relate their analysis to the following components: learnability, memorability, efficiency, errors and satisfaction. The latter three are determined by the following usability criteria: accuracy, response time and perceived difficulty, further expanded by the authors to distortion, content and presentation in a 3-dimensional framework. Evaluating various types of CAPTCHAs with it, led to the following general conclusions: (i) foreigners may be hampered in solving the text-based CAPTCHA, (ii) the predictability level of text sequences has the major effect on usability and security, as well as the use of the colour.

To further enhance the security of the text-based CAPTCHAs, Lupkowski and Urbański [16] proposed the users not only to recognise but also to understand the presented text. Introducing semantic priming, the researchers have proven that there is a significant dependence of the response time based on the users' experience with the newly proposed system. In the same time, the decrease of the response time does not influence the accuracy of solving the CAPTCHA. A subjective evaluation of the difficulty in solving it from the user's point of view was carried out on a 10-level scale. Less experienced users reported slightly higher levels of difficulty and that result seems to be highly correlated with the registered higher response times.

In [13], Ince et al. estimated the execution times of the interactive 3D CAPTCHA using a keystroke level model. Various system usage scenarios were tested. This proved possible to predict the necessary time of accomplishing specific tasks by the users. It includes up to 8 distinctive steps to perform all registered by their execution times. Upper limits for them are found along with the average action time for a complete solving of the CAPTCHA. Three types of errors are detected during the experimentation with their estimated frequency occurrence. However, no statistical analysis is performed against the users' response times.

Users' experience and solution performance on the reCAPTCHA system are statistically investigated more deeply by Beheshti and Liatsis [5]. Taking into account a 3 level model including distortion, content and presentation, the authors conducted a user survey with 13 questions. They considered gender, sex, age, glasses worn by the users, and the type of used monitor. The quantitative performance is represented by the number of needed attempts for a successful solution, the time needed for it along with the used character size and lengths. Some subjective measures announced by each user are the level of willingness to solve similar tasks again, the difficulty in recognising symbols and the experienced ambiguity level. Also, the personal preference on the language of the text and the level of interaction with the system were measured. No precise relation was declared among any of these parameters of the study and no attempt was made to predict the performance of the users in any future activity based on their properties.

Alsuhibany [3] tested a recently introduced optimiser within the CAPTCHA employing the collapsing mechanism over the text to find the effect on the users' performance. An improvement is thought to be statistically significant for both the solution accuracy and time. Age, sex and affiliation background are taken into account during the experiments. The experimental results include average accuracy and solution time with common statistical derivatives before and after the optimisation. Complete distributions among all users of these parameters are also presented. A subjective level of difficulty in solving the CAPTCHA prior and after the improvement is also provided as a feedback by the users. A considerably higher personal comfort is reported after the optimisation. No relation was presented between the users' properties and the achieved performance.

A significantly more complete study [18] over the usability of the CAPTCHA, the Dynamic Cognitive Game (DCG) one, in particular, and its relation to stream relay attacks is made by Nguyen. Presenting a customised version of that system, the author undertook a test with 40 participants, primarily students, knowing their demographics. A scale from 1 to 5 was used to evaluate the subjective user experience. Additional questions were asked for a users' feedback. Completion time, non-successful completion part of all users, effects of objects number and speed in the test on the response time and accuracy were the objective parameters to register. Positive results in performance are reported from using the proposed system's enhancement but no relation with the users' properties has been investigated.

Extensive results on testing the DCG CAPTCHA are given in [17] by Mohamed et al. Exploring the usability and security of the system in terms of completely automated attacks, relay attacks based on human interaction and hybrid types of interference, reveal that it remains usable and stays resilient in the first case, no matter of the access device type, stationary or mobile. Some vulnerability is discovered for the latter two groups of attacks. Demographics of all 40 participants in the test were taken into consideration, in particular the gender, age and education. Response time, success rate and subjective user experience were measured and statistically processed but no correlation to the users' demographics has been shown.

Another investigation on the usability of the CAPTCHA is presented in [23] concerning the application of Chinese characters in the tasks presented to the users. An analytical comparison is performed over test-cases including common alphanumeric labels and Chinese ones apart trying to get a deeper understanding of the cognitive processes involved during the solution. Only the age of the participants in the tests has been considered. Software and hardware properties, such as display size, of the testing platforms were also taken into account. Extensive statistical parameters from the processing of the test data are presented which prove the comparable level of usability of both CAPTCHAs and useful guidelines of designing a Chinese system were derived. No relation to the users' age or other demographic features was presented. By contrast, the age discrimination on the user performance was studied by Guerrar et al. [11] for CAPTCHAs solved on mobile devices. The dependency of the response time, accuracy, pleasantness, solvability, input mechanism type, understandability, suitability, memorability, and preference from distinctive age ranges is presented from which useful guidelines could be given for the future use of CAPTCHAs based on that user feature. All statistical analysis of the data presented in the aforementioned works could be unified by the introduction of a recently proposed robust metric for the comparison based on a multiagent system modelling [12].

In different works [6–8], Brodić et al. presented results from a recent study which aims to investigate the CAPTCHA usability not only from a point of view of the supporting software and hardware adopted by the users but also based on a variety of demographic features which describe them. In one of the tests, a user-centric approach is presented for which 190 participants were gathered to solve the Dice CAPTCHA on both laptops and tablets [7]. Age, gender and education level were taken into consideration during a statistical derivation of the related dependence of the response time. General conclusions were drawn about the usability of the Dice CAPTCHA and its closeness to an "ideal" CAPTCHA. An attempt of predicting the response time to solve image and interactive CAPTCHAs was made in [6] based on age, education level and Web use level of a population of 114 users. A regression tree was used to evaluate the prediction accuracy which appeared to be high enough for practical purposes of future CAPTCHA designs targeted to specific user groups. An advanced statistical analysis was also implemented based on a study with 197 subjects registered with their age and Web use level solving the Dice CAPTCHA on a tablet or laptop [8]. It was based on association rule mining with the response time and the number of solution tries as dependent variables. The co-occurrence of factors affecting the Dice CAPTCHA usability may be established using this approach which helps in understanding which type of Dice CAPTCHA is closer to an "ideal" CAPTCHA.

In this paper, we propose an artificial neural network model which could be trained and then tested to predict the Dice CAPTCHA response time from known characteristics of the users who solve the CAPTCHA, i.e. age, Web use in years and used device type. In comparison to the previous works [6–8], we propose the following novelties: (i) a predictability analysis on a different type of CAPTCHA tested with a different prediction model, and (ii) an extension of the usability analysis of the Dice CAPTCHA via predictability of its response time given known users' characteristics. It will provide new results on the usability of the Dice CAPTCHA and useful insights for designing future CAPTCHAs which could be closer to the "ideal" CAPTCHA.

The rest of the paper is organised as follows. In Sect. 3 the Dice CAPTCHA is described with its two used types. Then, in Sect. 4, the developed artificial neural network model is presented, followed by a description of the experimental setup in Sect. 5. Experimental results are given and discussed in Sect. 6. At the end, in Sect. 7 conclusions are drawn.

3 The Dice CAPTCHA

Dice CAPTCHA is a puzzle-based CAPTCHA where the user needs to roll a dice and enter the numbers which are visualised on the faces of the dice, or their sum in a given field [10]. If the user correctly solves the Dice CAPTCHA, then he/she will be considered as a human, otherwise he/she will be considered as a bot and his/her request to access a web form will be denied.

There are two types of Dice CAPTCHA: (1) Homo-sapiens Dice (Dice 1), where the challenge of entering the sum of the digits shown on the faces of the dice is presented to the user (see Fig. 1 (a)), and (2) All-the-rest Dice (Dice 2), where the user needs to enter the exact numbers as they are presented on the dice in a given field (see Fig. 1 (b)).

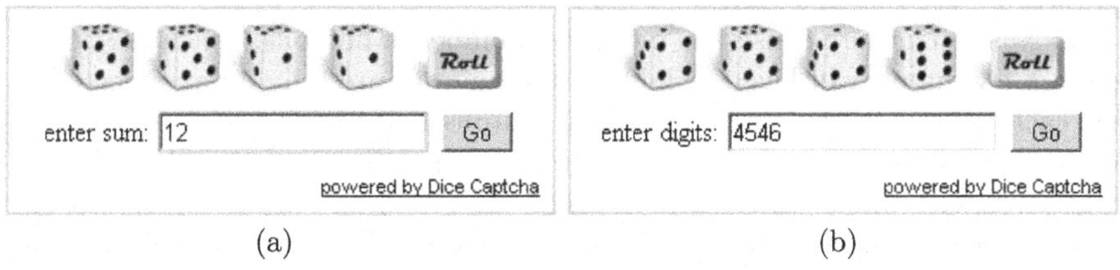

(a) (b)

Fig. 1. (a) Dice 1 CAPTCHA (Homo-sapiens Dice), (b) Dice 2 CAPTCHA (All-the-rest Dice)

Dice CAPTCHA is designed with a variety of colour skins as presented in Fig. 2. In this case, it is easy to presume that the colour can have an effect on the users' response time of solving the CAPTCHA. When designing colour CAPTCHAs, it is assumed that different colour schemes can serve as a defence against attacks, in particular attacks made by an OCR software [22]. However, the use of the colour when designing CAPTCHAs should be taken with caution, as adding colour can sometimes have a negative impact on usability and security [22]. Interested parties that would like to use the Dice CAPTCHAs for protecting their websites from the bots can choose the number of the dice their Dice CAPTCHA will consist of.

Fig. 2. Dice CAPTCHA colour skins

4 The Artificial Neural Network Model

An Artificial Neural Network (ANN) model is used for predicting the response time to solve the Dice 1 and Dice 2 CAPTCHAs from known personal and demographic characteristics of the users who solve the CAPTCHA. The response time can be influenced by many factors. From the previous study [8], the age of the user, the device type on which the CAPTCHA is solved and the Web use (in years) of the user are marked as the main influencing factors. Consequently, they will be used in this study.

ANN is a structure consisting of a large number of neurons, which are organised in a few number of layers. The layers of neurons are fully interconnected so that each neuron in the current layer of neurons is connected with all neurons from the previous one, as well as all neurons in the following layer. ANN has an input layer with one neuron for each input value and an output layer with one neuron for each output value. In this case, there will be 3 neurons in the input layer of the ANN, which represent: (i) age, (ii) device type and (iii) Web use. Also, ANN has just one output neuron in the output layer which represents the CAPTCHA response time (see Fig. 3 (a)).

The number of hidden layers and the number of neurons in each of them is not known in advance. But the processing ability of the ANN depends on the number of layers of hidden neurons and their number. Although there exist some heuristic methods for determining this number, the only certain method for resolving this problem is the trial-and-error approach. It is a critical design parameter because the performance of the ANN may not be adequate with an insufficient number of layers and neurons, while a large number of layers and neurons causes poor generalisation on the new data [20].

This kind of ANNs is sometimes called Feedforward Artificial Neural Network, because the information only travels forward (with no loops), through the input nodes, then through the hidden nodes and finally through the output nodes.

The performance of one neuron is pretty simple. It sums up the signals from the neurons which lay in the previous layer multiplied with interconnection weights and biases, forming in that way the neuron potential. The activation function produces the output from the neuron, according to the potential of the neuron. The activation function, also known as transfer function, invokes nonlinearity into the ANN, which enables in that way modelling very complicated relationships among input and output parameters. This can be represented by the following equations:

$$a_i = \sum_{j=1}^{n} w_{ij} \cdot x_j + b_i, \qquad y_i = f(a_i) \tag{1}$$

where a_i is the potential of the i-th neuron, w_{ij} is the adjustable interconnection weight between the j-th neuron in the previous layer and the i-th neuron in the current layer, x_j is the output from the j-th neuron serving as input into the i-th neuron, n is total number of inputs into the i-th neuron, y_i is the output from the i-th neuron, and f represents the activation function (transfer function).

The ANN has to be trained according to a training data set, i.e. known input/output pairs. The training data set must be representative, so that the desired accuracy of the ANN could be achieved. The training process is initialised by assigning random values to weights and biases. The input values are presented to the ANN, so that it can calculate the output value. The difference between the desired and calculated value represents the error, which has to be reduced. The values of the weights and biases are changed in that way to minimise the overall error. The neural networks are usually trained to provide targeted outputs for specific inputs. The network is adjusted, based on the comparison between outputs and target values, until the match between the outputs and target values is satisfactory. The algorithm of the ANN training is shown in Fig. 3 (b).

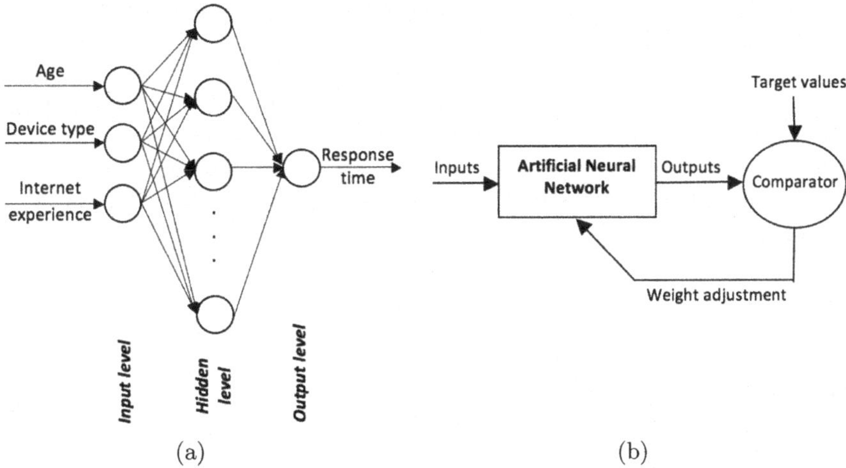

Fig. 3. (a) Architecture of the used ANN, (b) Algorithm of ANN training

5 Experiment

The aim is to determine if the response time of solving the Dice CAPTCHA can be efficiently predicted based on users' personal and demographic features. In that case, the investigated CAPTCHA cannot be considered as an "ideal" one, since its response time can be easily predicted from users' features.

The experiment involves a population of 197 Internet users with the Dice 1 and Dice 2 CAPTCHAs to solve on a laptop and tablet computer. The laptop used for the experiment has the following characteristics: (i) 15.6" wide screen, (ii) CPU Quad-core 2.4 GHz, (iii) 4 GB of RAM, (iv) 500 GB of internal memory, and (v) operating system Microsoft Windows 7. By contrast, the tablet used for the experiment has the following characteristics: (i) 7" wide screen, (ii) CPU Quad-core 1.2 GHz, (iii) 1 GB of RAM, (iv) 16 GB of internal memory, and (v) operating system Android.

5.1 Data Gathering and Dataset Creation

The users voluntarily participated in this study and agreed that their data would be anonymously used for research purposes. They were involved through personal email. Before starting the experiment, the users gave their consent through an online form. In order to avoid bias effects, the participants were not informed about the aim of the study. For each user, the response time to correctly solve both Dice CAPTCHAs was measured in seconds, from the beginning of the task until the end of the task. The measured times were then registered in a dataset. Accordingly, there are 197 instances consisting of 4 variables: (1) age, (2) type of device where the CAPTCHAs are solved (tablet or laptop), (3) Web use in years, and (4) response time.[1]

From these 197 users, 100 users solved the CAPTCHA on a tablet computer, while 97 users used a laptop computer for solving the CAPTCHA. Around 62% of the users were male, while the rest of 38% were female. The age of the users who were involved in the experiment ranges between 28 and 62 years, while the Web use ranges between 1 and 19 years. Figure 4 shows the distribution of the values of the ages and Web use of the participants.

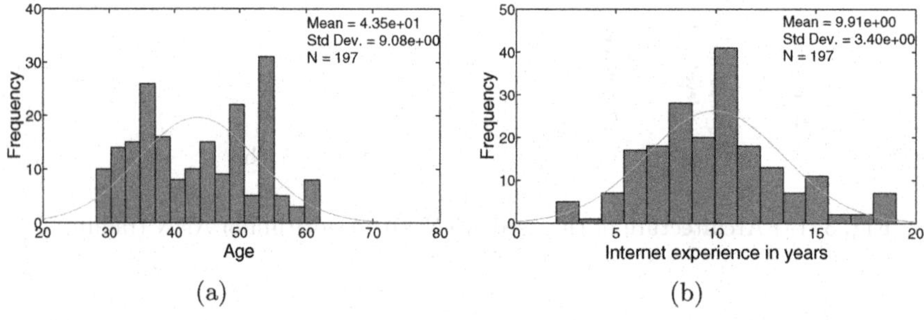

Fig. 4. Distribution of the values of (a) ages and (b) Web use of the participants [8]

From Fig. 4 (b), it is worth noting that the distribution of the Web use has a Gaussian like shape [8]. By contrast, the distribution of the ages in Fig. 4(a) is deviant from the ideal normal distribution [8], with the highest frequency between 32 and 40 years, and for 50 and 54 years.

Considering the response time, the users solved the Dice 2 faster than the Dice 1 CAPTCHA. Also, the mean value of the response time for the Dice 1 CAPTCHA is 9.48 s, and for the Dice 2 CAPTCHA is 7.34 s. The median values are 8.00 s and 6.00 s for the Dice 1 and Dice 2 CAPTCHAs, respectively.

[1] The gathered data is freely available at: https://sites.google.com/site/alessiaamelio/software-tools/dice-captcha-dataset.

5.2 Experimental Setting

Before the analysis, the collected values for the measured variables have been normalised in the range [0,1], using the following equation:

$$x_1 = \frac{x - min_x}{max_x - min_x} \tag{2}$$

where x_1 is the normalised value, x is the actual value, and min_x and max_x are the minimum and maximum values for the variable associated to x, respectively. After the normalisation, the prediction of the response time was made using the ANN. Then, the predicted values were denormalised using the inverse formula of Eq. (2) and compared to the actual response time values.

The number of layers and type of activation function were varied in the ANN. Since no meaningful changes were obtained, the simple ANN architecture 3-N_h-1 was selected, where N_h represents the number of the neurons in the hidden layer. Also, a trial-and-error approach was carried out for adjusting the number of neurons in the hidden layer. In particular, N_h was varied from 5 to 50 with intervals of 5 (5, 10, 15, 20, etc.). In that way, 10 different ANNs have been created and tested.

In order to check the ANN performance, some data was used for training, some for testing and the rest of data for ANN validation. The sizes of the adopted data sets are: 75% of instances for training, 10% of instances for validation and 15% of instances for testing. It is worth to say that the training, validation and test sets were varied, too. The adopted algorithm is the Levenberg–Marquardt algorithm [15], and the maximum number of epochs is 1000. The training of the ANN is repeated until the error function (in this case Mean Squared Error – MSE) between the predicted values and the desired (target) values is minimised.

In order to evaluate the prediction accuracy, the following measures are used: (i) Pearson's correlation coefficient [14] – R, which is computed between the desired (target) and predicted values, (ii) Error, which is the difference between the desired (target) and predicted values, and (iii) MSE.

6 Results and Discussion

The experimentation has been performed in Matlab R2017a and Weka version 3.7 on a laptop with Quad-core CPU 2.2 GHz, 16 GB of RAM and Unix operating system.

In the following, the results in terms of R coefficient of the trial-and-error procedure for detecting the best number of neurons in the hidden layer are discussed for Dice 1 and 2 CAPTCHA. Then, the prediction accuracy of the tuned ANN is analysed in terms of Error and R. Since close results are obtained by different combinations of training, validation and test sets, they will be reported for only one of these combinations. Finally, comparison results with other regression methods in terms of MSE and R are shown and discussed.

6.1 Analysis of the Hidden Layer

Table 1 reports the results of the trial-and-error procedure in terms of R coefficient for Dice 1 and 2 CAPTCHA on the test set. It is worth noting that the highest values of R correspond to hidden layer composed of 25 neurons for Dice 1 CAPTCHA, and 45 neurons for Dice 2 CAPTCHA. This same number of neurons corresponds to low MSE values of 0.02 and 0.04 for Dice 1 and 2 CAPTCHA, respectively.

Table 1. Pearson's correlation coefficient R on test set for Dice 1 and 2 CAPTCHA. The number of neurons in the hidden layer is varied from 5 to 50. The best values are marked in bold

	5n	10n	15n	20n	25n	30n	35n	40n	45n	50n
Dice 1	0.711	0.523	0.667	0.446	**0.804**	0.431	0.458	0.403	0.653	0.783
Dice 2	0.246	0.270	0.485	0.343	0.227	0.076	0.369	0.033	**0.542**	0.204

Accordingly, the ANN model with hidden layer composed of 25 neurons for Dice 1 CAPTCHA and 45 neurons for Dice 2 CAPTCHA will be in the focus for further analysis.

6.2 Analysis of the Prediction Accuracy

Figure 5 shows the histogram of the Error for Dice 1 and Dice 2 CAPTCHA. It is worth noting that both errors are far from zero. In the test set of Dice 1, most of instances show an error between −0.07 and 0.01. By contrast, in the test set of Dice 2, more instances are distributed in a larger error range between −0.11 and 0.10.

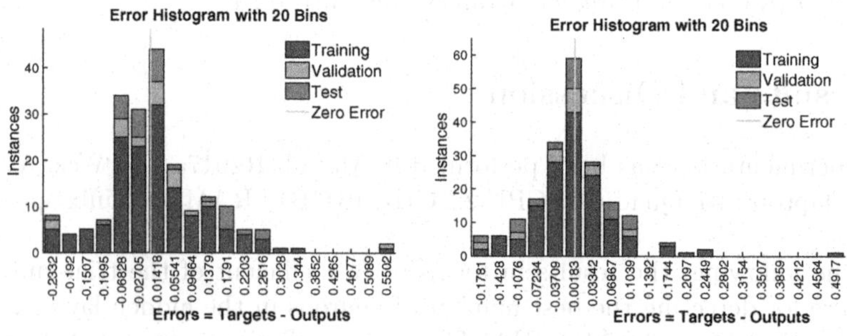

Fig. 5. Histogram of the Error for Dice 1 (left), and Dice 2 CAPTCHA (right)

In Fig. 6, the regression plots illustrate the network outputs with respect to target values in the test set for Dice 1 and 2 CAPTCHA, respectively. In order to obtain a perfect fit, the data should fall along a 45° line, which indicates that the network outputs are equal to the target values. It is worth noting that the fit is worst in Dice 2, with lower values of R than Dice 1 CAPTCHA (0.54 for Dice 2 vs. 0.80 for Dice 1).

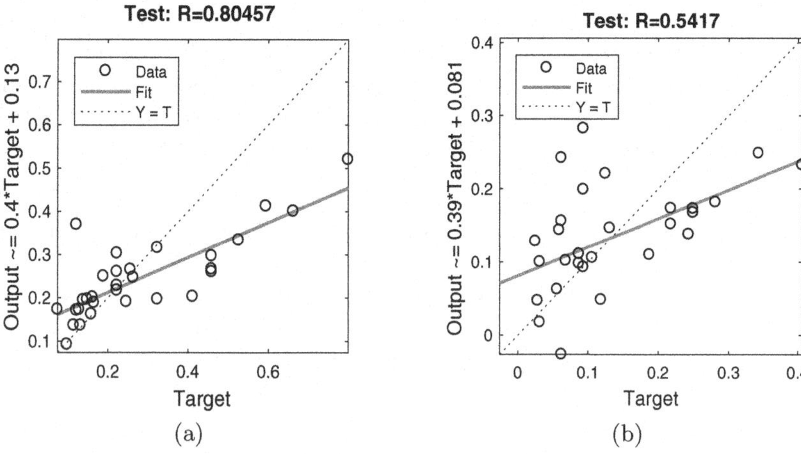

Fig. 6. Regression plots for (a) Dice 1 CAPTCHA (25 neurons in the hidden layer), and (b) Dice 2 CAPTCHA (45 neurons in the hidden layer)

From the results obtained by ANN, it is worth noting that the response time of both Dice 1 and 2 CAPTCHA is not perfectly predictable from known users' personal and demographic features: (i) age, (ii) type of device on which the CAPTCHA is solved, and (iii) years of Web use. In particular, the response time of Dice 2 is less predictable than Dice 1 CAPTCHA (higher Error and MSE, and lower R). Also, it is worth saying that Dice 2 CAPTCHA has an average and median response time which is less than 30 s. Still, from the previous study [8], Dice 2 was less dependent on the users' features than Dice 1 CAPTCHA. These results confirm that Dice 2 tends to be closer to an "ideal" CAPTCHA than Dice 1.

6.3 Comparison Results

The results obtained by ANN in terms of MSE and R coefficient are compared with results obtained by other two well-known regression methods: (i) Regression Trees (RT) [19], and (ii) Support Vector Machine Regression (SVMR) [9].

In Weka, SMOReg and REPTree algorithms with a 10-fold cross validation were applied on the dataset in order to predict the response time of Dice 1 and Dice 2 CAPTCHAs based on age, type of device, and Web use in years.

The SVMR is implemented in Weka through an improved SMOreg algorithm which finds the best fitted line that minimizes the cost function error.

The instances from the training set that are closest to that line are called support vectors. The training data was normalized during the application of the algorithm. A complexity parameter is set to 1 which means that the violations of the margin are allowed, and the polynomial kernel with exponent 1 was used, which makes it a linear kernel. Also, REPTree (Reduced Error Pruning Tree) uses different iterations to create multiple regression trees, after which the algorithm selects the best generated tree. The splitting criterion is the information gain, while reduced error pruning is used as a criterion for pruning the tree. The maximum tree depth was set to no restriction. The algorithm also used 3 folds for pruning the tree of Dice 1 CAPTCHA, and 4 folds for Dice 2 CAPTCHA.

Table 2 shows a comparison of the prediction results.

Table 2. Comparison results of response time prediction for Dice 1 and 2 CAPTCHA

	REPTree		SMOreg		ANN	
	MSE	R	MSE	R	MSE	R
Dice 1	20.25	0.51	20.69	0.51	0.02	0.80
Dice 2	12.37	0.27	11.93	0.31	0.04	0.54

It is worth noting that the results obtained by RT (REPTree) and SVMR (SMOreg) are consistent with ANN, since the response time is not perfectly predicted by the adopted users' features. In particular, it is visible that the response time of Dice 2 is less predictable than Dice 1 in terms of R coefficient (0.27 vs. 0.51 for REPTree and 0.31 vs. 0.51 for SMOreg). However, ANN proved to be the most reliable method for predictability analysis, since it obtains the best performances in terms of R and MSE.

7 Conclusions

This paper extended the study of the Dice CAPTCHA usability by analysing the predictability of its response time given known users' personal and demographic characteristics. This was accomplished by proposing a new ANN model for the evaluation of the prediction accuracy. According to the postulate of "ideal" CAPTCHA (response time should not depend on personal or demographic factors of solving users), a low predictability of time to complete implies a better quality of a CAPTCHA. The main result of this study is that response time of both Dice CAPTCHAs is not perfectly predictable from users' features. In particular, the response time to solve the Dice 2 is less predictable than Dice 1 CAPTCHA from the users' features. This implies that Dice 2 is closer to an "ideal" CAPTCHA than Dice 1.

Considering the difference between Dice 1 and Dice 2 and the features of the Dice CAPTCHA, some useful suggestions can be made for designing new CAPTCHAs which can be closer to an "ideal" one. They are the following: (i) visualisation is to prefer to calculation of some result in the CAPTCHA design, (ii) it is preferred to split the task in smaller steps (like in the Dice 2 where each digit must be recognised and reported).

Since there is not much literature about the effects of the colour of the CAPTCHA on its response time, future work will include testing the usability of different coloured Dice CAPTCHAs.

Acknowledgments. This work was partially supported by the Mathematical Institute of the Serbian Academy of Sciences and Arts (Project III44006). The authors are fully grateful to the participants to the experiment for anonymously providing their data. This paper is dedicated to our colleague and friend Associate Professor Darko Brodić with full gratitude.

References

1. von Ahn, L., Blum, M., Hopper, N.J., Langford, J.: Captcha: using hard AI problems for security. In: Biham, E. (ed.) Advances in Cryptology - EUROCRYPT 2003. LNCS, vol. 2656, pp. 294–311. Springer, Berlin Heidelberg (2003). https://doi.org/10.1007/3-540-39200-9_18
2. von Ahn, L., Blum, M., Langford, J.: Telling humans and computers apart automatically. Commun. ACM **47**(2), 56–60 (2004). https://doi.org/10.1145/966389.966390
3. Alsuhibany, S.A.: Evaluating the usability of optimizing text-based captcha generation methods. Int. J. Adv. Comput. Sci. Appl. **7**(8), 164–169 (2016)
4. Baecher, P., Fischlin, M., Gordon, L., Langenberg, R., Lützow, M., Schröder, D.: Captchas: the good, the bad and the ugly. In: Sicherheit, pp. 353–365 (2010)
5. Beheshti, S.M.R.S., Liatsis, P.: Captcha usability and performance, how to measure the usability level of human interactive applications quantitatively and qualitatively? In: 2015 International Conference on Developments of E-Systems Engineering (DeSE), pp. 131–136, December 2015. https://doi.org/10.1109/DeSE.2015.23
6. Brodić, D., Amelio, A., Ahmad, N., Shahzad, S.K.: Usability analysis of the image and interactive CAPTCHA via prediction of the response time. In: Phon-Amnuaisuk, S., Ang, S.P., Lee, S.Y. (eds.) MIWAI 2017. LNCS, vol. 10607, pp. 252–265. Springer, Cham (2017). https://doi.org/10.1007/978-3-319-69456-6_21
7. Brodić, D., Amelio, A., Draganov, I.R.: Statistical analysis of dice captcha usability. In: Proceedings of the Information, Communication and Energy Systems and Technologies - 52nd International Scientific Conference, ICEST 2017, Niš, Serbia, June 28–30, 2017, pp. 139–142 (2017)
8. Brodić, D., Amelio, A., Draganov, I.R., Janković, R.: Exploring the usability of the dice CAPTCHA by advanced statistical analysis. In: Agre, G., van Genabith, J., Declerck, T. (eds.) AIMSA 2018. LNCS, vol. 11089, pp. 152–162. Springer, Cham (2018)
9. Cortes, C., Vapnik, V.: Support-vector networks. Mach. Learn. **20**(3), 273–297 (1995). https://doi.org/10.1007/BF00994018

10. DiceCAPTCHA: http://dice-captcha.com/
11. Guerar, M., Merlo, A., Migliardi, M.: Completely automated public physical test to tell computers and humans apart: a usability study on mobile devices. Future Gener. Comput. Syst. **82**, 617–630 (2018). https://doi.org/10.1016/j.future.2017.03.012
12. Iantovics, L.B., Rotar, C., Nechita, E.: A novel robust metric for comparing the intelligence of two cooperative multiagent systems. Procedia Comput. Sci. **96**, 637–644 (2016). https://doi.org/10.1016/j.procs.2016.08.245. knowledge-Based and Intelligent Information & Engineering Systems: Proceedings of the 20th International Conference KES-2016
13. Ince, I.F., Salman, Y.B., Yildirim, M.E., Yang, T.: Execution time prediction for 3D interactive captcha by keystroke level model. In: 2009 Fourth International Conference on Computer Sciences and Convergence Information Technology, pp. 1057–1061, November 2009. https://doi.org/10.1109/ICCIT.2009.105
14. KentStateUniversity: Pearson's correlation coefficient. https://libguides.library.kent.edu/SPSS/PearsonCorr
15. Levenberg, K.: A method for the solution of certain non-linear problems in least squares. Quart. J. Appl. Math. **II**(2), 164–168 (1944). https://doi.org/10.1090/qam/10666
16. Lupkowski, P., Urbanski, M.: Semcaptchauser-friendly alternative for ocr-based captcha systems. In: 2008 International Multiconference on Computer Science and Information Technology, pp. 325–329, October 2008. https://doi.org/10.1109/IMCSIT.2008.4747260
17. Mohamed, M., Gao, S., Sachdeva, N., Saxena, N., Zhang, C., Kumaraguru, P., van Oorschot, P.C.: On the security and usability of dynamic cognitive game captchas. J. Comput. Secur. **25**, 205–230 (2017). https://doi.org/10.3233/JCS-16847
18. Nguyen, T.T.: Studies of Dynamic Cognitive Game CAPTCHA Usability and Stream Relay Attacks. Doctoral dissertation, California State Polytechnic University, Pomona (2017)
19. Rokach, L., Maimon, O.: Data Mining With Decision Trees: Theory and Applications, 2nd edn. World Scientific Publishing Co. Inc, River Edge (2014)
20. Tanikić, D., Marinković, V., Manić, M., Devedžić, G., Randelović, S.: Application of response surface methodology and fuzzy logic based system for determining metal cutting temperature. Bull. Pol. Acad. Sci. Tech. Sci. **64**(2), 435–445 (2016). https://doi.org/10.1515/bpasts-2016-0049
21. Wikipedia: The captcha test. http://en.wikipedia.org/wiki/CAPTCHA
22. Yan, J., El Ahmad, A.S.: Usability of captchas or usability issues in captcha design. In: Proceedings of the 4th Symposium on Usable Privacy and Security, pp. 44–52. SOUPS 2008. ACM, New York (2008). https://doi.org/10.1145/1408664.1408671
23. Yu, J., Ma, X., Han, T.: Usability investigation on the localization of text captchas: take chinese characters as a case study. In: Proceedings of the Transdisciplinary Engineering - 24th ISPE Inc., International Conference, vol. 5, pp. 233–242. IOS Press, Singapore (2017)

Digital Libraries and Archives

Water to the Thirsty Reflections on the Ethical Mission of Libraries and Open Access

Matilde Fontanin(✉) and Paola Castellucci

University La Sapienza, Rome, Italy
{matilde. fontanin, paola. castellucci}@uniromal. it

Abstract. The shift to digital information determines a parallel shift in access modes, and digital libraries are called to action by the ethical foundations of their mission. Open Access makes information potentially available not just to researchers, but to everyone, yet there are still barriers to be overcome in terms of technical infrastructures, points of access, digital and cultural divide.

The mission of libraries, as stated by IFLA Manifesto for Digital Libraries and IFLA/FAIFE Code of Ethics for Librarians and other Information Workers, converges with the mission and ethics of the BBB declarations on Open Access: it is about delivering information to everyone, from scholars to the "curious minds", and librarians can be mediators in the wide diffusion, at all levels of society, of scientific, scholarly knowledge, to foster "active" and "scientific" citizenship.

Keywords: Digital libraries · Open access · Ethical mission · Accessibility · IFLA CODE on ethics · BBB declarations

1 Digital Information Landscape: Open to Researchers/Open to Everybody

1.1 Digital Information and Library Mission

Since most of the information and knowledge started circulating in a digital format, life has not been the same for all sorts of libraries, as the growth is exponential: Floridi [1, 2] pointed out that "*Every day, enough data are being generated to fill all US libraries eight times over. [...] we shall have 8* ZB *of data by 2015*". ICT devices are allowing us to navigate this ocean of data "*but at the same time they are the sources of further data, which in turn require, or make possible, more ICTs. It is a self-Reinforcing cycle and it would be unnatural not to feel overwhelmed*". Naturally, Floridi refers to data of all sorts, not necessarily the sort of data libraries organise, yet the scenario raises questions: is it imaginable that libraries – or any other subject – succeed in organizing that data?

Digital libraries, especially research libraries, are probably busy enough with the preservation and dissemination of research in the digital ecosystem; librarians do not only honour their historical commitment to "serving", but accomplish their more recent role – stemmed from the new competencies necessary to manage digital libraries, collections and Open Access– of mediators between science and society. They can

P. Manghi et al. (Eds.): IRCDL 2019, CCIS 988, pp. 61–71, 2019.
https://doi.org/10.1007/978-3-030-11226-4_5

greatly contribute to efficiently disseminating the results of scientific research, as it was the case for the partnership between Charlotte Hess and Elinor Olstrom. Their work was originated by the *Workshop on Scholarly Communication As a Commons*, led by Olstrom at the University of Indiana in 2004, an attempt to define the concept of *commons* from a multidisciplinary point of view. Knowledge as a commons is a shared resource, like natural resources, but, unlike water or fisheries, it is impossible to exclude someone from knowledge once it has been made public- whereas the book it is written in is a piece of private property. At the time they wrote, they were Director of the Digital Library of the Commons at Indiana University and 2009 Nobel Prize in Economic Sciences: the book [3] resulting from the workshop contains papers from those who were to become the most prominent experts and advocates of Open Access.

As librarians develop into researchers, the ethics of science, prime mover of research, gets closer to the basic principles of the library mission, mainly allowing people to find the information they need to advance their knowledge and become active citizens [4]. Commitment to objective quality, to unbiased neutrality, to the rejection of personal gain in the choices, in other words “science for science sake”, are common core for librarians choosing resources and for scientists struggling with the citation system [8].

Librarians are not the only new stakeholders on the scene of Open Access: citizens are invited too, as they become gradually more aware of their “worthiness” to be informed of scientific information and research results. The Budapest Open Access Initiative [9] aims at *world-wide electronic distribution of the peer-reviewed journal literature and completely free and unrestricted access to it by [...] curious minds*; the “What you can do to Help” section asks citizens to advocate for Open Access demanding that research paid for by taxpayers be made public.

This new “scientific” or “active” citizenship has been acknowledged for some time now in many countries and is expressed in the participation to referenda on scientific issues such as nuclear energy or medically assisted procreation, which imply citizens are informed, and therefore have formed an opinion. In Italy, the patient is asked to sign an “informed” medical release form to authorise therapies. Yet, without being truly informed, it would be a blank check. Pietro Greco [10] underlines the need to raise citizens’ awareness on scientific issues, they need to know before they make decision on their health or on their environment; a model for this attitude is Al Gore’s engagement both in environmental communication and popularization [11] – for which he was awarded the 2007 Nobel Prize for Peace - and in converting MEDLINE to PubMed under the Clinton Administration in 1997, thus making a precious informational resource available on Open Access to everyone worldwide, not just to the taxpayers. Advancement in science cannot happen without democracy [10], as they share the same basic principles: during Hitler’s regime, science moved from Nazi Germany to the USA, where democracy was granted. Science is the prime mover of technology and economics, and no government can hope to succeed if they decide to harness it.

Libraries are ideally poised to mediate science from the specialist to the layman through their reference services. As an example, patients’ libraries offer services to help retrieve information on specific conditions, thus allowing the patient to become proficient in his/her own illness. Librarians mediate both researches on databases – be they proprietary or Open Access as PubMed - and search engines as Google, not forgetting resources in the library. Gaetana Cognetti, director of the Biblioteca Maceratini in Rome and Ivana Truccolo [12], director of the library at the specialized cancer center CRO Aviano (PN) were prominent in establishing an alliance of health libraries in Italy, from which a search engine specific for information on cancer was started.

Probably we are at the point that the distinction between digital and analogic libraries is superfluous, as all libraries, be they digital or not, need to come to terms with digital information.

The sheer mass of information available does not make libraries themselves redundant. The exponential growth of Internet services in the 1990s had raised a debate on the nearing extinction of librarians, who would have become useless: the more user-friendly technology, the less librarians needed, was the perspective. We can appreciate nowadays how this point of view was wrong: as Wiener [13] had already pointed out in the 1950s, machines can carry out better and faster than humans repetitive tasks, but creativity, ethics, empathy and imagination are human, and, as a NESTA report [14] underlines, are core skills to be successful on the job market.

Proceeding from Floridi, recently Bawden [15] argued that in 50 years' time probably computer rooms will be outdated, as everyone will wear their own digital devices, but libraries will still be needed, to help people make sense of the technology. The more information available, the more it needs to be mediated by someone who is interested in filtering it objectively and without judging it, simply discriminating what is reliable and what is not. Researchers are interested in content, librarians are interested in context and reliability, their look is supposed to be objective and unbiased according to their Code of Ethics. The mission of libraries is thus described by IFLA FAIFE's Code of Ethics [16]: *Librarians and other information workers organize and present content in a way that allows an autonomous user to find the information s/he needs. Librarians and other information workers help and support users in their information searching*, and, according to IFLA/UNESCO [4] *The mission of the digital library is to give direct access to information resources, both digital and non-digital, in a structured and authoritative manner and thus to link information technology, education and culture in contemporary library service.*

Thinking in this perspective about the aims of the Open Access movement clarifies immediately why libraries are a stakeholder in this scenario; besides, the Budapest Open Access Initiative [9] invites libraries, among the others who share the same vision, *to join us in the task of removing the barriers to Open Access and building a future in which research and education in every part of the world are that much more free to flourish.* Open Access pioneers set once more an example, as Harnad [17] and his concept that any piece of information shared on the Internet is written in the sky for everyone to see, meaning that it can be shared regardless of borders, obstacles, economic, social and intellectual gaps. Harnad names his blog "Open Access Archivangelism", because everyone can advocate for OA principles according to his/her means and skills, there are no exceptions and no weak or powerful allies. It is a bottom-up process and everyone is invited in.

Marchionini [18] recently remarked that data and information science is a small fish in a big sea, as the ratio is that for 100.000 jobs in data science there are 1 million in the sciences themselves (that is biology, engineering, a.s.o.), but still the field plays the important role of curating and bridging research data to the people. To be more effective, the action should be carried out in collaboration with other specialists – such as information technology or subject specialists – who may be involved in data production and in the technical aspects of preservation, but who do not need to be involved in the same ethical choices around data curation that directly involve libraries. This convergence would allow library and information professionals to tell the story of what they can do for the organisation, preservation, and consistent construction of metadata to represent data themselves. The benefits of such open attitude, apart from the collaboration between Ostrom and Hess mentioned above, are demonstrated in the case of Luisella Goldschmidt-Clermont (1925–2013), librarian at CERN and sociologist, whose pre-print [19], though never published at the time, was fully acknowledged in the light of the OA movement, as the author's meta-reflection contributes to highlighting the mutual growth that could result for physics, anthropology and library science from the mutual exchange: being married to a scientist, she had the privilege of observing the physicists' community in action. Moreover, the role of libraries is visible in the reasons and benefits that led Ginsparg to transfer arXiv from Los Alamos to the University of Cornell as well as in the contribution of librarians in IRIS, the Italian archive for scholarly publications, where librarians are in charge of the curation, the creation of metadata, the advocacy of the repository among scholars and their training.

The above-mentioned IFLA/UNESCO Manifesto for Digital Libraries mentions the importance to overcome the Digital divide to pursue the Millennium Development Goals, and states that *the dissemination of information enables citizens to participate in life-long learning and education*; in line with other IFLA/FAIFE Code of Ethics and other IFLA documents, user education is one of the missions of every sort of library, and the education to digital content, or media literacy, is carried out by all species of libraries for their different audiences. Academic and research libraries can help researchers use digital collections for their purposes; public libraries help citizens finding and making sense of the information they need for their health, business, or to enforce their rights as citizens.

1.2 Open Access Accessibility: Water to the Thirsty

Telling our story from the perspective of Cultural History [20], a novel by Roth [21] could be used as an example to represent the distribution of knowledge. We are at the beginning of the 20th century; the main character in the novel, David, who had migrated with his family to the USA a few years previously, now is six years old. In his kitchen, he is staring at the water tap which is too high for him to reach:

Standing before the kitchen sink and regarding the bright brass faucets that gleamed so far away, each with a bead of water at its nose, slowly swelling, falling, David again became aware that this world had been created without thought of him. He was thirsty, but the iron hip of the sink rested on legs tall almost as his own body, and by no stretch of arm, no leap, could he ever reach the distant tap. Where did the water come from that lurked so secretly in the curve of the brass? Where did it go, gurgling in the drain? What a strange world must be hidden behind the walls of a house! But he was thirsty.

The water from the tap could be compared to information. Water is distributed freely to everyone in the place where the main character is, though it is not so for other countries at the time – for example the countries of origin of most migrants in the novel, for whom the United States are the golden land. Yet, in the case of David, the tap is too high for him to drink, but he is thirsty. Open Access publications are delivered, as the water is, to everyone, free of charge. The reflection leads the reader to considering that the general public, like David, is unable to take full advantage of that resource. People are not always able to reach out to that knowledge, as there are many obstacles to sharing knowledge worldwide, even after research results, in the form of publications or data are – as the Open Access movement advocates – made freely available. The nature of such obstacles to accessibility regards the digital divide, the cultural (and social) divide, the accessibility issues and the organization and validation of knowledge, *but they must be faced to remove the barriers to Open Access and building a future in which research and education in every part of the world are that much more free to flourish, thus building the basis for scientific and active citizenship extended to all curious minds* [9].

2 Accessibility Issues

2.1 Digital Divide

The IFLA/UNESCO manifesto for digital libraries [4] states that *Bridging the digital divide is a key factor in achieving the Millennium Development Goals of the United Nations. Access to information resources and the means of communication supports health and education as much as cultural and economic development.* The digital divide could merely consist in the lack of a digital device or access to the Internet: back in 2007, when the IFLA delegates visited it, the Mpumalanga Public Library in Kwala-Zulu Natal (South Africa) offered a series of computers to its users. They had been paid for by a nearby factory, which had an interest that young people in the area acquired digital competencies, and the library was the ideal place to do this, as it had space, electricity, Internet connection and staff to help users in their learning needs. This is one of the ways libraries can help overcome that particular sort of divide: access to digital information has a physical dimension.

Even when the connection is present and the device is available, though, there could be a different sort of digital divide: those who are able to use information critically and those who are not, the latter being unable to reach informed judgements. Marchionini [18] stated that democracy is endangered both by too little and by too much information – and science may be damaged by the spread of uncontrolled resources, especially if they are easier to reach than the serious, fact-checked and well-grounded scientific production available through Open Access. Making people information literate is the goal libraries pursue through user education, a topic which will be touched upon in the next paragraph.

2.2 Cultural Divide

There is more hindering the access to open knowledge: cultural (and social) differences matter. Without an adequate background it is probably unlikely that common citizens reach a database such as PubMed, and, even if they do and retrieve the documents they need, they require certain competencies to understand them. The documents contained in PubMed, ArXiv, ERIC are not written for the ordinary public, though it could be argued that there are differences. While the others aim mostly at being understandable for the scholarly community, PubMed must be understandable for a wider audience, if we agree that knowledge about health could be defined as a commons. Actually, the development from Index Medicus – started in 1876 - to its digitization in MEDLARS - available from 1964 at the National Library of Medicine in Bethesda - to MEDLINE, since 1971 the online version of MEDLARS, draw a timeline leading to increased opening and availability of medical information. A dramatic acceleration to the trend was given in 1997 when the government decided to pay for the database, considered a necessary public resource, so the domain changed from .com to .gov and the name updated to PubMed. After this, to increase the findability and overcome cultural barriers, PubMedPlus, multilingual, was started in 1998, with a Spanish interface and a thesaurus mediating between medical specialized terms and common language; in 2000 PubMedCentral added a collection of full-text documents to the bibliographic database. MeSH (Medical Subject Headings) must not be forgotten: started in Index Medicus, it strives to increase accessibility and normalize the vocabulary; the Unified Medical Language System (UMLS), besides, since 1986 strived to mediate among various languages, language registries and communities.

The story of Lorenzo's oil [20], the true story of Augusto and Michaela Odone, constitutes an example of the layman's use of medical information. These two parents were in search for a cure for their son Lorenzo's adrenoleukodystrophy (ALD), and their story, incidentally, was the subject of a 1992 film by George Miller. The Odones were told that the rare illness of their son would have taken him to death in two years' time: they were educated people, they decided to research. The father went to the library in the first place; at the time – the end of the 1960s – there was no Internet available to common citizens. Besides, geography favoured them: the nearest library was the one of the National Institute of Health, in Bethesda, Maryland, the greatest medical library in the world. Though not being medical practitioners themselves, they were people with a higher education background and the husband, Augusto, worked at the World Bank, in an international context. They had acquired the right competencies to look for documentation in their fields of expertise, but now they needed to search in an unknown field. The illness of their son made them transfer those skills into another area, and these skills proved successful: they were able to conduct cross-searches on Medline, other biomedical databases and Index Medicus, which were all, at the time, proprietary tools whose use was dearly paid for. For six months, in line with the code of ethics of the library service, the Bethesda Library enabled the Odones to use those advanced research tools for free, within the library premises – it should be noted, besides, that Bethesda was the place where Medline server was physically located. At the end, the mixture they came up with, the so-called "oil", allowed Lorenzo to live 20 years longer. Their remedy still rises many eyebrows in the professional health field, it produced no protocol and is strongly criticized, but these facts are of little importance to our present scope: we are more interested in the documentation process, as this story is an example of advanced documentation retrieval. Researchers will just need someone to point them to the right database and will have the competency to understand the results, whereas common citizens who do not have the same skills can ask a specialist for help – or an information specialist, that is a librarian.

This is the same thing happening to David, who needs his mum to help him get to the water and quench his thirst. He is too short, he feels the world around has been *created without thought of him*, his mother is tall enough to get him a glass of water, or, in other words, to act as a mediator and to supply for the lack of accessibility of the resource. This point is developed in the next paragraph.

2.3 Design for All: Web Accessibility

Basically, the world of digital information is still heavily dominated by words and text and therefore subject to some of the same patterns applicable to language. Most of the information offered by libraries at the moment still requires that we sit in front of a computer or use our smartphone and type in text when looking for information, only the space we explore is the infosphere, made of cyberspace, but also including offline and analogue spaces of information.

Text in itself is not clear to everyone, nor are images or the information on the screen. For people with visual impairments, for example, the screen is not that clear, unless it is carefully planned. IFLA has a Libraries Serving Persons with Print Disabilities Section which developed many guides for library services to special communities. Electronic Information for Libraries (EIFL) prepared guidelines for the implementation of the Marrakesh Treaty, a WIPO treaty for persons with print disabilities [22]. The ICT4IAL [23] developed the “Guidelines for Accessible Information, an Open Educational Resource (OER) to support the creation of accessible information in general and for learning in particular.”, and the World Wide Web Consortium itself is very attentive to special needs and prepares many Guidelines to accessibility [24]. Without standardized procedures on text writing, XML, description of images, subtitles for the deaf and provisions for special psychological, neurological and physical needs, Open Access resources risk being closed to a meaningful part of the population.

What is more, the concept of accessibility is for all [24], as better-designed resources are an advantage also for people without disabilities – web pages designed for cognitive disorders result clearer for everyone – whether they are using the Internet on mobile devices or with temporary hindrances.

2.4 Knowledge Organization and Validation

The tap David is staring at channels water that comes from different sources (lakes, rivers, basins) but is basically channeled into the same system: it could be correct to say that the same water arrives everywhere in the city of New York.

On the contrary, though there are many databases available on Open Access, there is not only one tap. On the web it is possible to find incredible Open Access resources, millions of data, articles, papers, videos, images and more. The problem is that, even when they are produced by similar institutions, they are generally based on different platforms. The question is, how is a citizen to know they are all there? This is one of the needs the library community can answer to, differentiating its action according to the population served.

In the case of the scholarly community, the mentoring usually implied in the researchers' career contributes to pass on the discipline-related knowledge on digital and information resources. This system is not flawless: a certain tendency to relying on what is already known overseeing what is not yet known is normal, when one is busy on research: subject librarians can help fill in that particular gap.

As it is the librarians' job to become acquainted with information resources, they can always point library users to those which answer their needs, but this solution works only for the people who actually go to the library or check on the library website. Olijhoek and Tennant [25] advocate users' education, and librarians do precisely that, as it is in their mission and in their code of ethics.

The majority of the Internet users will turn once more to search engines – Google first of all. Search engines can make themselves perfectly understandable, but reliability is not their mission. Google's original mission statement in 1998 was *to organise the world's information and make it universally accessible and useful*. In 2014 Larry Page expressed his doubts that the company probably needed a new statement, but he was not sure which one would actually fit in with what they were doing at the time. Google may be born under the star of that initial mission, but in order to thrive offering free tools it relied on advertisers. Naturally, the mission of every business company is to support itself: Google made and is still making many amazing projects feasible, many of them in and with libraries, yet it would be irresponsible to put a company in charge of organizing, preserving and granting access to world knowledge, this is a task for governments and people's institutions [26–28]. As an aside, the concept of Open Access and free of charge are not overlapping: scholarly publications can be offered free of charge because they have been publicly funded, and therefore belong to the community, they are a commons, unlike resources which are offered free of charge because some company or corporation is trying to get to the consumers through them.

Digital libraries should contribute to raise awareness and increase knowledge, and they definitely strive to do so, also acting as advocates of Open Access, by encouraging authors to deposit in open repositories and making directories of such repositories widely known [29]. They make wonderful collections available, yet these collections are not always visible to the population at large, at least not among the first twenty hits. Admittedly, this search string is quite superficial, yet, this is the way people search - unless they are librarians of professional researchers. This means that many Open Access resources remain invisible to the large public, and all field-specialized databases even more so.

Thinking back of David, so thirsty and waiting for water: what would happen if the water turned out to be polluted? Recently a German magazine [30] published an investigation demonstrating, according to the authors, that Open Access research is not necessarily of scholarly quality. The investigators made up a Mr. R. Funden - "Erfunden" in German means "made up, invented" - gave him life, and he received some invitations from predatory publishers in the seven months the investigation lasted. The findings might be interesting and made a case in Germany, but they are not news to those into scholarly publishing. According to the authors, the investigation would prove that, provided anyone has the money, they can make themselves a scholarly reputation and be published along with highly-reputed scholars, whose names are sometimes simply used without their knowledge and at other times before they realized who they were publishing with. Other, better informed, sources [25] recall previous similar enquiries and underline the poor data support in the present investigation and state that such examples should not undermine the whole OA movement. Taking the story with the necessary caution, this goes back to what we were saying above: the increase in the information available does not make libraries redundant. Since the main commitment of the librarians is to organize information itself, more than using it to create knowledge in a specific disciplinary field, they are more and more needed on the digital scenario to select sources and train users.

Would David's mother be able to understand that the water is poisoned? Probably not, but she has more chances of becoming aware of that than David himself does: she is in charge of the household after all, whereas he is simply in charge of growing up.

3 Conclusion

The digital revolution is on, as well as the Open Access movement, which, through the three declarations (Budapest, Bethesda, Berlin) made great steps forward.

The huge amount of online free information does not push the libraries out of the game, on the contrary it makes them even more useful, as when everybody is producing open knowledge the mechanisms for distribution that otherwise rely on large private companies cannot be taken for granted.

Great investment is required from the research institutions and the libraries to face the issues related to the accessibility and the usability of the resources – and their preservation too, though this article chose not to did not deal with the latter. Efforts towards grouping of all resources in common large containers is advisable, though simply putting many things in a box does not help with their retrieval: information should be allowed to flow as water does, channeled to the taps in David's and everyone else's homes, and, being a free commons, the costs should be sustained by the institutions with the aim of fostering a larger societal growth. To face all these issues, the long-term competencies of librarians in data organization and curation will be an asset to preserve and maintain open knowledge.

Librarians are bound by their mission to give direct access to information resources, both digital and non-digital, in a structured and authoritative manner and thus to link information technology, education and culture in contemporary library service [4] and in this respect they converge with the aims of the Open Access Initiative, to provide the public with unrestricted, free access to scholarly research—much of which is publicly funded […] free of charge and without most copyright and licensing restrictions—in the belief that such process will accelerate scientific research efforts and allow authors to reach a larger number of readers [9]. In becoming advocates for the process of Open Access, librarians contribute with their competencies in information organization and dissemination, are involved in the research process and become researchers themselves, thus creating a new vision of science, as the one inaugurated when Paul Ginsparg opened the arXiv repository to the digital humanities.

References

1. Floridi, L.: The 4th Revolution: How the Infosphere is Reshaping Human Reality. Oxford University Press, New York (2014)
2. Floridi, L.: The Ethics of Information. Oxford University Press, Oxford (2015)
3. Hess, C., Ostrom, E. (eds.): Understanding Knowledge as a Commons: From Theory to Practice. MIT Press, Cambridge (2006)
4. IFLA/UNESCO Manifesto for Digital Libraries. https://www.ifla.org/publications/iflaunesco-manifesto-for-digital-libraries. Accessed 14 Sept 2018
5. Solimine, G.: Senza sapere: il costo dell'ignoranza in Italia. GLF editori Laterza, Roma (2014)
6. Solimine, G.: La biblioteca: scenari, culture, pratiche di servizio. GLF editori Laterza, Roma (2004)
7. Ridi, R.: Etica bibliotecaria: Deontologia professionale e dilemmi morali. Editrice Bibliografica, Milano (2011)
8. Cronin, B.: The Hand of Science: Academic Writing and Its Rewards. Scarecrow Press, Lanham (2005)
9. Budapest Open Access Initiative. https://www.budapestopenaccessinitiative.org. Accessed 14 Sept 2018
10. Greco, P.: Scienza e (è) democrazia, 24 novembre 2017. Accessed 14 Sept 2018. https://bit.ly/2CUbfGx
11. Guggenheim, D.: An Inconvenient Truth (2006)
12. Truccolo, I., Cognetti, G. et al.: National Cancer Information Service in Italy: an information points network as a new model for providing information for cancer patients. Tumori J. **97**(4), 510–516 (2011)
13. Wiener, N.: The human Use of Human Beings: Cybernetics and Society. Eyre and Spottiswoode, London (1950)
14. Bakshi, H.: Creativity versus robots : the creative economy and the future of employment Nesta (2015)
15. Bawden, D.: Never again the in the history of humanity: information education for onlife. In: Aparac-Jelušić, T., Casarosa, V., Macevičiūtė, E. (eds.). The Future of Education in Information Science: Proceedings from FEIS – International EINFOSE Symposium, Pisa, Italy, 10–11 September 2018
16. IFLA FAIFE: Freedom of Access to Information and Freedom of Expression. IFLA Code of Ethics for Librarians and other Information Workers (2012). https://www.ifla.org/publications/node/11092. Accessed 14 Sept 2018
17. Harnad, S.: Scholarly skywriting and the prepublication continuum of scientific inquiry. Psychol. Sci. **1**, 342–343 (1990)
18. Marchionini, G.: Information science roles in data science. In: Aparac-Jelušić, T., Casarosa, V., Macevičiūtė, E. (eds.) The Future of Education in Information Science: Proceedings from FEIS – International EINFOSE Symposium, Pisa, Italy, 10–11 September 2018
19. Goldschmidt-Clermont, L.: Communication patterns in high-energy physics. High Energy Physics Libraries Webzine 6 (2002)

20. Castellucci, P.: Carte del nuovo mondo: banche dati e Open Access. Il mulino, Bologna (2017)
21. Roth, H.: Call it Sleep. Robert O. Ballou, New York (1934)
22. Marrakesh Treaty to Facilitate Access to Published Works for Persons Who Are Blind, Visually Impaired or Otherwise Print Disabled. http://www.wipo.int/treaties/en/ip/marrakesh . Accessed 14 Sept 2018
23. ICT4IAL: Guidelines for Accessible Information. https://www.ict4ial.eu/guidelines-accessible-information. Available in 26 languages. Accessed 14 Sept 2018
24. W3C: Introduction to Web Accessibility. https://www.w3.org/WAI/fundamentals/accessibility-intro/#what. Accessed 14 Sept 2018
25. Olijhoek, T., Tennant, J.: The "problem" of Predatory Publishing Remains a Relatively Small One and Should Not be Allowed to Defame Open Access, 25 September 2018. https://bit.ly/2QW6fVe. Accessed 25 Sept 2018
26. Vaidhyanathan, S.: The Googlization of Everything: (And Why We Should Worry), Updated edn. University of California Press, Berkeley (2012)
27. Battelle, J.: The Search: How Google and Its Rivals Rewrote the Rules of Business and Transformed Our Culture. Portfolio, New York (2005)
28. Darnton, R.: The Case for Books: Past, Present, and Future. Public Affairs, New York (2009)
29. OPEN DOAR. http://v2.sherpa.ac.uk/opendoar/. Accessed 14 Sept 2018
30. Wagner, L., Langhans, K., Kropshofer, K., Bauer, P., Krause, T.: Das Schein-geschäft : Angriff auf die Wissenschaft. Süddeutsche Zeitung Magazin (29), 10–24 (2018)

Computational Terminology in eHealth

Federica Vezzani[1(✉)] and Giorgio Maria Di Nunzio[2]

[1] Department of Linguistic and Literary Studies, University of Padua, Padua, Italy
federica.vezzani@phd.unipd.it

[2] Department of Information Engineering, University of Padua, Padua, Italy
giorgiomaria.dinunzio@unipd.it

Abstract. In this paper, we present a methodology for the development of a new eHealth resource in the context of Computational Terminology. This resource, named TriMED, is a digital library of terminological records designed to satisfy the information needs of different categories of users within the healthcare field: patients, language professionals and physicians. TriMED offers a wide range of information for the purpose of simplification of medical language in terms of understandability and readability. Finally, we present two applications of our resource in order to conduct different types of studies in particular in Information Retrieval and Literature Analysis.

1 Introduction

Computational Terminology (CT) is a recent field of study gathering the interest of researchers who have experienced the need to improve communication, or to access domain-related information [3]. CT is closely related to the organization and management of linguistic data for different purposes and, for this reason, several types of terminological resources have been implemented in order to satisfy these needs, such as specialized dictionaries, terminological databases and glossaries. Moreover, scientific needs in fast growing domains (such as biomedicine, chemistry and ecology) and the overwhelming amount of textual data published daily demand that terminology is acquired and managed systematically and automatically.

In the medical field, the need to manage data is increasingly evident, in particular in the context of health practice through the support of mobile and portable tools and in the physician-patient interactions. According to GSMA,[1] there are four major customers in the eHealth market: health-care providers, payers (both public and private health-care insurers), governments, and Healthcare consumers, each of whom have different priorities and needs. Focusing on health-care consumers, the main priority is to manage one's own health in order to have access to reliable and comprehensible medical information. For this reason, there are freely available resources [18,35], as for example *Everyday Health*[2]

[1] https://www.gsma.com/mobilefordevelopment/wp-content/uploads/2012/05/Role-and-Value-of-MNOs-in-eHealth1.pdf.

[2] https://www.everydayhealth.com/.

P. Manghi et al. (Eds.): IRCDL 2019, CCIS 988, pp. 72–85, 2019.
https://doi.org/10.1007/978-3-030-11226-4_6

which offers personalized health advice, tools, and communities, or *Medscape*,[3] offering medical information for specialists, physicians, and industry professionals. These tools are based on the need for effective communication between various actors and the transmission of information in a clear and understandable way. Therefore, terminology is an important issue to be considered because medical language is often characterized by a complex lexicon difficult to understand. Many studies [6,7,14,30] point out problems related to medical terminology such as semantic ambiguity, incorrect use of suffixes, archaism maintaining, redundancy in the formation of compounds, and etymological inconsistencies. As a result, patients and in general non-experts in medicine are often exposed to medical terms that can be semantically complex and hardly understandable [38].

Public libraries have a long history of providing community outreach programs and services to their diverse user population, including aiding access to reliable consumer health information and electronic health resources and offering health-information literacy programs [39]. Acquiring this knowledge, from public libraries as well as the availability of free and publicly available online resources, and organizing it into a digital library would ease the problem of health literacy defined as 'the degree to which individuals have the capacity to obtain, process, and understand basic health information and services needed to make appropriate health decisions' [16]. Such digital library would also facilitate medical practitioners in the discovery of novel treatments or diseases. However, building an ontology for a medical digital library is not a trivial task since it requires a significant amount of time and manual effort.

In this paper, we describe the motivations and the methodology behind the development of TriMED, an eHealth resource based on terminological and linguistic features [41]. This terminological database responds to the information needs of different categories of users within the health-care field: patients, language professionals and physicians. This tool is composed of multilingual terminological records offering a wide range of information depending on the user identification in three languages: English, Italian and French. This kind of terminological resource and, in particular, the model of terminological record designed for this tool, can be exploited in order to conduct different types of studies in a variety of research areas: not only medical terminology analysis and simplification, but also identification and retrieval of relevant medical documents and linguistic analysis of medical terms in literature.

The reminder of this paper is organized as follows: in Sect. 2, we present the state-of-the-art from two points of view in the context of eHealth: CT and Digital Library (DL). In Sect. 3, we describe the requirements of the terminological eHealth resource focusing on the definition of a medical terminological record and its structure. Then, in Sect. 4, we show the applications of these terminological records in two different domains: Information Retrieval and Literature analysis. Finally in Sect. 5, we give our conclusions and some hints on future works.

[3] https://www.medscape.com/.

2 Related Works

In this section, we present the state-of-the-art relating to the eHealth field from two different perspectives: Computational Terminology and Digital Libraries.

2.1 Computational Terminology

The medical field gathers people of different social statuses, such as students, pharmacists, biologists, nurses and mainly doctors and patients [34]. Despite their different levels of expertise, these people need to interact and understand each other; but, unfortunately, the communication is not always easy and effective [15,24,31]. The recent contributions of CT aim to (i) the simplification of medical texts in terms of readability and understandability and to (ii) the implementation of resources and applications in order to facilitate patient-doctor dialogue in situations of medical diagnosis. Text simplification is closely linked to the readability studies [12], the purpose of which is to address the ease with which a document can be read and understood by people. In medical texts, one source of difficulty may be due to the specific and specialized notions that are used. Indeed, the medical field conveys very specific and often opaque notions (e.g., *myocardial infarction, cholecystectomy, abdominal strangulated hernia, galactose urine*), that are difficult to understand by lay people. Numerous studies address these issues from different perspectives and following different computational approaches for the analysis of medical terminology such as:

1. the automatic identification of specialized and non-specialized terms;
2. the identification of equivalents lay terms;
3. the identification of the level of technicality;
4. the realization of terminological resources.

In [42], the authors propose an automatic method in order to distinguish between specialized and non-specialized occurrences of verbs in medical corpora. This method uses a contrastive automatic analysis of such verbs based on the semantic annotation of the verbs nominal co-occurrents. The results show that some verbs regularly co-occur with specialized terms in a given context or corpus, while the same verbs mostly occur with general language words in a different corpus. These kinds of observations fit in the context of readability: verbs which co-occur frequently with specialized terms can be considered as sources of reading difficulties for non-experts in the medical field. Other approaches [2] try to assess the level of technicality of a term through the combination of learning-to-rank techniques with statistical and linguistic features, that is the specialization degree to each of the entries given in a list of synonym terms. In [22], the authors propose a method for the classification of term technicality considering term variation in the medical field. Authors focused on the different degree of specialization of a term and term variation in the characterization of clinical sublanguages by analyzing the language used in a corpus of Belgian Electronic Health Records (EHRs). Each sections of these records vary systematically with regard to their lexical, terminological and semantic composition, as well as their potential for term variation, so that they distinguished between vernacular (e.g. 'buik', 'belly') and specialized (e.g. 'abdomen') terms.

The study presented in [20] highlights the need for reliable terminological resources in this field. This study presents how to build specific lexicon in which the words are rated according to whether they are *understandable* or *non-understandable*. French medical words have been rated by human annotators on a scale with three positions: *I can understand, I am not sure, I cannot understand*. In this way, the *I cannot understand* category may be associated with specialized words, while the *I can understand* category may be associated with non-specialized words.

At present, one of the most reliable terminological resource providing patient-oriented information is SNOMED CT,[4] that is an international standard for the interoperability in Digital Health; it can be used to represent clinically relevant information consistently and to support the development of comprehensive high-quality clinical content in health records. Another open access and collaborative resource is the Consumer Health Vocabulary (CHV)[5] developed by the Department of Biomedical Informatics at the University of Utah. The purpose of this project is to translate technical terms into popular language by linking informal and common health words and expressions to technical terms used by health professionals. Such kind of resources may help both in the detection of parts of medical documents containing complex and non-understandable terms, and in the patient-physician communication by highlighting such terms that should be explained to patients in order to make the communication more successful and easy.

2.2 Digital Libraries

The existence of large digital libraries containing medical documents has given the opportunity to develop text mining techniques for the automatic extraction of knowledge from unstructured text. In [27], the authors identified typical cue-phrases and structural indicators that introduce definitions of medical terms through an analysis of a set of consumer-oriented medical articles. Building an ontology of medical concepts requires times and effort; the authors of [28] propose a method to reduce these costs by starting with a small (or seed) ontology and enrich it with concepts and semantic relations acquired from medical abstracts. Concept Mapper [45] combines an ontology together with an automatic generated thesaurus based on document term co-occurrences in order to provide users with suggestions for query expansion.

Patients usually experience difficulty when they use health information retrieval systems due to the vocabulary gap between their request and the corresponding controlled vocabulary terms used to index the health information retrieval system [44]. It is therefore important to evaluate the difficulty of a

[4] https://www.snomed.org/.

[5] http://consumerhealthvocab.chpc.utah.edu/CHVwiki/.

term in order to provide recommended terms for an effective query formulation. In [29], the authors propose a metric to label text difficulty levels and focus on a lexical measure about term familiarity. The work presented in [25] analyzes user generated terms and compare them to those generated by professionals. This study also show that most health information users have low levels of health literacy which means that users are not able to access health information effectively and understand the information.

There are examples of successful systems that support users in the search of medical digital libraries. PERSIVAL (PErsonalized Retrieval and Summarization over Images, Video and Language) is a medical digital library which provides access to literature that is clinically relevant to the patient under their care at the point of patient care [32]. This information includes the medical history, laboratory results, procedures performed and diagnoses, which can be used to pinpoint articles that can provide the physician with the latest results relevant to the patient under care. MedSearch is a retrieval system for medical literature based on a Semantic Similarity Retrieval Model (SSRM) which suggests discovering semantically similar terms in documents and queries using term ontologies [23]. The SINAMED and ISIS projects focused on information access on patient clinical records and related scientific documentation [4]. These projects integrate automatic text summarization and categorization algorithms to improve access to bilingual information in the biomedical domain. In this way, the combination of a medical information system with the electronic clinical record would help doctors to take decisions, to decrease the mistakes and the clinical variability and to increase the patient's safety.

3 TriMED: A Terminological eHealth Resource

In this context, we are developing a new eHealth resource in order to tackle the problem of the complexity of medical terminology by considering different level of communications. The multilingual resource is named TriMED [41]: it is a database collecting terminological records compiled over a set of technical terms manually extracted by experts in linguistics and terminology from a corpus of documents. These documents concerning the oncology field and, in particular, breast cancer treatments. are selected from specialized online magazine reviews based with the highest impact factor value, such as "Breast Cancer research and treatment"[6] for English language, from national associations websites such as "AIMaC - Associazione Italiana Malati di Cancro"[7] for Italian, and the "Association Francophone pour les Soins Oncologiques de Support (AFSOS)"[8] for French.

Terminological records are the core of our methodology and provide different kinds of information depending on the user identification.

[6] http://www.springer.com/medicine/oncology/journal/10549.
[7] https://www.aimac.it.
[8] http://www.afsos.org.

3.1 Users

We have identified three categories of people that are mostly affected by the complexity of medical language and they can benefit from the use of this resource: patients, language professionals (translators and interpreters) and physicians.

Patients: Patients, or more in general lay people, find a considerable difficulty in understanding information, both oral and written, about their own health [1,13, 21,26]. As a consequence, they need to understand medical technical terms using their correspondent in the popular language or using an appropriately calibrated language for the communication to be effective. For this reason, they are the first category of users who can benefit from the use of TriMED because this eHealth resource provides the equivalent of the technical term in the popular language, that is the term most frequently used (as for example *fever* for *pyrexia*) and provides an informative definition respecting a non-specialized level of register.

Translators and Interpreters: There are several language related factors that need to be taken into consideration in the correct transmission of health information [18]. The need to use interpreters in the health-care domain becomes increasingly evident especially referring to the immigration phenomena. TriMED is designed to support 'language professionals', such as translators and interpreters who work in emergency situations. TriMED offers terminological records providing the translation into three languages (English, French and Italian) of the technical term and all the linguistically relevant information for the process of decoding and transcoding it in its oral and written forms. In this way, professionals can immediately consult a reliable translation of the term in an easy and quick way. The objective is indeed to try to reduce the time of terminological research by offering a regularly updated and reliable digital resource.

Physicians: The international scale release of medical knowledge implies that most of the scientific texts are produced in English [33]. In terms of spreading new health care protocols and scientific discoveries, language could be a barrier to service transactions among medical specialists speaking different languages because perfect knowledge and mastery of the foreign language is not an expected outcome. In order to overcome these language barriers and to satisfy the peer-to-peer communication, TriMED offers the possibility to consult the translation of the technical term respecting the specialized linguistic register.

The definition of the three categories of users allowed us to design the structure of TriMED as a user-friendly resource. A user can select one of the three category and then access the related information need. Currently, the eHealth resource contains about 328 terminological records that, at present time, are under a review process performed by terminologists and translators. After the review process, records will be openly available; a demo of the application with some examples of terminological records in English an French is available online.[9]

[9] https://gmdn.shinyapps.io/TriMED/.

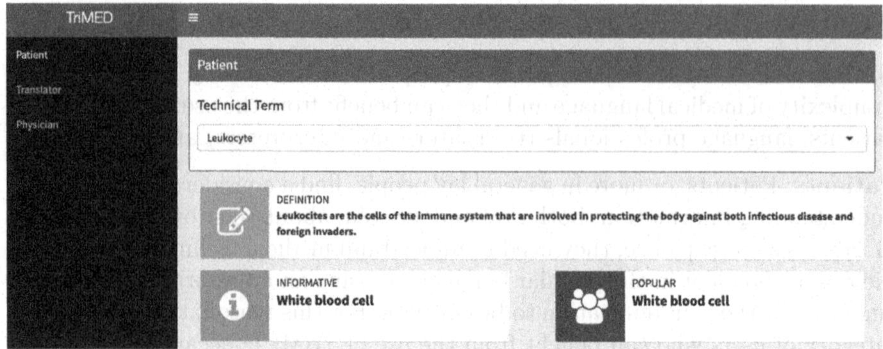

Fig. 1. Patient visualization for the technical term *Leukocyte* and its equivalent in popular language *White Blood Cell.*

3.2 Terminological Record

Our methodology is based on the formulation of a new model of terminological record which is designed to satisfy the information needs of the above mentioned categories of users both from inter and intra-linguistic viewpoints. Terminological records are commonly used in terminology and linguistics as a tool for the collection of linguistic data referring to a specific concept [19]. We designed the new records in order to extend the SNOMED CT records and Consumer Health Vocabulary (CHV) records. In particular, we link our terminological records to the SNOMED CT concepts by means of the SNOMED concept identifiers; then, on the basis of the CHV we propose not only the technical term and its equivalent in popular language, but also intra and inter-linguistic medical information in French and Italian which are not currently supported by those terminological resources. In Fig. 1 we present the terminological record visualization for a patient, while in Fig. 2 the linguistic analysis for technical terms in source and target languages are shown for language professionals. All the information provided are necessary for the technical-scientific translator in order to decode (interpret) and then transcode (transfer) the meaning of a technical term and help the professional choosing the correct translating candidate. TriMED terminological record is structured around four axes of analysis of the technical term:

1. Formal features;
2. Semantics;
3. Corpus;
4. References.

Regarding the formal and lexical framework of the term, we provide information such as: gender, spelling, pronunciation in the International Phonetic Alphabet (IPA) and other information about the etymology, such as derivation and composition of the term. In addition, we propose the spelling variant and the related acronyms which are currently used in medical language. Finally, based on the WordNet resource,[10] the record contains all the nouns, verbs, adjectives, and adverbs deriving from the analyzed term and which fall into the same semantic sphere.

The second section focuses on the semantic features of the term. First, we propose a definition extracted from reliable resources such as Merriam-Webster Medical Dictionary,[11] MediLexicon[12] especially for acronyms and abbreviations, TERMIUM Plus,[13] or "Enciclopedia Salute" from the Italian Ministry of Health.[14] In addition, we provide the semic analysis of the term [36] that is a methodology used in compositional semantics in order to decompose the meaning of technical terms (lexematic or morphological unity) into minimal units of meaning: the semes. Moreover, in order to evaluate the semantic behavior of a term, we collect the phraseology of the term by considering cases of collocations [17] and colligations [37]. Finally, we provide the synonymic variants of the term: in this way, we categorize terms and their semantic relations.

In the corpus section, we provide all specialized contexts where technical terms have been extracted and then we proceed through the identification of the domain and the register of communication of the term (popular, slang, familiar, current or standard and specialized). The term and its definition, therefore, take on meaning when they are connected to a specific domain: in our analysis, we identify the domain and subdomains of the text (such as surgery, pathology, pharmacology, etc). Finally, since all of this information has been extracted from different sources, we provide references to each source.

4 Applications

The TriMED application was realized in R and the user interface implemented with the Shiny R package [5]. The 328 records were loaded by experts in linguistics and terminology and the current structure of each record follows the tidy data approach [43] that uses dataframes as the main unit of data storage and analysis.

In this Section, we present two different applications of the TriMED terminological records; our aim is to show that a structured collection of terminological data can be useful and effective in order to conduct researches related to the medical field for different domain of interest: Information Retrieval and Literature Analysis.

4.1 Information Retrieval

Our first experiment in the application of detailed terminological records in order to improve the description of the medical lexicon was the participation to the

[10] https://wordnet.princeton.edu/.
[11] https://www.merriam-webster.com/.
[12] https://www.medilexicon.com/.
[13] https://www.btb.termiumplus.gc.ca/tpv2alpha/alpha-fra.html.
[14] http://www.salute.gov.it/portale/home.html.

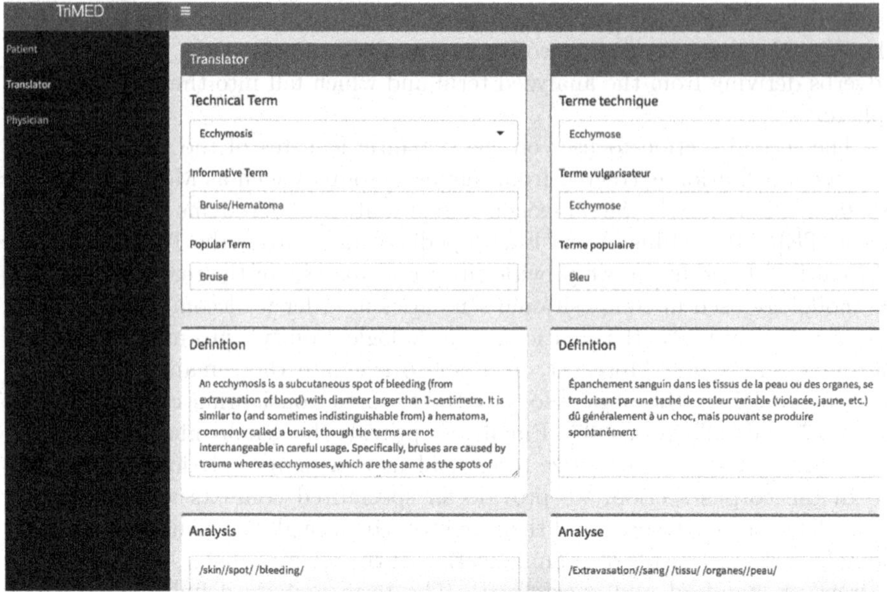

Fig. 2. Translator visualization for the technical term in the source language (EN) *Ecchymosis* and its equivalent in the target language (FR) *Ecchymose.*

Cross-Language Evaluation Forum eHealth Task on "Technologically Assisted Reviews in Empirical Medicine" [9–11]. The main goal of the task was to find the most relevant medical publications by means of a manual query rewriting approach. Our query reformulation methodology was based on a purely terminological approach, proposing variants based on a detailed linguistic analysis of the technical terms presented in the initial query. This starting point allowed us to see the usefulness of a digital terminological and multilingual resource for the retrieval of medical information [8].

In these experiments, we asked two experts in linguistics to rewrite the initial query provided with the experimental collection through a terminological methodology based on the following steps:

1. Identification of technical terms;
2. Manual extraction of technical terms;
3. Linguistic and semantic analysis;
4. Formulation of terminological records;
5. Query rewriting.

After the extraction of technical terms, the two linguists started to formulate TriMED terminological records in order to write two variants of the original query. The first variant was written with the aim of creating a list of keywords resulting from the semic analysis, that is the study of meaning in linguistic units, of the technical terms extracted from the initial query. The second variant was

Table 1. Query reformulation: keyword and readable variants

Variant	Query
Information need	First rank symptoms for schizophrenia
Expert keywords	Diagnosis, diagnostic, first rank symptoms, symptom, schizophrenia, FRS, international pilot study, IPSS, schneider, schneiderian, schizophrenics, non-schneiderian
Expert readable	Diagnostic accuracy of one or multiple FRS for diagnosing schizophrenia as a psychotic disorder

written with the aim of reformulating the information need into a humanly readable sentence using alternative terms such as synonyms, orthographic variants, related forms and/or acronyms. The two experts worked independently from each other by following this structured linguistic methodology and focusing on different terminological aspects. We name these two experiments with "keywords" and "readable": in Table 1, an example of query reformulation is shown for the initial query about *First rank symptoms for schizophrenia.*

This approach in combination with Technology-Assisted Review system allowed us to achieve a perfect recall on almost all the topics provided for the CLEF task [8]. Therefore, the linguistic approach based on terminological record has contributed to an effective and efficient reformulation for the retrieval of the most relevant documents for the research.

4.2 Literature Analysis

In this section, we present the second application of the new model of terminological record for linguistic analysis in the literature domain [40]. This is an innovative approach combing quantitative and qualitative analyses in order to study medical terminology in literary texts. In particular, we focused on the works of Conan Doyle and our case study was the entire collection of adventures of Sherlock Holmes, starting from 'A Study in Scarlet' (1887) to 'The Casebook of Sherlock Holmes' (1927), freely available on the Project Gutenberg website.[15] We initially proceeded with the semi-automatic extraction of 98 English technical terms, as well as their collocations by means of the tidytext R package for text analysis.[16] After the identification of medical terms, we proceeded with the formulation of TriMED terminological records by focusing on different linguistic aspects of such literary texts such as:

1. The level of technicality of a term, dividing popular terms from technical ones such as 'St. Vitus's dance' for *Chorea minor*, 'Heart Disease' for *Cardiopathy* or 'Nosebleed' for *Epistaxis*. In this way, we could analyze changes in the linguistic register by focusing on the diastratic variation resulting from

[15] https://www.gutenberg.org.

[16] https://cran.r-project.org/web/packages/tidytext/.

the specialized-popular dualism in order to bridge the gaps between various registers;
2. The semantic behavior of a term in a diachronic sense, evaluating how a specialized term can change its meaning over time and by comparing the use of the term in the past and its current use, such as ‘Consumption’ used to indicate the process of general decay of the organism in place of the current *cachexia* or *wasting syndrome*. Likewise, we can evaluate the disuse of a term as ‘brain fever’ used until the first half of the nineteenth century to indicate the association between an irregular set of neurological symptoms;
3. The syntactic behavior of technical terms in the literary corpus through the analysis of collocations, as a sequence of terms that frequently co-occur, as for example *asphyxia by confinement* vs *asphyxia in a confined space*.

This innovative study constitutes a first attempt aiming to show that TriMED and its terminological records are valid digital supports not only for specialized documents, but also for literary corpora. Moreover, this kind of study led us to evaluate different features of medical terminology, in particular, by considering the diachronic variation of the technical term consisting in a formal or semantic change over time.

5 Conclusions and Future Works

In this paper, we described the development of an eHealth resource, named TriMED, that is a digital library of multilingual terminological records designed to satisfy the information needs of different categories of users within the healthcare field. This resource provides information at multiple levels of linguistic register with the main purpose of simplification of medical language in terms of understandability and readability. Indeed, the new model of terminological record we propose allows to provide different information in order to (i) satisfy the peer-to-peer communication between medical experts, (ii) facilitate the comprehension of medical information by patients, and (iii) provide a regularly updated resource for scientific translators. The data as well as the source code of the application will be available under OSI-approved licenses.[17]

Moreover, we presented two different applications in order to show that a structured collection of terminological data can be effective in multiple fields of study related to the medical domain for different purposes, such as Information Retrieval and Literature Analysis. TriMED terminological record proved to be a useful support tool for the identification of the most relevant medical publications according to a specific topic and for the linguistic analysis of medical terminology in Conan Doyle literary works.

As future work, in order to ease the manual work of the terminologists and translators, we are studying a method to create automatically a draft version of a record by reusing pieces of information already available in the online resources.

[17] https://opensource.org/licenses.

References

1. Ali, T., Schramm, D., Sokolova, M., Inkpen, D.: Can I hear you? Sentiment analysis on medical forums. In: IJCNLP, pp. 667–673 (2013)
2. Bouamor, D., Llanos, L.C., Ligozat, A., Rosset, S., Zweigenbaum, P.: Transfer-based learning-to-rank assessment of medical term technicality. In: Proceedings of the Tenth International Conference on Language Resources and Evaluation, LREC 2016, Portorož, Slovenia, 23–28 May 2016 (2016)
3. Bourigault, D., Jacquemin, C., L'Homme, M.: Recent Advances in Computational Terminology. Natural Language Processing. J. Benjamins Publishing Company (2001). https://books.google.it/books?id=0eX8HtA7mQIC
4. de Buenaga, M., Maña, M., Gachet, D., Mata, J.: The SINAMED and ISIS projects: applying text mining techniques to improve access to a medical digital library. In: Gonzalo, J., Thanos, C., Verdejo, M.F., Carrasco, R.C. (eds.) ECDL 2006. LNCS, vol. 4172, pp. 548–551. Springer, Heidelberg (2006). https://doi.org/10.1007/11863878_65
5. Chang, W.: Shiny: Web Application Framework for R (2015). http://CRAN.R-project.org/package=shiny, r package version 0.11
6. Cimino, J.J.: Terminology tools: state of the art and practical lessons. Methods Inf. Med. **40**(04), 298–306 (2001)
7. Detmar, S.B., Muller, M.J., Schornagel, J.H., Wever, L.D., Aaronson, N.K.: Health-related quality-of-life assessments and patient-physician communication: a randomized controlled trial. JAMA **288**(23), 3027–3034 (2002)
8. Di Nunzio, G.M.: A study of an automatic stopping strategy for technologically assisted medical reviews. In: Pasi, G., Piwowarski, B., Azzopardi, L., Hanbury, A. (eds.) ECIR 2018. LNCS, vol. 10772, pp. 672–677. Springer, Cham (2018). https://doi.org/10.1007/978-3-319-76941-7_61
9. Di Nunzio, G.M., Beghini, F., Vezzani, F., Henrot, G.: An interactive two-dimensional approach to query aspects rewriting in systematic reviews. IMS unipd at CLEF ehealth task 2. In: Working Notes of CLEF 2017 - Conference and Labs of the Evaluation Forum, Dublin, Ireland, 11–14 September 2017 (2017). http://ceur-ws.org/Vol-1866/paper_119.pdf
10. Di Nunzio, G.M., Ciuffreda, G., Vezzani, F.: Interactive sampling for systematic reviews. IMS unipd at CLEF 2018 ehealth task 2. In: Working Notes of CLEF 2018 - Conference and Labs of the Evaluation Forum, Avignon, France, 10–14 September 2018 (2018)
11. Di Nunzio, G.M., Vezzani, F.: Using R markdown for replicable experiments in evidence based medicine. In: Bellot, P., et al. (eds.) CLEF 2018. LNCS, vol. 11018, pp. 28–39. Springer, Cham (2018). https://doi.org/10.1007/978-3-319-98932-7_3
12. DuBay, W.H.: The principles of readability. Online Submission (2004)
13. Elhadad, N., Sutaria, K.: Mining a lexicon of technical terms and lay equivalents. In: Proceedings of BioNLP Workshop, pp. 49–56. ACL (2007)
14. Epstein, R.M., et al.: Measuring patient-centered communication in patient-physician consultations: theoretical and practical issues. Soc. Sci. Med. **61**(7), 1516–1528 (2005)
15. Eysenbach, G.: Poverty, human development, and the role of ehealth. J. Med. Internet Res. **9**(4), e34 (2007)
16. Ferguson, L.A., Pawlak, R.: Health literacy: the road to improved health outcomes. J. Nurse Pract. **7**(2), 123–129 (2011). https://doi.org/10.1016/j.nurpra.2010.11.020. http://www.sciencedirect.com/science/article/pii/S1555415510005519

17. Firth, J.R.: A synopsis of linguistic theory, 1930–1955. In: Studies in Linguistic Analysis (1957)
18. Gibbons, M.C.: eHealth Solutions for Healthcare Disparities, 1st edn. Springer Publishing Company, Incorporated, New York (2007)
19. Gouadec, D.: Terminologie: constitution des données. AFNOR gestion, AFNOR (1990). https://books.google.it/books?id=cRrnAAAAMAAJ
20. Grabar, N., Hamon, T.: A large rated lexicon with French medical words. In: LREC (Language Resources and Evaluation Conference) (2016)
21. Grabar, N., Van Zyk, I., De La Harpe, R., Hamon, T.: The comprehension of medical words. In: Proceedings of the International Joint Conference on Biomedical Engineering Systems and Technologies - Volume 5, BIOSTEC 2014, pp. 334–342. SCITEPRESS - Science and Technology Publications, Lda, Portugal (2014). https://doi.org/10.5220/0004803803340342
22. Grön, L., Bertels, A.: Clinical sublanguages: vocabulary structure and its impact on term weighting. Terminology **24**(1), 41–65 (2018)
23. Hliaoutakis, A., Varelas, G., Petrakis, E.G.M., Milios, E.: *MedSearch*: a retrieval system for medical information based on semantic similarity. In: Gonzalo, J., Thanos, C., Verdejo, M.F., Carrasco, R.C. (eds.) ECDL 2006. LNCS, vol. 4172, pp. 512–515. Springer, Heidelberg (2006). https://doi.org/10.1007/11863878_56
24. Jimison, H., et al.: Barriers and drivers of health information technology use for the elderly, chronically ill, and underserved. Evid Rep Technol Assess (Full Rep) **175**, 1–1422 (2008)
25. Joo, S., Choi, Y.: Content analysis of social tags generated by health consumers. In: II, P.L.B., et al. (eds.) Proceedings of the 15th ACM/IEEE-CE Joint Conference on Digital Libraries, Knoxville, TN, USA, 21–25 June 2015, pp. 249–250. ACM (2015). http://doi.acm.org/10.1145/2756406.2756959
26. Keselman, A., Tse, T., Crowell, J., Browne, A., Ngo, L., Zeng, Q.: Assessing consumer health vocabulary familiarity: an exploratory study. J. Med. Internet Res. **9**(1), e5 (2007)
27. Klavans, J., Muresan, S.: Evaluation of DEFINDER: a system to mine definitions from consumer-oriented medical text. In: Proceedings of the ACM/IEEE Joint Conference on Digital Libraries, JCDL 2001, Roanoke, Virginia, USA, 24–28 June 2001, pp. 201–202. ACM (2001). http://doi.acm.org/10.1145/379437.379488
28. Lee, C.-H., Na, J.-C., Khoo, C.: Towards ontology enrichment with treatment relations extracted from medical abstracts. In: Sugimoto, S., Hunter, J., Rauber, A., Morishima, A. (eds.) ICADL 2006. LNCS, vol. 4312, pp. 419–428. Springer, Heidelberg (2006). https://doi.org/10.1007/11931584_45
29. Leroy, G., Endicott, J.E.: Term familiarity to indicate perceived and actual difficulty of text in medical digital libraries. In: Xing, C., Crestani, F., Rauber, A. (eds.) ICADL 2011. LNCS, vol. 7008, pp. 307–310. Springer, Heidelberg (2011). https://doi.org/10.1007/978-3-642-24826-9_38
30. Rouleau, M.: La terminologie médicale et ses problèmes. Tribuna, vol. IV, n. 12 (2003)
31. McCray, A.: Promoting health literacy. J. Am. Med. Infor. Ass. **12**, 152–163 (2005)
32. McKeown, K.R., Elhadad, N., Hatzivassiloglou, V.: Leveraging a common representation for personalized search and summarization in a medical digital library. In: Proceedings of the ACM/IEEE 2003 Joint Conference on Digital Libraries (JCDL 2003), 27–31 May 2003, Houston, Texas, USA, p. 159. IEEE Computer Society (2003). https://doi.org/10.1109/JCDL.2003.1204856

33. Neveol, A., Grosjean, J., Darmoni, S., Zweigenbaum, P.: Language resources for French in the biomedical domain. In: Proceedings of the LREC 2014. ELRA, Reykjavik, Iceland, May 2014
34. Parker, R.M., et al.: Health literacy-report of the council on scientific affairs. JAMA-J. Am. Med. Assoc. **281**(6), 552–557 (1999)
35. Ranck, J. (ed.): Disruptive Cooperation in Digital Health. Springer, Cham (2016). https://doi.org/10.1007/978-3-319-40980-1. https://books.google.it/books?id=mGfVjwEACAAJ
36. Rastier, F.: Sémantique interprétative. Formes sémiotiques, Presses universitaires de France (1987). https://books.google.it/books?id=BnuyAAAAIAAJ
37. Sinclair, J.: Reading Concordances: An Introduction. Pearson Longman, New York (2003)
38. Street Jr., R.L.: Information-giving in medical consultations: the influence of patients' communicative styles and personal characteristics. Soc. Sci. Med. **32**(5), 541–548 (1991)
39. Tu-Keefner, F.: The value of public libraries during a major flooding: how digital resources can enhance health and disaster preparedness in local communities. In: Morishima, A., Rauber, A., Liew, C.L. (eds.) ICADL 2016. LNCS, vol. 10075, pp. 10–15. Springer, Cham (2016). https://doi.org/10.1007/978-3-319-49304-6_2
40. Vezzani, F., Di Nunzio, G.M., Henrot, G.: (not so) elementary, my dear Watson! In: Coronato, R., Gesuato, S. (eds.) Filling Gaps, Building Bridges: Qualitative and Quantitative Approaches to the Study of Literature, Padova, June 2018
41. Vezzani, F., Di Nunzio, G.M., Henrot, G.: TriMED: a multilingual terminological database. In: Proceedings of the Eleventh International Conference on Language Resources and Evaluation LREC 2018, Miyazaky, Japan, 7–12 May 2018 (2018, in press)
42. Wandji Tchami, O., Grabar, N.: Towards automatic distinction between specialized and non-specialized occurrences of verbs in medical corpora. In: Proceedings of the 4th International Workshop on Computational Terminology (Computerm), pp. 114–124. Association for Computational Linguistics and Dublin City University, Dublin, Ireland, August 2014. http://www.aclweb.org/anthology/W14-4814
43. Wickham, H.: Tidy data. J. Stat. Softw. **59** (2014). http://www.jstatsoft.org/v59/i10/
44. You, S., DesArmo, J., Mu, X., Lee, S., Neal, J.C.: Visualized related topics (VRT) system for health information retrieval. In: IEEE/ACM Joint Conference on Digital Libraries, JCDL 2014, London, United Kingdom, 8–12 September 2014, pp. 429–430. IEEE Computer Society (2014). https://doi.org/10.1109/JCDL.2014.6970209
45. Zhu, B., Leroy, G., Chen, H., Chen, Y.: MedTextus: an intelligent web-based medical meta-search system. In: Proceedings of the ACM/IEEE Joint Conference on Digital Libraries, JCDL 2002, Portland, Oregon, USA, June 14–18 2002, p. 386. ACM (2002). http://doi.acm.org/10.1145/544220.544333

Connecting Researchers to Data Repositories in the Earth, Space, and Environmental Sciences

Michael Witt[1(✉)], Shelley Stall[2], Ruth Duerr[3], Raymond Plante[4], Martin Fenner[5], Robin Dasler[5], Patricia Cruse[5], Sophie Hou[6], Robert Ulrich[7], and Danie Kinkade[8]

[1] Purdue University, West Lafayette, IN, USA
mwitt@purdue.edu
[2] American Geophysical Union, Washington DC, USA
sstall@agu.org
[3] Ronin Institute, Montclair, NJ, USA
ruth.duerr@ronininstitute.org
[4] National Institute of Standards and Technology, Gaithersburg, MD, USA
raymond.plante@nist.gov
[5] DataCite, Hannover, Germany
{martin.fenner,robin.dasler,
patricia.cruse}@datacite.org
[6] National Center for Atmospheric Research,
University Corporation for Atmospheric Research, Boulder, CO, USA
hou@ucar.edu
[7] Karlsruher Institut für Technologie, Karlsruhe, Germany
robert.ulrich@kit.edu
[8] Woods Hole Oceanographic Institution, Woods Hole, MA, USA
dkinkade@whoi.edu

Abstract. The Repository Finder tool was developed to help researchers in the domain of Earth, space, and environmental sciences to identify appropriate repositories where they can deposit their research data and to promote practices that implement the FAIR Principles, encouraging progress toward sharing data that are findable, accessible, interoperable, and reusable. Requirements for the design of the tool were gathered through a series of workshops and working groups as a part of the Enabling FAIR Data initiative led by the American Geophysical Union that included the development of a decision tree that researchers may follow in selecting a data repository, interviews with domain repository managers, and usability testing. The tool is hosted on the web by DataCite and enables a researcher to query all data repositories by keyword or to view a list of domain repositories that accept data for deposit, support open access, and provide persistent identifiers. Metadata records from the re3data.org registry of research data repositories and the returned results highlight repositories that have achieved trustworthy digital repository certification through a formal procedure such as the CoreTrust Seal.

P. Manghi et al. (Eds.): IRCDL 2019, CCIS 988, pp. 86–96, 2019.
https://doi.org/10.1007/978-3-030-11226-4_7

Keywords: Research data management · FAIR principles · Geosciences · Repositories · Data facilities · Recommender systems

1 Background

The Enabling FAIR Data initiative[1] was organized by the American Geophysical Union (AGU) with a goal of promoting the adoption of the FAIR Principles: sharing research datasets in the domain of Earth, space, and environmental sciences and making them findable, accessible, interoperable, and reusable [1]. It accomplished its work through a series of two stakeholder meetings, two workshops, and six working groups (called targeted adoption groups, or TAGs) that engaged over three hundred researchers, publishers, funders, professional societies, repository managers, librarians, and other data professionals over the course of twelve months between November 2017 and October 2018.

There were many notable outcomes from the initiative and the work of the TAGs. Building on the past efforts of the Coalition on Publishing Data in the Earth and Space Sciences (COPDESS), the "Enabling FAIR Data Commitment Statement in the Earth, Space, and Environmental Sciences"[2] was drafted and outlined responsibilities for repositories; publishers; societies, communities, and institutions; funding agencies and organizations; and individual researchers to sign and commit to strive for FAIR data in their domain. A set of guidelines were developed for journals and publishers[3] to instruct their authors to deposit data in FAIR-aligned repositories (e.g., instead of including data as supplementary files with their articles); to cite and link to data in their articles; to include a data availability statement; and to provide open access to data that support published findings except in cases of ethical or legal constraints. The Data Management Training Clearinghouse[4] began collecting information about educational materials related to research data management and the data lifecycle through a novel approach of crowdsourcing events; this resource will continue to be developed and maintained through the Earth Science Information Partners (ESIP) with a subsequent grant from the Institute of Museum and Library Services. Other efforts included the definition of workflows around persistent identifiers such as Digital Object Identifiers (DOIs) between data repositories and publishers [2]; discussion and outreach related to creating a change in culture by giving proper credit to those who enable FAIR data; and the establishment of a program with funds to support a cohort of repositories in the Earth, space, and environmental sciences to pursue CoreTrustSeal certification[5] and become formally recognized as trustworthy digital repositories.

In this context, the Repository Guidance TAG was motivated by the use case of a researcher who is producing data and trying to identify appropriate domain repositories

---

[1] http://www.copdess.org/enabling-fair-data-project.

[2] http://www.copdess.org/enabling-fair-data-project/commitment-to-enabling-fair-data-in-the-earth-space-and-environmental-sciences.

[3] http://www.copdess.org/enabling-fair-data-project/author-guidelines.

[4] http://dmtclearinghouse.esipfed.org.

[5] https://www.coretrustseal.org.

that will accept their data for deposit. A secondary motivation was to promote practices that implement or otherwise support the FAIR Principles, in particular, among data repositories. Through a series of online discussions and work in person, the group diagrammed the decisions that a researcher commonly faces when selecting a repository to deposit their data. An interview protocol was also developed, and interviews were conducted with eleven repository managers to better understand the current state of domain repositories in implementing or planning to implement the FAIR Principles. Requirements were derived from these two activities to design an online, web-based tool that would be simple and easy for researchers to identify and select an appropriate repository. The tool, Repository Finder[6], queries the re3data registry of research data repositories[7] using Elasticsearch. Wireframing and software development took place in the final six months of the initiative in collaboration with the AGU and DataCite. Repository Finder was inspired, in part, by the Digital Research Infrastructure for the Arts and Humanities (DARIAH) Data Deposit Recommendation Service that provides a similar tool for European arts and humanities researchers that enables users to select their research discipline and country from drop-down lists and presents a list of repositories in their domain and locale that may accept their data [3]. A prototype of the Repository Finder was introduced, and three usability studies resulted in feedback from users that was incorporated into the tool. Although challenges and constraints were met throughout the process, the tool has been well-received by the Earth, space, and environmental sciences research community, and opportunities exist for future work in expanding the tool to cover other domains and extending its functionality to meet additional needs that were expressed by users during usability testing and early adopters of the tool in production.

2 Design and Development

2.1 Decision Tree

The starting place for the group was to imagine a researcher who is producing data and to diagram at a high level what decisions that researcher would make as they select a repository to deposit their data. Researchers could be writing proposals, for example, to funding agencies that require data management plans in which repositories must be specified; or, they could be further along in performing their research at a point when they are submitting papers for publication with journals that require supporting data be shared and archived in a repository (Fig. 1).

In all cases, researchers will be compelled to follow any mandates or recommendations of specific repositories that are made by their funder, publisher, journal, or institution. If this is not the case, researchers should consider what domain-specific repositories are commonly used in their area of research or for the type of data they are producing. They should contact the repository or otherwise confirm whether they can deposit their data and what the parameters for using the service are, e.g., what metadata

---

6 http://repositoryfinder.datacite.org.

7 http://re3data.org.

When selecting a repository to deposit their data, researchers in the Earth, space and environmental sciences should:

1. Follow the mandate or recommendation of their funder / publisher / journal / institution / etc.
2. Use a domain repository that adheres to norms of their research community*
3. Use a certified repository*%
4. Use the repository with the highest level of curation*
5. Use an institutional repository*
6. Use a general repository

* that will take their data based on the repository's terms of use or direct interaction between the researcher and the repository staff

% leveraging this opportunity to encourage/facilitate repositories who are are not certified to pursue certification, e.g., CoreTrustSeal

Fig. 1. Ordered list of principles distilled from the decision tree.

and formats do they require, do they charge a fee, file size limits, etc. A repository that is certified is preferable to one that is not because it has demonstrated through a formal process such as the CoreTrustSeal or ISO 16363 [4] that it has an adequate and sustainable organizational infrastructure, digital object management, and technology to provide the services that it advertises. Furthermore, repositories that provide higher levels of curation are preferable to repositories that provide lower levels of curation. In the context of CoreTrustSeal, four levels of curation are defined [5]. The lowest level of curation is to simply accept and distribute content as-is deposited. Basic curation may involve a simple check of the data before it is accepted and the addition of some basic metadata or documentation. Enhanced curation may additionally include format conversion and more detailed metadata or documentation. The highest level, or data-level, curation includes enhanced curation with editing and quality assurance of the data or other, additional services. If a domain repository is not available or is unable to accept the researcher's data, they may use a data repository that is offered by their institution or a general-purpose data repository such as Dryad[8], figshare[9], Harvard Dataverse[10], Mendeley Data[11], Open Science Framework[12], and Zenodo[13]. Likewise for institutional or general-purpose data repositories, certification and higher levels of curation

[8] http://datadryad.org.

[9] https://figshare.com.

[10] https://dataverse.harvard.edu.

[11] https://data.mendeley.com.

[12] https://osf.io.

[13] https://zenodo.org.

are preferred. In many research organizations, researchers can consult librarians for assistance in navigating these options and for help in selecting an appropriate repository for their data [6], and further guidance is offered by resources such as the Digital Curation Centre's Checklist for Evaluating Data Repositories [7].

2.2 Interviews with Data Facilities

Initiated by the Lorentz Workshop[14] in 2014, members of the broader research community collaborated to develop and publish the FAIR Principles in 2016 [1], and work has continued through the GO FAIR initiative[15] towards defining metrics for evaluating and measuring implementation of the Principles or the "FAIRness" of data and metadata. To get a better, practical sense of FAIR adoption among data repositories in the Earth, space, and environmental sciences, the TAG designed an interview guide [8] and conducted one-hour interviews with domain repository managers who were engaged in the Enabling FAIR Data initiative. These included the Ag Data Commons (United States Department of Agriculture), Alabama Geological Survey, Biological and Chemical Oceanography Data Management Office (Woods Hole Oceanographic Institution), Dash (California Digital Library), Deep Carbon Observatory, Interdisciplinary Earth Data Alliance (Columbia University), Helmholtz Centre Potsdam GFZ German Research Centre for Geosciences, PANGAEA, Socioeconomic Data and Applications Center (NASA), Research Data Archive (National Center for Atmospheric Research), and VTechData (Virginia Polytechnic Institute and State University).

The questions were developed from discussions within the TAG (including those who would be interviewed) and reflect what they considered FAIR implementation to resemble in current repository practice that are salient within the domain. For each practice, repositories were asked if they had implemented the practice, had plans to implement it, or did not have plans for implementation. Common practices among repositories in the domain included providing a search/browse user interface; provisioning landing pages for datasets; minting Digital Object Identifiers (DOIs) for datasets and/or data collections; providing human-readable and machine-actionable metadata describing datasets; linking datasets to related, published literature; supporting interfaces for metadata export and harvesting; identifying authors using ORCID identifiers; describing datasets with temporal, geospatial, and other domain-specific metadata; suggesting citations to encourage users to cite data; providing support services around data (e.g., help desk); enabling direct machine access to data (e.g., ftp, THREDDS, OPeNDAP, SPARQL, OGC); ascribing open access licenses for data reuse; registering their repositories with re3data; and supporting functionality to include data housed by the repository in peer review workflows. All repositories recognized the importance of certification: approximately half were already certified (primarily through the World Data System[16] or CoreTrustSeal) or were actively

[14] http://www.lorentzcenter.nl/lc/web/program.php3?jaar=2015.

[15] https://www.go-fair.org.

[16] https://www.icsu-wds.org.

pursuing certification, with the other half either planning to or interested in pursuing certification in the near future. Only some repositories embed machine-actionable metadata in landing pages (e.g., JSON-LD, HTML meta tags); linked or otherwise referenced datasets in their repositories to related data elsewhere; captured provenance of data in their custody; or furnished citations to related literature in their DOI metadata, e.g., such that could be used by Scholix[17] or other services that relate data and literature, quantify impact measures of data, etc. Interestingly, while most repositories responded that they do not provide machine-actionable citations for their data, these were effectively provided by the DOI for many applications such as citation management software clients.

2.3 re3data Schema Mapping and Tool Design

The primary purpose of the decision tree and interview exercises were to inform the design and development of the Repository Finder: to make it easy for a researcher to identify an appropriate domain repository to deposit their data and, in the process, to tacitly promote the FAIR Principles both in terms of awareness for the researcher and to begin to recognize emerging "FAIR" practices by data repositories (Fig. 2).

311-01 Astrophysics and Astronomy	311 Astrophysics and Astronomy	32 Physics	3 Natural Sciences
313-01 Atmospheric Science	313 Atmospheric Science, Oceanography and Climate Research	34 Geosciences (including Geography)	
313-02 Oceanography			
314-01 Geology and Palaeontology	314 Geology and Palaeontology		
315-01 Geophysics	315 Geophysics and Geodesy		
315-02 Geodesy, Photogrammetry, Remote Sensing, Geoinformatics, Cartography			
316-01 Geochemistry, Mineralogy and Crystallography	316 Geochemistry, Mineralogy and Crystallography		
317-01 Physical Geography	317 Geography		
317-02 Human Geography			
318-01 Hydrogeology, Hydrology, Limnology, Urban Water Management, Water Chemistry, Integrated Water Resources Management	318 Water Research		

Fig. 2. Relevant domain Deutsche Forschungsgemeinschaft (DFG) subject classifications.

The re3data registry currently manages metadata records describing 2,200 data repositories across all domains of research and around the world. Each repository is cataloged using forty-one descriptive attributes that are explained and can be validated in XML[18] using version 3.0 of the Metadata Schema for the Description of Research Data Repositories [9]. A subset of records pertaining to the Earth, space, and environmental sciences was established by limiting to relevant subjectID attributes based on the Classification of Subject Area, Review Board, Research Area and Scientific Discipline (2016–2019) from the Deutsche Forschungsgemeinschaft (DFG)[19], which is used by re3data. SubjectID is a required attribute in the schema. In addition, results are implicitly limited to only repositories that accept data for deposit (dataUploadType is "open" or "restricted") and those that are domain repositories (type is "disciplinary").

[17] http://www.scholix.org.

[18] https://www.re3data.org/schema.

[19] http://dfg.de/download/pdf/dfg_im_profil/gremien/fachkollegien/fk-wahl2015/2015_fachsystematik_2016_2019_en.pdf.

Guided by the interview and user test results, repositories that provide open access to their data (dataAccessType is "open") and persistent identifiers (pidSystem is true) were included in the criteria for inclusion to recognize practices that are working towards FAIR that are currently and widely adopted (Fig. 3).

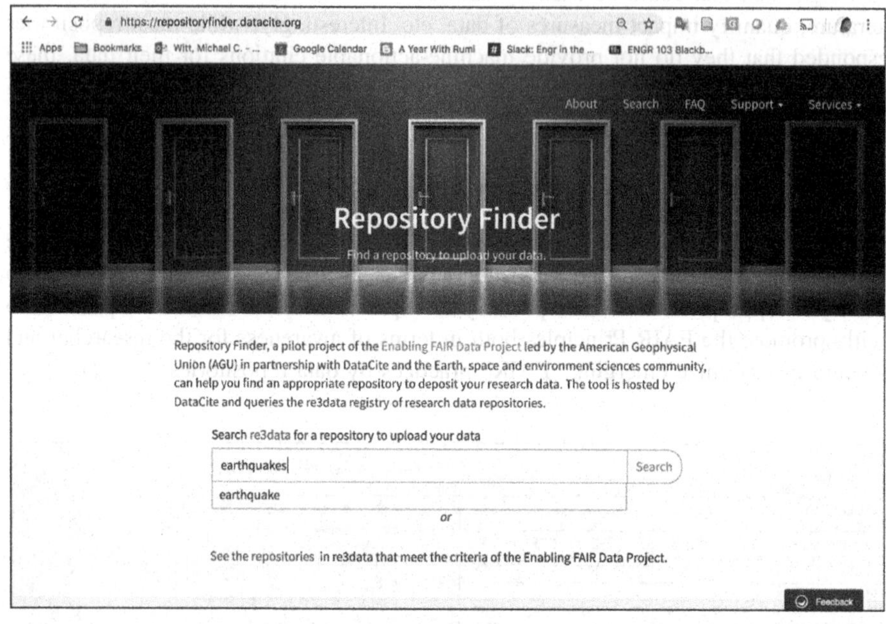

Fig. 3. Web-based user interface of the repository finder.

Initial design documents and discussions were incorporated into a wireframe using Balsmiq[20] that was iterated through biweekly online meetings of the project team. The software was developed as two separate applications: an API integrated with the re3-data Elasticsearch index using the Ruby on Rails[21] framework, and a frontend for this API using the EmberJS[22] framework. The work was done over the course of four monthly development sprints, and the tool is hosted by DataCite with its source code openly accessible on github[23,24]. The application queries re3data using Elasticsearch match phrase prefix queries[25] on the repositoryName, description, and keyword fields. Repository Finder begins with a short explanation of the tool and then presents two

[20] https://balsamiq.com.

[21] https://rubyonrails.org.

[22] https://www.emberjs.com.

[23] https://github.com/datacite/dackel.

[24] https://github.com/datacite/schnauzer.

[25] https://www.elastic.co/guide/en/elasticsearch/reference/current/query-dsl-match-query-phrase-prefix.html.

options: the user can (1) initiate a search by entering keywords that are auto-completed and receive results ranked by relevance of all repositories that accept deposit of data, provide open access, and use persistent identifiers. Alternatively, the user can (2) click a link to see repositories that meet the criteria of the Enabling FAIR Data community. These results are ordered alphabetically and include only repositories in the domain of Earth, space, and environmental sciences that meet the above criteria, highlighting repositories that have achieved certification with a "seal" icon. After results are displayed, the user has the ability to narrow the results by keyword; subsequent results are ranked by relevance. Each individual result displays the name of the repository; its description, subjects, and keywords; and a switch to display more details about the repository, including links to the repository, contact information, and its full registry entry in the native re3data interface. At the end of the result list, institutional and general-purpose repositories are suggested to be used for cases where a domain repository is not available or will not accept the researcher's data (Fig. 4).

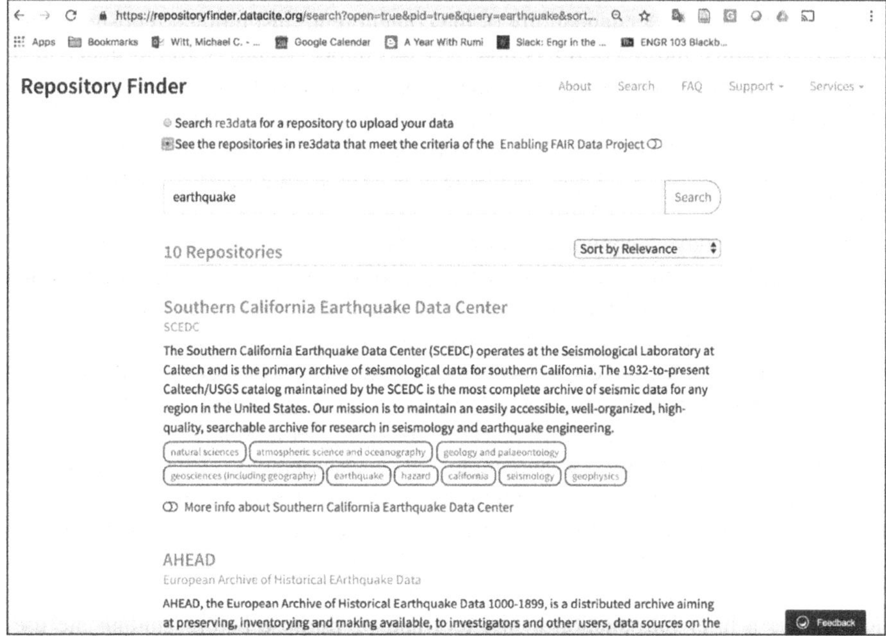

Fig. 4. Search results in the repository finder.

2.4 User Testing

In between the third and fourth development sprints, a prototype of the tool was made available for the purpose of user testing, which occurred in three, separate studies. The first two studies were held at the 2018 ESIP Summer Meeting to leverage the diversity of the attendees' data roles and responsibilities. The first study that was conducted by the ESIP Usability Cluster[26] engaged fifteen users in a session with a focus on usability that combined the focus group and user study techniques so that the users could provide feedback regarding specific, task-based interactions with the tool in a moderated fashion. The second study was conducted by the ESIP Usability Cluster Chair and Fellow using the one-on-one, in-person user study technique with a total of five users who fit the general "researcher" persona. During the user study session, each subject was first asked to tell a "user story" and describe a goal they would like to accomplish when looking for a repository. The subject was then asked to use the tool to perform specific, defined tasks based on the "user story" scenario and the goal. The subject was asked to think aloud while performing the tasks, so that the subject could share the thought process as they determine how to use the tool to accomplish the tasks. Feedback from users identified several concerns that aligned with usability issues that are outlined and discussed in Jakob Nielsen's 10 Usability Heuristics for User Interface Design [10]. In particular, users indicated that improvement in the following areas could have significant impact on the user interface and experience of the tool: the identity and messaging of the tool (e.g. what can the tool do, and why would I use it?), the authenticity and understandability of the content (e.g., institutional repositories not included in results, too many filters that only repository managers would understand, and lack of information regarding how the repositories' records are curated and can be updated in re3data); and the overall design approach (e.g. be more user-centric by providing visibility of system status, minimizing use of jargons, adding support documentation such as an FAQ, and implementing user friendly aesthetics for the user interface).

In the third study, a commercial firm was hired to interview users while guiding them through use of the tool. Subjects were recruited by project team members and included twenty-four individuals who identified themselves as either domain researchers or repository "champions" such as librarians, curators, data facility staff, or other data professionals. Test subjects described their backgrounds coming from Astronomy, Astrophysics, Atmospheric Sciences, Ecology, Environmental Science, Geodesy, Geography, Geoinformatics, Geology, Geomorphology, Geophysics, Hydrogeology, Hydrology, Oceanography, Paleoceanography, Palaeontology, and Polar Science. All subject classifications from the selected DFG subject areas were represented by at least one user with the exception of 316-01 Geochemistry, Mineralogy, and Crystallography. Online web sessions were conducted and recorded using Zoom with each session lasting between twenty and thirty minutes each. An interviewer gave a brief introduction to the tool and its purpose before guiding the user through the task of searching for a repository to deposit their data. Users were asked if the terminology and prompts were clearly understood as well as to evaluate the results for accuracy and relevance. Were there any repositories that were not relevant in the result list, and were the top results the most relevant? Were there any repositories they would expect to see in the results that were not there? Lastly, interviewers asked if the user's expectations were met by the tool and to share any additional input, ideas, or improvements that could be incorporated in the final development cycle of the tool or

[26] http://wiki.esipfed.org/index.php/Usability.

potential future development. Recordings of the sessions and interview notes were analyzed and a summary report reaffirmed users' perception of the need for such a tool and suggested improvements needed to the utilization of space and level of detail presented in the user interface, the mechanism for searching, and the metadata quality and completeness of the information about repositories in re3data. The user interface was refined to give collapsed results that can be expanded to show more detail, and the original hierarchical drop-down list of subjects was replaced with an auto-completing keyword search and a simple link to display a list of repositories that meet the criteria of the Enabling FAIR Data community initiative. The quality of the results given by the tool are impacted directly by the quality and completeness of metadata describing each repository in the re3data registry. To begin to address concerns with metadata, the re3data editorial board met for a two-day workshop hosted by the Karlsruhe Institute of Technology to focus on enhancing and bringing more consistency to the records for repositories in the Earth, space, and environmental sciences. They collectively edited a representative sample of records and compared notes to discuss issues and build consensus around editorial practices, in particular, for the repository attributes that impact Repository Finder and other tools like it in the future that may be built using re3data's API. The most accurate information about a repository can be provided to re3data by the repository managers themselves; to encourage their participation, a one-page guidance document was prepared and disseminated to the community by AGU. Users of Repository Finder and re3data continue to submit enhancements and corrections that refine and improve the quality of the registry and the results provided by the tool.

3 Challenges and Future Work

The project faced familiar constraints of a short timeline and limited resources; while we were able to engage a significant cross-section of stakeholders who work with data in the context of scholarship in Earth, space, and environmental sciences, it was not representative of the domain as a whole. Input was not statistically significant and relied on convenience samples of parties engaged in the initiative with a strong representation bias from North America and Europe. More time and broader engagement would result in a more robust consensus. The decision tree, interviews, and user tests were intended to inform the development of the tool in a practical and direct manner; they were not designed to stand alone as formal research studies. Problems related to metadata extended beyond the completeness of records in re3data: differences in terminology and the lack of widely adopted controlled vocabularies for the domain and subdomains as well as data types raised concerns in user testing and limited the potential functionality of the tool, e.g., the ability to search repositories by the type of data they accept. In particular, the DFG subject classification was limiting, for example, by not including commonly used subject terms such as "environmental science". Within the re3data schema, the most flexibility to overcome this limit exists in adding a variety of different keywords that represent the same subjects with different names and in the description, in particular, to add very specific subdomain terminology, instrumentation, and data formats. There is an inverse relationship between the number of attributes that are used to filter searches and the quantity of results those searches will produce. In terms of promoting FAIR, many of the practices that were reported by repositories were either not widely adopted, or in some cases, not cataloged in the registry. For example, an early iteration of the tool limited results to only certified repositories, but this excluded too many repositories that researchers recognized as being relevant to their research, and in some cases, yielded no results at all. There is also an important role for repositories and data facilities that are provided locally by institutions; however, the tool does not know the affiliation of the user, so it was not possible to include relevant institutional repositories in the results. The current version of Repository Finder was limited in scope to the use case of a researcher selecting a repository to deposit their data, but discussions with other TAGs and from user testing suggested many other use cases that could be motivated by publishers, journals, funders, societies, and other drivers that could be explored. Other potential future work includes updating the criteria to reflect the metrics coming out of GO FAIR and other, related initiatives as well as extending this approach to other domains outside of the Earth, space, and environmental sciences and to other lists of recommendations that may exist or emerge in the future.

Acknowledgements. Enabling FAIR Data was made possible by a grant from the Laura and John Arnold Foundation to the American Geophysical Union; program manager, Shelley Stall. Sabbatical support for Michael Witt was provided in part by the Pufendorf Institute of Advanced Studies at Lund University.

References

1. Wilkinson, M.D., et al.: The FAIR guiding principles for scientific data management and stewardship. Sci. Data **3**, 160018 (2016)
2. Cruse, P., Servilla, M.: Workflow Recommendations for Enabling FAIR Data in the Earth, Space, and Environmental Sciences, Zenodo (2018). http://doi.org/10.5281/zenodo.1445839
3. Buddenbohm, S., De Jong, M., Priddy, M., Moranville, Y., Ribbe, P.: Open Data in the Humanities Platform: Humanities at Scale: Evolving the DARIAH ERIC, DARIAH; DANS-KNAW (2017). https://hal.archives-ouvertes.fr/hal-01686320
4. ISO 16363:2012 - Space data and information transfer systems – Audit and certification of trustworthy digital repositories (2012). https://www.iso.org/standard/56510.html
5. Core Trustworthy Data Repositories Extended Guidance (2018). https://www.coretrustseal.org/wp-content/uploads/2017/01/20180629-CTS-Extended-Guidance-v1.1.pdf
6. Witt, M.: Co-designing, co-developing, and co-implementing an institutional data repository service. J. Libr. Adm. **52**(2), 172–188 (2012)
7. Whyte, A.: Where to Keep Research Data: DCC Checklist for Evaluating Data Repositories Version 1.1, Digital Curation Centre (2016). http://www.dcc.ac.uk/resources/how-guides-checklists/where-keep-research-data/where-keep-research-data
8. Plante, R., Witt, M.: Interview Questions for Determining Data Repository FAIR Compliance, Zenodo (2018). http://doi.org/10.5281/zenodo.1432515
9. Rücknagel, J., et al.: Metadata Schema for the Description of Research Data Repositories: version 3.0, p. 29 (2015). http://doi.org/10.2312/re3.008
10. Nielsen, J.: 10 Heuristics for User Interface Design, Nielsen Norman Group (1995). https://www.nngroup.com/articles/ten-usability-heuristics

Learning to Cite: Transfer Learning for Digital Archives

Dennis Dosso[1], Guido Setti[2], and Gianmaria Silvello[1](✉)

[1] Department of Information Engineering, University of Padua, Padua, Italy
{dosso,silvello}@dei.unipd.it

[2] Department of Mathematics, University of Padua, Padua, Italy

Abstract. We consider the problem of automatically creating citations for digital archives. We focus on the learning to cite framework that allows us to create citations without users or experts in the loop. In this work, we study the possibility of learning a citation model on one archive and then applying the model to another archive that has never been seen before by the system.

1 Introduction

Scientific research relies more and more on data for conducting advanced analysis and support discoveries and empirical findings. Nowadays, scientific datasets constitute the backbone of the system of the sciences and are critical factors for conducting high-quality research. Hence, open and shared datasets constitute first-class objects of the scientific process and need to be retrieved, accessed and cited as traditional scientific articles are. Moreover, the creation, curation, and preservation of scientific datasets require a great deal of investment and human-effort that need to be recognized and assessed by the scientific community [9].

For these reasons, there is a strong demand [1,5] to give databases the same scholarly status of traditional references. Recently, data citation has been defined as a computation problem [3], where the main issues to be tackled are: (i) the unique and persistent identification of a dataset or a data subset; (ii) the temporal persistence of the data as well as of the data citations; and, (iii) the automatic creation of text snippets (references) citing data subsets.

In this work, we focus on the automatic creation of text snippets for citing datasets with a variable granularity. This problem has been tackled with rule-based/deterministic approaches from a relational [11], hierarchical [4] and graph [2,7] database perspective or with a machine learning approach – i.e. the *Learning to Cite* (LtC) approach – for XML [8]. Pros and cons of these two approaches are specular ones to the other. The LtC approach has the main advantage of not requiring expert intervention to define citation policies and rules required by rule-based systems; on the other hand, the citations produced are not "exact" as those produced by rule-based systems.

P. Manghi et al. (Eds.): IRCDL 2019, CCIS 988, pp. 97–106, 2019.
https://doi.org/10.1007/978-3-030-11226-4_8

In [8], we introduced the LtC approach and we tested it on digital archives (i.e. XML Encoded Archival Description (EAD) files). We decided to testbed the LtC approach on this domain because archives usually lack resources and present a high data heterogeneity also within the same archive; these aspects make the LtC approach particularly valuable in the archival context. In [8] we showed that the LtC approach allows us to produce entirely accurate citations with small training sets, thus requiring minimum effort to database administrators and domain experts.

In this work, we move one step ahead by studying if *"it is possible to learn a citation model on an archive A and apply it to an unseen archive B"*. The goal is to learn a citation model on an archive where there are enough economic and human resources to build a training set and maintain a citation model (e.g. the LoC archive) and to apply it to other – possibly a broad spectrum – archives with lower resources.

Hence, in this work, we study the problem of transfer learning from an archive to another by using the LtC approach presented in [8] as a baseline. We conduct two experiments: (i) we train a citation model on a uniform and consistent training set (i.e. EAD files coming from a single archive) and we create citations for EAD files coming from five different heterogeneous archives; and, (ii) we train a citation model on a training set composed of the union of five heterogeneous archives and we create citations for a single archive not present in the training set. These two tests define a task harder than a traditional transfer learning task because the training and the test sets we consider are entirely disjointed. We show that the LtC approach has the potential to be applied in a transfer learning scenario, even though there is a performance drop concerning a classic learning scenario where training and test sets are sampled from the same archival collection.

The rest of paper is organized as follows: in Sect. 2 we briefly describe how data citation applies to the archival domain and summarize the main approaches to data citation. In Sect. 3 we describe at a high-level the LtC approach and explain how we model transfer learning for data citation. In Sect. 4 we define the experimental setup, describe the datasets and the experiments we conduct and in Sect. 5 we present the results of the evaluation. Finally, in Sect. 6 we draw some conclusions and outline future work.

2 Related Work

2.1 Digital Archives

Archives are composed of unique records where the original order of the documents is preserved because the context and the order in which the documents are held are as valuable as their content. Archival documents are interlinked and their relationships are required to understand their informative content. Therefore, archives explicitly model and preserve the provenance of their records by means of a hierarchical method, which maintains the context in which they have been created and their relationships.

Archival descriptions are encoded by means of the Encoded Archival Description (EAD) which is an XML description of a whole archive; EAD files resemble the description of the archival material and provide a means to represent the internal logic of an archive.

The EAD files represent a good test-bed for the LtC approach because they are deep files not easy to navigate and understand for the users, there is a wide variability in the use of tags that makes it difficult to set up citation rules across files and every node in an EAD file is a potential citable unit.

2.2 Data Citation Approaches

A recent and detailed overview of the theory and practice of data citation can be found in [9]. It has been highlighted that the manual creation of citation snippets is a barrier towards an effective and pervasive data citation practice as well as a source of inconsistencies and fragmentation in the citations [10]. Indeed, especially for big, complex and evolving datasets, users may not have the necessary knowledge to create complete and consistent snippets.

Recently, some solutions to tackle the problem of automatically creating citation snippets have been proposed. There are two main approaches: (i) rule-based and, (ii) machine-learning based.

Within the first approach, one of the first methods has been proposed by [4]. This method requires that the nodes corresponding to citable units are identified and tagged with a rule that is then used to generate a citation. This method was extended by [3] which defined a view-based citation method for hierarchical data. The idea is to define logical views over an XML dataset, where each view is associated to a citation rule, which if evaluated generates the required citation snippet according to a predefined style. This approach has been further formalized and extended also for the relational databases in [11]. In the same vein by exploiting database views, [2] proposed a system for citing single RDF resources by using a dataset on the medical domain as use-case.

The machine-based approach has been proposed for the first time by [8] with the Learning to Cite (LtC) framework that we present below.

3 Creation of Data Citations Based on Machine Learning

3.1 Learning to Cite

The aim of the LtC approach is to automatically create a model that can produce human- and machine-readable citation from XML files (EAD files for our use-case) without manual interventions of the data curators and without any modification to the data to be cited.

The LtC framework is composed of six main blocks as shown in Fig. 1: the training data, the learner, the citation model, the citation systems, the test data and the output reference.

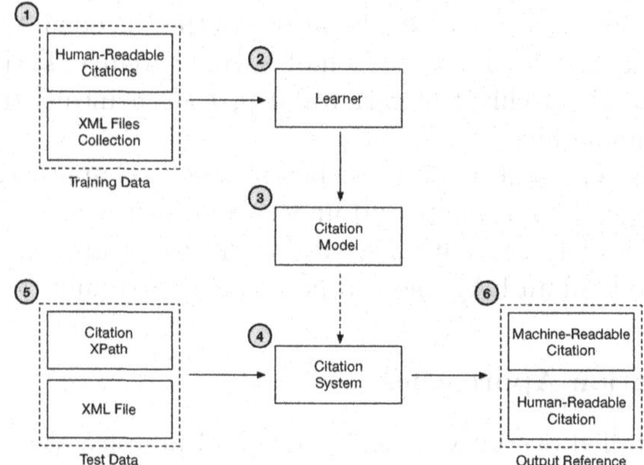

Fig. 1. The building blocks of the "Learning to Cite" framework [8].

The training set is composed of a collection $\mathcal{C}$ of XML files. Given two sets $T = \{t_1, t_2, \ldots, t_n\}$ of XML trees and a set $\mathcal{H} = \{H_1, H_2, \ldots, H_m\}$ of human-readable citations, the *learner* component takes as training data a set of pairs $<t_i, H_i>$. In particular, each citation $H_i \in \mathcal{H}$ is associated to one and only one XML tree $t_i \in T$, while each tree has at least one associated citation (but potentially more than one).

From the training data the *learner* produces a *citation model* able to create human-readable citations. In particular, the test data are a set of pairs $<p_t, t_t>$ where t_t is a XML tree with a citable unit referenced by the XPath p_t. The *citation system* parses the XPath p_t and creates a human-readable citation for the user exploiting the data inside the XML.

In particular, for the validation phase, the system can use a function to evaluate the effectiveness of the citation system and tune the parameters. These functions are *precision*, *recall* and *fscore*. Let $MC_k = \{p_1, p_2, \ldots, p_n\}$ be a machine readable citation generated by the system for the element $e_k = < p_k, t_k >$. $\{p_1, p_2, \ldots, p_n\}$ are the paths composing the citation. Let $GTC_k = \{p'_1, p'_2, \ldots, p'_m\}$ be the ground-truth machine-readable citation for the same element, i.e. the set of paths that correctly form the citation for e_k. Then we can define:

$$precision = \frac{|MC_k \cap GTC_k|}{|MC_k|}$$

$$recall = \frac{|MC_k \cap GTC_k|}{|GTC_k|}$$

$$f\text{-}score = 2 * \frac{precision * recall}{precision + recall}$$

Precision is the ratio between the total number of correct paths in the generated citation with the total number of generated paths, while recall is the ratio between the total number of generated correct paths and the total number of correct paths. Both are in the $[0, 1]$ interval, just like the fscore, which is a synthesis measure.

The framework uses one of these function in a k-fold validation strategy to find the best parameters for the system.

3.2 Transfer Learning

As defined in [6], given a source domain $\mathcal{D}_S$ with a learning task $\mathcal{T}_S$ and a target domain $\mathcal{D}_T$ with a learning task $\mathcal{T}_T$, *transfer learning* aims to help improve the learning of the target predictive function $f_T(\cdot)$ in $\mathcal{D}_T$ using the knowledge in $\mathcal{D}_S$ and $\mathcal{T}_S$, where $\mathcal{D}_S \neq \mathcal{D}_T$ or $\mathcal{T}_S \neq \mathcal{T}_T$.

In order to apply transfer learning to the LtC approach, it is necessary to define the domains and task at hand:

- The *source domain* $\mathcal{D}_S$ is the couple $\{\mathcal{C}_S, P(X_S)\}$, where $\mathcal{C}_S$ is a collection of XML files and X_S is a sub-collection sampled from $\mathcal{C}_S$;
- The *source task* $\mathcal{T}_S$ is the couple $\{\mathcal{Y}_S, f_S(\cdot)\}$, where $\mathcal{Y}_S$ is the set of ground truth machine-readable citations for $\mathcal{C}_S$, and $f_S(\cdot)$ is the function represented by the model built from the training data obtained from $\mathcal{C}_S$;
- The *target domain* $\mathcal{D}_T$ is the couple $\{\mathcal{C}_T, P(X_T)\}$, where $\mathcal{C}_T$ is a different collection of XML files, and X_T is a sub-collection sampled from $\mathcal{C}_T$.
- The *target task* $\mathcal{T}_T$ is a couple $\{\mathcal{Y}_T, f_T(\cdot)\}$, where $\mathcal{Y}_T$ is the set of ground truth machine-readable citations for $\mathcal{C}_T$, and $f_T(\cdot)$ is the model build from the training data of $\mathcal{C}_T$.

Thus, we can use the knowledge coming from the source domain and source task to learn the predictive function $f_T(\cdot)$, which corresponds to a citation model for the target collection. In the case we are considering, source and target domain are different, and so are source and target tasks.

4 Experimental Setup

4.1 Experimental Collections

The first experimental collection we consider is based on the Library of Congress (LoC)[1] EAD files and it has been defined in [8]; it consists of training, validation and test set. The training and validation sets are composed of XML tree and human-readable citation pairs. The validation set is obtained with k-fold cross validation from the training set. The test set is made of XML tree and machine-readable citation pairs. The human- and machine-readable citations were all built manually. The full LoC collection is composed of 2,083 files. In order to build the training and validation set, 25 EAD files were randomly selected, and from each of these files 4 citable units were extracted. For each citable unit, a human-readable and machine-readable citation was manually created to be used to train the citation system and to build the ground-truth to be used for validation purposes respectively. The test set was built by following a similar

[1] http://findingaids.loc.gov.

procedure. In this case, a ground-truth machine-readable citation was manually built for every randomly sampled citable unit. A new collection of EAD files is created in order to test Transfer Learning. Five different and heterogeneous source archives are selected:

1. University of Chicago Library finding aids (chicago);
2. University of Maryland Libraries finding aids (MdU);
3. Nationaal Archief, Den Haag (NL-HaNA);
4. Syracuse University finding aids (syracuse);
5. WorldCat aggregate collection aids (worldcat). This is a very heterogeneous collection of digital archives from all across the United States.

10 citable units are randomly selected from each of these collections, creating a new collection of 50 citable units from different sources. This new collection is called ***EAD various*** in the rest of the paper.

We conduct two experiments. In the first one, the source collection $\mathcal{C}_S$ is the LoC collection and the target task is to produce a set of citations for the target collection $\mathcal{C}_T$ which is the EAD various collection. The EAD various collection is only used as test set, hence a model $f_T(\cdot)$ cannot be directly built. $f_S(\cdot)$ will be used in order to learn the target predictive function $f_T(\cdot)$ for the target task $\mathcal{T}_T$. The second experiment reverses experiment one since we train on EAD various and test on LoC.

For each experiment, the citation model is built using the training and validation sets of the source collection and a 5-fold cross-validation is used to choose the best parameters of the model, with the f-score as optimization measure. The whole training and test procedure are repeated with different training sizes – i.e. the number of citable units contained in the training set – ranging from 20 to 80 with step 10. The citation model is then tested against the target collection and the procedure is repeated 5 times for each training size. The final measures presented are the average over the results of the five repetitions.

5 Evaluation

In the first experiment, we trained a citation model on the uniform LoC collection and we tested both on the LoC (classic learning procedure) and the EAD-various (transfer learning) test set.

In Table 1 we can see the precision, recall, and f-score obtained by the LtC approach with different training set sizes over the two considered test collections. As expected, the citation model produces generally better citations for the LoC collection, while for the EAD various collection the performances are usually halved. It is particularly interesting how a training set size of 20 immediately obtains acceptable values in all three measures. This is true for both the collections. This is consistent with the results presented in [8].

We conduct an ANOVA statistical test to check if the performance difference between LoC and EAD various are statistically significant. Figure 2a shows that the difference between the evaluation measure of the LoC collection and the

Table 1. Experiment 1: From homogeneous to heterogeneous. Precision, recall and f-score values obtained in the two test collections with f-score as optimization measure.

Training set size	Precision		Recall		f-score	
	LoC	EAD various	LoC	EAD various	LoC	EAD various
20	0.8819	0.5289	0.8232	0.4188	0.8441	0.4584
30	0.9034	0.5283	0.8089	0.4101	0.8465	0.4525
40	0.8748	0.5282	**0.8312**	**0.4254**	0.8447	**0.4623**
50	0.9239	0.5277	0.8045	0.4043	**0.8531**	0.4488
60	**0.9333**	**0.5414**	0.7723	0.3955	0.8366	0.4474
70	0.9012	0.5284	0.8106	0.4131	0.8462	0.4547
80	0.9152	0.5281	0.8055	0.4065	0.8506	0.4503

EAD various collection are statistically significant and not due to chance. This means that the citation model built using the LoC is missing some knowledge regarding the target EAD various collection.

Given that the performances of the citation model are worse for the EAD various collection, we performed the Tukey's HSD test to check if the model is statistically different over the 5 subsets of citation units comprising the *EAD various* collection. The results, presented in Fig. 2b, shows that the citation model built with the LoC collection training data (using 50 citation units) behaves with no significant difference with regard to f-score on the 5 sub-collections (the same result is obtained with precision and recall).

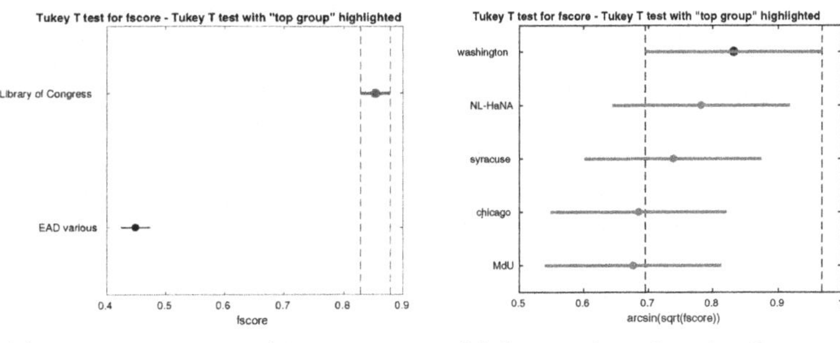

(a) fscore of LoC vs EAD various (b) fscore of single subcollections

Fig. 2. (a) The Tukey's HSD test for fscore of LoC vs *EAD various* (b) The Tukey's HSD test for fscore for the different sub-collections of *EAD various*. Training size is 50.

The second experiment builds the citation model with the *EAD various* collection and tests it on the LoC collection. The aim of this experiment is to discover if one of the five sub-collections of *EAD various* is more informative than the other in an LtC setting. The citation model has been built six times. One using all *EAD various* as training set, and the remaining five times by leaving out of the training set one sub-collection at a time.

Table 2. Precision, recall, and f-score values obtained from 5 different citing models trained on the *EAD various* collection, leaving out each time one of the sub-collections. f-score is the optimization measure. The training set is 40.

Collection left out	Precision	Recall	fscore
none	0.4143	**0.4531**	0.4199
chicago	0.4366	0.4498	0.4334
MdU	**0.4577**	0.4518	**0.4439**
NL-HaNA	0.4191	0.4530	0.4236
syracuse	0.4144	0.4430	0.4178
worldcat	0.4204	0.4485	0.4238

Table 2 shows that the performances obtained with the full EAD various collection are comparable to those obtained by leaving out one sub-collection. These are probably due to the heterogeneity of the training collection and to the different employment of tags among the sub-collections with respect to the LoC collection. Moreover, as shown in Fig. 3b the differences between the sub-collections are not statistically significant.

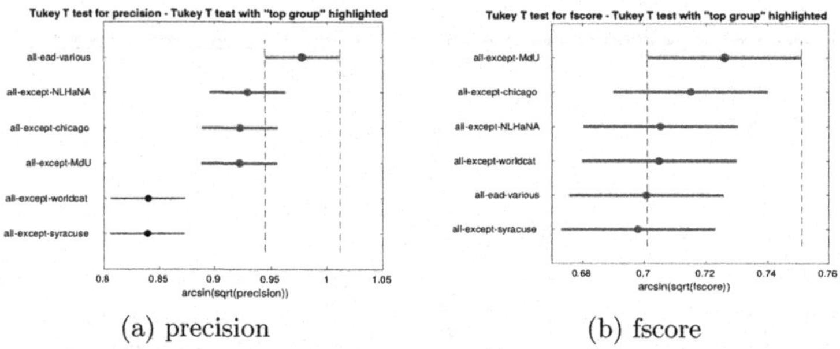

(a) precision (b) fscore

Fig. 3. The Tukey's HSD tests for the measures of precision and fscore of the models trained on the whole *EAD various* collection (all-ead-various) and on different sub-collections, obtained with the leave-one-out method, and tested on the LoC collection. Training size of 40 (except for the all-ead-various).

Nevertheless, let's note that there the sub-collection worldcat and syracuse appear to be determinant for the performances of the model in terms of precision (Fig. 3a). In fact, when we remove them from the training set, the performances are significantly lower. Also, the recall measure doesn't highlight any significant difference (thus omitted from the plots).

6 Final Remarks

The transfer learning experiments we conducted highlight that different digital archives employ the EAD standard differently and use the tags in a heterogeneous way. This aspect impacts the LtC approach which behaves very well within the same archive, but fairly less when we try to apply the same model on a heterogeneous collection.

We see that the impact of a single sub-collection in the training set is marginal even though some collections bring key contributions that help to improve the citation model – see the role of the highly heterogeneous "worldcat" sub-collection in the second experiment. On the one hand, this means that the LtC framework performs at best when trained on the collection where it will be applied. On the other hand, the framework adapts well to heterogeneous collections provided that the test set not to be composed of EAD files coming from archives not considered in the training set. Finally, we confirm that the LtC approach does not require big the training sets as it was shown for a homogeneous setting in [8].

Future work will investigate the role of expert users in a reinforcement learning setting, where the citations produced by the system are corrected and revised by experts. We plan to dynamically change the citation model when a user modifies a citation in order to add a new learning layer to the system.

Acknowledgments. The work was partially funded by the "Computational Data Citation" (CDC) STARS-StG project of the University of Padua.

References

1. Task Group on Data Citation Standards and Practices, Out of Cite, Out of Mind: The Current State of Practice, Policy, and Technology for the Citation of Data, vol. 12. CODATA-ICSTI, September 2013
2. Alawini, A., Chen, L., Davidson, S.B., Portilho Da Silva, N., Silvello, G.: Automating data citation: the eagle-i experience. In: ACM/IEEE Joint Conference on Digital Libraries, JCDL 2017, pp. 169–178. IEEE Computer Society (2017)
3. Buneman, P., Davidson, S.B., Frew, J.: Why data citation is a computational problem. Commun. ACM (CACM) **59**(9), 50–57 (2016)
4. Buneman, P., Silvello, G.: A rule-based citation system for structured and evolving datasets. IEEE Data Eng. Bull. **33**(3), 33–41 (2010)
5. FORCE-11: Data Citation Synthesis Group: Joint Declaration of Data Citation Principles. FORCE11, San Diego, CA, USA (2014)
6. Pan, S.J., Yang, Q., et al.: A survey on transfer learning. IEEE Trans. Knowl. Data Eng. **22**(10), 1345–1359 (2010)
7. Silvello, G.: A methodology for citing linked open data subsets. D-Lib Magazine 21(1/2) (2015). https://doi.org/10.1045/january2015-silvello
8. Silvello, G.: Learning to cite framework: how to automatically construct citations for hierarchical data. J. Am. Soc. Inf. Sci. Technol. (JASIST) **68**(6), 1505–1524 (2017)

9. Silvello, G.: Theory and practice of data citation. J. Am. Soc. Inf. Sci. Technol. (JASIST) **69**(1), 6–20 (2018)
10. Thorisson, G.A.: Accreditation and attribution in data sharing. Nat. Biotechnol. **27**, 984–985 (2009)
11. Wu, Y., Alawini, A., Davidson, S.B., Silvello, G.: Data citation: giving credit where credit is due. In: Proceedings of the 2018 SIGMOD Conference, pp. 99–114. ACM Press, New York (2018). https://doi.org/10.1145/3183713

Exploring Semantic Archival Collections: The Case of Piłsudski Institute of America

Laura Pandolfo[1(✉)], Luca Pulina[1], and Marek Zieliński[2]

[1] Dipartimento di Chimica e Farmacia, Università di Sassari, via Vienna 2, 07100 Sassari, Italy
{laura.pandolfo,lpulina}@uniss.it

[2] Piłsudski Institute of America, 138 Greenpoint Avenue, Brooklyn, NY 11222, USA
MZielinski@pilsudski.org

Abstract. Over the last decades, a huge amount of available digital collections have been published on the Web, opening up new possibilities for solving old questions and posing new ones. However, finding pertinent information in archives often is not an easy task. Semantic Web technologies are rapidly changing the archival research by providing a way to formally describe archival documents.

In this paper, we present the activities employed in building the semantic layer of the Piłsudski Institute of America digital archive. In order to accommodate the description of archival documents as well as historical references contained in these, we used the ARKIVO ontology, which aims at providing a reference schema for publishing Linked Data. Finally, we present some query examples that meet the domain experts' information needs.

Keywords: Semantic technologies for digital archives · Ontologies · Linked data

1 Introduction

Semantic Web (SW) technologies [1,2] have been offering new opportunities and perspectives in their use in historical research and, more in general, in the humanities. Until recently, the overall historical documents was scattered among different archives, each of which holds a specific and unique collection of information separated from the others. Historians and scholars had to physically visit archive repositories each time they wanted to consult primary sources, try to get relevant information and then manually assemble cross-references. Today, the huge amount of available digital collections, usually converted in interchangeable formats, makes it feasible to access resources from any place at any time, by offering users the possibility to have direct access to information regardless of where they are physically located. Also, the publication of several datasets on the Web provide a comprehensive picture of historical and social patterns

P. Manghi et al. (Eds.): IRCDL 2019, CCIS 988, pp. 107–121, 2019.
https://doi.org/10.1007/978-3-030-11226-4_9

by allowing historians to explore unknown interactions between data that could reveal important new knowledge about the past.

In the last decades, there has been a great amount of effort in designing vocabularies and metadata formats to catalogue documents and collections, such as Dublin Core (DC)[1], Functional Requirements for Bibliographic Records (FBRB)[2], MAchine-Readable Cataloging (MARC)[3], Metadata Object Description Schema (MODS)[4], and Encoded Archival Description (EAD)[5], just to cite a few well-known examples. While DC is particularly suited for enabling searches of library catalogs of digital collections, metadata such as FRBR, EAD and MODS seem to be more devoted to human consumption rather than machine processing [3]. Concerning MARC, some experts experienced that it is not suitable neither for machine processable nor for actionable metadata [4,5]. Also, MODS is focused on objects such as books, and EAD, even reflecting the hierarchy of an archive, is focused on finding aids and the support for digitized objects is limited.

Despite the wide range of metadata standards, there is an ongoing lack of clarity regarding the use of these resources, which leads to the conclusion that in absence of a standardized vocabulary or ontology, different institutions will continue to use their own distinct systems and different metadata schemas. Notice that both vocabulary and ontology describe the way human beings refer to things in the real world, but they are different in a number of aspects. For instance, vocabularies may have no formal semantics, no defined interrelationships between different terms, and consequently no automatic reasoning technique can be exploited. On the contrary, ontologies are usually specified using the Web Ontology Language OWL [6] language, which has its logical grounding in Description Logics (DLs) [7]. Their formal semantics allows humans and computer systems to exchange information without ambiguity as to their meaning, and also makes it possible to infer additional information from the facts stated explicitly in an ontology [8].

In this paper, we present the activities employed in building the semantic layer of the Piłsudski Institute of America digital archive. In order to accommodate the description of archival documents, supporting archive workers by encompassing both the hierarchical structure of archival collections and rich metadata created during the digitization process, we used the ARKIVO ontology for modeling the Piłsudski archival collections. ARKIVO aims at providing a reference schema for publishing Linked Data [9] about archival documents as well as to describe historical elements referenced in these documents, by giving the opportunity to represent meaningful relationships between data.

The paper is organized as follows. Section 2 includes some preliminaries that will be used in the rest of the paper, and some relevant work in the field of digital

[1] http://dublincore.org/.
[2] http://www.cidoc-crm.org/frbroo/.
[3] https://www.loc.gov/marc/.
[4] http://www.loc.gov/standards/mods/.
[5] https://www.loc.gov/ead/.

archives. Section 3 describes all the aspects related to the use case, including the ARKIVO ontology for modeling resources and the connection to external datasets. Section 4 is dedicated to present some query examples that meet the domain experts' information needs. Finally, Sect. 5 concludes the paper with some final remarks and future work.

2 Background and Related Work

2.1 Preliminaries

An ontology is usually defined as a formal specification of domain knowledge conceptualization [10]. Ontologies can be defined by ontology languages such as the Resource Description Framework Schema (RDFS) [11] and the Web Ontology Language OWL [6]. While RDF is suitable for modeling simple ontologies, OWL is considered a more expressive representation language. The latest version of OWL is OWL 2, which addresses the complexity issue by defining profiles [12], namely fragments for which at least some reasoning tasks are tractable. OWL 2 DL, the version of the Web Ontology Language we focus on, is defined based on Description Logics (DL), which is a family of formal knowledge representation languages that models concepts, roles, individuals and their relationships. In DL, a database is called a knowledge base. In particular, if $\mathcal{K} = \langle \mathcal{T}, \mathcal{A} \rangle$ is a knowledge base, then the Tbox $\mathcal{T}$ is a set of *inclusion assertions*, i.e., concept descriptions in $\mathcal{AL}$ or some of its extensions, whereas the Abox is a set of *membership assertions* of the form $A(x)$ and $R(x, y)$ where A is some atomic concept, R is some atomic role and x, y are objects of a domain. Some OWL 2 constructors with the corresponding DL syntax are listed in Table 1.

Table 1. OWL 2 constructors and the corresponding DL syntax.

Constructor	DL syntax
Class	C
SubClassOf (C D)	$C \sqsubseteq D$
EquivalentClasses ($C_1 ... C_n$)	$C_1 \equiv ... \equiv C_n$
DisjointClasses ($C_1 ... C_n$)	$C_i \sqcap C_j \sqsubset \perp$ $i \neq j$ $i, j \in \{1, ..., n\}$
DisjointUnion (C $C_1 ... C_n$)	$C = C_1 \sqcup ... \sqcup C_n$
objectProperty	R
datatypeProperty	T
ObjectInverseOf (R)	R^{-}
ObjectSomeValuesFrom (R C)	$\exists$R.C

RDFS is considered as the basic representation format for developing the SW. It represents sentences in the form of triples, which consist of a subject, a predicate and an object. Triples can also be represented using the Turtle notation [13], which provides a slightly more readable RDFS serialization. As shown in the example below, Turtle syntax separates the data into two parts: a list of URIs and their abbreviated prefixes, and a list of the triples. In this example, the three triples express that the subject in these is a book, identified by a specific URI, which has its title and an author.

```
@prefix ex:  <http://example.com> .
@prefix book:<http://books.com> .
 book:uri rdf:type   ex:Book ;
          ex:title   "The Whale" ;
          ex:author  "Herman Melville".
```

The standard query language is SPARQL [14], whose latest version, namely SPARQL 1.1, includes many new language features such as aggregates, subqueries, a new suite of built-in functions, and path expressions. SPARQL queries typically consist of various clauses and blocks, which specify basic graph patterns to be matched along with keywords that join, filter and extend the solution sequences to these patterns.

```
PREFIX dbp: <http://dbpedia.org>
PREFIX dcterms: <http://purl.org/dc/terms/>
SELECT ?title ?author ?publisher ?date
WHERE {
         ?book dbp:title      ?title .
         ?book dbp:author     ?author .
         ?book dcterms:publisher ?publisher .
         OPTIONAL {?book dbp:releaseDate ?date}
        }
```

Considering the SPARQL query example above, the keyword `PREFIX` declares a namespace prefix, similar to @prefix in Turtle. The keyword `SELECT` determines the general result format, while the statements after `SELECT` refer to the remainder of the query. The listed names are identifiers of variables for which return values are to be retrieved. The above query returns all values for the variables `?title`, `?author`, `?publisher`. The actual query is initiated by the keyword `WHERE`. It is followed by a simple graph pattern, enclosed in curly braces. Intuitively speaking, these identifiers represent possible concrete values that are to be obtained in the process of answering the query. Finally, the keyword `OPTIONAL` refers to the subsequent group pattern. Optional patterns are not required to occur in all retrieved results, but if they are found, may produce bindings of variables – in our case `?date` – and thus extend the query result [2].

SPARQL 1.1 allows to use many other operators, such as, e.g, `FILTER` to restrict the set of matching results and `SERVICE` to support queries that merge data distributed across the Web. For the full list of operators, please refer to [14].

2.2 Semantic Digital Archives: A Brief Survey

Although digital archives and digital libraries may appear similar, a number of distinctions can be identified. The main difference lies in the focus on history in archives work, since they usually house collections of unique and unpublished materials not available anywhere else. Moreover, digital archive catalogues have to reproduce in some way their hierarchical structure composed of different layers, in which *fonds* represent the highest level of that structure, while *item* the lowest. Notwithstanding these differences, both are facing new challenges in order to overcome traditional data management and information browsing. In this context, SW technologies can improve the annotation metadata process by adding semantic capabilities, which increase the quality of the information retrieval process. Moreover, the use of shared ontologies can enable interoperability and promote consistency between different systems [15,16].

Since the late 1990s, after a great digitization effort, several digital archives on the Web have been developed with the aim of facilitating the document storage and retrieval processes. Europeana[6] represents the most visible effort to link cultural heritage resources and their metadata across several cultural institutions throughout Europe. The data are represented in the Europeana Data Model (EDM) [17], which is based on SW languages. EDM ensures a suitable level of interoperability between the datasets from different institutions, but the automatic conversion process into new data formats causes loss of the original metadata [18].

Pergamos[7] is a Web-based digital library implemented by the University of Athens that offers a uniform platform for managing, documenting, preserving and publishing heterogeneous digital collections. Pergamos provides even old and rare historical material in PDF format and the users can browse this collection and also visualize biographic and bibliographic information. A beta version of its open data platform has been published recently.

The Franklin D. Roosevelt (FDR) Library and Digital Archives[8] represent one of the most significant collections of historical material concerning the history of America and the world in the 20th century. In the context of this digital library, the FDR/Pearl Harbour project was intended to develop means to support enhanced search and retrieval from a specific set of documents included in the FDR library which refer to the history of the Pearl Harbour attack. The main goal of the FDR/Pearl Harbor project was to provide new search methods for historians based on an ontology in the background, which supported the retrieval process not only on the basis of specific names and events but also by category and/or role [19].

Another example of digital archive is the Józef Piłsudski Archive created by the Piłsudski Institute of America[9], which has been used as use case in this paper and it will be described in details in the next Section.

---

[6] https://www.europeana.eu/portal/en.

[7] https://pergamos.lib.uoa.gr/uoa/dl/frontend/en/index.html.

[8] http://www.fdrlibrary.marist.edu/archives/collections.html.

[9] http://www.pilsudski.org/portal/en/about-us/history.

3 The Piłsudski Institute of America Digital Collections

The Józef Piłsudski Institute of America was set up in 1943 in New York City for the purpose of continuing the work of the Institute for Research of Modern History of Poland, established in Warsaw in 1923. After Poland regained its independence at the end of the Great War, a group of historians and officers begun to travel around the country to collect archival documentation. At the beginning of World War II, part of the archives were evacuated and landed in Washington, eventually creating the seed of the Institute archival collections, which grew in time by donations from politicians, officers and organizations of prewar Poland and Polish diaspora. From its establishment, the Institute was to be a cultural and historical research center that would gather archives in order to disseminate the history of Poland [20].

Today, the Institute is devoted to collecting, safe-keeping and preserving the documents and other historical memorabilia as well as to make these resources accessible to researchers and visitors by providing support to scholars during archival queries on site. To give some idea of the range of archival material, the collections occupy about 240 linear meters, namely 2 million pages of documents covering mostly the Polish, European and American history of late 19th and 20th century. The majority of archival documents are written in Polish, but the amount of documents in other languages (e.g., Italian, English, Russian, French, Portuguese, and others) is not trivial. The international character of the archival resources draws the attention of a large number of experts and visitors coming from different countries. The collections include not only archival documents but also photographs, films, posters, periodicals, books, personal memoirs of diplomats as well as collection of paintings by Polish and European masters. In the last years, the archival collections have been annotated, digitized, full-text indexed, and gradually put online on the website of the Institute. The annotation process has been carried out in two steps. In the first step, archive workers have manually annotated each document with relevant entities (e.g., title, author, date of creation, etc.). In the second step, the annotations has been regularly validated and stored in a database. Considering the maturity reached in the development of Semantic Web technologies and Linked Data applications, the Piłsudski Institute of America started to link the archival data to external resources.

3.1 Modeling Archival Collections with ARKIVO Ontology

ARKIVO [21] is an ontology designed to accommodate the archival description, supporting archive workers by encompassing both the hierarchical structure of archives and the rich metadata attributes used during the annotation process. The strength of ARKIVO is not only to provide a reference schema for publishing Linked Data about archival documents, but also to describe the historical elements contained in these documents, e.g., giving the possibility to represent relationships between people, places, and events. We used ARKIVO ontology to model the Piłsudski digitized archival collections.

The ontology development process has been carried out according to a top-down strategy, which consists first in identifying the most abstract concepts of the domain and then in specializing the specific concepts. Given the specificity of the archival field, domain experts and archivists often used real scenarios to validate the design of ARKIVO ontology throughout its development process. In the light of reusability principle [22], we selected some existing standard meta-data, such as, e.g., `Dublin Core` and `schema.org`[10] for describing and cataloguing both physical resources, `BIBO` ontology[11] in order to have a detailed and exhaustive document classification, `FOAF`[12] for describing agents, `Geonames`[13] for linking a place name to its geographical location and `LODE`[14] for representing events. Throughout this paper, prefixes, such as `dc` for Dublin Core, `foaf` for FOAF, `schema` for schema.org, and `bibo` for BIBO ontology, are used to abbreviate URIs. The empty prefix is used for `arkivo`.

ARKIVO has been developed using the OWL 2 DL profile [23]. In the following, we describe some of the classes, properties and axioms of the ontology[15]. Furthermore, a graphical representation of ARKIVO is shown in Fig. 1.

Some of the main classes in ARKIVO are `bibo:Collection`, which represents the set of documents or collections, and `:Item`, which is the smallest indivisible unit of an archive. In order to model the different categories of collections as well as describe the structure of the archive, different subclasses of the class `bibo:Collection` are asserted, as shown below using the DL syntax:

$$
\begin{aligned}
:Fonds &\sqsubseteq bibo:Collection \\
:File &\sqsubseteq bibo:Collection \\
:Series &\sqsubseteq bibo:Collection
\end{aligned}
$$

Using existential quantification property restriction (`owl:someValuesFrom`), we define that the individuals of class `:Item` must be linked to individuals of class `:Fonds` by the `schema:isPartOf` property:

$$:Item \sqsubseteq \exists\ schema:isPartOf.:Fonds$$

This means that there is an expectation that every instance of `:Item` is part of a collection, and that collection is a member of the class `:Fonds`. This is useful to capture incomplete knowledge. For example, if we know that the individual `:701.180/11884` is an item, we can infer that it is part at least of one collection.

[10] http://schema.org.
[11] http://bibliontology.com.
[12] http://www.foaf-project.org.
[13] http://www.geonames.org/ontology/documentation.html.
[14] http://linkedevents.org/ontology/.
[15] The full ARKIVO documentation is available at https://github.com/ArkivoTeam/ARKIVO.

We also define union of classes for those classes that perform a specific function on the ontology. In this case, we used `owl:unionOf` constructor to combine atomic classes to complex classes, as we describe in the following:

$$:CreativeThing \equiv bibo:Collection \sqcup\ :HistoricalEvent \sqcup\ :Item$$

This class denotes things created by agents and it includes individuals that are contained in at least one of the classes `bibo:Collection`, `:HistoricalEvent` or `:Item`.

$$:NamedThing \equiv schema:Place \sqcup\ :Date \sqcup foaf:Agent$$

It refers to things, such as date, place and agent, and it includes individuals that are contained in at least one of the classes `schema:Place`, `:Date` or `foaf:Agent`. Individuals of class `:NamedThing` are connected to individuals of class `:CreativeThing` using the `schema:mentions` object property.

$$:GlamThing \equiv bibo:Collection \sqcup\ :Item$$

GLAM is the acronym of Galleries, Libraries, Archives and Museums. This class denotes individuals that are or can be stored in a GLAM institution. It includes individuals that are contained in at least one of the classes `bibo:Collection` or `:Item`.

3.2 Piłsudski Archival Collections to Linked Data

In order to support data integration process of combining data residing at different sources, we have used external identifiers. In this way, the resources of Piłsudski Digital Archival Collections have been linked to external datasets of the Linked Data in order to enrich the information provided with each resource. We have selected, among others, the Wikidata[16] and VIAF (Virtual International Authority File)[17], as the most common source of identifiers of people, organizations and historical events. In particular, VIAF is a system that is managed by the Online Computer Library Center (OCLC) with the goal to increase the utility of library authority files by matching and linking widely-used authority files and making that information available on the Web. These datasets appear to be stable, suggesting longevity, and data rich, which increase a chance of finding resources.

For example, we can express in Turtle notation that individuals Pius V (person), Józef Piłsudski Institute of America (organization) and Kampania

[16] https://www.wikidata.org/wiki/Wikidata:Main_Page.
[17] https://viaf.org.

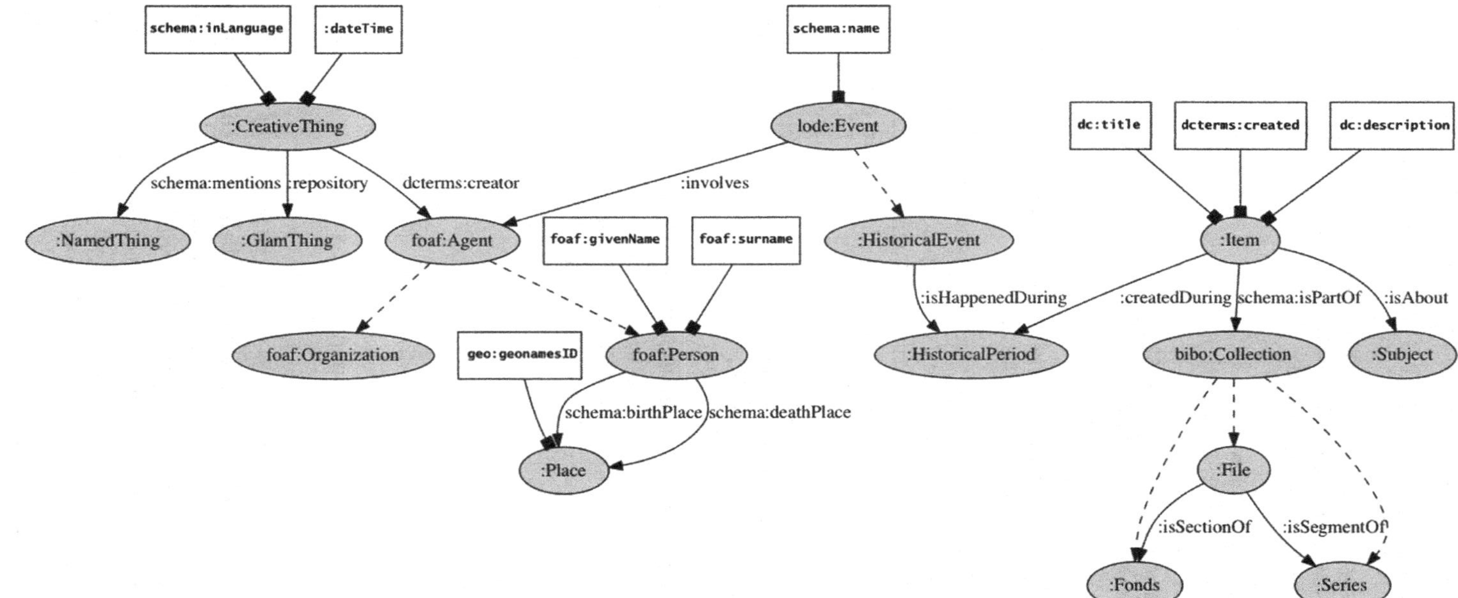

Fig. 1. Graph representation depicts some of the main classes and properties of the ARKIVO ontology. The classes are drawn as labeled ellipses and object properties between classes are shown as labeled edges, while dashed edges represent “is a” relationships. Finally, boxes represent data properties.

wrzesniowa (historical event) are linked to the corresponding Wikidata and VIAF resources as follows:

```
:P11373 a foaf:Person;
         schema:name "Pius V"^^xsd:string;
         owl:sameAs wikidata:Q131945;
         owl:sameAs viaf:76309925.

:ORG01 a foaf:Organization;
                          schema:name "Józef Pilsudski Institute of
  America"^^xsd:string;
        owl:sameAs wikidata:Q6320631;
        owl:sameAs viaf:151002901.

:R10001 a :HistoricalEvent;
         schema:name "Kampania wrzesniowa"^^xsd:string;
         owl:sameAs wikidata:Q150812.
```

Concerning geographical places, other than Wikidata and VIAF, we link the resources to Geonames[18], an open-license geographical database that provides RDF description about eight million locations and exposes them as Linked Data. In the following, we report as the place Warszawa is linked to external data:

```
:G10003 a schema:Place;
         schema:name "Warszawa"^^xsd:string;
         owl:sameAs geonames:756135;
         owl:sameAs wikidata:Q270;
         owl:sameAs viaf:146267734.
```

The process of linking the Piłsudski resources to other datasets is still ongoing and we are aiming to enrich our data with more external data sources. The triple store has been implemented using Stardog 5 Community edition [24], and currently the semantic archival collection of the Institute consist of more than 300 K triples.

4 Use Case Queries

In this Section, we describe the exploration of the Piłsduski archival collection with typical domain experts and historians information needs. Concerning the main information needs in querying archival collections, we can identify the following categories:

Collection. One of the main challenges is to detect the type of collections, such as fonds, file, and series, which are relevant to their research. In this context, also the collections' characteristics can provide meaningful cues. Moreover, relationships among records represent a primary issue.

Agent. People, organizations and authors are part of this category. Domain experts are interested, e.g., in people mentioned in documents, authors of documents as well as organizations that hold specific archival collection.

[18] http://www.geonames.org/ontology/.

Repository. The provenance of an archival collection plays a central role when accessing archival materials. The creator or the institution holding the collection, together with the name of the creator, are among the most common information used in archival queries.

Date and Place. Date and places may indicate specific references to the document. This data can be related with collections, e.g., date of creation, place mentioned in documents, or with biographical data.

Topic Information. Topics provide a way to find more content about a subject and do targeted searching in archival collections. In this regard, abstracts and descriptions of collections are used to reduce the amount of time spent in research.

We collected a set of queries formulated by domain experts. In the following, we illustrate some queries and their results. Notice that for each query in natural language, we wrote a corresponding query in SPARQL language (Table 2).

Query 01. Find all items, created between 1950 and 1955, that mention people with the surname "Churchill" and the place"Polska". Thus, return the title of the item, the title of the collection to which it belongs and possibly the name of its author.

```
SELECT distinct ?itemTitle ?collectionTitle ?author
WHERE {
        ?item a :Item .
    ?item dc:title ?itemTitle .
    ?item schema:isPartOf ?collection .
    ?collection dc:title ?collectionTitle .
    ?item dcterms:created ?d .
         FILTER (?d >"1950"^^xsd:gYear && ?d < "1955"^^xsd:gYear) .
    ?item schema:mentions ?p .
    ?p foaf:surname "Churchill" .
    ?item schema:mentions ?place .
    ?place a schema:Place .
    ?place schema:name "Polska" .
             OPTIONAL {?item dcterms:creator ?name .
                   ?name schema:name ?author } .
     }
```

Table 2. SPARQL query **01** results

?itemTitle	?collectionTitle	?author
Wycinek z Orła Białego: Słowa papieża o Polsce	Wycinki prasowe dotyczace Watykanu	
15 rocznica śmierci Józefa Piłsudskiego	Artykuły prasowe na temat Józefa Piłsudskiego	
Sprawozdanie prezesa Rady Ministrów	Projekt zjazdu dyplomatów	Odzierzyński, Roman

Query 02. Return the number of items that belong to collection focused on the historical event "Kampania wrześniowa" (Invasion of Poland, in English). Return also the collection title and the name of the institution which houses that collection (Table 3).

```
SELECT ?title ?collection ?archive (count(distinct ?item) as ?triple)
WHERE {
    ?item a :Item .
    ?item schema:isPartOf ?collection .
    ?collection a :CreativeThing .
    ?collection :isAbout ?event .
    ?collection dc:title ?title .
    ?event a :HistoricalEvent .
    ?event schema:name "Kampania wrzeniowa" .
    ?organization :repository ?collection .
    ?organization schema:name ?archive .
     }
GROUP BY ?title ?collection ?archive
```

Table 3. SPARQL query **02** results

?title	?collection	?archive	?triple
Wojny Polskie	http://pilsudski.org/resources/A701.025	Piłsudski Institute of America	184

Query 03. Find all items created before or in 1936, which belong to a file collection and mention both Benito Mussolini and Adolf Hitler. Moreover, from the external dataset of the Italian Chamber of Deputies find information about the Premier office held by Mussolini and eventually some data pertaining his bio. Thus, return the title of the items, their creation date, the file resources, information about Mussolini's Premier office and his biography data (Table 4).

```
PREFIX ocd: <http://dati.camera.it/ocd/>
SELECT ?title ?date ?file ?office ?bio
WHERE {
    ?item a :Item .
    ?item schema:isPartOf ?file .
    ?file a :File .
    ?item dcterms:created ?date .
        FILTER (?date <= '1936'^^xsd:gYear) .
    ?item dc:title ?title .
    ?item schema:mentions ?p .
    ?p schema:name ?person1 .
    ?item schema:mentions ?otherperson .
    ?otherperson schema:name ?person2 .
        FILTER (?person1 = "Mussolini, Benito" && ?person2 = "Hitler, Adolf").
SERVICE <http://dati.camera.it/sparql> {
     ?s owl:sameAs <http://dbpedia.org/resource/Benito_Mussolini> .
     ?s ocd:rif_presidenteConsiglioMinistri ?off .
     ?off dc:title ?office .
         OPTIONAL {?s dc:description ?bio }.
      }
     }
```

Table 4. SPARQL query **03** results

?title	?date	?file	?office	?bio
Kariera Józefa Piłsudskiego	1935-05-13	A701.001.087	Presidente del Consiglio dei Ministri dal 31.10.1922 al 25.07.1943	Insegnante di scuole superiori, Pubblicista / Giornalista

5 Conclusions and Future Work

In this paper, we have presented our work in building the semantic layer of the Piłsudski Institute of America digital archive, which included the development of ARKIVO ontology, the representation of the Piłsudski archival collections with ARKIVO, the connection of these resources with external datasets and finally some of the domain experts' queries.

It is well-known that in order to be successfully and efficiently used both from end-users and service providers in practical cases, digital archives entail the need to deal with some critical issues. The first issue is related to the problem of maintaining updated an ontology-based application. In fact, manual ontology population is a time consuming task and it requires professional expertise for detecting extractable data. As future work, we will investigate methodologies for the automatizing of the ontology population process exploiting the techniques presented in [25,26]. The second issue deals with query answering over large ontology-enriched datasets. Query answering is not a simple retrieval procedure of explicit facts but involves some inference mechanism capable of discovering new information. In this context, our aim will be to provide fast and efficient query answering over large knowledge bases and thus allow user to build complex queries. The third issue concerns the ability to access, retrieve and use data by non-expert users, namely those who lack technical or domain knowledge skills. In this respect, we are planning to provide some visual tools for querying semantic data that would support users to easily explore all the interesting relationships that arise from encountering a single document in the archive.

References

1. Berners-Lee, T., Hendler, J., Lassila, O., et al.: The semantic web. Sci. Am. **284**(5), 28–37 (2001)
2. Hitzler, P., Krotzsch, M., Rudolph, S.: Foundations of Semantic Web Technologies. CRC Press, Boca Raton (2009)
3. Alemu, G., Stevens, B., Ross, P., Chandler, J.: Linked data for libraries: benefits of a conceptual shift from library-specific record structures to rdf-based data models. New Libr. World **113**(11/12), 549–570 (2012)
4. Coyle, K., Hillmann, D.: Resource description and access (RDA): cataloging rules for the 20th century. D-Lib. **13**(1/2) (2007)
5. Tennant, R.: MARC must die. Libr. J. New York **127**(17), 26–27 (2002)
6. Antoniou, G., Van Harmelen, F.: Web ontology language: owl. In: Handbook on Ontologies, pp. 91–110. Springer, Heidelberg (2009). https://doi.org/10.1007/978-3-540-24750-0_4

7. Baader, F., Lutz, C.: Description logic. In: Studies in Logic and Practical Reasoning, vol. 3, pp. 757–819. Elsevier, Amsterdam (2007)
8. Krötzsch, M., Simancik, F., Horrocks, I.: A description logic primer. arXiv preprint arXiv:1201.4089 (2012)
9. Bizer, C., Heath, T., Berners-Lee, T.: Linked data - the story so far. In: Semantic Services, Interoperability and Web Applications: Emerging concepts, pp. 205–227 (2009)
10. Guarino, N., Oberle, D., Staab, S.: What is an ontology? In: Staab, S., Studer, R. (eds.) Handbook on Ontologies. IHIS, pp. 1–17. Springer, Heidelberg (2009). https://doi.org/10.1007/978-3-540-92673-3_0
11. Brickley, D., Guha, R.V., McBride, B.: RDF schema 1.1. W3C Recommendation **25**, 2004–2014 (2014)
12. Motik, B., Grau, B.C., Horrocks, I., Wu, Z., Fokoue, A., Lutz, C., et al.: Owl 2 web ontology language profiles. W3C Recommendation **27**, 61 (2009)
13. Beckett, D., Berners-Lee, T., Prud'hommeaux, E., Carothers, G.: RDF 1.1. turtle-terse RDF triple language. W3C Recommendation (2014)
14. Harris, S., Seaborne, A., Prud'hommeaux, E.: SPARQL 1.1 query language. W3C Recommendation **21**(10), 806 (2013)
15. Kruk, S., Haslhofer, B., Piotr, P., Westerski, A., Woroniecki, T.: The role of ontologies in semantic digital libraries. In: European Networked Knowledge Organization Systems (NKOS) Workshop (2006)
16. Kruk, S.R., McDaniel, B.: Semantic Digital Libraries. Springer, Heidelberg (2009). https://doi.org/10.1007/978-3-540-85434-0
17. Doerr, M., Gradmann, S., Hennicke, S., Isaac, A., Meghini, C., van de Sompel, H.: The europeana data model (EDM). In: World Library and Information Congress: 76th IFLA General Conference and Assembly, pp. 10–15 (2010)
18. De Boer, V., et al.: Supporting linked data production for cultural heritage institutes: the Amsterdam museum case study. In: Simperl, E., Cimiano, P., Polleres, A., Corcho, O., Presutti, V. (eds.) ESWC 2012. LNCS, vol. 7295, pp. 733–747. Springer, Heidelberg (2012). https://doi.org/10.1007/978-3-642-30284-8_56
19. Ide, N., Woolner, D.: Exploiting semantic web technologies for intelligent access to historical documents. In: LREC, Citeseer (2004)
20. Pietrzyk, P.: A brief history of the mission and collections of the piłsudski institute of America for research in the modern history of Poland. Pol. Am. Stud. **60**, 91–98 (2003)
21. Pandolfo, L., Pulina, L., Zielinski, M.: Towards an ontology for describing archival resources. In: Proceedings of the Second Workshop on Humanities in the Semantic Web (WHiSe II) Co-located with 16th International Semantic Web Conference (ISWC 2017), Vienna, Austria, pp. 111–116, 22 October 2017
22. Gangemi, A., Presutti, V.: Ontology design patterns. In: Handbook on Ontologies, pp. 221–243. Springer, Heidelberg (2009). https://doi.org/10.1007/11574620_21
23. Grau, B.C., Horrocks, I., Motik, B., Parsia, B., Patel-Schneider, P., Sattler, U.: Owl 2: the next step for owl. Web Semant. Sci. Serv. Agents World Wide Web **6**(4), 309–322 (2008)
24. Inc., C.: Stardog 5: The manual (2017). http://docs.stardog.com/. Accessed June 2018

25. Pandolfo, L., Pulina, L., Adorni, G.: A framework for automatic population of ontology-based digital libraries. In: Adorni, G., Cagnoni, S., Gori, M., Maratea, M. (eds.) AI*IA 2016. LNCS (LNAI), vol. 10037, pp. 406–417. Springer, Cham (2016). https://doi.org/10.1007/978-3-319-49130-1_30
26. Pandolfo, L., Pulina, L.: ADnOTO: a self-adaptive system for automatic ontology-based annotation of unstructured documents. In: Benferhat, S., Tabia, K., Ali, M. (eds.) IEA/AIE 2017. LNCS (LNAI), vol. 10350, pp. 495–501. Springer, Cham (2017). https://doi.org/10.1007/978-3-319-60042-0_54

Digital Libraries for Open Science: Using a Socio-Technical Interaction Network Approach

Jennifer E. Beamer[1,2(✉)]

[1] University of Hawaii at Manoa, Honolulu, HI, USA
jbeamer@hawaii.edu
[2] The Claremont Colleges Library, Claremont, CA, USA

Abstract. This paper argues that using Socio-Technical Interaction Networks to build on extensively-used Digital Library infrastructures for supporting Open Science knowledge environments. Using a more social -technical approach could lead to an *evolutionary* reconceptualization of Digital Libraries. Digital Libraries being used as knowledge environments, built upon on the document repositories, will also emphasize the importance of user interaction and collaboration in carrying out those activities. That is to say, the primary goal of Digital Libraries is to help users convert information into knowledge; therefore, Digital Libraries examined in light of socio-technical interaction networks have the potential to shift Digital Libraries from individual, isolated collections to more interoperable, interconnected knowledge-creating repositories that support an evolving relationship between open science users and the Digital Library environment.

Keywords: Digital libraries · Open science · Socio-Technical Interaction Networks

1 Digital Libraries as Socio-Technical Systems

The purpose of this short paper is to suggest that the use of a social informatics framework could be helpful in examining the potential ways in which Digital Libraries (DLs) may support the practices of open science. DLs have become increasingly fundamental to conducting research [1, 2], and there is a corresponding need for them to not only support intellectual work, but also to transform into sites of collaborative knowledge production. The structure of this paper is as follows: First, it argues that DLs are socio-technical systems that deserve study as such. Next, there is a brief introduction to the underlying premise of social informatics (SI) and the strategy of socio-technical interaction networks (STIN) for examining how DLs can be examined. This is followed by a concise analysis, concluding with what may be some outcomes of using this underutilized strategy for open science. It should be noted that this paper is introductory in nature. Its objective is to argue for the refocusing of technical infrastructure to include more socio-technical elements. Thus, this short paper only presents a preliminary framework, and does not include specific evidence; future work will include research questions, data, and findings.

P. Manghi et al. (Eds.): IRCDL 2019, CCIS 988, pp. 122–129, 2019.
https://doi.org/10.1007/978-3-030-11226-4_10

DLs can be thought of as "socio-technical systems" composed of an "interrelated and interdependent combination of people, their social and work practices, the norms of use, hardware and software, the support systems that help users, the maintenance systems that keep them operating" [3]. That is to say, technical systems are interacting within an institutional and cultural context, and as such the technology informs the social and vice versa. Furthermore, these socio-technical processes essentially demonstrate collaboration between human and nonhuman actors, as they are assembled and reassembled in different ways to different ends [4].

In contrast, open science and the researchers engaging in the practices of open science operate in a similar socio-technical knowledge ecosystem. Open science practices may vary with the individual, but nevertheless rely heavily on collaboration within communities of practicing researchers. This collaboration among themselves is facilitated by the dependence upon an ever-improving and advancing digital infrastructure—often to the point of success or failure of their entire projects [5]. Researchers may practice in communities or groups, or teams, embracing the groundwork created by those before them, or be a pioneer themselves incorporating flexible (or sometimes work-around) features of DLs. Open science relies on DLs to support, construct, and build these different kinds of knowledge communities that use their content and services [6].

While prior DL research has thoroughly explored social-community practices, or the technical-system features of DLs, a comprehensive search of the literature shows that it has rarely intersected to include both the social and the technical. The socio-technical exploration, i.e., the mutual, concurrent, and reciprocal shaping of technology and society [7], has largely been under researched. This paper is proposing that this intersection is precisely what should be considered for future exploration. DLs have an opportunity to contribute to open science by improving already existing DL platforms and tools, thereby enhancing their open science practices, and their interconnected communities and collaborations.

Already in the past few decades, DLs and their architects have largely transformed and modernized scholarly publishing, the philosophy behind academic and research libraries and universities, the methods of access to information resources, intellectual property practices, and the very relationships between authors, libraries, publishers and readers [3]. Thus, it is argued that *by conducting a holistic examination into the relationship between the social and technical, the outcome will provide more* ***meaningful*** *data on the implications for DLs to generate more support for open science communities and collaborative practices.* The socio-technical approach I propose is not new (it is in fact an underutilized social informatics approach), and it is a strategy for identifying, organizing and comparatively analyzing (a) the patterns of social interaction within a system's development, and (b) the configuration of components that constitute an information system [8].

2 Social Informatics and the Emergence of Socio-Technical Interaction Networks

The premise of SI is that it focuses upon the relationships between information and communication technologies (ICTs) and the larger social context in which they exist [9]. For decades, DL programmers, librarians, systems specialists, users, scientists, researchers, and institutions have already been working collaboratively to build, innovate and sustain DLs. Specifically, conducting SI research means a shift to reframe the focus on understanding "the interdisciplinary study of the design, uses and consequences of information technologies that take into account their interaction with institutional and cultural contexts" [10]. SI researchers hold several premises. First, CTs and the social and organizational settings in which they are embedded are in a relationship of mutual shaping [10]. Second, their analyses frequently challenge commonly-held assumptions about information technologies, and often attempt to improve the lives of the people who work and play with ICTs [10].

Designed to provide a specific tool for understanding socio-technical systems in a way that advantages neither the social nor the technical aspects of a system, the STIN strategy was proposed as a framework for SI analysis [413]. In the early 2000s STIN was used to examine topics in which we are concerned with today DLs and the advancement of open; scholarly communication forums [ibid], democratization of scholarly publishing [12], web information systems [13], online communities [14], and DLs [15].

The most extensive study was conducted by Kling et al. in 2003 [9], where they conducted one of the most extensive analysis using their STIN strategy. They examined what they called electronic scholar communication forums (eSCFs). At the time these might have been considered to be DLs in their own right: arXiv.org, Flybase, ISWORLD, and CONVEX. One of their conclusions was that "technological developments themselves will not overcome issues embedded in the social contexts into which the technologies are introduced" [9]. Another important finding was that an understanding of the business models of the supporting organizations was necessary to understand the STIN, and that an understanding of the social relationships imbedded in the STIN was helpful in understanding how the technological innovations of electronic publishing were used and sustained. Their findings highlight the interconnected nature of knowledge creation, i.e., the many stakeholders and the interactions, organizations, systems and relationships that support the eSCFs.

Philosophically, there are two main rationales for embracing a SI approach. First, the goals and achievements of SI are congruent with the researchers' objectives and motivations. Second, a holistic method of investigation assumed by SI research provides more meaningful data. SI researchers aim to develop "reliable knowledge about information technology and social change based on systematic empirical research, in order to inform both public policy issues and professional practice" [16].

Kling et al. established a series of theoretical models and frameworks for supporting the transition between descriptive data, interviews, observations, and results that would be useful to wider communities [11]. The STIN strategy drew from other established SI theories such as the Social Construction of Technology (SCOT) [17] and in parallel to, but independently of, Actor Network Theory [18, 19].

3 Using STIN Strategy to Examine Digital Libraries

STIN is not traditionally referred to as a theory because it doesn't lead to strong predictions [11]. Instead, it is typically referred to as a framework or a strategy [20]. For the purposes of examining DLs, the elements used in conducting a STIN study may form a theoretical viewpoint, in that they are arranged in a way that implies a pattern of relations among concepts or even possibly the basis of a theory. The elements could define how the researcher perceives the issue and then how the researcher could address the challenge of answering the research questions.

All of the various elements involved in a network are considered nodes. These nodes are likely to include people, groups, organizations, devices, infrastructures, resources, processes, content, and policies. The nodes are not static elements, but interactors. The networks are dynamic, and the focus is on the relationships between elements.

STIN research is implemented by following the eight heuristics and include:

H1. Identify interactors (likely actors, their roles, and their needs);
H2. Identify core interactor groups;
H3. Identify incentive structures (such as a business model or motivation);
H4. Identify excluded actors and undesired interactions;
H5. Identify existing communication forums (communications systems or ecologies) and their relationships to this STIN;
H6. Identify resource flows (following the money);
H7. Map architectural choice points (technological features or social arrangement in which the designer has historically selected alternatives);
H8. Describe viable configurations and trade-offs.

From the eight heuristics above, a standard model is built and then subsequently disassembled. Its purpose is to abstract a series of underlying commonly-held assumptions about the information system's design of study. For example, for Kling [11], the standard model was built from literature about electronic scholarly communication forums. By building a standard model, researchers can incorporate conceptions that are incomplete or left out of the standard models. "What is left out of the standard models are important features of very specific technologies and settings in which people try to use them, the organizational complexity in which IT-based services are provided and embedded" [11: 49]. In contrast to the standard model, the alternative STIN model helps "to map some of the key relationships between people and people, between people and technologies, between technologies and their infrastructures and between technologies" [11: 49].

4 STIN Analysis for DLs

The usefulness of the STIN heuristics is entrenched in thirty years of technology analysis. First, H1 interactors are understood to include both human and non-human actors [11: 66], as well as non-material elements such as standards [21] and processes and traditions, potentially including dispositifs [21: 61]. Instructing the researcher to group these interactors as evident in H2 draws attention to their interactions. The organizational relationships between groups of people may have a greater impact within the STIN than dyadic human-computer interactions [21, 22].

Incentive structures H3 are identified as business models at a macro level, while at a more micro-, personal level, they need to be considered in terms of motivations.

For example, open science researchers adopting a new technology for open publishing need to consider how time spent on this will have an impact on the time available for activities which traditionally further their career, such as publishing papers in closed high-tier journals for promotion or tenure. Kling et al. [11: 57-8] use the term "communications systems" for H5, communication ecologies and existing communication forums to describe the participant's communications systems, including non-digital systems. These are predominantly understood as networks of people, rather than devices and wires [13, 21].

One of the strengths of the STIN approach for studying systems is the direction to look beyond the network [24]—first by identifying those who are the excluded actors under H4, and then by identifying the wider communication ecologies in H5 which interact with the STIN. The external elements can reveal vital perspectives, both in terms of the impacts of a system and influences on its development and use. These attentions are important where exclusion is a concern and successful participation requires the interaction of diverse stakeholder group in DLs and open science communities. Identifying undesired interactions within H4 draws attention to the experiences supported by the system. Interactions should also be considered in terms of privacy and surveillance [11: 57].

While it is useful to consider resource flows H6 in terms of following the money, the researcher is also reminded to think in terms of "resource dependencies" and "account-taking dependencies" [11, 13]. "Resource dependencies" relate to interactions which need funding, knowledge, skills, prestige or trust; "account-taking dependencies" relate to links or interactions based upon some kind of social rating [13: 102]. Resource flows also draw attention to infrastructural elements, as sooner or later these need skilled attention and financial investment.

Mapping architectural choice points under H7 relates to technical systems, but it can also refer to social processes. The researcher is directed towards the history of the system, to look at the points where choices have been made which may be considered as forks in the path of the development of the system.

Finally, H8 describes viable configurations and trade-offs. This step supports the researcher to think beyond the present system and consider potential changes (alternative configurations).

The data on which STIN models are based may be gathered through various methods, including interviews, observation, and studying materials associated with the network [9: 66]. If a STIN approach is established before data collection, the eight heuristics can be used to inform the design of instruments, such as the interview protocols.

There are several limitations that are worthy of awareness with STIN and with SI research in general. The first stems from STINs use of a variety of data collection methods: "combining the need for extensive data collection with the complex conceptualizing of socio-technical phenomena means it is a difficult methodological toolkit for many scholars" [23: 12]. A second STIN limitation is the talent to successfully identify and analyze STINs, which is deeply dependent on the interview skills of the researcher and their ability to obtain information from respondents, not to mention gaining access to individuals and organizations.

5 Can STIN Help Us Build Better Digital Libraries for Open Science?

As the goal of using SI and STIN strategy is understanding more thoroughly the relationships between social and DL design (ultimately to provide more meaningful support and facilitate open science communities and collaborative practices), there is much diversity within the different DL and open science communities. There are even more ways of collaborating, and the considerable numbers of stakeholders in both communities emphasize the need for a more holistic approach to supporting and understating how the two can work together. For example, computer scientists may see DLs as relative to databases, networks, retrieval engines, and other empowering technologies. Librarians might view DLs as extensions of the library, or as a tool for energizing and accessing information and knowledge. Policymakers often regard DLs as tools for lessening digital divides and providing equal access. Open scientists may wish for DLs to play a central role in providing access to information—tools that may assist them in developing and expanding human knowledge and sharing that knowledge.

Nevertheless, after more than a decade of research, there is some scholarly acknowledgement [6, 19, 22] that the capabilities of DLs to achieve a role advancing open science has, in large part, been constrained by its current social and technological state. Since DLs were initially intended and built to curate, search, and act as networked repositories of digital resources, they have largely remained in this form. This is not to suggest that these goals are not well-intentioned. DLs were mainly influenced by their traditional library counterparts (both humans and library systems) as they selected, collected, organized, managed, stored, preserved, and facilitated access to information. These activities remain important, and they emphasize developing, maintaining, and improving a collection of digital resources. However, if we wish to support the practices of open sciences, the next phase of DL development must include an emphasis on how people *work* with DL resources to pursue various knowledge-related goals.

In examining and practicing STIN DLs, we consider what people do, i.e., how they interact with digital resources and each other, and with organizations; and also, who is excluded. By doing this, DLs can transform into more than just searchable document repositories of knowledge; they become ecosystems that help people *create* knowledge. DLs are workspaces with rich content and tools, where people can work independently or collaborate with others to learn and to solve their problems within the interfaces of the DL.

Using STIN to build on already existing DLs, particularly those that are extensively used as a successful knowledge environment, will increase the kinds of activities that DLs support. This in turn could lead to an *evolutionary* reconceptualization of DLs. DLs as knowledge environments, built upon the document repositories, will broaden the kinds of activities that DLs support, and emphasize the importance of interaction in carrying out those activities. The primary goal of DLs is helping users convert information into knowledge. DLs examined in light of STIN have the potential to shift DLs from individual, isolated collections to more interoperable, interconnected repositories that support an evolving relationship between open science users and the digital library environment.

Acknowledgements. Thank you to my fellow Ph.D. colleagues for their advice and collegial discussions about theory and methodology. Thanks especially to Rich Gazan, D.B. and Wiebke Reile.

References

1. Blandford, A., Buchanan, G., Jones, M.: Usability of digital libraries. Int. J. Digit. Libr. **4**(2), 69–70 (2004)
2. Borgman, C.L., et al.: Knowledge infrastructures in science: data, diversity, and digital libraries. Int. J. Digit. Libr. **16**(3–4), 207–227 (2015)
3. Borgman, C.: What are digital libraries? Competing visions. Inf. Process. Manage. **35**, 227–243 (1999)
4. Bearman, D.: Digital libraries. Ann. Rev. Inf. Sci. Technol. **41**, 223–272 (2007)
5. Latour, B.: Reassembling the Social: An Introduction to Actor-network Theory. Oxford University Press, New York (2005)
6. Munafò, M.R., et al.: A manifesto for reproducible science. Nat. Hum. Behav. **1**(1), 0021 (2017)
7. Kling, R., Scacchi, W.: The web of computing: computer technology as social organization. Adv. Comput. **21**, 1–90 (1982)
8. Scacchi, W.: Socio-technical interaction networks in free/open source software development processes. In: Acuna, S.T., Juristo, N. (eds.) Software Process Modeling, pp. 1–27. Springer Science & Business Media Inc., New York (2005). https://doi.org/10.1007/0-387-24262-7_1
9. Kling, R., Rosenbaum, H.: Social informatics in information science: an introduction. J. Am. Soc. Inf. Sci. **49**, 1047–1052 (1998)
10. Lamb, R., Sawyer, S., Kling, R.: A social informatics perspective on soc10- technical networks. In: Chung, H.M. (ed.) Proceedings of the Americas Conference on Information Systems. Long Beach, CA (2000)
11. Kling, R., McKim, G., King, A.: A bit more to IT: scholarly communication forums as socio-technical interaction networks. J. Am. Soc. Inform. Sci. Technol. **54**(1), 46–67 (2003)
12. Meyer, E., Kling, R.: Leveling the playing field, or expanding the bleachers? Socio-Technical Interaction Networks and arXiv.org (Center for Social Informatics Working Paper Series WP-02-10) (2002)
13. Eschenfelder, K., Chase, L.: Socio-technical networks of large, post- implementation web information systems: tracing effects and influences. In: 35th Hawaii International Conference on System Sciences. Big Island, Hawaii (2002)
14. Barab, S., Schatz, S., Scheckler, R.: Using activity theory to conceptualize online community and using online community to conceptualize activity theory. Mind Culture Activity **11**(1), 25–47 (2004)
15. Joung, K., Rosenbaum, H.: Digital libraries as socio-technical interaction networks: A study of the American Memory Project. In Paper presented at the ASIST 2004 Annual Meeting; 'Managing and Enhancing Information: Cultures and Conflicts' (ASIST AM 04), Providence, Rhode Island (2004)
16. Williams, R., Edge, D.: The social shaping of technology. Res. Policy **25**, 856–899 (1996)
17. Pinch, T., Bijker, W.: The social construction of facts and artifacts: or how the sociology of science and the sociology of technology might benefit each other. In: Bijker, W., Hughes, T., Pinch, T. (eds.) The Social Construction of Technological Systems: New Directions in the Sociology and History of Technology, pp. 17–50. MIT Press, Cambridge (1987)

18. Law, J.: After ANT: complexity, naming and topology. In: Law, J., Hassard, J. (eds.) Actor Network Theory and After, pp. 1–14. Maiden, Blackwell. (1999)
19. Meyer, E.T.: Socio-Technical Perspectives on Digital Photography: Scientific Digital Photography Use by Marine Mammal Researchers. Indiana University, Bloomington (2007)
20. Star, S.L.: This is not a boundary object: reflections on the origin of a concept. Sci. Technol. Hum. Values **35**(5), 601–617 (2010)
21. Contractor, N., Monge, P., Leonardi, P.: Multidimensional networks and the dynamics of sociomateriality: bringing technology inside the network. Int. J. Commun. **5**(39), 682–720 (2011)
22. Lamb, R., Kling, R.: Reconceptualizing users and social actors m information systems research. MIS Q. **27**(2), 197–235 (2003)
23. Meyer, E.T.: Examining the hyphen: the value of social informatics for research and teaching. In: Fichman, P., Rosenbaum, H. (eds.) Social Informatics: Past, Present and Future, pp. 56–73. Cambridge Scholars Publishing, Cambridge (2014)
24. Sawyer, S.: Social informatics: overview, principles and opportunities. Bull. Am. Soc. Inf. Sci. Technol. **31**(5), 9–12 (2005)

Information Integration

OpenAIRE's DOIBoost - Boosting Crossref for Research

Sandro La Bruzzo[1], Paolo Manghi[1], and Andrea Mannocci[2(✉)]

[1] Institute of Information Science and Technology - CNR, Pisa, Italy
{sandro.labruzzo,paolo.manghi}@isti.cnr.it
[2] Knowledge Media Institute – The Open University, Milton Keynes, UK
andrea.mannocci@open.ac.uk

Abstract. Research in information science and scholarly communication strongly relies on the availability of openly accessible datasets of scholarly entities metadata and, where possible, their relative payloads. Since such metadata information is scattered across diverse, freely accessible, online resources (e.g. Crossref, ORCID), researchers in this domain are doomed to struggle with (meta)data integration problems, in order to produce custom datasets of often undocumented and rather obscure provenance. This practice leads to waste of time, duplication of efforts, and typically infringes open science best practices of transparency and reproducibility of science. In this article, we describe how to generate DOIBoost, a metadata collection that enriches Crossref with inputs from Microsoft Academic Graph, ORCID, and Unpaywall for the purpose of supporting high-quality and robust research experiments, saving times to researchers and enabling their comparison. To this end, we describe the dataset value and its schema, analyse its actual content, and share the software Toolkit and experimental workflow required to reproduce it. The DOIBoost dataset and Software Toolkit are made openly available via Zenodo.org. DOIBoost will become an input source to the OpenAIRE information graph.

Keywords: Scholarly communication · Open science · Data science · Data integration · Crossref · ORCID · Unpaywall · Microsoft Academic Graph

1 Introduction

Research in information science and scholarly communication strongly relies on the availability of openly accessible datasets of metadata and, where possible, of relative payloads. In the context of literature publishing, Crossref is certainly playing a central role as mediator between publishers of scientific literature and consumers, which are often also producers in this process. Publisher services publish scientific literature, mint a DOI from Crossref, and push into the system a complete bibliographic record according to Crossref metadata scheme. In turn, Crossref provides CC-BY 4.0 access to

P. Manghi et al. (Eds.): IRCDL 2019, CCIS 988, pp. 133–143, 2019.
https://doi.org/10.1007/978-3-030-11226-4_11

its entire metadata collection via REST APIs[1]. Due to its longitudinal, pan-publisher and up-to-date content, this metadata collection has become the pivot of several other initiatives willing to *(i)* enrich/complete the collection with further information, not necessarily provided by publishers to Crossref, or *(ii)* willing to enrich their own collection(s) with DOIs and metadata from Crossref. Several well-known examples can be mentioned, such as Google Scholar, Dimensions, SemanticScholar, Microsoft Academic Graph, AMiner, OpenAIRE, ORCID, Unpaywall; many of them make their content freely available for research purposes, under CC-BY or CC-0 license. Researchers can either download or access via APIs such metadata collections and perform their experiments, but only after non-trivial efforts of (meta)data integration, cleaning, and harmonization. Efforts often given for granted by major players in scholarly knowledge analytics and dismissed in one sentence where a list of data sources, often behind paywall and thus not available to the general public, is provided; e.g. [5]. Typically, such integration efforts differ from experiment to experiment, where, violating principles of Open Science, provenance and lineage of data are often undocumented. This general misalignment spoils quality, and evaluation and comparison of different research endeavours, which should be rather based on common input data collections, transparently generated and recognized by the community.

In response to this general demand, this paper presents DOIBoost [6], a collection of metadata records resulting from a transparent process of integration, harmonization, and cleaning of *Crossref* with *Microsoft Academic Graph*[2] (via *Azure Data Lake Store*), *ORCID*,[3] and *Unpaywall*.[4] Such sources can considerably impact on the quality and richness of Crossref by adding publication access rights information, missing abstracts, author identifiers, and precious authors' affiliations equipped with organization identifiers. The result of our integration efforts, the DOIBoost dataset, is here described, i.e. its input sources, its data model (JSON schema), together with the methodology to generate the dataset, and the actual software (DOIBoost Software Toolkit) and machinery used to produce it. Both DOIBoost dataset and software are published in Zenodo.org [6, 7] and made available for research purposes under CC-BY 4.0. DOIBoost will become an input source to the OpenAIRE information graph.[5]

2 The Dataset

DOIBoost is constructed by enriching Crossref records as shown in Fig. 1: the input sources described in Table 1 are collected and integrated by using Crossref DOIs as pivot for the data integration process. A final cleaning step is applied, to get rid of the records whose quality is too low or that are leftovers inserted in Crossref for testing

[1] *Crossref APIs*, https://www.crossref.org/services/metadata-delivery/rest-api.

[2] *Microsoft Academic Graph*, https://aka.ms/msracad.

[3] *ORCID*, http://orcid.org.

[4] *Unpaywall*, http://unpaywall.org.

[5] OpenAIRE EXPLORE, http://explore.openaire.eu.

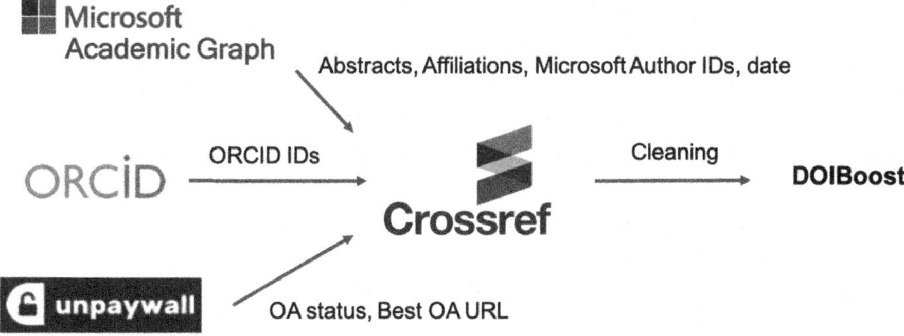

Fig. 1. DOIBoost: dataset construction workflow.

reasons and never removed. In the following sections, we provide details on the input sources and describe the DOIBoost data model.

2.1 Input Dataset Sources

The input data sources are described in Table 1. Their metadata is provided under free-to-reuse and distribute license, although with slightly different constraints, which however do not prevent the dissemination of the collection. Such sources are relevant to Crossref due to the following reasons:

- *Unpaywall* by ImpactStory [1] attempts to identify the Open Access records in Crossref by also crawling from the Web (e.g. from institutional repositories) the best Open Access URLs they can find for each record. Crossref DOIs can be enriched with such Open Access instances.
- *Microsoft Academic Graph, via Azure Data Lake Store (ADLS)* [2] uses "…AI-powered machine readers to process all documents discovered by Bing crawler and extract scholarly entities and their relationships to form a knowledge base…". When possible, MAG links to DOIs and can therefore enrich Crossref with extra information, e.g. author identifiers, affiliation identifiers, abstracts.
- *ORCID* [3] builds a world-wide record of researchers by providing them with a persistent identifier and allowing them to populate a publicly accessible curriculum, inclusive of article DOIs. As a result, ORCID gathers many more associations between articles in Crossref and ORCID IDs than Crossref is actually collecting from publishers.

2.2 Dataset Model

Crossref, as well as the other sources, are integrated into a common (meta)data model and JSON schema, initially populated with Crossref records. The model is illustrated via an example in Listing 1 (*For record types please refer to* https://api.crossref.org/v1/types).

Table 1. DOIBoost: input datasets.

Source	License	Protocol & format	Approximate size	Download date
Crossref	CC0	API, JSON[a]	250 GB	Nov 2018
ORCID	CC0 1.0	Download, CSV (txt)[b]	32 GB (zipped)	Oct 2018
MAG (ADLS)	ODC-BY	Download, CSV (txt)[c]	120 GB (relevant DB tables)	May 2018
Unpaywall	CC0	Download, CSV (txt)[d]	6 GB (zipped)	Jun 2018

[a]*Crossref APIs*, http://api.Crossref.org.
[b]*ORCID download*, https://orcid.org/content/download-file.
[c]*Microsoft Academic Graph* obtained via the *Azure Data Lake Store (ADLS)*, https://azure.microsoft.com/en-us/services/storage/data-lake-storage.
[d]*Unpaywall download*, https://unpaywall.org/products/snapshot.

Data integration is relevance-driven in the sense that from the input data sources only a few properties, regarded as particularly important, are selected for integration into the Crossref dataset. Accordingly, the model has been conceived to include a set of Crossref properties, as provided by the relative dataset, and a set of properties that can be integrated from other sources, as described in Fig. 1. Each one of these "inheritable" properties is equipped with a *provenance* field, whose value currently includes "Crossref", "MAG", "Unpaywall", and "ORCID" in order to trace the origin of the information. Provenance plays a key role when processing a dataset in order to account for the origin of any possible misbehaviour or unexpected result and to fine-tune processing based on the data model and on specific provenance of given fields. More specifically, the properties are:

- *Identifiers of authors*: authors can be assigned identifiers from different "authorities", for example internal identifiers as provided by Microsoft or persistent identifiers as provided by ORCID. Accordingly, the model allows to gather multiple identifiers for the same author; to facilitate programmatic interpretation, for each identifier *value* the model includes the respective *schema*, intended as the authority issuing the identifier.
- *Affiliations of authors*: authors are affiliated to an institution (or more), which is the organization of the author at the moment of publishing; the model allows the collection of different affiliations for the same author since these may be collected from different sources (e.g. Crossref and MAG); in turn, each institution may be associated to different identifiers provided by the same source, e.g. MAG may provide organization IDs internal to MAG as well as organization persistent identifiers released by the Global Research Identifier Database[6] (hence, same *provenance*, but different *schema*).
- *Dates*: publications in Crossref often miss the publishing date which we can collect from Crossref and MAG (provenance for this field is missing);
- *Abstracts*: abstracts can be provided by different sources, e.g. Crossref or by MAG, hence require provenance information to track down their origin.

[6] GRID database, https://www.grid.ac.

```
{  "title":"My Title",
   "authors":[
      {  "given":"Marco",
         "family":"Rossi",
         "fullname": "Marco Rossi",
         "identifiers":[
            {  "schema":"ORCID",
               "value":"https://..../0000-0002-3337-2025",
               "provenance":"ORCID" },
            {  "schema":"MAG ID",
               "value":"https://.../1278293695",
               "provenance":"MAG" } ],
         "affiliations":[
            {  "value":"My Affiliation Name",
               "official-page":"www.affiliation.org",
               "identifiers":[
                  {  "schema":"grid.ac",
                     "value":"https://.../grid.12345.a" },
                  {  "schema":"microsoftID",
                     "value":"https://.../4213412341" },
                  {  "schema":"wikipedia",
                     "value":"https:///wiki/my_affiliation" }],
               "provenance":"MAG" } ] },
      {  "given":"Giuseppe",
         "family":"Trovato",
         "fullname": "Giuseppe Trovato",
         "identifiers":[],
         "affiliations":[] } ],
   "issued":"2016-07-01",
   "abstract":[
      {  "value":"Abstract Text", "provenance":"MAG" },
      {  "value":"Abstract Text", "provenance":"Crossref" } ],
   "subject":["Agronomy and Crop Science", "Forestry"],
   "type":"journal-article",
   "license":[
      {  "url":"http://www.elsevier.com/tdm/userlicense/1.0/",
         "date-time":"2011-07-01T00:00:00Z",
         "content-version":"tdm",
         "delay-in-days":0 } ],
   "instances":[
      {  "url":"http://unkonwonInstance.org",
         "access-rights":"UNKNOWN", "provenance":"Crossref" },
      {  "url":"http://openAccessInstance.org",
         "access-rights":"OPEN", "provenance":"Unpaywall" } ],
   "published-online":"2016-08-01",
   "published-print":"2016-07-01",
   "accepted":"2016-01-01",
   "publisher":"Publisher Name",
   "doi":"10.1016/j.ffhfhgfhf",
   "doi-url":"http://dx.doi.org/10.1016/j.ffhfhgfhf",
   "issn":[ { "type":"print", "value":"01234-5678" } ],
   "collected-from":[ "Crossref", "MAG", "Unpaywall", "ORCID" ],
   "record-quality-report": "complete"
}
```


Listing 1. DOIBoost: JSON record example.

- *Instances of the DOI work*: instances represent the location of the files of a given DOI work at different source sites. Since these may represent different manifestations - e.g. the published journal version, the open access version of an article in an institutional repository - each instance has its own list of files (*URLs*) and *access rights*[7].
- *Record quality report:* in order to filter out "invalid" records when importing the dump into the OpenAIRE system, the records are marked with a report of quality. This information may be useful also to scientists re-using the data and is therefore captured in the model. The property can have the following values: *incomplete* (the record misses one or more of the OpenAIRE mandatory properties, i.e. Title, Authors, or Date); *mock* (mock records are very frequent in the scholarly communication, typically created by operators at publishers or institutional repositories to verify system functionalities and then never removed); *complete* (when the record is neither marked as *incomplete* nor *mock*).

3 Methodology

Due to the large number of records, in the order of hundreds of millions, our solution relies on in-memory parallel processing techniques. To this end, the software we developed, named DOIBoost Software Toolkit [7], is deployed over the infrastructure depicted in Fig. 2. The architecture workflows support two distinct phases of *(i)* data collection and preparation for integration and *(ii)* data integration to deliver DOIBoost. In the following we described the actions involved in these two phases; knowledge on HDFS and Spark terminology and technologies is strongly advisable to fully understand the internals.

3.1 DOIBoost Toolkit Deployment

The infrastructure underlying DOIBoost Toolkit is shown in Fig. 2 and features: 20 virtual machines (VMs) for Apache HDFS Data Nodes and Spark workers, each VM with 16 cores, 32 GB of ram, and 250 GB of disk; plus 3 dedicated virtual machines for HDFS Name Nodes, each one with 8 cores, 16 GB of ram, and 40 GB of disk.

Apache HDFS is used as the main storage for the objects and files collected from the sources, in order to exploit its fast writing and reading rates. Apache Spark is used to *(i)* read such content from HDFS in order to manipulate and transform it into Spark DataFrames that match the DOIBoost data model, and *(ii)* to perform the data integration pipeline that produces DOIBoost, by joining the data source DataFrames. All workflows are implemented and orchestrated via Apache Oozie[8].

---

[7] The field "access-rights" can assume the values OPEN, EMBARGO, RESTRICTED, CLOSED, UNKNOWN.

[8] *Apache Oozie*, http://oozie.apache.org.

The DOIBoost Toolkit is written in PySpark under AGPL Open Source license[9] and is available for download and citation on Zenodo.org [7]. The package contains the scripts required to implement such workflows and reproduce the collection, which will be described in the following sections.

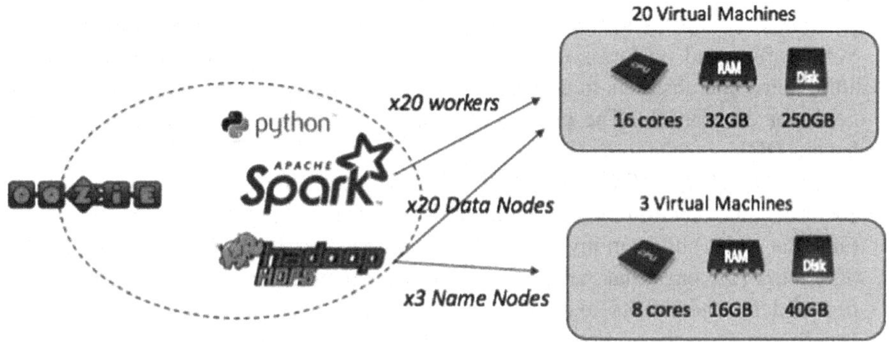

Fig. 2. DOIBoost Toolkit: deployment.

3.2 Data Collection and Preparation for Integration

As anticipated in the previous sections, each source is collected according to different methods, then transferred into HDFS as a corresponding sequence file, and finally manipulated in-memory via Spark jobs (*generateXDataFrame.py*), in order to produce a relative DOIBoost Spark DataFrame.

We assume in the following that the datasets are manually collected and transferred into HDFS via Shell, creating corresponding sequence files: JSON format for Crossref and CSV text format for MAG, ORCID, and Unpaywall. More specifically:

- Crossref is downloaded from the relative APIs using the GitHub repository *Crossref REST API*[10] made available by Crossref; the execution of the script results in a dump on the file system.
- ORCID and Unpaywall are manually downloaded as CSV text files on the file system. Each line in the dump from ORCID represents an author with his/her publication list and in Unpaywall represents a DOI entry with the relative OA status and URL access information.
- MAG is manually downloaded from ADLS as a set of CSV text files, where each CSV is the content of one relational database[11] table in MAG and each line represents a row in the table. For the enrichment of DOIBoost we downloaded content from the following relevant tables: *Papers*, *PapersAuthorAffiliation*, *Authors*, *Affiliation*, *PaperAbstractsInvertedindex*.

---

9 *Affero General Public License*, https://en.wikipedia.org/wiki/Affero_General_Public_License.

10 *Crossref REST API - GitHub*, https://github.com/Crossref/rest-api-doc.

11 *MAG Schema*, https://microsoftdocs.github.io/MAG/Mag-ADLS-Schema.

Such dumps can be uploaded to HDFS as sequence files with a simple shell command ("hdfs dfs -put fileName pathHDFS"). Once the sequence files are created, the "preparation to integration" phase is performed by executing (in any order) the following Spark jobs:

- *generateCrossrefDataFrame.py* The script reads from the Crossref sequence file and transforms the JSON records into a respective DOIBoost DataFrame.
- *generateMAGDataFrame.py* The script generates DataFrames corresponding to the MAG tables and performs the joins required to recombine articles with authors, affiliations, and abstracts to deliver a DOIBoost DataFrame that only contains such fields for each article. The process also filters out articles from MAG that do not have a DOI.
- *generateORCIDDataFrame.py* The ORCID sequence file contains rows relative to ORCID author identifiers, each followed by the list of publications of the author. First, the script builds an inverted list, where the key is the DOI followed by the list of authors (the ones that can be found in the sequence file for the DOI) with their first and second names and ORCID ID. Finally, the script builds a DOIBoost DataFrame from these representations, which only contain author information for each article: *given, family, fullname, and identifier (schema, value, provenance).*
- *generateUnPayWallDataFrame.py* The Unpaywall sequence file contains rows relative to Crossref DOIs and their Open Access information[12] as extracted by Unpaywall. The Spark script transforms the file in a DOIBoost DataFrame where articles are equipped with the *instances* derivable from each row (*URL* and *access-rights*) and are empty on other fields.

The execution times of these jobs, given our current architectural specifications, are reported in Table 2 below.

Table 2. DOIBoost generation: workflow execution times.

Execution step	Execution time
generateCrossrefDataFrame.py	6.1 min
generateMAGDataFrame.py	1.1 h
generateORCIDDataFrame.py	30 s
generateUnpaywallDataFrame.py	20 s
createDOIBoost.py	35 min

3.3 DOIBoost Integration Pipeline

Once all DOIBoost DataFrames for the input sources are generated a final integration script can be executed, named *createDOIBoost.py*. The script performs a join by DOI, starting from Crossref, and adding in sequence: MAG, ORCID, and Unpaywall. Each step of the pipeline progressively enriches DOIBoost DataFrame with one data source

[12] *Unpaywall data format*, https://unpaywall.org/data-format.

at a time (by performing joins on DOIs). Given an input DOIBoost record and one matching its DOI, two kinds of enrichments are possible:

- *Publication-level update*: this happens when the joined data source adds incrementally information to the record, such as Unpaywall, which patches the input DataFrame by adding an Unpaywall *instance* or a *date* to the DOI, and MAG, which adds an *abstract* or a *date* to the record.
- *Author-match-dependent update*: this happens when the information to be added by the data source is relative to the authors of a DOIBoost record (*author identifiers* and *author affiliations*); in this case the authors of the two records to be joined must be matched to find the correspondence and thus complete the information in the proper places; the match is string based and considered positive when the Levenshtein distance[13] between author names is above 0.8. Note that to avoid quadratic performance issues, author-to-author match is not performed for records whose number of authors is greater than 300 (around 12,000 records). In such cases the authors from MAG are simply used as the authoritative set.

In both cases, the information is added together with the appropriate provenance information. Finally, the last step of the workflow generates a DOIBoost dump in JSON format on the file system, to be openly shared and to be ingested into OpenAIRE. This step also marks the record with a quality report (*complete, incomplete, mock)*, specified by the property *record-quality-report*. Currently, the validation steps identify two cases of mock records:

- *Basic test records*: a record is considered as such if by normalizing the title (i.e. lower-case strings and removal of articles, special characters, etc.) and removing the word "test" the resulting string is empty;
- *Structured test records*: a record is considered as such if an occurrence of the word "test" appears both in the title and at least in the name of one author.

Table 2 reports on the execution time of the individual steps. Note that the final step *createDOIBoost.py*, performing a join between 105 million records in Crossref and 74 million from MAG, 11 million from ORCID, and 97 million from Unpaywall, runs in around 35 min. The records marked as *incomplete* or *mock* are around 25 million.

4 Evaluation

In Table 3 we report the measure of the "boost" that each data source gives to the original dataset as obtained via Crossref APIs. For each property involved in the aggregation, we report both the number of records with a Crossref DOI that was enriched with the property and the number of records that was effectively "boosted", i.e. records for which the property was missing.

[13] *Levenshtein Distance*, https://en.wikipedia.org/wiki/Levenshtein_distance.

Table 3. Input datasets and contributing properties.

Source	Properties	# of Crossref DOIs enriched by the source with a property	Boost: # of Crossref DOIs enriched by the source with a missing property
ORCID	Author IDs (ORCID)	11,345,996	9,666,098
MAG	DOIs	71,654,334	68,561,516
	Affiliation (GRID.ac)	45,670,806	45,670,806
	Affiliation (Microsoft)	51,630,810	47,528,221
	Abstract	45,407,968	43,857,752
	Author ID (Microsoft)	74,582,104	68,561,516
	Date	71,654,334	2,542,773
Unpaywall	Instances	97,751,914	22,328,223
Crossref	All fields	100,507,347	91,365,868

Table 4. Authorships enhancement in DOIBoost.

Indicator	Crossref	DOIBoost
# authorships assigned an identifier	3,060,804	212,291,232
# authorships assigned an affiliation	25,941,421	165,271,110

For the sake of example, in Table 4 we quantify the "boost" for authors in DOIBoost. To this end, we define *authorship* as the contribution a single author has in the context of a given paper. Hence, if a paper p has three authors $\{a1, a2, a3\}$, we count three authorship in total. This said, the entire Crossref corpus rounds up 263,869,225 authorships; of these, only the 1.15% has is equipped with an author identifier in Crossref, while in DOIBoost the percentage jumps to 80.45%, thanks to the joint integration effort of both MAG and ORCID. Similarly, only the 9.83% of authorships is assigned an affiliation in Crossref, while in DOIBoost we reach the 62.63%.

5 Conclusions

In this paper, we presented our reproducible data integration efforts in creating DOIBoost, an open dataset in support of research in the field of scholarly communication and scholarly knowledge mining. The contribution of this work is twofold: first, the dataset itself, together with the description of its value and its content, i.e. the data sources involved in the integration process; secondly, in order not to fall in the perpetration of the infamous "yet another resource" series, the description of the methodology to generate it, embodied in an open source software toolkit that can be used to recreate, extend and update the DOIBoost dataset.

Acknowledgements. This work could be delivered thanks to the Open Science policies enacted by Microsoft, Unpaywall, ORCID, and Crossref, which are allowing researchers to openly collect their metadata records for the purpose of research under CC-0 and CC-BY licenses. The MAG dataset is available with ODC-BY license thanks to the Azure4research sponsorship signed between Microsoft Research and KMi. This work was partially funded by the EU projects OpenAIRE2020 (H2020-EINFRA-2014-1, grant agreement: 643410) and OpenAIRE-Advance H2020 project (grant number: 777541; call: H2020-EINFRA-2017) [4].

References

1. Chawla, D.S.: Unpaywall finds free versions of paywalled papers. Nature News (2017)
2. Sinha, A., et al.: An overview of Microsoft Academic Service (MAS) and applications. In: Proceedings of the 24th International Conference on World Wide Web (WWW 2015 Companion), pp. 243–246. ACM, New York (2015)
3. Haak, L.L., Fenner, M., Paglione, L., Pentz, E., Ratner, H.: ORCID: a system to uniquely identify researchers. Learn. Publish. **25**, 259–264 (2012). https://doi.org/10.1087/20120404
4. Manghi, P., Bolikowski, L., Manold, N., Schirrwagen, J., Smith, T.: OpenAIREplus: the European scholarly communication data infrastructure. D-Lib Mag. **18**(9), 1 (2012)
5. Fortunato, S., et al.: Science of science. Science **359**(6379), eaao0185 (2018)
6. La Bruzzo, S., Manghi, P., Mannocci, A.: DOIBoost Dataset Dump (Version 1.0) [Data set]. Zenodo (2018). http://doi.org/10.5281/zenodo.1438356
7. La Bruzzo, S.: DOIBoost Software Toolkit (Version 1.0). Zenodo, 1 October 2018. http://doi.org/10.5281/zenodo.1441058

Enriching Digital Libraries with Crowdsensed Data
Twitter Monitor and the SoBigData Ecosystem

Stefano Cresci[1], Salvatore Minutoli[1], Leonardo Nizzoli[1,2], Serena Tardelli[1,2](✉), and Maurizio Tesconi[1]

[1] Institute of Informatics and Telematics, IIT-CNR, Pisa, Italy
{stefano.cresci,salvatore.minutoli,leonardo.nizzoli,serena.tardelli, maurizio.tesconi}@iit.cnr.it
[2] Department of Information Engineering, University of Pisa, Pisa, Italy

Abstract. SoBigData is a Research Infrastructure (RI) aiming to provide an integrated ecosystem for ethic-sensitive scientific discoveries and advanced applications of social data mining. A key milestone of the project focuses on data, methods and results sharing, in order to ensure the reproducibility, review and re-use of scientific works. For this reason, the Digital Library paradigm is implemented within the RI, providing users with virtual environments where datasets, methods and results can be collected, maintained, managed and preserved, granting full documentation, access and the possibility to re-use.

In this paper, we describe the results of our effort for integrating the Twitter Monitor, a tool for gathering messages from the Twitter Online Social Network, into the SoBigData RI. The Twitter Monitor provides a simple user interface, enabling researchers and stakeholders, without programming skills, to seamlessly (i) select relevant messages out of the huge Twitter stream by means of language, keyword, user tracking and geographical filters, (ii) store data on user personal Workspace, (iii) and publish them in the SoBigData Resource Catalogue, which implements all the aforementioned Digital Library features.

Thanks to the seamless integration in the SoBigData RI, the Twitter Monitor allows researchers and stakeholders, belonging to different areas and having different backgrounds, to exploit the crowdsensing paradigm for enriching the SoBigData Digital Library. In this way, crowdsensing acquires the key features of openness, accessibility, interoperability and interdisciplinarity that characterize the Digital Libraries framework.

Keywords: Digital libraries · Resource sharing · Online social networks · Crowdsensing

1 Introduction

In the last two decades, *eScience* designed a new research paradigm aiming to produce innovation in collaborative, computationally- or data-intensive research across all disciplines [13,17]. In this context, data sharing plays a key role: the

P. Manghi et al. (Eds.): IRCDL 2019, CCIS 988, pp. 144–158, 2019.
https://doi.org/10.1007/978-3-030-11226-4_12

availability of research datasets, published in open, accessible, fully documented online repositories, ensures the reproducibility of experiments, facilitates the review process and enables re-use for further research [7]. In this open and multi-disciplinary scenario, collaboration and sharing between different disciplines, institutions and scientists become vital.

The *eInfrastructure* paradigm emerged as the most promising approach for enabling those best practices [16]. It is defined as a framework enabling (i) secure, (ii) cost-effective and (iii) on-demand resource sharing across different organizations [8,14]. Within eInfrastructures, it is possible to provide scientists with *Virtual Research Environments* (VRE), defined as *"web-based, community-oriented, comprehensive, flexible, and secure working environments conceived to serve the needs of modern science"* [9]. eInfrastructures also enable the implementation of *Digital Libraries*, virtual environments where research datasets, methods and results can be collected, mantained, managed and preserved, granting full documentation, access and the possibility to perform further analysis [10].

SoBigData[1], a Research and Innovation Action funded by the European Commission under the Horizon 2020 program, creates such eScience ecosystem through the deployment of a Research Infrastructure (RI), which provides an integrated environment for ethic-sensitive scientific discoveries and advanced social data mining and big data applications [15]. As an open research infrastructure, SoBigData promotes repeatable and open science in multiple research fields, including mathematics, ICT, human, social and economic sciences. Interoperability by design enables easy comparison, re-use and integration of state-of-the-art big social data, methods, and services [18]. Hence, SoBigData implements the features of a Digital Library, including accessible and fully documented datasets, open source methods and services, which may impact industrial and other stakeholders (e.g. agencies, non-profit organisations, funders, policy makers).

The SoBigData eInfrastructure grants seamless access to tools, applications, datasets, services, algorithms, catalogues through VREs. The *Twitter Monitor* is a tool, included in the so-called SoBigDataLab VRE, that allows end-users and stakeholders to build, document and share new datasets. It collects data from Twitter in a focused way, by specifying gathering criteria to retrieve only relevant information. This tool is based on the disruptive crowdsensing paradigm, in which people publishing contents on social media platforms act as *social sensors* [2]. Such data can be leveraged to gather information on users activities, preferences, and tastes [1], and to extract public opinion about different topics concerning economy, politics, security, society, and finance [3–5,11,12]. Once retrieved, data can be enriched, documented and published in the SoBigData catalogue, which ensures all the features mentioned as best practices for a Digital Library framework.

Contribution. The contribution of this work is to present our experience in integrating the Twitter Monitor within the SoBigData RI. The purpose of the tool is to enrich and expand the volume and variety of Digital Libraries content, particularly with crowdsensed data. In detail, we provide an example of how a

[1] http://www.sobigdata.eu.

social scientist, laking programming skills, can use the tool to easily perform a data collection task. We then show how the customized datasets of Twitter data can be easily shared in the Digital Library framework implemented in the SoBigData RI. Moreover, We compare the workflow that would have been necessary without using the Twitter Monitor and the SoBigData RI, and we provide a cost-benefit analysis.

Roadmap. This paper is organized as follows: Sect. 2 describes in details the Twitter Monitor sensing tool and its integration in the SoBigData eInfrastructure. Section 3 describes a use-case workflow of an end-user leveraging the Twitter Monitor for a multidisciplinary project developed in his/her VRE. Section 4 focuses on how the Twitter Monitor may contribute in a Digital Library framework. Finally, Sect. 5 draws conclusions and highlights promising directions for future research and experimentation.

2 Twitter Monitor: Features and Integration in the SoBigData RI

Among the aims of SoBigData, there is the capability to provide a set of readily available datasets and methods to scientific communities. Typically, users of the SoBigData eInfrastructure can discover and leverage any of the datasets, released within the SoBigData RI itself, or upload, document and share their owns. The SoBigData RI takes care of hosting, maintaining and granting full, seamless and open access to all the included datasets and methods. In this way, distinguishing features of the eScience and Digital Libraries paradigms, such as collaboration, interdisciplinarity, resource sharing, interoperability, open and seamless access and cost-effectiveness are fulfilled. Recently, another alluring possibility emerged, where end-users and stakeholders are directly given the possibility to build and share new personalized datasets – all within the eInfrastructure – without the need for technical expertise. This novel solution greatly empowers scientists and end-users of the eInfrastructure, thus ultimately further contributing to collaboration, interdisciplinarity and resource sharing, that are fundamental points of the eScience and Digital Libraries paradigms.

The Twitter Monitor, integrated within the SoBigData eInfrastructure, – that we describe in this section – represents one of the first examples of this novel approach. It represents a new data-entry point to the whole eInfrastructure, thus acting as a catalyst for collaboration and sharing between platform users. Given the aims of the SoBigData project, the Twitter Monitor allows easy data collection from social media sources, and in particular, from Twitter[2]. Social media platforms are the most effective, sophisticated and powerful way to gather preferences, tastes, and activities of groups of users in the context of Web 2.0. In turn, this large amount of information may generate in-depth knowledge about topics of interest. As such, because of their massive number of users, their real-time features, and their ease-of-use, social media platforms, such as Twitter, have become a major source of information [1].

[2] https://twitter.com/.

2.1 Twitter Monitor and the Crowdsensing Landscape

In the paradigm of crowdsensing, the crowd of social network users becomes a distributed network of social sensors [1]. Specifically, depending on their awareness and their involvement in the system, users are confronted with either an opportunistic or a participatory sensing approach.

- Participatory crowdsensing: users willingly choose to give their contribution of sensory information to form a body of knowledge. They consciously opt to meet an application request, and they are aware of the sensing action (e.g. by photographing locations or discussing events or by intentionally sending such information to the sensing system). Systems exploiting participatory crowdsensing require intentional participation and must therefore provide incentives to the users to perform such actions.
- Opportunistic crowdsensing: users spontaneously collect and share data as they go for their daily life. In this scenario, relevant data is sensed, intercepted, and collected without user intervention and, in some cases, even without the users explicit knowledge. Opportunistic crowdsensing platforms do not require a specific user base, since they rely on already publicly-available data.

Social networking platforms, such as Twitter, are one of the main source of information for many crowdsensing systems. The Twitter Monitor tool gathers data from Twitter, leveraging the opportunistic crowdsensing approach.

2.2 Features and Usage of the Twitter Monitor

The Twitter Monitor is an interactive tool designed to access the Twitter stream by exploiting the public Twitter Streaming APIs[3], which opens a persistent connection with a stream of tweets. In this way, the tool collects new tweets containing the keywords, plus real-time replies and retweets, until the end of the connection. The tool is able to manage concurrent monitors: it is possible to launch parallel listening sessions (i.e., more than one Twitter crawler at a time) with personalized parameters to collect different sets of data. The Twitter Monitor also offers a set of functionalities, aimed to minimize the loss of data due to network or local machine problems. It is also capable of alerting, detecting and recovering from errors, such as streaming connection failures. In particular, it can automatically handle rate limits imposed by the Twitter APIs[4]. Specifically, the Twitter Monitor accepts three different types of searching parameters, thus allowing high flexibility to the end-users of the eInfrastructure:

- Keywords (so-called *Track* mode): collects tweets containing specific keywords. It is possible to specify simple words, hashtags, by adding the '#' character in front of the word, mentions, by adding the '@' character in front of the word, etc. It is also possible to retrieve data published during the previous week from the crawler start date, thanks to the implementation of the Twitter Search API in the tool. A maximum number of 400 keywords per crawler can be specified.

[3] https://developer.twitter.com/en/docs.html.
[4] https://developer.twitter.com/en/docs/basics/rate-limiting.html.

- Users (*Follow* mode): collects tweets published by or mentioning a specific set of Twitter users. This mode focuses on the users instead of the content of tweets. A maximum number of 5.000 users per crawler can be specified.
- Rectangles (*Location* mode): collects geolocated tweets published within a specific geographical area, defined by the lon/lat coordinates of the corners of a bounding box. The bounding box is represented as a geographical rectangle. A maximum number of 25 bounding boxes per crawler can be specified.

The main limitations of the Twitter Monitor are related to the APIs needed for data acquisition. The Streaming API opens a persistent connection to the real-time tweet stream, therefore tweets published before the opening of the connection cannot be retrieved. To overcome this restriction, we exploit the Search API, which returns the tweets produced no more than one week prior to the crawler start date, but it gives access only to a subset of all the tweets published on the platform. In addition, the search parameters have some limitations in flexibility and extensibility. For example, it's not possible to use regular expressions to retrieve tweets, to search for all inflections of a keyword.

2.3 Twitter Monitor Integration into the SoBigData eInfrastructure

The Twitter Monitor application has been seamlessly integrated in the SoBigData RI as a tool included in the `SoBigDataLab` VRE. It was implemented as a collection of modules. It leverages many functionalities[5] made available by the SoBigData RI, which is build on top of the D4Science eInfrastructure [8], supported by the gCube software system [18]. The key benefits, allowed by the presence of the Twitter Monitor within the SoBigData eInfrastructure, are achieved via a combination of functions of the Twitter Monitor itself, and by means of a tight integration with the functionalities offered by the eInfrastructure. The main functionalities of the SoBigData RI, used in this application, are (i) the management of user interaction, (ii) the management of a user Workspace, (iii) the management of processing modules hosted on a set of nodes, and (iv) the management of database systems. The Twitter Monitor application is composed of three main modules: `TwMonScheduler`, `TwMonCron` and `TwMonCrawler`. In particular, the `TwMonScheduler` is visible to the users in the list of available Algorithms in the SoBigData environment. The `TwMonCron` is launched periodically by the SoBigData RI, by means of appropriate configurations. The `TwMonScheduler` is launched, when needed, by the `TwMonCron` by means of SoBigData RI APIs. Figure 1 shows the structure of the application and the interaction of the modules with the SoBigData RI.

The `TwMonScheduler` is a Statistical Manager Algorithm, and it extends the `StandardLocalExternalAlgorithm` class by overriding methods that allows it to interact with the SoBigData RI. It displays a user interface for collecting the

[5] The documentation for all the platform libraries, functions and methods, mentioned in this subsection, can be found at https://gcube.wiki.gcube-system.org/gcube/GCube_Documentation.

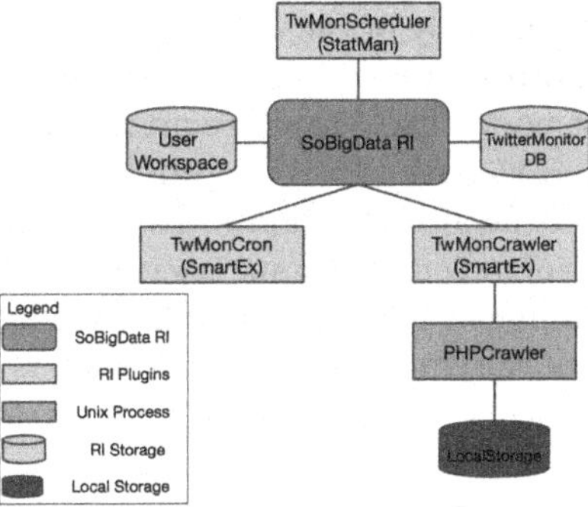

Fig. 1. Twitter Monitor integration in the SoBigData RI environment.

input parameters that will be used to filter the Twitter messages. The user interface is built by the SoBigData RI, based on settings specified by the module. In particular, the SoBigData RI calls a method `setInput`, that the module is required to implement. This method must define the list of needed parameters, along with each own type. Based on this list, the SoBigData RI displays, for each parameter, an appropriate widget to let the user enter the corresponding value. This module stores the parameters in a database called `TwitterMonitorDB`, managed by the SoBigData RI, containing a record for each crawler launched. The reference to this database is obtained by means of a service discover procedure: the `ICFactory` class is used to obtain a `ServiceEndpoint`, given the database identifier (in our case `TwitterMonitorDB`, unique among the SoBigData RI) and the needed credentials. The SoBigData RI finds the node on which the database is currently deployed, and it returns all the information that the `TwMonScheduler` actually needs to connect to the database. The database record also contains a unique identifier for the crawler, the state of the crawling process and a link to the final results. The `TwMonScheduler` periodically queries the database to check if the crawling process terminated, and, when the output result is available, it updates the user interface to notify the user with a message and with a link to download the output file. The output file is stored in the user Workspace available to each registered user so that they can also access it later. Since the processing time could be very long, depending on the period of time selected by the user, he/she is allowed to disconnect from the platform. The crawling process still continues to run until the specified end time.

The `TwMonCron` is a process (actually, a `SmartExecutor` plugin) started periodically by the SoBigData RI. Each time it is launched, it queries the TwitterMonitorDB database to check the state of the crawling processes (called `TwMonCrawler` and described later). It manages to stop each process that reached its end time, and to start the new crawlers inserted by `TwMonScheduler`. It can also detect if some process has terminated before its end time, possibly due to an error. In this case, it launches it again. In order to check, start and stop the `TwMonCrawler`, the `SmartExecutorProxy` API is used: this API allows to manage the state of plugins independently of the actual node on which they are running. More than one TwMonCrawler can run on the SoBigData RI, and each one generally runs in a different node. The SmartExecutor API manages to run a new TwMonCrawler on the most convenient node, and find a particular instance of TwMonCrawler, among all the available nodes, given its unique ID. In particular, its methods getStateEvolution and getPluginState return information on whether the plugin is running or not. The SmartExecutorProxy.launch method allows starting the TwMonCrawler, with given parameters. The SmartExecutorProxy.stop method is used to stop a TwMonCrawler, when the end time has been reached.

The TwMonCrawler, a SmartExecutor plugin, is the process that actually collects the information required by the user. It is launched by the SoBigData RI, on behalf of a TwMonCron request: it retrieves the crawling information from the TwitterMonitorDB database and runs a PHP script, as a separate process, providing it with all the needed parameters. The PHP process connects to the Twitter services to receive the selected messages, and it stores them in a local file. The TwMonCrawler continuously monitors this PHP process and, if it stops before the defined end time, it will promptly run it again. When the end time is reached, the TwMonCrawler copies the local output file into the user Workspace. This is done by using the HomeLibrary, that allows accessing the Workspace of the user who launched the crawling process. The JCRWorkspaceFolder API is then used to create folders (createFolder) and the WorkspaceUtil API is used to create files in the user Workspace (createExternalFile). The FolderItem.getPublicLink creates an HTTP link useful to quickly download the output file, without traversing the Workspace folders. It also creates a link (functionality provided by the SoBigData RI) to this output file, and stores it in the database. The crawling process is finally marked as finished in the database.

3 Twitter Monitor Use-Case in the SoBigData Research Infrastructure

In this section, we describe a simple use-case of the Twitter Monitor within the SoBigData RI. The purporse of this example is to show how the seamless integration of the Twitter Monitor into the SoBigData RI enables researchers, lacking programming skills, to benefit of the crowdsensing approach for gathering Online Social Media data, and to share them contributing to enrich a Digital Library.

We imagine a social scientist, with very basic Computer Science skills, trying to discover which are the most mentioned locations on Twitter related to the *World Tourism Day* (the 27th of September) trending topic. Firstly, we show a general layout of the SoBigData RI components involved in the process, namely the SoBigDataLab and the ResourceCatalogue VREs, summarizing the main available features. Secondly, we describe what the user should do to perform this task *without* the Twitter Monitor and SoBigData RI. Then, we highlight how our tool, interacting with the SoBigData RI, *greatly simplifies* the process. In both cases, we suppose that the user has already created a Twitter App and obtained the tokens necessary to access the Twitter APIs. Finally, we carry out an explicit cost-benefit analysis.

3.1 SoBigDataLab and ResourceCatalogue VREs Features and Usage

Figure 2 depicts a general layout of the features and interactions of two among the many VREs provided by the SoBigData RI, precisely those involved in our use-case example. The SoBigDataLab VRE provides users with a collection of methods and tools, included in the shared Method Engine library, and a personal Workspace, hosting his/her own datasets and results, and accessible only to him/her. Datasets and results can enter the Workspace by means of (i) an upload from the user filesystem, (ii) an import from the shared ResourceCatalogue Digital Library, (iii) an output from a method included in the Method Engine Library. The user can also send data, hosted in his/her Workspace, as an input to a method, and he/she can publish them, together with proper documentation, to the ResourceCatalogue Digital Library. All the aforementioned operations can be performed by means of a web-based, user-friendly interface, provided by the SoBigData RI.

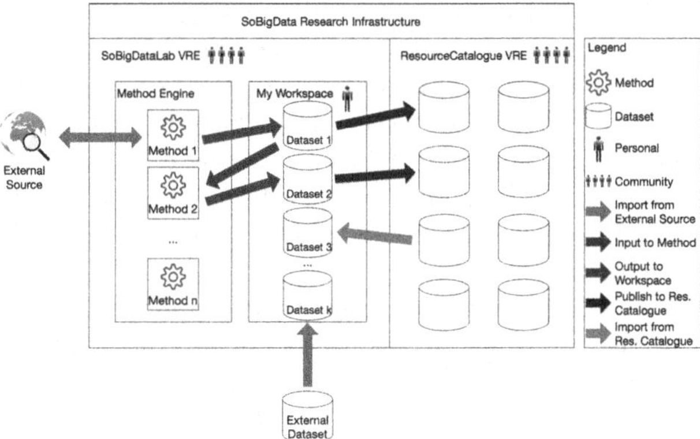

Fig. 2. Layout of the SoBigDataLab and ResourceCatalogue VREs. Each user can access open source methods in the SoBigDataLab VRE. Method engines take datasets as input and perform different tasks. They can acquire information from external sources. Outputs and results are saved into the user personal Workspace, where the user can also upload external datasets. Research data can be shared and published to the ResourceCatalogue VRE, directly from the Workspace.

3.2 Enriching a Digital Library with Crowdsensing Data Without the Twitter Monitor and the SoBigData RI

Twitter, as well as all other popular social media, provides companies, developers and users with programmatic access to its data through Twitter APIs. To use the APIs, collect and store large datasets, one must be familiar with pivotal technologies, such as basic programming languages, Web knowledge, REST and API concepts, JSON[6], user authentication standards such as OAuth[7], and database structures. In particular, the user must be able to (i) authenticate via the OAuth protocol, (ii) establish and maintain a connection to the streaming APIs, specifying the proper parameters to obtain the desired messages, (iii) handle various Twitter errors[8] related to rate limits, connection failures, etc., (iv) consume all messages as soon as they are provided by Twitter APIs, and (v) store the dataset in a proper repository. Therefore, users without proper programming skills are prevented to access this type of data. Moreover, the user should also be able to extract mentioned locations by applying Named-Entity Recognition (N.E.R.) techniques. Finally, the scientist must find a suitable platform for sharing data (e.g. Zenodo[9] or Figshare[10]) and results, in order to enable reproducibility, validation and re-use.

3.3 Enriching a Digital Library with Crowdsensing Data with the Twitter Monitor and the SoBigData RI

The SoBigData RI provides users with various VREs, giving access to many datasets, tools, methods and services. In this way, the task of the social scientist is greatly simplified. The key VREs for our use-case are the SoBigDataLab VRE and the ResourceCatalogue VRE (cfr. Subsect. 3.1). The SoBigDataLab VRE provides personal user Workspace and a set of tools, in this case the Twitter Monitor and the N.E.R. tools. The ResourceCatalogue VRE gives access to a rich set of datasets, and it enables the user to easily make his/her data and results available to the scientific community.

Figure 3 shows a schema of the workflow to accomplish the task in the SoBigData RI. Firstly, the user must access the SoBigDataLab VRE and choose the Twitter Monitor tool in the Method Engine panel[11]. Here, by means of a web-based, user-friendly interface (cfr. Fig. 4), the user can set general parameters of the crawler:

- the name of the crawler, to label and easily retrieve the collected dataset. In this case, the user names it "WTD_Crawler";
- the language of the tweets to be retrieved (optional). In this case, "en";

[6] http://www.json.org/.
[7] https://oauth.net/.
[8] https://developer.twitter.com/en/docs/basics/response-codes.html.
[9] https://zenodo.org/.
[10] https://figshare.com/.
[11] https://sobigdata.d4science.org/group/sobigdatalab/method-engine.

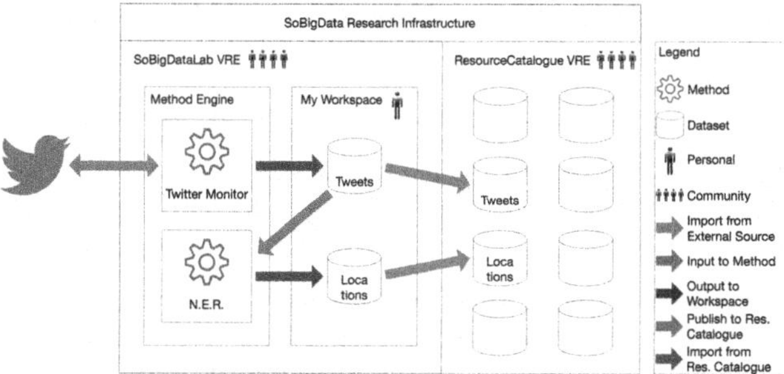

Fig. 3. Workflow of the use-case: the user accesses the SoBigDataLab VRE and launches a Twitter Monitor crawler. The data retrieved is saved into his/her personal Workspace and can be used to initialize a N.E.R. task to extract locations from tweets. The results are again saved into the Workspace. The user may want to publish data and results into the ResourceCatalogue VRE, to make it accessible to the community.

Fig. 4. The user must set general parameters to launch a Twitter Monitor crawler (e.g., tweet language and keywords).

- the type of searching parameters ("track", "follow" or "location" mode, cfr. Subsect. 2.2). In this case, the user uses the "track" mode;
- the list of parameters for filtering the messages that the user wants to collect. In this case, the user chooses the keyword "WorldTourismDay", which is the official hashtag of the event;
- the user tokens to authenticate via the Twitter OAuth protocol;
- the crawler end date and time.

At the end of the crawling process, the user has collected 1,000 English tweets containing the desired keyword.

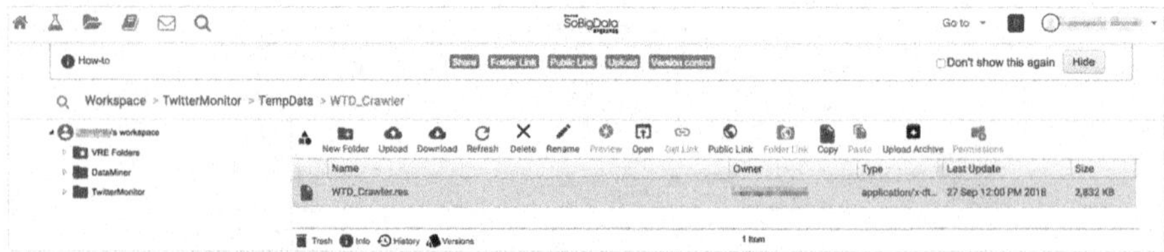

Fig. 5. In the Workspace, the user can find all his/her datasets and results, perform some basic actions (rename, delete, open, copy files, etc.), download files in local, publish his/her datasets and results into the ResourceCatalogue, and retrieve datasets to re-use from the SoBigData ResourceCatalogue or other external sources.

The dataset is automatically saved in the user personal Workspace[12], as shown in Fig. 5. The platform interface allows the user to download it, or to use it as an input for another method available in the VRE.

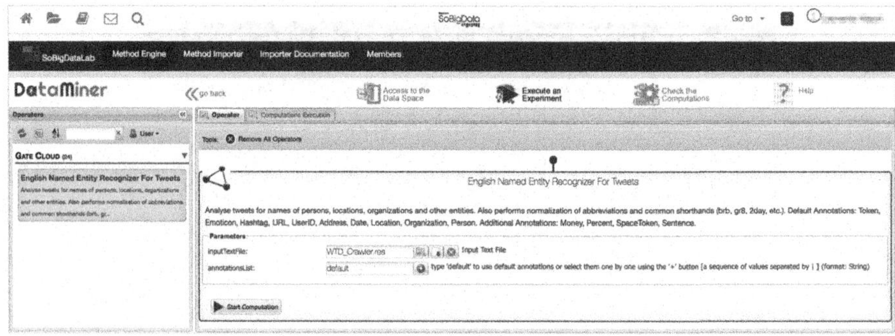

Fig. 6. Example of a dataset re-use for a Name Entity Recognition task.

In this case, the user wants to extract locations mentioned inside the text of collected tweets. To do so, he/she can leverage the N.E.R. Method Engine available in the VRE [19]. This tool allows the user to input data from his/her Workspace, in this case the dataset just created, and perform the task with a simple click of a button, as shown in Fig. 6. The results are again saved in the user Workspace. The user has therefore completed the task without the need of writing a single line of code and, most importantly, by investing only a small amount of work time.

Datasets and results can be used for further analysis, such a simple visualisation (Fig. 7), and they can be uploaded in the ResourceCatalogue VRE, where other scientists can use them to validate the work or to perform further research (Fig. 8).

[12] https://sobigdata.d4science.org/group/sobigdata-gateway/workspace.

Fig. 7. World Tourism Day locations wordcloud.

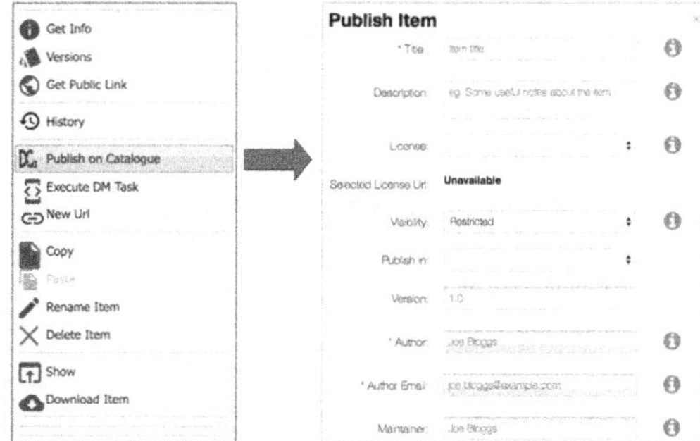

Fig. 8. The user can publish datasets and results into the catalogue directly from his/her Workspace.

3.4 Cost-Benefit Analysis of the Usage of the Twitter Monitor Tool Integrated in the SoBigData RI

Figure 9 shows a qualitative cost-benefit analysis of the usage of the Twitter Monitor tool for a user aiming to enrich the Digital Library with crowdsensing data.

The common starting point of the two approaches consists in creating a Twitter App and obtaining the tokens, necessary to access the Twitter APIs. This can be easily done leveraging an ad-hoc Web interface[13]; hence, it is not a difficult or time-consuming activity for a user with no technical expertise. Then, the user needs to set the parameters necessary to authenticate to the APIs and to filter the relevant messages. This task does not require much effort, nevertheless it can be a first obstacle for a user that is totally unaware of the basics of programming. As shown in Subsect. 3.3, Twitter Monitor provides a dedicated web-based, user-friendly interface to accomplish this task (cfr. Fig. 4). Much more effort is required for the authentication, via the OAuth protocol, and the connection to the Twitter Stream APIs, which implies to handle all the possible errors and to timely consume and store the retrieved data. Implementing this workflow is far beyond the possibilities of an unskilled user. Instead, all the above mentioned operations are automatically performed in the background by the Twitter Monitor, requiring no effort to the user.

Finally, it is possible to leverage the features provided by the SoBigData RI, in which the Twitter Monitor tool is integrated, to publish the obtained dataset to the SoBigData ResourceCatalogue, which implements all the aforementioned features of a Digital Library. Also in this case, this can be done by means of the platform interface. Otherwise, the user would have to upload data on an external service (e.g.: Zenodo), which can be a time consuming operation in case of large datasets.

[13] https://apps.twitter.com/.

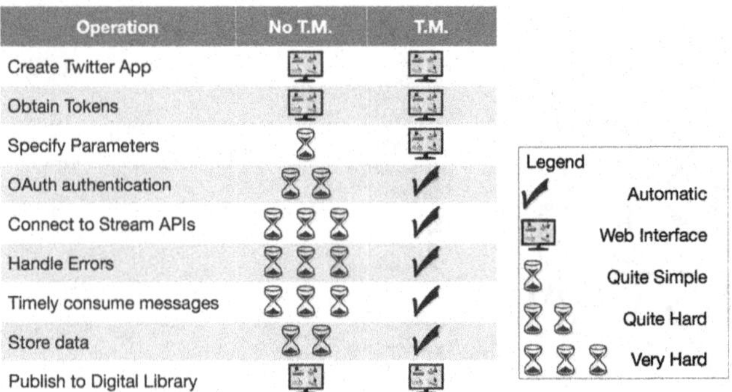

Fig. 9. Cost-benefit analysis of the usage of the Twitter Monitor tool for a user, lacking programming skills, aiming to enrich the Digital Library with crowdsensing data.

4 The Twitter Monitor as a Source for Digital Libraries

The release of research data to other potential users has been extensively discussed in literature [6, 7]. The complexity that arises in making research data available is mainly threefold:

1. the difficulty in getting people to collaborate and share data, due to their concerns about the potential misuse of their work, intellectual property rights and credit attribution [6]. Thanks to the SoBigData RI, people can specify the type of license for each resource that they publish in the catalogue (Fig. 8). Furthermore, research data remains within the SoBigData community, as people need to have an account to access openly available datasets;
2. the need of data owners to personally benefit from data sharing and to be incentived in terms of ease of sharing [7]. Data sharing is a way of increasing collaboration and citation rate. To encourage users to share, the SoBigData RI includes the ResourceCatalogue VRE, which act as a Digital Library and makes the publishing task very simple;
3. the uncertainty of how combined sets of data can operate together once shared [7]. The SoBigData RI provides open source methods and services, enabling easy comparison, re-use and integration of shared data into new research, which will, in turn, be shared. In this way, data owners can actually see the contribution of their work to other research.

Because of these reasons, SoBigData RI facilitates data sharing and integration in a variety of scenarios.

The dataset catalogue service, hosted by the ResourceCatalogue VRE in the SoBigData RI, enables users to discover, in a seamless way, information and metadata on the available datasets and datasets itself. The VRE is, to all effects, a Digital Library, in which datasets are accessible to other researchers or stakeholders. In this way, research publications, dataset descriptions and the actual datasets can be linked. This is important to validate the processes applied to data collection, treatment and analysis. Moreover, data and results can be reused, allowing new applications and further research.

The data collected with the Twitter Monitor can be published and made available to the community. This task can be performed in a very straightforward way, by means of the SoBigData RI. Datasets can be published together with proper documentation and metadata, and the infrastructure itself takes care of maintenance and accessibility. In this way, the Twitter Monitor contributes to enrich the SoBigData Digital Library with Twitter datasets, enabling users to apply the crowdsensing paradigm to their research activities.

In the era of big data as the new oil of the digital world, the tight integration of a data-acquisition tool – such as the Twitter Monitor – within an eInfrastructure, contributes to bridge the gap between data and non-technical research communities. In turn, this effort further strengthens the collaboration, sharing and interdisciplinarity within the flourishing eScience ecosystems.

5 Conclusions

In this paper, we described how the Twitter Monitor tool can enrich the Digital Library hosted in the SoBigData RI, with data collected from the Twitter Streaming APIs. We showed the features of the tool, and we described how we seamlessly integrated it within the SoBigData RI. By means of a simple use-case and a cost-benefit analysis, we provided a practical example of workflow, enabling a non-specialist user to retrieve social media content, store it in his Workspace, re-use it for further analysis and share data and results on the SoBigData Resource Catalogue, which implements the functionalities of a Digital Library. The Twitter Monitor contributes to the Digital Library framework by enabling research that exploits the crowdsensing paradigm.

Aknowledgements. This research is supported in part by the EU H2020 Program under the schemes `INFRAIA-1-2014-2015: Research Infrastructures` grant agreement #654024 *SoBigData: Social Mining & Big Data Ecosystem.*

References

1. Avvenuti, M., Bellomo, S., Cresci, S., La Polla, M.N., Tesconi, M.: Hybrid crowdsensing: a novel paradigm to combine the strengths of opportunistic and participatory crowdsensing. In: Proceedings of WWW 2017 Companion, pp. 1413–1421. ACM (2017)
2. Avvenuti, M., Cimino, M.G., Cresci, S., Marchetti, A., Tesconi, M.: A framework for detecting unfolding emergencies using humans as sensors. SpringerPlus **5**(1), 43 (2016)

3. Avvenuti, M., Cresci, S., Del Vigna, F., Fagni, T., Tesconi, M.: CrisMap: a big data crisis mapping system based on damage detection and geoparsing. Inf. Syst. Front. 1–19 (2018)
4. Avvenuti, M., Cresci, S., Marchetti, A., Meletti, C., Tesconi, M.: Predictability or early warning: using social media in modern emergency response. IEEE Internet Comput. **20**(6), 4–6 (2016)
5. Avvenuti, M., Cresci, S., Nizzoli, L., Tesconi, M.: GSP (Geo-Semantic-Parsing): geoparsing and geotagging with machine learning on top of linked data. In: Gangemi, A., et al. (eds.) ESWC 2018. LNCS, vol. 10843, pp. 17–32. Springer, Cham (2018). https://doi.org/10.1007/978-3-319-93417-4_2
6. Bezuidenhout, L., Chakauya, E.: Hidden concerns of sharing research data by low/middle-income country scientists. Glob. Bioeth. **29**(1), 39–54 (2018)
7. Borgman, C.L.: The conundrum of sharing research data. J. Am. Soc. Inf. Sci. Technol. **63**(6), 1059–1078 (2012)
8. Candela, L., Castelli, D., Pagano, P.: D4Science: an e-infrastructure for supporting virtual research environments. In: Proceedings of IRCDL 2009, pp. 166–169 (2009)
9. Candela, L., Castelli, D., Pagano, P.: Virtual research environments: an overview and a research agenda. Data Sci. J. **12**, GRDI75–GRDI81 (2013)
10. Candela, L., et al.: Setting the foundations of digital libraries. D-Lib Mag. **13**(3/4), 1082–9873 (2007)
11. Cresci, S., Di Pietro, R., Petrocchi, M., Spognardi, A., Tesconi, M.: Social fingerprinting: detection of spambot groups through DNA-inspired behavioral modeling. IEEE Trans. Dependable Secure Comput. **15**(4), 561–576 (2018)
12. Cresci, S., Lillo, F., Regoli, D., Tardelli, S., Tesconi, M.: $FAKE: evidence of spam and bot activity in stock microblogs on Twitter. In: Proceedings of ICWSM 2018, pp. 580–583. AAAI (2018)
13. Deelman, E., Gannon, D., Shields, M., Taylor, I.: Workflows and e-Science: an overview of workflow system features and capabilities. Future Gener. Comput. Syst. **25**(5), 528–540 (2009)
14. Foster, I., Kesselman, C., Tuecke, S.: The anatomy of the grid: enabling scalable virtual organizations. Int. J. High Perform. Comput. Appl. **15**(3), 200–222 (2001)
15. Giannotti, F., Trasarti, R., Bontcheva, K., Grossi, V.: SoBigData: social mining & big data ecosystem. In: Proceedings of WWW 2018 Companion, pp. 437–438. ACM (2018)
16. Hey, T., Trefethen, A.E.: Cyberinfrastructure for e-Science. Science **308**(5723), 817–821 (2005)
17. Newman, H.B., Ellisman, M.H., Orcutt, J.A.: Data-intensive e-science frontier research. Commun. ACM **46**(11), 68–77 (2003)
18. Simeoni, F., Candela, L., Lievens, D., Pagano, P., Simi, M.: Functional adaptivity for digital library services in e-infrastructures: the gCube approach. In: Agosti, M., Borbinha, J., Kapidakis, S., Papatheodorou, C., Tsakonas, G. (eds.) ECDL 2009. LNCS, vol. 5714, pp. 51–62. Springer, Heidelberg (2009). https://doi.org/10.1007/978-3-642-04346-8_7
19. Tablan, V., Roberts, I., Cunningham, H., Bontcheva, K.: GATECloud.net: a platform for large-scale, open-source text processing on the cloud. Phil. Trans. R. Soc. A **371**(1983), 20120071 (2013)

Populating Narratives Using Wikidata Events: An Initial Experiment

Daniele Metilli(✉), Valentina Bartalesi, Carlo Meghini, and Nicola Aloia

Istituto di Scienza e Tecnologie dell'Informazione "A. Faedo" – CNR, Pisa, Italy
{daniele.metilli,valentina.bartalesi,carlo.meghini,
nicola.aloia}@isti.cnr.it

Abstract. The study presented in this paper is part of our research aimed at improving the search functionalities of current Digital Libraries using formal narratives. Narratives are intended as sequences of events. We present the results of an initial experiment to detect and extract implicit events from the Wikidata knowledge base in order to construct a narrative in a semi-automatic way. Wikidata contains many historical entities, but comparably few events. The reason is that most events in Wikidata are represented in an implicit way, e.g. by listing a date of birth instead of having an event of type "birth". For this reason, we decided to generate what we call the Wikidata Event Graph (WEG), i.e. the graph of implicit events found in Wikidata. We performed an initial experiment taking as case study the narrative of the life of Italian poet Dante Alighieri. Only one event of the life of Dante is explicitly represented in Wikidata as instance of the class *Q1190554 Occurrence*. Using the WEG, we were able to automatically detect 31 more events of Dante's life that were present in Wikidata in an implicit way.

Keywords: Wikidata · Narratives · Semantic Web · Ontology · Digital Libraries

1 Introduction

Currently, Digital Libraries (DLs) offer search functionalities that respond to a user's web-like query with a list of digital objects based only on their metadata descriptors. We believe that DLs should be able to provide *narratives* to their users in addition to lists of objects. We intend narratives as sequences of events defined by a narrator, endowed with factual aspects (who, what, where, when) and semantic relations. Narratives would allow DLs to provide more sophisticated information services to their users, going beyond the current state.

In order to introduce narratives in DLs, we developed an ontology to formally represent narratives [2], based on the CIDOC CRM standard [4]. Subsequently, we built a semi-automated Narrative Building and Visualising Tool (NBVT)[1],

[1] https://dlnarratives.eu/tool.html.

P. Manghi et al. (Eds.): IRCDL 2019, CCIS 988, pp. 159–166, 2019.
https://doi.org/10.1007/978-3-030-11226-4_13

which allows the user to construct a narrative as a sequence of events. The tool has been used to construct four narratives[2] about different subjects: the life of Florentine poet Dante Alighieri, the life of Austrian painter Gustav Klimt, the history of the giant squid, and the history of climate change.

While building the narrative in NBVT, the user can add to each event some entities (e.g. people, places, objects) related to the subject of the narrative. These entities can be automatically imported from the Wikidata[3] knowledge base. Wikidata is a collaborative project hosted by the Wikimedia Foundation [10]. Containing more than 50 million entities, it is one of the largest general-purpose knowledge bases. In order to facilitate the user's work when building a narrative, we developed a mapping between our ontology and the Wikidata ontology which can be applied to import entities and events into our tool [1].

Unfortunately, the number of events (instances of the class *Q1190554 Occurrence*) contained in the knowledge base is relatively low, because Wikidata's ontology is not event-based. The knowledge about events is present in Wikidata, but it is generally represented in an implicit way. For instance, the birth of the Florentine poet Dante Alighieri is not represented as an event "Birth of Dante Alighieri", but instead the knowledge base contains a statement of the form "Dante Alighieri *place of birth* Florence" which directly links the poet to the city he was born in.

To solve this issue, we have decided to extract the events implicitly contained in the knowledge base, generating a graph that we call the Wikidata Event Graph (WEG). This graph can then be used to import events into NBVT in order to populate our ontology for narratives.

In the following, we present the generation of a subset of the WEG focused on events about people's lives, and an initial experiment to verify how much the events contained in it can improve the narrative building process. Section 2 describes our reasons for choosing Wikidata as reference knowledge base. Section 3 describes the extraction of the event graph from Wikidata. Section 4 describes the initial experiment about the narrative of Dante's life, and its results. Finally, Sect. 5 reports our conclusions and future works.

2 Wikidata as Reference Knowledge Base

In our formal representation, a narrative consists of three main elements: (i) *fabula*, i.e. the sequence of events in chronological order, (ii) *narration(s)*, i.e. one or more texts that express the narrative, and (iii) *reference function* that connects the narrations to the fabula, allowing the derivation of the *plot*. In the fabula, each event is endowed with entities such as people, places, and physical objects. When representing such events and entities through Semantic Web technologies, it is good practice to re-use IRIs (Internationalized Resource Identifiers) from existing knowledge bases, when possible [3].

[2] https://dlnarratives.eu/narratives.html.

[3] https://wikidata.org.

In order to import existing IRIs into our ontology and our tool, we investigated three of the most popular knowledge bases: Wikidata, DBpedia [7], and YAGO [9]. A recent study has compared the quality of these knowledge bases[4] according to various metrics [6]. The results of this study highlight that Wikidata is the top-rated knowledge base on the average of the considered metrics, with especially high scores on trustworthiness, consistency, timeliness, relevancy, and licensing. On the basis of these results and of an analysis we performed, we chose Wikidata as reference knowledge base, for the following reasons:

- it contains the largest number of entities (currently more than 50 million) when compared to the other knowledge bases;
- it is compatible with Semantic Web technologies such as RDF(S), OWL, and SPARQL [5];
- it is fully multilingual, with more than 39% of the entities having labels in multiple languages;
- it aims to collect not just statements about entities, but also the primary sources behind those statements (referenced statements are currently more than 75% of the total);
- it is fully integrated into Wikipedia and other Wikimedia projects, such as Wikimedia Commons, from which we can easily import non-structured data such as text and images;
- it adopts a Creative Commons Zero[5] license, equivalent to the public domain, making it easier to re-use the knowledge contained in it.

Notice that Wikidata also has a significant potential downside when compared to the other knowledge bases, i.e. its open and collaborative nature, similar to that of Wikipedia. The users of Wikidata can freely add and edit knowledge, including the class hierarchy, thus altering the ontology in unpredictable ways. However, both humans and bots frequently check the ontology for errors that can be due to users' mistakes or deliberate acts of "vandalism", and correct them.

3 The Wikidata Event Graph

Ideally, a suitable knowledge base for our purposes should contain: (i) historical entities such as people, places, and physical objects (ii) historical events connecting those entities. However, in most existing knowledge bases, including Wikidata, events are often represented in an implicit way. For instance, the knowledge base currently contains 4.52 million entities about people, but only 6,360 events of type "death", because most people's deaths are expressed implicitly through properties such as *P570 date of death*.

Many historical events, such as World War II, are represented explicitly in Wikidata, but they make up just 3% of the total number of entities. This is still

[4] We did not consider the other two knowledge bases analysed in the study (Freebase and OpenCyc), because they were both recently discontinued.

[5] https://creativecommons.org/publicdomain/zero/1.0/.

a significant number overall (1.92 million)[6], but it is not enough for our purposes because in our ontology *all* events are represented explicitly. Indeed, in the four narratives (see footnote 2) that were developed using our tool, the percentage of events that could be directly matched to Wikidata was less than 2%. This is significantly less than the percentage of related entities that could be found in Wikidata (69%).

In our view, the solution to this problem is the generation of what we call the Wikidata Event Graph (WEG), i.e. the Wikidata graph augmented with an explicit representation of all events implicitly expressed in it. Generating this graph would allow us to reference the events from our ontology and import them into our tool, offering the user a much more complete coverage of historical events.

In order to extract the WEG, we analysed all Wikidata properties[7] and compiled a list of the ones that, in our opinion, express implicit events. For instance, the property *P570 date of death* expresses an event of type "death".

We developed and implemented an algorithm that allows recognizing Wikidata properties that do not express events. From the current total of 5,234 properties, the algorithm removed several properties based on the following criteria:

1. the type of the property, i.e. meta-properties, properties that connect entities to other Wikimedia projects, obsoleted and deprecated properties, properties classified as "Wikidata property for an identifier", which simply link a Wikidata entity to an identifier in another knowledge base (for instance, the property *P214 VIAF ID* connecting an individual to its representation in the Virtual International Authority File[8]);
2. the datatype of the property's range literal, i.e. Web pages (datatype URL), numerical quantities (datatype Quantity), geographical features (datatypes GeoShape and GlobeCoordinate), media (datatype CommonsMedia), external IDs (datatype ExternalId), tabular data (datatype TabularData), and Wikidata properties (datatype WikibaseProperty).

At the end of this process, we obtained a list of about 1,000 candidate properties that could potentially express implicit events. Most of these (265) were applied to works, 158 were applied to people, 119 were applied to organisations, and the remaining ones were applied to other types of entities. In order to implement a case study, we decided to focus on the 158 properties about people. This would allow us to use as test case one of the narratives that had been previously constructed with our tool, i.e. the one about the life of Dante Alighieri[9].

---

[6] https://bit.do/ewP9w.

[7] The full list of properties is available at https://www.wikidata.org/wiki/Wikidata:List_of_properties. Another way to explore the properties is the Wikidata Property Explorer, available at https://tools.wmflabs.org/prop-explorer/.

[8] https://viaf.org.

[9] https://dlnarratives.eu/timeline/dante.html.

Table 1. Wikidata properties expressing implicit events about people's lives.

Event type	Property ID	Property name	Number of events
Baptism	P1290	godparent	1,840
	P1636	date of baptism	
Birth	P19	place of birth	4,519,957
	P22	father	
	P25	mother	
	P40	child	
	P569	date of birth	
Creation	P50	author	546,048
	P57	director	
	P58	screenwriter	
	P61	discoverer or inventor	
	P84	architect	
	P86	composer	
	P87	librettist	
	P110	illustrator	
	P161	cast member	
	P170	creator	
	P178	developer	
	P800	notable work	
Death	P20	place of death	1,651,865
	P157	killed by	
	P509	cause of death	
	P570	date of death	
	P1196	manner of death	
Education	P69	educated at	763,823
	P184	doctoral advisor	
	P185	doctoral student	
	P512	academic degree	
	P802	student	
	P812	academic major	
	P1066	student of	
Election	P726	candidate	25,775
	P991	successful candidate	
	P3602	candidacy in election	
Foundation	P112	founder	22,359
Marriage	P26	spouse	94,726
Membership	P54	member of sports team	712,299
	P102	member of political party	
	P463	member of	
Occupation	P6	head of government	3,310,621
	P35	head of state	
	P39	position held	
	P106	occupation	
	P108	employer	
	P210	party chief representative	
	P286	head coach	
	P803	professorship	
	P1075	rector	
Residence	P263	official residence	60,372
	P551	residence	

4 An Initial Experiment

To perform our initial experiment, we ordered the list of 158 Wikidata properties obtained in the previous step by usage in the knowledge base. Among the most used, we selected the first 50 that clearly expressed events about a person's life. The list of 50 properties we considered is reported in Table 1.

We developed a software that, through the Wikidata Query Service[10], automatically extracts all events that were expressed implicitly by the properties of Table 1 from the Wikidata graph. As expected, the number of birth events is the most numerous (4.52 million), since every person has a birth. The second most numerous type of event is occupation (3.31 million), followed by death (1.65 million). The total number of events contained in the subset of the WEG that we generated is 11.71 million, thereby increasing the number of Wikidata events that can be linked from our tool by more than 600%.

The software removes duplicate events, i.e. identical events that can be extracted more than once through multiple properties, by applying the following criteria implemented using rules:

1. if two entities are linked by a direct property and also by its inverse, e.g. the properties *P802 student* and *P1066 student of*, the two events extracted from the properties are merged;
2. if two entities are linked by a symmetric property, e.g. *P26 spouse*, in both directions, the two resulting events are merged;
3. when two properties express the same event, e.g. if the property *P569 date of birth* and the property *P19 place of birth* are applied to the same person, the two resulting events are merged.

In the first version (see footnote 10) of the narrative of the life of Dante Alighieri constructed using our tool, only one of 53 events (the Battle of Campaldino) was present in Wikidata as instance of the class *Q1190554 Occurrence*. After generating the WEG, we identified in it 31 more events that were present in the narrative. Therefore, the percentage of events in the narrative that could be automatically detected in Wikidata has increased from 1.9% (1 event) to 60.4% (32 events).

Major events such as the birth of Dante, the writing of the *Divine Comedy*, and the election of Pope Boniface VIII are all contained in the WEG, despite not being explicitly present in Wikidata as instances of the class *Q1190554 Occurrence*. Furthermore, the WEG contains 99 more events about Dante's life that are not present in the narrative built using our tool. Many of these are minor events, e.g. the writing of a sonnet, but it can still be useful to propose them to the user during the narrative building process.

We consider these results very promising, and anticipate that the coverage can be improved further by including more properties in our study. Furthermore, as more knowledge is added to Wikidata every day, the number of events in the WEG will increase.

[10] https://query.wikidata.org.

5 Conclusions and Future Works

In this paper we have presented an initial study on the population of formal narratives through the import of events from the Wikidata knowledge base. We have analysed all Wikidata properties and used a subset of them to generate the Wikidata Event Graph (WEG), i.e. the graph of events that are expressed in an implicit way in the knowledge base.

As case study, we have taken into account one of the narratives that were built using our Narrative Building and Visualising Tool (NBVT), i.e. the life of Florentine poet Dante Alighieri. For this reason, we have focused on the detection of events about people's lives from Wikidata. Furthermore, we have generated a subset of the WEG containing 11.71 million events related to people's lives, thereby increasing the number of Wikidata events that can be linked from our tool by more than 600%. From this subset of the WEG we have extracted a subgraph of events related to the life of Dante, allowing us to increase the number of events that could be automatically detected in Wikidata from 1.9% (1 event) to 60.4% (32 events).

As future work, we plan to take into account other Wikidata properties related not only to people's lives but also to other topics of narratives such as scientific experiments and historical events, and generate a larger subset of the WEG from these properties. In order to perform a preliminary evaluation of our approach, we are also working to automatically extract events from Wikidata related to the other narratives that have been constructed using our tool.

Another issue that we aim to study is how to automatically identify events related to the subject of the narrative and propose them to the users for import in their narratives. In addition, we are currently investigating automatic narrative extraction from text. We believe that the WEG will prove very useful in this context, in particular to increase the recall of entity linking algorithms [8] applied to narrative texts.

References

1. Bartalesi, V.: An ontology for narratives. Ph.D. thesis, University of Pisa (2017)
2. Bartalesi, V., Meghini, C., Metilli, D.: A conceptualisation of narratives and its expression in the CRM. Int. J. Metadata Semant. Ontol. **12**(1), 35–46 (2017)
3. Bizer, C., Heath, T., Berners-Lee, T.: Linked data: the story so far. In: Sheth, A. (ed.) Semantic Services, Interoperability and Web Applications: Emerging Concepts, pp. 205–227. IGI Global, Hershey (2011)
4. Doerr, M.: The CIDOC Conceptual Reference Module: an ontological approach to semantic interoperability of metadata. AI Mag. **24**(3), 75 (2003)
5. Erxleben, F., Günther, M., Krötzsch, M., Mendez, J., Vrandečić, D.: Introducing Wikidata to the linked data web. In: Mika, P., et al. (eds.) ISWC 2014. LNCS, vol. 8796, pp. 50–65. Springer, Cham (2014). https://doi.org/10.1007/978-3-319-11964-9_4
6. Färber, M., Bartscherer, F., Menne, C., Rettinger, A.: Linked data quality of DBpedia, Freebase, OpenCyc, Wikidata, and YAGO. Semant. Web **9**(1), 1–53 (2017)

7. Lehmann, J., et al.: DBpedia–a large-scale, multilingual knowledge base extracted from wikipedia. Semant. Web **6**(2), 167–195 (2015)
8. Shen, W., Wang, J., Han, J.: Entity linking with a knowledge base: issues, techniques, and solutions. IEEE Trans. Knowl. Data Eng. **27**(2), 443–460 (2015)
9. Suchanek, F.M., Kasneci, G., Weikum, G.: YAGO: a core of semantic knowledge. In: Proceedings of the 16th International Conference on World Wide Web, pp. 697–706. ACM (2007)
10. Vrandečić, D., Krötzsch, M.: Wikidata: a free collaborative knowledgebase. Commun. ACM **57**(10), 78–85 (2014)

Metadata as Semantic Palimpsests: The Case of PHAIDRA@unipd

Anna Bellotto and Cristiana Bettella(✉)

The University Library Centre "ULC", University of Padova, Via Anghinoni, 3, 35121 Padua, PD, Italy
{anna.bellotto, cristiana.bettella}@unipd.it

Abstract. This paper illustrates the experience of the Library System of the University of Padova in reviewing the data model of Phaidra (Permanent Hosting, Archiving and Indexing of Digital Resources and Assets), the digital repository for the long-term management and preservation of digital objects in place since 2010, whose system was created and developed by the University of Vienna. In order to provide better informational representation and visualisation of data, both in terms of metadata quality and display, this re-examination consisted in a critical analysis of the foundational metadata profile of Phaidra, its mapping and conversion into the Dublin Core metadata schema (Dublin Core Metadata Element Set 1.1) and, at prototype level, into the Metadata Object Description Schema (MODS). This paper discusses the evidence of the identified solutions being guided by two core principles: on the one hand, the distinctive valorisation of the dual analogue-digital nature of the Phaidra cultural heritage object, on the other, the metadata reuse in the visual function for the graphic updating of the new web interface, which is being done in order to encourage the discovery, even serendipitously, of its content by the digital researcher. Finally, the presentation considers the development activities being carried out by the Phaidra working groups of the Universities of Padova and Vienna, focused on the semantic evolution of the concept of metadata to open data, by presenting here an unpublished example of the Simple Knowledge Organization System (SKOS) prototype and last, but not least, suggesting the definition of a new Phaidra data model.

Keywords: Cultural heritage object metadata · Crosswalk · Data model · Web of data

1 Introduction

Phaidra (Permanent Hosting, Archiving and Indexing of Digital Resources and Assets) is the platform of the University Library System of the University of Padova for the long-term archiving of digital objects and collections, currently hosting a vast range of 390,000 digital objects including antiquarian books, manuscripts, photographs, wall charts, maps, learning objects, films, archival material and museum objects [1].

Designed and developed by the University of Vienna[1] [2] beginning in 2008 based on the digital architecture of the Fedora open source system, Phaidra was adopted by the

[1] Phaidra has arisen from the cooperation between the Computer Centre of the University of Vienna, the University Library of Vienna and the Centre for Teaching and Learning. Project management is located at the University Library.

P. Manghi et al. (Eds.): IRCDL 2019, CCIS 988, pp. 167–184, 2019.
https://doi.org/10.1007/978-3-030-11226-4_14

University of Padova in 2010, when the two institutions signed a bilateral collaboration agreement which led to the creation of the organisational structure and the formation of the Phaidra.org network infrastructure [3], which gradually continued to grow, both locally and internationally, by hosting cultural institutions such as Galleries, Libraries, Archives, and Museums, also known by the acronym GLAM [4, 5] (See Fig. 1).

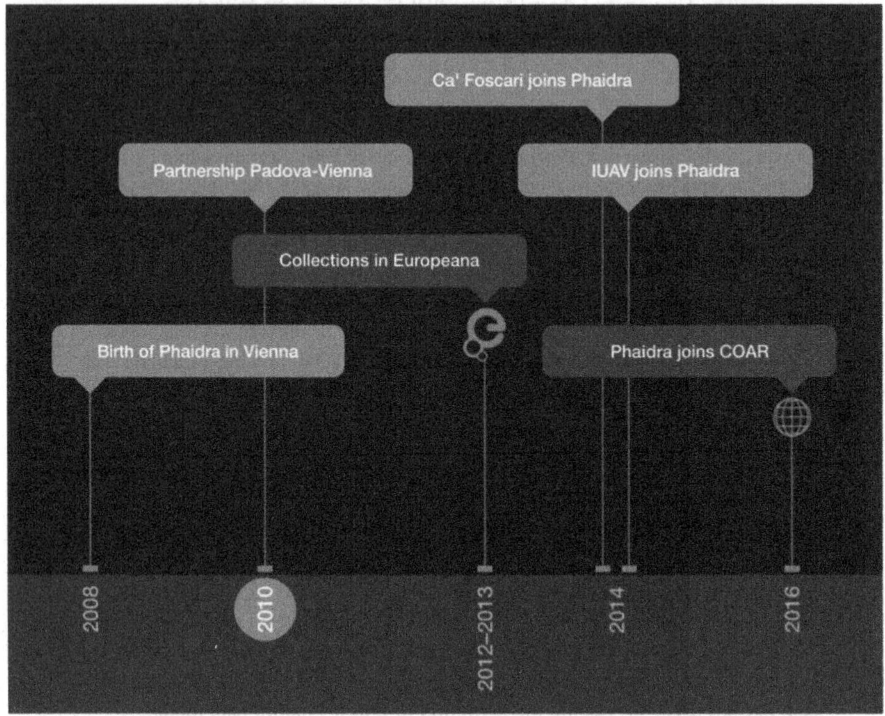

Fig. 1. Phaidra@unipd.it timeline.

The distinctive characterisation of the Paduan instance of Phaidra since its inception has on the one hand been the illustrative and heterotopic[2] valorisation of the heterogeneous richness of the University's digital collections of cultural heritage, such as

[2] Heterotopic, from heterotopia, a placeless place that refers to all other spaces, to every conceivable space, according to the meaning that the philosopher Michel Foucault gave to the medical term in a conference held in March 1967 and published later under the title "Des espaces autres" in the magazine Architecture-Mouvement-Continuité, n. 5, October 1984 (translated as: "Of other spaces" in Diacritics, Vol. XVI, n. 1, 1986, available online at https://foucault.info/documents/heterotopia/foucault.heteroTopia.en/). The extension of the spatial concept of heterotopia to libraries and digital collections – the library is among the Foucauldian examples of heterotopia – would deserve a reflection of its own with respect to the objective that we propose in this paper. See: Bruno, G. Atlas of Emotions. Journeys in Art, Architecture, and Film, Verso (2002) and Wikipedia entry https://en.wikipedia.org/wiki/Heterotopia_(space).

those from departments and research centres, archives and museums, as well as from libraries' digitisation projects [6]. On the other hand, it acts as an attraction for other academic institutions in the region[3], triggering a virtuous cycle of cultural and technological infrastructural osmosis which has conferred upon Phaidra, in addition to its primary function as a Digital Asset Management system, as well as the inter-institutional aggregator, an organisation that collects and aggregates, creates and administers metadata from multiple content providers.

Given the definition of aggregator, Phaidra serves at the same time as a service provider, through its portal and Web API [4, 7][4], and as a data provider to external service providers, exposing its metadata through the OAI-PMH protocol [8, 9]. The expansion of this aggregative and meta-aggregative function of heterogeneous metadata from similarly heterogeneous origins has raised the urgent need for a critical analysis of the foundational data model of Phaidra Universität Wien metadata (hereinafter UWmetadata), both from the point of view of its mapping and conversion into the Dublin Core metadata scheme aimed at its publication in the OAI-PMH Phaidra data provider, as well as the visualisation and presentation of data in the Phaidra web interface [10].

This presentation provides evidence of the solutions which were identified and their outcomes, aimed on the one hand at the distinctive valorisation of the dual analogue-digital identity of the Phaidra cultural heritage object, highlighting its profile from the authorial point of view (people → Who), from the physical-digital materiality of the work being described (works → What), from the space-time dimension (Where and When) and from the traceability of the provenance; and, on the other hand, it is aimed at metadata reuse as a visual function and for accessibility to content, used in the conception of the new graphic design of the web interface, which is being done in order to encourage discovery, even serendipitously, of the content found in Phaidra by digital researchers and browsers.

Coherent to a process intended to be evolutionary and seamless, the implementation project of the Metadata Object Description Schema (MODS) standard in Phaidra will also be illustrated. Through the prototype processing of mapping from UWmetadata, this has allowed for a retrospective and recursive review of some coding choices previously defined in the mapping between the UWmetadata schema and the Dublin Core elements set, resulting in the updating to a new version of the profile and regeneration of Dublin Core metadata in the Phaidra web interface [11].

Finally, we intend to highlight how the MODS implementation is also functional in the prospects of ongoing and future development of the Phaidra platform, focused on Resource Description Framework (RDF) migration and adoption of standards and their technologies of the Semantic Web, in line with the semantic evolution of the concept of metadata to linked open data, meant as a new informational entity which necessarily

[3] The Universities of Ca' Foscari and IUAV of Venice are a part of Phaidra since 2014.

[4] "A set of public APIs, REST-compliant, used to provide search services, content management of digital objects and sampling and handling of metadata, is also available on Phaidra. Anyone who wants to develop an application that presents digital objects in a customised way, can freely use these APIs. An example of such an application is the Collection Viewer, developed for sharing and browsing in digital collections on Phaidra in an external site through embedding" [4] (See: http://bibliotecavallisneri.cab.unipd.it/collezioni-digitali/zoologische-wandtafeln-von-prof-dr-paul-pfurtscheller).

eludes the identity and exclusiveness of a single catalogue, a single digital repository, or a single digital library system, by presenting here an unpublished example of the Simple Knowledge Organization System (SKOS) prototype and last, but not least, suggesting the definition of a new Phaidra data model.

2 The PHAIDRA_DC Profile (and PHAIDRA_MODS Profile)

The foundational data model of Phaidra, called Universität Wien metadata and abridged as UWmetadata, informs the design of Phaidra metadata, both in terms of representation of the values as well as the description of the contents [12]. It is the result of the expansion of the IEEE Learning Object Metadata (LOM) standard (IEEE 1484.12.1 – 2002), and the combination of elements of different metadata namespaces. This places UWmetadata among the examples of application profile (AP), which for example include the data profile of the portal for CulturaItalia PICO, the data profile of the portal for Europeana E(uropeana)D(ata)M(odel) and the former E(uropeana)S(emantics)E(lements) as well as the application of EDM in the context of the Digital Public Library of America and the German Digital Library.

In general, the LOM schema is a data model, usually encoded in XML, used to describe learning objects or digital resources for educational purposes such as learning supports. LOM, as its UWmetadata application profile, structures the metadata in accordance with a hierarchy of elements defined in nine top-level categories, and containing groups of attributes in a tree structure. In the following images (Figs. 2, 3 and 4), see respectively the LOM conceptual map [13], the explanation of its top-level categories and an XML snippet of UWmetadata schema:

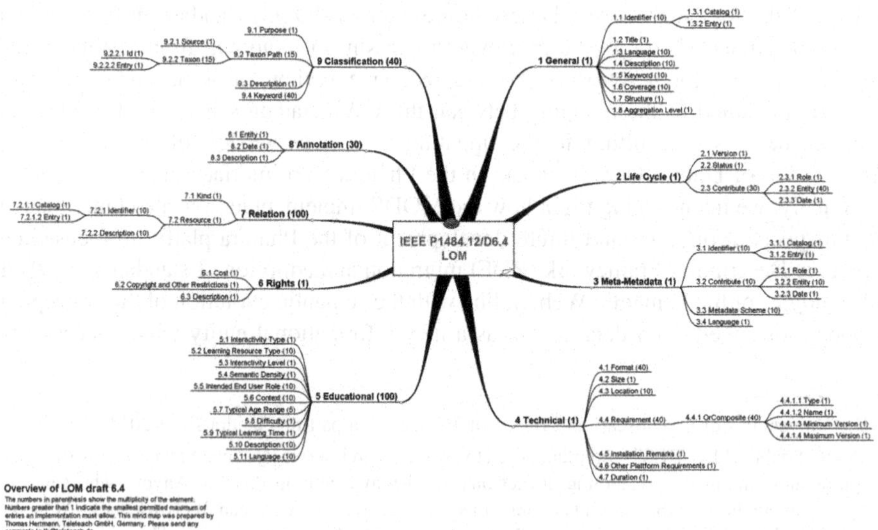

Fig. 2. Overview of LOM. Mind map prepared by Thomas Herrmann (Source: [13])

LOM top level category	Explanation
General	This category groups the general information that describes the learning object as a whole.
Lifecycle	This category describes the history and current state of the learning object and those entities that have affected the learning object during its evolution.
Meta-metadata	This category describes how the metadata instance can be identified; who created this metadata instance; and how, when, and with what references.
Technical	This category describes the technical requirements and characteristics of the learning object.
Educational	This category describes the key educational or pedagogic characteristics of the learning object.
Rights	This category describes the intellectual property rights and conditions of use for the learning object.
Relation	This category defines the relationship between a learning object and other learning objects, if any.
Annotation	This category provides comments on the educational use of the learning object, and information on when and by whom the comments were created.
Classification	This category describes where the learning object falls within a particular classification system. To define multiple classifications there may be multiple instances of this category.

UWmetadata extends the LOM schema with further additional categories aiming to represent primary data stored in Phaidra (Contextual allegation and Provenience respectively)[5], digital books (Digital book)[6], and electronic theses (eThesis)[7]:

[5] The Institute History of Arts at the University of Vienna asked for these new sections [12].

[6] Connected to The Vienna University Library eBook on demand (EOD) service: https://bibliothek.univie.ac.at/en/eod.html. Moreover, the Digitalbook sub-elements, if completed, have a bearing on the way the book information frame appears in the Book Viewer, for instance: Place of publication, Publisher, Date of publication, Catalogue URL, Number of pages, or volume no. By way of example, see: https://fc.cab.unipd.it/fedora/objects/o:387557/methods/bdef:Book/view?language=en#page/1/mode/2up.

[7] The eThesis category has not been implemented at Phaidra@unipd since theses are currently hosted at the EPrints repositories Padua@thesis (http://tesi.cab.unipd.it/) and Padua@research (http://paduaresearch.cab.unipd.it/), the latter specifically devoted to doctoral dissertations.

UWmetadata	Explanation
Contextual allegation	This category defines the physical description of primary data
Provenience	This category defines the provenance of primary data
Digital Book	This category describes the bibliographic information of digital books

Fig. 3. LOM (Source: [14]) and UWmetadata top-level categories.


```
-<ns0:uwmetadata>
  -<ns1:general>
     <ns1:identifier>o:358241</ns1:identifier>
     <ns1:title language="it">Rilevamento geologico di Pieve di Cadore</ns1:title>
     <ns1:language>it</ns1:language>
   -<ns1:description language="it">
      Rilevamento disegnato sulla base di: Pieve di Cadore - Foglio 12 della Carta d'Italia, II. N.E., scala 1:25.000 (S.l.: IGM, 1888 - ediz. riservata fuori
      commercio). Firma di Antonio De Toni sul lato destro della carta
     </ns1:description>
   -<ns1:description language="en">
      Survey drawn on the basis of: Pieve di Cadore - Foglio 12 della Carta d'Italia, II. N.E., scala 1:25.000 (S.l.: IGM, 1888 - ediz. riservata fuori commercio).
      Antonio De Toni's signature on the right side of the map
     </ns1:description>
     <ns1:keyword language="it">Antonio De Toni</ns1:keyword>
     <ns1:coverage language="it">1914?</ns1:coverage>
   -<ns2:identifiers>
      <ns2:resource>1552151</ns2:resource>
      <ns2:identifier>003051864</ns2:identifier>
     </ns2:identifiers>
   -<ns2:identifiers>
      <ns2:resource>1552151</ns2:resource>
      <ns2:identifier>PUV1493414</ns2:identifier>
     </ns2:identifiers>
  </ns1:general>
```


Fig. 4. UWmetadata_XML: General.

The analysis of mapping between the UWmetadata schema source and the Dublin Core target schema has established, as each of metadata crosswalk activities, the mapping of the correspondences of elements, the syntax and semantics of the two schemas involved, adopting a relative translation mode, namely trying to map each source element into at least one of the target elements, in order to avoid as much as possible any loss of information recorded in the source schema.

Each correspondence has also determined, depending on the encoding purposes, an inter-schema relationship such as one-to-one, one-to-many, many-to-one, and many-to-many, *a fortiori* if one considers the conversion of a descriptive schema organised in blocks, or nuclei, semantic and nested like UWmetadata in a flat schema such as the Dublin Core metadata schema.[8]

---

[8] There is not a full overlapping among the two metadata schemas. For instance, the unrefined element `<dc:relation>` encoded the system of relationships currently handled in Phaidra, which are not represented in UWmetadata (See: https://github.com/phaidra/phaidra-api/wiki/Relations).

By way of example, the authorial entity has been defined both from the point of view of the intellectual level of contribution in the creation of the described resource (Creator, Contributor) and from that of the mode and form established for the value recorded in the source elements[9]:

UWmetadata_ Source	**1. Lifecycle** **Creator, Contributor_Person**

```
<ns1:lifecycle>
      <ns1:contribute seq="">
            <ns1:role>PHAIDRA role code
          for Creator, Contributor, per-
          son</ns1:role>
            <ns1:entity seq="">
                  <ns3:firstname>First-
                name</ns3:firstname>
                  <ns3:lastname>Last-
                name</ns3:lastname>
                  <ns3:type>per-
                son</ns3:type>
            </ns1:entity>
            <ns1:date>Date expressed as
          YYYY</ns1:date>
      </ns1:contribute>
</ns1:lifecycle>
```

Creator, Contributor_Institution

```
<ns1:lifecycle>
      <ns1:contribute seq="">
            <ns1:role>PHAIDRA role code
          for Creator, Contributor, in-
          stitution</ns1:role>
            <ns1:entity seq="">
                  <ns3:institution>In-
                stitution</ns3:institu-
                tion>
                  <ns3:type>institu-
                tion</ns3:type>
            </ns1:entity>
            <ns1:date>Date expressed as
          YYYY</ns1:date>
      </ns1:contribute>
</ns1:lifecycle>
```

[9] The value encoded in <ns1:role> is taken from Phaidra Roles Vocabulary, which relates to the role of the entities contributing to the creation of the (analogue or digital) resource (See further: Towards a semantic data modelling).

DC_Target	<dc:creator>ns3:lastname, ns3:firstname (ns1:role eng)</dc:creator> <dc:contributor>ns11:lastname, ns11:firstname (ns10:role eng)</dc:contributor>
	<dc:creator>ns3:institution (ns1:role eng)</dc:creator> <dc:contributor>ns11:institution (ns11:role eng)</dc:contributor>

Example	<dc:creator>Pellegrini, Giovan Battista</dc:creator> <dc:creator>Germania : Wehrmacht : Propaganda Staffel</dc:creator> <dc:contributor>Mari, Mario (Illustrator)</dc:contributor> <dc:contributor>Università di Padova - Centro di Ateneo per le Biblioteche (Digitiser)</dc:contributor> <dc:contributor>Facoltà di Scienze matematiche, fisiche e naturali (Curator)</dc:contributor> <dc:contributor>Bodrero, Emilio (Former owner)</dc:contributor> People Pellegrini, Giovan Battista (Author) Germania : Wehrmacht : Propaganda Staffel (Author) Mari, Mario (Illustrator) Università di Padova - Centro di Ateneo per le Biblioteche (Digitiser) Facoltà di Scienze matematiche, fisiche e naturali (Curator) Bodrero, Emilio (Former owner)

Each inter-schema encoding relationship has been described and reviewed following a system of standard analytical matrix accompanied by the following informational units: standard textual descriptions and definitions of the elements adapted to the Phaidra informational context; their unique identification (Uniform Resource Identifier, URI) and possible classification into the corresponding elements refined by DCMI Metadata Terms; the compulsoriness and replicability of conversion encoding; the version of the mapping, namely replacement of an earlier version; notes where the reasons for the encoding choices adopted are critically discussed, also in terms of historical stratification of the mapping, together with the formalisation of any logical conditions to be complied with for a correct writing of the conversion code; the exemplary extrapolation of XML snippets from source and target elements; the label adopted in the display element and its real representation from the point of view of the form prescribed for the value of the reference being converted [10]:

- Name
- Label (ita)
- Label (eng)
- Defined by
- Term_URI
- Definition (ita)
- Definition (eng)
- Refined by
- Obligation & Occurence
- Mapping version
- Replaces
- Comment (ita)
- UWmetadata_Source
- DC_Target
- Visualizzato come (ita)
- Visualised as (eng)
- Esempio
- Example.

As a reflection of the inter-schema complexity of mapping of the two schemas involved, we can use the example of encoding the Dublin Core Date element compared to its specular version in the temporal elements of the MODS standard, from which, however, the Dublin Core mapping has recursively derived benefits both in terms of information quality of the metadata and in their presentation.

2.1 Date

In the context of PHAIDRA_DC profile, the Date element `<dc:date>` translates a temporal event related to the lifecycle of the resource, certain or inferred, in terms of the date of publication (dateIssued) or creation (Created), which can be expressed either in exact form or as a time interval, open or closed, according to the formats that conform to the ISO 8601 Date and time format standard.

UWmetadata sources for coding the Date element are:

1. sub-element `<ns1:date>` of Contribute `<ns1:contribute>` in Lifecycle `<ns1:lifecycle>`
2. sub-elements `<ns10: date_from><ns10:date_to>` of Contribute `<ns10:contribute>` in Provenience `<ns10:provenience>`
3. the element `<ns12:releaseyear>` in Digitalbook `<ns12:digitalbook>`.

The conversion to `<dc:date>` of sub-elements `<ns10:date_from>` `<ns10:date_to>` from Contribute `<ns10:contribute>` in Provenience `<ns10: provenience>` was introduced in version 1.1 2018, on the basis of the encoding example of MODS temporal sub-elements, in order to permit the allocation of uncertain or inferred dating to the described resource.

In fact, MODS provides granular and distinctive representation about the temporalisation of the resource by hosting in the upper element `<originInfo>` the sub-elements specific to each type of dating: `<dateIssued>`, `<dateCreated>`, `<dateValid>`, `<dateModified>`, `<copyrightDate>`, `<dateOther>`, partially also represented by qualified terms of the Dublin Core vocabulary.

By contrast, encoding of the Date `<dc:date>` element not only translates the values of heterogeneous source elements, but also if, and only if, there are the pre-determined conditions, which are in order:

1. `<ns12:releaseyear>` of `<ns12:digitalbook>`. If `<ns12:releaseyear>` is not filled, then:
2. `<ns1:date>` of `<ns1:contribute>` in `<ns1:lifecycle>` with `<ns1:role>` code 47 equal to Publisher type institution (`<ns3:type>institution</ ns3:type>`) OR with `<ns1:role>` code 1557141 of Printer type person or institution. If these elements are not populated, then:
3. the first occurrence `<ns1:date>` of `<ns1:contribute>` in `<ns1:lifecycle>` with `<ns1:role>` code 1552095 same as Author, whether the entity is a person or an institution. If these elements are not populated, then:
4. the first occurrence of `<ns1:date>` of `<ns1:contribute>` of `<ns1:lifecycle>` if the value of `<ns1:role>` has different code than 47 Publisher institution type, and from 1557141 Printer to code 1552154 Author of the digitisation, whether the entity is a person or an institution.

If the conditions described in paragraphs 1–4 are not met, then they take the values of the sub-elements Date from `<ns10:date_from>`; Date to, Date up to `<ns10:date_to>` of Contribute `<ns10:contribute>` in Provenience, which can represent an uncertain or inferred date of the resource, according to the following modes and forms:

5(a) `<ns10: date_from>` and `<ns10: date_to>` in `<ns10:provenience>`, where the two dates are equivalent if precise dates are being attributed (eg.: 1950)

5(b) `<ns10: date_from>` and `<ns10: date_to>` in `<ns10:provenience>`, where the two dates differ if it intends to assign a set interval of dates (eg.: 1950–1960)

5(c) `<ns10: date_from>` in `<ns10:provenience>` if an open date interval (eg.: 1950-) are being attributed.

If the conditions set out in paragraphs 1–5 are not met, the `<dc:date>` is omitted, and the date of publication of the digital object in PHAIDRA recorded in `<ns1:upload_date>` of `<ns1:lifecycle>` is not published.

See the example of display of the target elements, which significantly highlights the translational operation described, in particular by observing the outcome displayed:

DC_Target	<dc:date>ns12:releaseyear</dc:date> If not then: <dc:date>ns1:date</dc:date> → *as expressed by conditions 2) and 3)* If not then: <dc:date>ns10:date_from=ns10:date_to</dc:date> → *as expressed by conditions 5a)* If not then: <dc:date>ns10:date_from-ns10:date_to</dc:date> → *as expressed by conditions 5b)* If not then: <dc:date>ns10:date_from-</dc:date> → *as expressed by conditions 5c)*

Example	Date 1822 1820-1830 1822-

2.2 Some Remarks in the Margin

The mapping and conversion of UWmetadata to Dublin Core is *de facto* a chance conversion, sometimes acrobatic, aimed at informing a qualified and comprehensive informative aggregate in the conceptual simplification of the Dublin Core element, which has made it possible at once to identify the functional requirements needed to accommodate schemas of refined metadata, such as for example the MODS standard, whose prototype mapping analysis has made further refinement possible in the Dublin Core encoding choices.

Additionally, it has enhanced precision in the representation of data and information content of Phaidra by disclosing its data profile and conceptualising the source model of data by qualifying and formalising its core elements. It also encouraged reflection in evolutionary terms of its ontological structure, outlining where possible the classes of Persons, Works, Space, and Time.

It has clarified and characterised the different levels and the interdependence of the dimensional combination of physicality and digitality of the information content (and knowledge) conveyed by the Phaidra cultural heritage object.

It has, in particular, made it possible to experience and evaluate the vital importance of standards, the adoption of which creates interoperability, leading to the decontextualisation of data from the scope of their original creation, accelerating their exposure and potential for reuse in different contexts and by different services, with the valorisation and development of the informative and cognitive value of which they are a memorial device.

It has helped to strengthen the methodological attitude for a correct reading of the data, or of reading of the data as "semantic palimpsests" given the stratified and permanent coexistence of heterogeneous data models, and their evolutionary and generative function in terms of schema, structure, profile, model, in aggregate form and as *corpora* of data, stressing the knowledge that each mapping activity is an inter-data conceptual negotiation which implies, more than anything else, a mutual understanding and compromise (See Fig. 5).

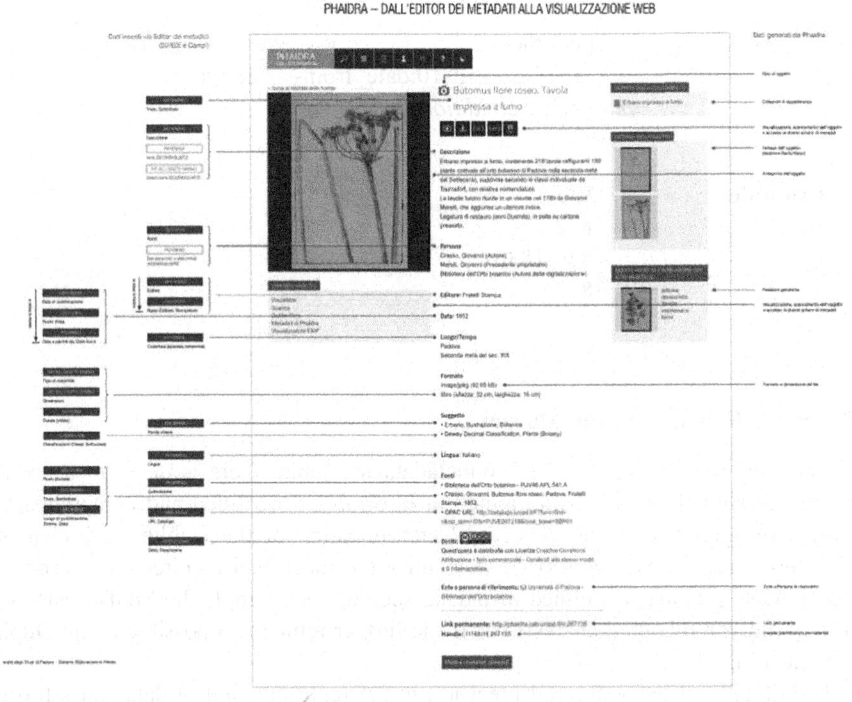

Fig. 5. From the Metadata editor to the web visualisation (http://phaidra.cab.unipd.it/static/campi-di-phaidra.pdf).

3 Towards a Semantic Data Modelling

"In libraries, metadata is a first-class object. Metadata doesn't just describe a library resource, it also connects that resource to entities such as people, places, events, and to other resources" [15]. The persisting validity of this statement in the context of digital repositories can be easily let it be understood. Rather, it is here considered of greater value to focus on how the technical set of established standards and technologies, collectively referred to as "Linked Data", are able to implement and increase the faceted connective potential of metadata.

Since 2016, within a broader workflow pursued by the team of the University of Vienna targeting an enhanced interoperability and accessibility of Phaidra, the development and implementation of a Classification Server has been assessed as one task needed to be carried out. Consisting of an external component to the digital asset management system, the Classification Server would handle and provide in one place all relevant thesauri, classification schemes, taxonomies and controlled vocabularies potentially needed for the assignment of well-defined metadata to digital objects [16] (see Fig. 6). The ideal goal of the Classification Server would be to ensure that during the upload of new items to the repository, when the user adds metadata information to these resources, as well as during the search for objects, when the user types terms in order to search for specific digital objects, Phaidra's users could have access to the main Knowledge Organization Systems (KOSs) as much as easy, comfortable and user-friendly as possible [16]. The opportunity represented by this tool to remarkably enrich both the platform usability and metadata interoperability of the repository was recognised by the working group of the University of Padova as well; this team thus decided in the last few months to start its own narrower implementation analysis of the new component in its local management system.

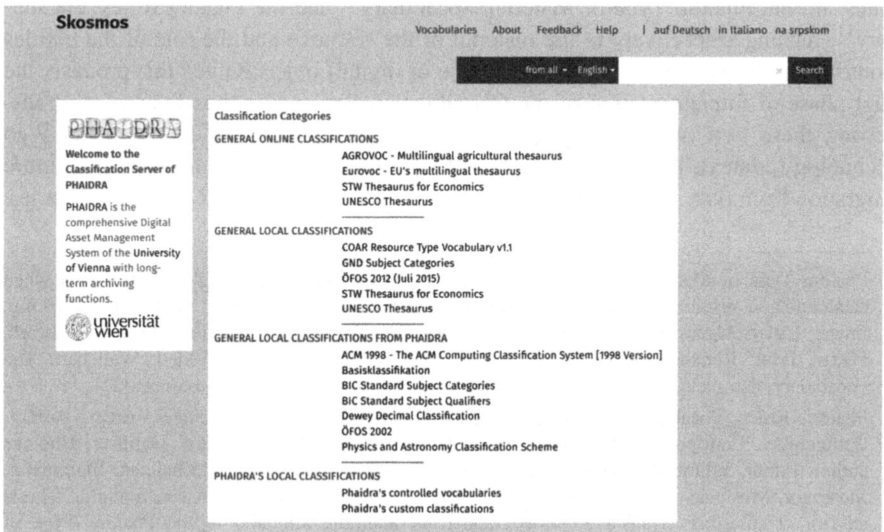

Fig. 6. Opening page of the Classification Server (Source: [19]).

From a technical point of view, the required import format for the various controlled vocabularies and classification schemes to be imported and locally managed by the database and the web application that form up the Classification Server architecture (see Fig. 7) is Simple Knowledge Organization System (SKOS) data model. This is defined as a data-sharing standard recommended by the W3C community for representing in Semantic Web and Linked Data technologies context, that is in Resource Description Framework (RDF) language, the many existing systems used to organise information. Based on the assumption that the Knowledge Organization Systems share a similar structure and content, SKOS allows them to be transformed from isolated and stand-alone entities of organized information into a global machine-readable network of highly integrated conceptual schemes, which are thus publishable in the Web, shareable, readable, wider re-usable and therefore automatically (and much more meaningfully) discoverable by software applications [17, 18].

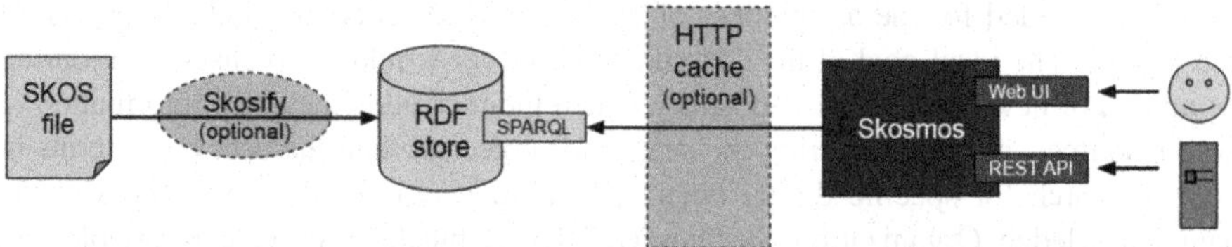

Fig. 7. Tehnical architecture of the Classification Server (Source: [20]).

To date, within Phaidra archival system, the most concrete attempt towards the use of standardised values as metadata has resulted into two locally-implemented lists of descriptors intended to index the catalogued objects and to facilitate their easy retrieval. They are the Phaidra Type of Material Vocabulary[10] and the Phaidra Roles Vocabulary[11], relating respectively to the material of the resource and the role of the entities contributing to the creation of the (analogue or digital) object. Given this premise, the first phase of implementation of the Classification Server was thus focused on transferring these two (not machine-readable) local vocabularies to the Semantic Web technology context. Their representation in SKOS format was tested towards their future migration from data silos to largely linkable and shareable Linked Open Vocabularies.

[10] Phaidra Type of Material Vocabulary includes the following terms available to selection when cataloguing a resource: Arrangement, Article of periodical, Atlas, Book, Book part, Drawing, Image, Letter, Manuscript, Map, Negative, Object, Other, Painting, Periodical, Picture, Postcard, Poster, Print, Remote sensing image, Score, Slide, Sound recording, Video, Wallchart. The vocabulary also includes other currently hidden terms, made accessable on request [21].

[11] Phaidra Roles Vocabulary currently includes 29 terms: Architect, Arranger, Artist, Author, Calligrapher, Cartographer, Composer, Curator, Data contributor, Dedicatee, Digitiser, Dubious author, Editor, Editor of compilation, Engraver, Former owner, Graphic technician, Illuminator, Illustrator, Musician, Other, Photographer, Printer, Publisher, Scientific advisor, Sculptor, Thesis advisor, Transcriber, Translator, Videographer. In addition, similarly to the Phaidra Type of Material Vocabulary additional currently hidden entries are made available at the request of the individual cataloguer [21].

Overall, during the prototypal encoding of these two lists of terms, the essential emphasis of SKOS data model on semantics rather than on terminology enabled the problematic and poorly interoperable approach of the "term" to be replaced with the less ambiguous and much more effectively understandable notion of the "concept". The concept is what constitutes the fundamental element of SKOS vocabulary: it is an abstract unit of thought, i.e. an idea, a meaning, a class of objects or events, uniquely identified by an URI and independent from the multiform expressions used to label it in natural language [17, 18]. The example in Fig. 8 visually displays the aforementioned theoretical core of SKOS standard: the concept of "calligrapher" (`<skos:Concept>`), contained in Phaidra Roles Vocabulary, is noticeably distinct from its corresponding bilingual terminological expressions, both the preferred lexical label (`<skos:prefLabel>`) and the alternative one (`<skos:altLabel>`), as well as from the explanatory note about the intended meaning of the concept (`<skos:definition>`).

```
<skos:Concept rdf:about="http://phaidra.org/vocabularies/roles/calligrapher">
  <skos:inScheme rdf:resource="http://phaidra.org/vocabularies/roles"/>
  <skos:topConceptOf rdf:resource="http://phaidra.org/vocabularies/roles"/>
  <skos:prefLabel xml:lang="en">calligrapher</skos:prefLabel>
  <skos:prefLabel xml:lang="it">copista</skos:prefLabel>
  <skos:altLabel xml:lang="en">scribe</skos:altLabel>
  <skos:altLabel xml:lang="it">scriba</skos:altLabel>
  <skos:definition xml:lang="en">A person who inscribe or copy texts, especially
    those who transcribed, copied, and edited manuscripts before mechanical printing
    technology was developed. </skos:definition>
  <skos:definition xml:lang="it">Una persona che copia testi; si riferisce
    in particolare a chi ha trascritto, copiato e curato un manoscritto prima
    dell'invenzione della stampa. </skos:definition>
</skos:Concept>
```

Fig. 8. Modelling of the concept "calligrapher" in SKOS standard.

Nevertheless, within a scenario of future feasibility, the true most valuable enhancement in terms of data association and integration lies on the mapping of semantic relations between concepts. The logic of the "Web of Data", consisting in expressing the relationships among data in order to define and describe the same data, mirrors the crucial features of SKOS data model. In this context, asserting which relationships exist between concepts of a single concept scheme and, more importantly, which links could be established between concepts of two or more different (but still semantically-related) schemes, constitutes the real key advantage for the different communities of Knowledge Organization Systems. Indeed, SKOS mapping properties would enable information retrieval tools to make use of a widely disseminated and heterogeneous web of Knowledge Organization Systems, causing concepts even supposedly modelled according to dissimilar principles and coming from different contexts to be automatically connected, compared and matched [17].

According to these terms, the step of specifying the semantic relations for each concept of the two local vocabularies of Phaidra, whether they be associative, hierarchical or equivalent links, gained a remarkable weight. By way of example, at the time of a search by type of material of the digital objects stored in Phaidra, the SKOS-formatted concept "photograph" shown below (see Fig. 9) not only would let the

Phaidra search engine to suggest the user all the available materially-related resources, i.e. all the digital objects labelled as "microfilm" or "negative" (as encoded in the tag `<skos:narrower>`). Additionally, the accessibility and visibility of the resources existing in the preservation system of the University of Padova would be increased by the potential interlinking of their metadata with external datasets in the Web, described according to concepts relatively similar or equivalent to the aforementioned local term "photograph". In the snippet represented in Fig. 9 see respectively `<skos:closeMatch>`, referencing to the concept "Fotografie" in *Nuovo soggettario* edited by the National Central Library of Florence, and `<skos:exactMatch>`, linking for example to the concept "Photographs" in *Art & Architecture Thesaurus® (AAT).*

```
<skos:Concept rdf:about="http://phaidra.org/vocabularies/typeofmaterial/photograph">
  <skos:inScheme rdf:resource="http://phaidra.org/vocabularies/typeofmaterial"/>
  <skos:topConceptOf rdf:resource="http://phaidra.org/vocabularies/typeofmaterial"/>
  <skos:prefLabel xml:lang="en">photograph</skos:prefLabel>
  <skos:prefLabel xml:lang="it">fotografia</skos:prefLabel>
  <skos:definition xml:lang="en">Still image produced from radiation-sensitive materials
    (sensitive to light, electron beams, or nuclear radiation), generally by means of the
    chemical action of light on a sensitive film, paper, glass, or metal. A photograph may
    be positive or negative, opaque or transparent. The concept includes photographs made by
    digital means. </skos:definition>
  <skos:definition xml:lang="it">Immagine prodotta da materiale sensibile alla radiazione
    (sensibile alla luce, fasci di elettroni, o radiazione nucleare), generalmente attraverso
    l'azione chimica della luce su una pellicola sensibile, carta, vetro, o metallo.
    Una fotografia potrebbe essere positiva o negativa, opaca o trasparente.
    Questo concetto include anche fotografie realizzate in modo digitale. </skos:definition>
  <skos:narrower rdf:resource="http://phaidra.org/vocabularies/typeofmaterial/microfilm"/>
  <skos:narrower rdf:resource="http://phaidra.org/vocabularies/typeofmaterial/negative"/>
  <skos:exactMatch rdf:resource="http://vocab.getty.edu/aat/300046300"/>
  <skos:exactMatch rdf:resource="http://rdaregistry.info/termList/RDACarrierEU/1025"/>
  <skos:closeMatch rdf:resource="http://purl.org/bncf/tid/1578"/>
</skos:Concept>
```

Fig. 9. Modelling of the concept "photograph" in SKOS standard.

3.1 Future Outcome

Despite the limited extent of this case study, it is well-known that standards as RDF, SKOS and SPARQL, key means as ontologies, controlled vocabularies and authority files, and back-end architectures such as triplestores and reasoners, are comprehensively pivotal. They all would be equally demanded for a long-term digital archive, as is Phaidra, to be migrated to the "Web of Data" in an actual and full manner. An unparalleled data interoperability and a serendipitous networked knowledge discovery would be the granted benefits (see Fig. 10).

But at least, this is the promising outcome, and efforts are now set on this future perspective. The whole work which has been done so far on the theoretical mapping of UWmetadata schema to MODS was undertaken by both the Universities of Padova and Vienna in the light of a broader outlook, namely the announcement of a development and implementation of a new version of Fedora web-architecture, i.e. Fedora 4, which would have stored metadata in RDF standard. Mostly on the basis of recommendations and discussions guided by an international community of institutions engaged in transitioning their MODS-based digital repository systems to RDF [22], both the

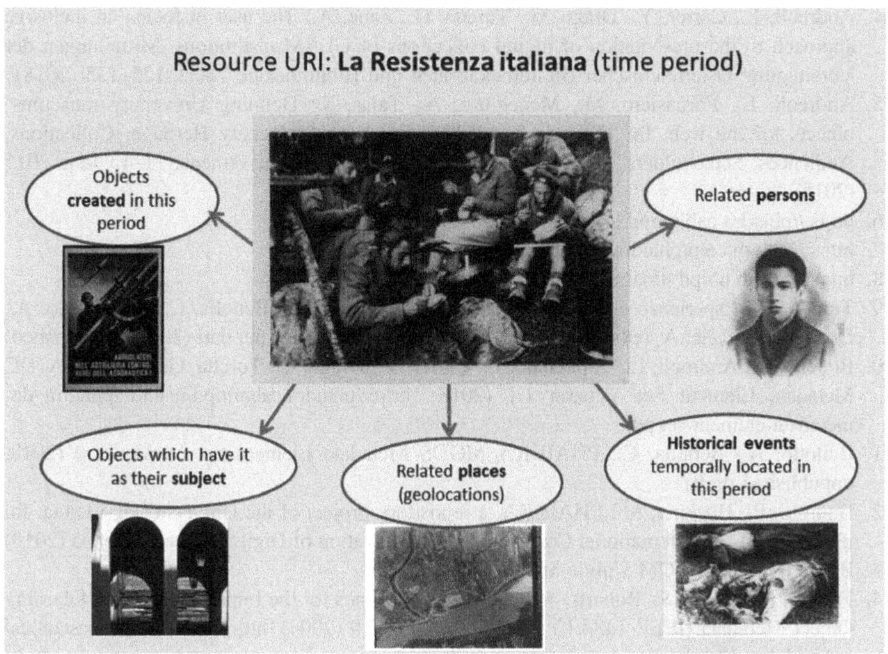

Fig. 10. Potential example of Semantic Web data in the digital repository of the University of Padova.

working groups of Phaidra are currently involved in outlining a new foundational data model represented in RDF triples. By the potential use of an arbitrary number of external vocabularies and ontologies, along with the possibility of RDF graphs to be extended with new nodes and new relationship types effortlessly, this new semantics-embedding model would be much more flexible, extendable to every future needs as well as highly interoperable.

In these terms, the forthcoming achievement of such a framework might thus exactly represent the most effective means to disclose the associative potential of metadata that was cited at the beginning of Sect. 3.

Acknowledgements. A pivotal thank you goes to the team of Phaidra, University of Padova – Lorisa Andreoli, Linda Cappellato, Yuri Carrer, Gianluca Drago, Giulio Turetta, and Antonella Zane – without whom the work illustrated in this paper would have never been existed.

References

1. https://phaidra.cab.unipd.it/
2. https://phaidra.univie.ac.at/
3. https://www.phaidra.org/community/phaidra-partners/

4. Andreoli, L., Carrer, Y., Drago, G., Turetta, G., Zane, A.: The user in focus: an inclusive approach to the presentation of digital collections of GLAM institutions. Mitteilungen der Vereinigung Österreichischer Bibliothekarinnen und Bibliothekare **71**(1), 125–135 (2018)
5. Andreoli, L., Fornasiero, M., Menegazzi, A., Talas, S.: Defining University museums' objects for the web. In: "Turning Inside Out European University Heritage: Collections, Audiences, Stakeholders". Proceedings of the 16th Universeum, Athens, 11–13 June 2015 (2015)
6. https://phaidra.cab.unipd.it/info/impressum
7. https://github.com/phaidra/phaidra-api/wiki/Documentation
8. https://fc.cab.unipd.it/oaiprovider/
9. Turetta, G.: Esperienze e modelli di dati: il caso Phaidra. In: Bettella, C., De Robbio, A., Duzzin, M., Zane, A. (eds.) Corso di formazione La biblioteca dei dati (2017, unpublished)
10. Bettella, C., Andreoli, L., Cappellato, L., Carrer, Y., Drago, G., Turetta, G.: PHAIDRA_DC Metadata Element Set Version 1.1 (2018). http://phaidra.cab.unipd.it/static/phaidra_dc-metadata-element-set.pdf
11. Bellotto, A., Bettella, C.: PHAIDRA_MODS Metadata Element Set Version 1.0 (2018, unpublished draft)
12. Budroni, P., Höckner, M.: PHAIDRA, a repository project of the University of Vienna. In: iPRES 2010, 7th International Conference on Preservation of Digital Objects, Vienna (2010)
13. Budin, G., et al.: LOM Univie Schema, April 2006
14. Friesen, N., Fisher, S., Roberts, A.: CanCore Guidelines for the Implementation of Learning Object Metadata (IEEE 1484.12.1-2002), Version 2.0 (2004). http://cancore.athabascau.ca/en/guidelines.html
15. Powell, J., Hopkins, M.: A Librarian's Guide to Graphs, Data and the Semantic Web, p. 130. Chandos Publishing, Waltham (2015)
16. Kopácsi, S., Hudak, R., Ganguly, R.: Implementation of a classification server to support metadata organization for long term preservation systems. In: Mitteilungen der Vereinigung Österreichischer Bibliothekarinnen und Bibliothekare Bd. 70, Nr. 2 (2017)
17. World Wide Web Consortium (W3C): SKOS Simple Knowledge Organization System Primer. Working Group Note (2009)
18. World Wide Web Consortium (W3C): SKOS Simple Knowledge Organization System Reference. W3C Recommendation (2009)
19. Skosmos Homepage. http://vocab.phaidra.org/skosmos/en/?clang=en
20. Suominen, O.: Publishing SKOS concept schemes with Skosmos. AIMS Webinar 6th April 2016, Slide 25 (2016)
21. Cappellato, L.: Linee guida per la compilazione dei metadati (2018, revised edition, forthcoming)
22. Samvera MODS to RDF Working Group: MODS to RDF Mapping Recommendations. v.0.1 - Draft for Review & Comment (2018). https://docs.google.com/document/d/1FZI8KJiW4qSKYUUKe0mAwqlx0ppVRFyPtsfLDqQE5T8/edit

In Codice Ratio: Machine Transcription of Medieval Manuscripts

Serena Ammirati[1], Donatella Firmani[2(✉)], Marco Maiorino[3], Paolo Merialdo[2], and Elena Nieddu[2]

[1] Department of Humanities, Roma Tre University, Rome, Italy
serena.ammirati@uniroma3.it
[2] Department of Computer Science, Roma Tre University, Rome, Italy
{donatella.firmani,paolo.merialdo,elena.nieddu}@uniroma3.it
[3] Vatican Secret Archives, Vatican City, Italy
m.maiorino@asv.va

Abstract. Our project, *In Codice Ratio*, is an interdisciplinary research initiative for analyzing content of historical documents conserved in the Vatican Secret Archives (VSA). As most of such documents are digitized as images, Machine Transcription is both an enabler to the application of Knowledge Discovery techniques, as well as a useful tool to the paleographer for speeding up the transcription process. Our approach involves a convolutional neural network to recognize characters, statistical language models to compose and rank word transcriptions, and crowdsourcing for scalable training data collection. We have conducted experiments on pages from the medieval manuscript collection known as the Vatican Registers. Our results show that almost all the considered words can be transcribed without significant spelling errors.

1 Introduction

The research project *In Codice Ratio* has the goal of supporting humanities scholars in the content analysis and knowledge discovery activities on large collections of historical documents. Thanks to novel methods and tools that we aim at developing, paleographers, philologists and historians will be able to conduct data-driven studies at a large scale by quantitatively analyzing trends and evolution of writings and languages across time and countries, and by examining and discovering facts and correlations among information spread in vast corpora of documents. Our project concentrates on the collections preserved in the Vatican Secret Archives (VSA), one of the largest and most important historical archives in the world. In an extension of 85 km of shelving, it maintains more than 600 archival collections of historical sources on the Vatican activities – such as, official correspondence of the Vatican, account books, correspondence of the popes – starting from the end of the eighth century. We are currently working on the collection of the Vatican Registers, which record the inbound and outbound

This work is an extended abstract of [4].

P. Manghi et al. (Eds.): IRCDL 2019, CCIS 988, pp. 185–192, 2019.
https://doi.org/10.1007/978-3-030-11226-4_15

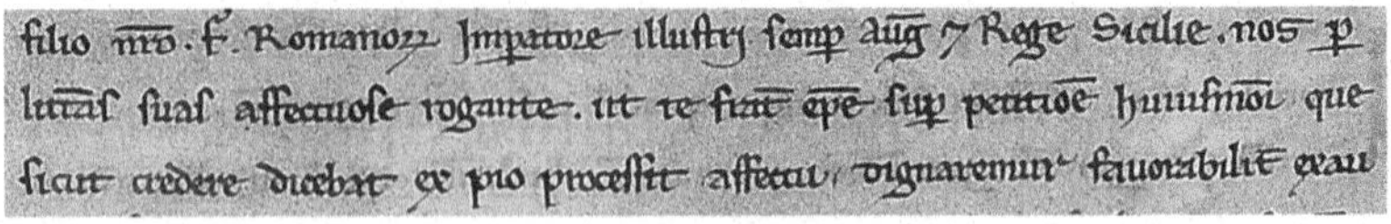

Fig. 1. Sample text of the "Liber septimus regestorum domini Honorii Pope III".

correspondence of the popes. A small sample is shown in Fig. 1. These registers have been continuously and systematically preserved since the middle age, hence most of these documents are *manuscripts.* The VSA has begun to acquire digital images of these documents but, unfortunately, complete transcriptions for the earliest registers do not exist. Therefore, a first fundamental step to develop any form of data-driven content analysis is to perform a transcription of the manuscripts. The problem is challenging: on the one hand, a manual transcription is unfeasible (at least in a reasonable amount of time), due to the volume (hundreds of thousands of pages) of the collection. On the other hand, although these manuscripts are written with a uniform style (a derivation of the *Caroline* style), traditional OCR does not apply here, because of irregularities of hand-writing, ligatures and abbreviations.

Since segmenting words in characters is tricky with handwritten texts, recent automatic transcription approaches typically aim at recognizing entire words. However, because of the variability and the size of the lexicon, they need a huge amount of training data, i.e., hundreds of fully transcribed pages. To illustrate this problem, consider Fig. 2: it reports the distribution of the occurrences of words in a corpus composed by a partial transcription of the Registers of Innocent III (in total, it is about 68,000 words). Observe that a few words (just 9) occur more than 100 times (the most occurring word is *"et"*, the Latin conjunction that corresponds to "and"), while the majority of words have less than 10 occurrences.

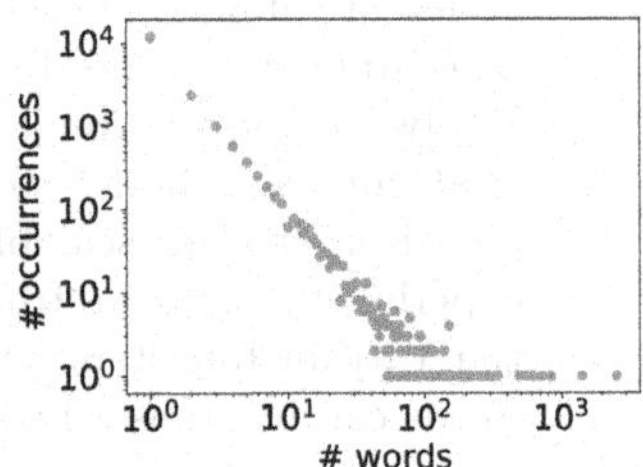

Fig. 2. Word count.

We follow a different approach, based on character segmentation. Our idea is to govern imprecise character segmentation by considering that correct segments are those that give rise to a sequence of characters that more likely compose a Latin word. We have therefore designed a principled solution that relies on a convolutional neural network classifier and on statistical language models. For every word, we perform a segmentation that can produce more segments than those actually formed by the characters in the word. Every segment is labeled by a classifier, which essentially recognizes the most likely character. We then organize the sequence of segments in a directed acyclic graph: the paths of such a graph represent candidate transcriptions for the word, and the most likely solution is selected based on language statistics.

Structure of this Paper. Section 2 contains an overview of our approach. Detailed description of our algorithms can be found in [4]. Main experimental results of [4] are reported in Sect. 3. Finally, Sects. 4 and 5 contain related work and concluding remarks. *In Codice Ratio* was introduced in [1]. All the code and data of the project is publicly online.[1]

2 Overview

We start from a set of high-quality scanned images of whole manuscript *pages*. Each page undergoes three standard pre-processing steps:

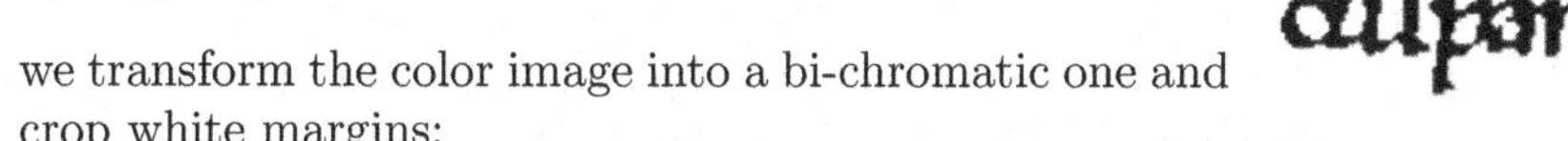

1. we transform the color image into a bi-chromatic one and crop white margins;
2. we correct *skew* and *slant*, i.e., page distortions due to acquisition process and calligraphy;
3. we crop lines and words according to horizontal and vertical white spaces, respectively.

Fig. 3. A typical input image for our system.

Each word image is finally submitted to our transcription system. Figure 3 shows a pre-processed word image, of size 178×67 pixels. The correct transcription of the word in the figure is the Latin word "culpam" – the accusative singular of "culpa", that means "crime".

System Architecture. Our pipeline consists of four main components.

- **Training samples collector.** We implemented a custom crowd-sourcing platform, and employed 120 high-school students to label the dataset. To overcome the complexity of reading ancient fonts, we provided the students with positive and negative examples of each symbol. We trained a deep convolutional neural network character classifier on this dataset.
- **Character recognizer.** Recognizing characters within a handwritten word is challenging, due to *ligatures*. To this end, we first partition the input word into elementary text segments. Most segments contain actual characters, but there are also segments with spurious ink strokes. Then, we submit all the segments to the trained classifier. Computed labels are very accurate when the input segment contains an actual character, but can be wrong otherwise. We take into account minuscule characters of the Latin alphabet.
- **Transcription generator.** We reassemble noisy labels from the classifier into a set of candidate word transcriptions. Specifically, we select the best m candidate transcriptions for the input word image, using language models.
- **Word decoder.** We consider the m transcriptions from the previous step and revise character recognition decisions in a principled way, by solving a specific decoding problem on a high-order hidden Markov model. The most promising transcriptions are finally returned to the user.

[1] www.inf.uniroma3.it/db/icr/.

Discussion. It is worth noting that compared to a segmentation-free approach, training the classifier requires labeled examples for the limited set of character symbols, with a twofold advantage. First, the size of the training set is several order of magnitude smaller, as we need to provide examples only for the limited set of character symbols, and not for a rich lexicon of words. Second, producing the examples is much easier, as it does not require to transcribe whole words, an activity that can be carried on by expert paleographers. In our system, the production of the training set is accomplished by a crowdsourcing solution that consists of simple visual pattern matching tasks, similar to captchas.

3 Experiments

For our experiments we use annotations from 2 pages of Vatican Register 12. This results in approximately 15K characters. Characters with less than 1K examples were augmented to match the required quantity and balance the training set. The augmentation process involves slight random rotation, zooming, shearing and shifting, both vertical and horizontal. The final dataset comprises 23K examples evenly split between 23 classes. We test our system on four pages belonging to the same Vatican Register, but spanning different ages and writers, transcribed entirely by volunteer paleographers. After undergoing the pre-processing, each word is transcribed independently by the system. Our system currently considers only word images without *abbreviated forms*. This is further discussed in Sect. 5. Our language model is composed of 716 ancient Roman Latin texts, spanning different ages and subjects, for a total of over 14M words. It is worth observing that the Latin language used in the Vatican Registers exhibits some differences with the ancient Roman Latin, which is typically used in publicly available corpora. These differences introduce some drawbacks, that we are currently overcoming, as we discuss later in Sect. 5.

Set-Up. We define the **m-precision** as the fraction of word images in our test set, for which the correct transcription is (i) generated by our system, and (ii) ranked in the top m positions. Classical definition of precision is captured by 1-precision. For the top few transcriptions, we provide edit distance statistics (**ED**) with respect to the correct transcription. Specifically, we use the distance metric in [3]. Our experiments are summarized below.

Results. In the *character recognition* step, average precision and recall of our neural network among all classes are both 96%. Precision ranges from 86% to 99%, whereas recall ranges from 74% to 99%. As frame of comparison, we trained a logistic regression model on the same dataset. Such baseline scored 80% and 79% average precision and recall. More results on this are in [5].

In the *transcription generation* step, the fraction of words for which our system yields the correct transcription is ≈65% (decoding can recover the correct transcription of approximately 9% of the remaining 35%), compared to much lower 20% achieved by the baseline in [1]. When the correct transcription is available, *language models* can rank the correct transcription of almost all the word images in the top 5. For remaining 35%, 16% of first-ranked transcriptions is at edit distance 1 from the correct transcription, 15% at distance 2 and 28% at distance 3. Figure 4 shows a sample word image of the 15% group, for which the first-ranked transcription is at distance 2 from the correct transcription.

The purple bars in Fig. 5 show the 1-precision and 3-precision of our system for different q-gram sizes in the language model. The bar labeled as "NoLM" shows ranking results obtained without taking language models into account. The NoLM ranking was produced by multiplying network classification scores for each character. Figure 5b considers top 3 transcriptions of all the word images in the test set. We observe that, by using 6-g, almost 80% of our results are away from correct transcriptions by no more than 2 characters, and approximately 60% corresponds exactly to the underlying manuscript word. Figure 5a reports the corresponding results when considering only top 1 transcriptions. Another way for reading results in Fig. 5a is the following. Consider the 65% of the word images in our dataset for which we generate the correct transcription. Approximately 77% of the word images have the correct transcription ranked at position 1 when using 6-g (which is our default setting), but approximately 23% does not get the optimal ranking. Correct transcription, when generated, is in the top 5 for almost all the word images. Improving on the ranking produced requires a better model of the language used in the Vatican Register, included models of sentences, and is discussed in Sect. 5.

Fig. 4. The correct transcription of this word image is "asseritis", while the first-ranked transcription is "afferitis".

Consider now the 35% of word images for which our system does *not* generate the correct transcription is approximately.[2] Decoding can recover the correct transcription of approximately 9% of such word images. Other effects of the decoding phase is that top-ranked transcriptions become closer to correct transcriptions. For instance, the amount of word images having correct transcription

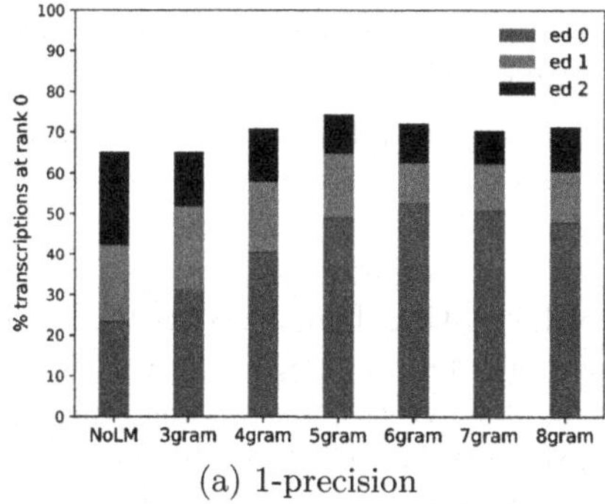

(a) 1-precision

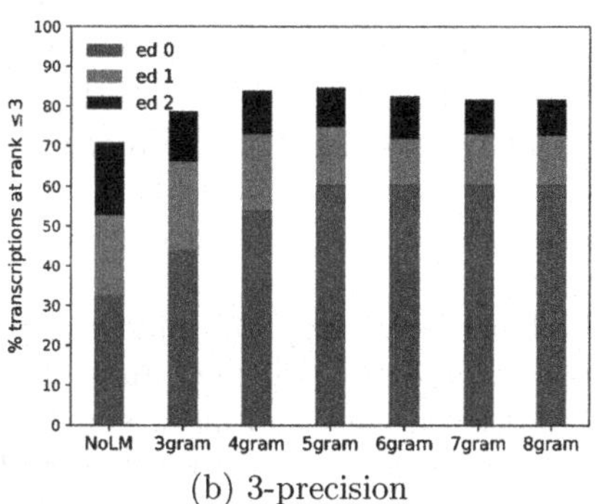

(b) 3-precision

Fig. 5. Different values of q in the language model. "NoLM" represents ranking without language model, relying on character classification score only. (Color figure online)

[2] For such word images, most of first-ranked transcriptions have $\leq$3 spelling errors.

ranked as second increases by 30%. Overall, the amount of word images having correct transcription ranked as first does not change significantly.

4 Related Works

Handwritten Text Recognition (or HTR) is a research topic concerning the automatic transcription of handwritten text. Even though it extends to live-captured handwriting (online recognition), that is clearly not the case for historical documents. Offline recognition is generally regarded as harder than the online, due to the lack of temporal information: online handwriting recognition can leverage the order and timing of character strokes, while offline recognition cannot. Due to the many challenges involved in a fully automatic transcription system of historical handwritten documents, many researchers in the last years have focused on solving sub-problems, including word spotting [11], and text line segmentation [10]. Our goal is rather the creation of a full-fledged off-line HTR system: an effort shared by several ongoing projects, as more and more libraries and archives worldwide digitize their collections [7,13]. These systems generally work by a segmentation-free approach, where it is not necessary to individually segment each character. To deal effectively with ambiguity in segmentation and transcription, we map each word image to a lattice, whose source-to-sink paths represent alternative segmentations and corresponding transcriptions. Our approach is close to the technique in [8].

Crowdsourcing. Crowdsourcing solution for cultural heritage has been experienced in many projects. One of the pioneering initiative to crowdsource the transcription of manuscripts is the *Transcribe Bentham* project, a collaborative platform for crowdsourcing the transcription of the philosopher Jeremy Bentham's unpublished manuscripts [2]. Also the Transcriptorium project [12] exposes HTR tools through specialized crowd-sourcing web portals, supporting collaborative work. Our solution is more focused than the above ones: since it aims at producing training data, it relies on a much simpler solution based on visual pattern matching task that can be performed by unskilled workers.

Neural Networks. Our approach employs a convolutional neural network for character image classification. There has been an interest in applying recent results in recurrent and convolutional neural networks to achieve improved classification accuracy: [14] performs word spotting through a deep convolutional neural network, outperforming various word spotting benchmarks; while [6] adopts a bidirectional Long Short-Term Memory neural network to transcribe at word level, with high accuracy. In order to achieve complete transcriptions, these approaches would need thousands of word-level annotations, which is not a scalable task due to the expertise required. We will come back on this point when discussing future research directions for our project.

5 Conclusions and Future Work

Fig. 6. A word (*patrono*rum) containing an abbreviation (in black).

Data science can deeply contribute to analyze and understand our historical and cultural heritage. Data acquisition and preparation from manuscript historical documents is done by means of a transcription process, whose scalability is limited, as it must be performed by expert paleographers. In this paper, we have presented a system, developed in the context of the *In Codice Ratio* project, to support the transcription of medieval manuscripts in order to improve the scalability of the process. We have followed an original approach that requires minimal training effort, and that is able to produce correct transcriptions for large portions of the manuscripts. Our approach, which relies on word segmentation, neural convolutional network, and language models, has been successfully experimented on the Vatican Registers.

We are currently working on the system in order to extend the set of symbols, and hence to improve the overall effectiveness of the process. In particular, we are adding the most frequent abbreviations, i.e., short-hands used by the scribes to save room or to speed up writing. In our process, the main issue with abbreviations is the lack of statistics on their occurrences, which prevents us to effectively apply the language models. Gathering statistics for the abbreviation is not trivial: the usage of these symbols depends both on the age and on the domain of the manuscripts. For instance, in the Vatican Registers, which have diplomatic and legal contents, some abbreviations are more frequent than in manuscripts with of literary works, even from the same age. Indeed, we have already collected training samples for the classifier also for many abbreviations: our crowdsourcing approach to collect labeled examples worked well also for these symbols, as it is based on simple visual pattern matching tasks. Figure 6 shows an example of a one of the most frequent abbreviations. The last symbol, in black, is a shorthand for the Latin desinence *"rum"*: notice that it is simple, given some sample images, to recognize it also without any paleography knowledge. Also the neural network performs well with the extended set of symbols, as abbreviations are typically well distinguishable from other symbols.

Our plan to collect statistics for the abbreviations is to use our current system to produce partial transcriptions for a number of pages, a few dozens, highlighting the words where the character classifier recognizes an abbreviation. Then, we will ask to the paleographers to transcribe these words. Based on these semi-automatic transcriptions, we will progressively update the language models. So far, we took a probabilistic approach on language modeling: we plan, however, to investigate character-level neural language modeling, similarly to [9].

Acknowledgments. We thank NVIDIA Corporation for the donation of a Quadro M5000 GPU, and Regione Lazio (Progetti di Gruppi di Ricerca) and Roma Tre University (Piano Straordinario di Sviluppo della Ricerca di Ateneo) for supporting our project "In Codice Ratio".

References

1. Ammirati, S., Firmani, D., Maiorino, M., Merialdo, P., Nieddu, E., Rossi, A.: In codice ratio: scalable transcription of historical handwritten documents. In: Proceedings of the 25th Italian Symposium on Advanced Database Systems, Squillace Lido (Catanzaro), Italy, 25–29 June 2017, p. 65 (2017)
2. Causer, T., Terras, M.: 'Many hands make light work. Many hands together make merry work': transcribe Bentham and crowdsourcing manuscript collections. Crowdsourcing Our Cultural Heritage, pp. 57–88 (2014)
3. Cohen, W.W., Ravikumar, P., Fienberg, S.E.: A comparison of string distance metrics for name-matching tasks. In: Proceedings of the 2003 International Conference on Information Integration on the Web, IIWEB 2003, pp. 73–78 (2003)
4. Firmani, D., Maiorino, M., Merialdo, P., Nieddu, E.: Towards knowledge discovery from the Vatican secret archives. In codice ratio - episode 1: machine transcription of the manuscripts. In: Proceedings of the 24th ACM SIGKDD International Conference on Knowledge Discovery & Data Mining, KDD 2018, London, UK, 19–23 August 2018, pp. 263–272 (2018)
5. Firmani, D., Merialdo, P., Nieddu, E., Scardapane, S.: In codice ratio: OCR of handwritten Latin documents using deep convolutional networks. In: Proceedings of the 11th International Workshop on Artificial Intelligence for Cultural Heritage (2017)
6. Fischer, A., et al.: Automatic transcription of handwritten medieval documents. In: 15th International Conference on Virtual Systems and Multimedia. IEEE (2009)
7. Flaounas, I., et al.: Research methods in the age of digital journalism: massive-scale automated analysis of news-content-topics, style and gender. Digit. J. **1**(1), 102–116 (2013)
8. Keysers, D., Deselaers, T., Rowley, H.A., Wang, L.-L., Carbune, V.: Multi-language online handwriting recognition. IEEE Trans. Pattern Anal. Mach. Intell. **39**(6), 1180–1194 (2017)
9. Kim, Y., Jernite, Y., Sontag, D., Rush, A.M.: Character-aware neural language models. In: Proceedings of the Thirtieth AAAI Conference on Artificial Intelligence, AAAI 2016, pp. 2741–2749. AAAI Press (2016)
10. Likforman-Sulem, L., Zahour, A., Taconet, B.: Text line segmentation of historical documents: a survey. Int. J. Doc. Anal. Recogn. **9**(2), 123–138 (2007)
11. Puigcerver, J., Toselli, A.H., Vidal, E.: ICDAR 2015 competition on keyword spotting for handwritten documents. In: 13th International Conference on Document Analysis and Recognition (ICDAR), pp. 1176–1180. IEEE (2015)
12. Sánchez, J.A., et al.: tranScriptorium: a European project on handwritten text recognition. In: Proceedings of the 2013 ACM Symposium on Document Engineering, pp. 227–228. ACM (2013)
13. Sánchez, J.A., Romero, V., Toselli, A.H., Vidal, E.: ICFHR 2014 competition on handwritten text recognition on tranScriptorium datasets (HTRtS). In: 2014 14th International Conference on Frontiers in Handwriting Recognition (ICFHR), pp. 785–790. IEEE (2014)
14. Sudholt, S., Fink, G.A.: PHOCNet: a deep convolutional neural network for word spotting in handwritten documents. In: 15th International Conference on Frontiers in Handwriting Recognition (ICFHR), pp. 277–282. IEEE (2016)

Open Science

Foundations of a Framework for Peer-Reviewing the Research Flow

Alessia Bardi(✉), Vittore Casarosa, and Paolo Manghi

Institute of Information Science and Technologies - CNR, Pisa, Italy
{alessia.bardi, vittore.casarosa, paolo.manghi}@isti.cnr.it

Abstract. Traditionally, peer-review focuses on the evaluation of scientific publications, literature products that describe the research process and its final results in natural language. The adoption of ICT technologies in support of science introduces new opportunities to support transparent evaluation, thanks to the possibility of sharing research products, even inputs, intermediate and negative results, repetition and reproduction of the research activities conducted in a digital laboratory. Such innovative shift also sets the condition for novel peer review methodologies, as well as scientific reward policies, where scientific results can be transparently and objectively assessed via machine-assisted processes. This paper presents the foundations of a framework for the representation of a peer-reviewable research flow for a given discipline of science. Such a framework may become the scaffolding enabling the development of tools for supporting ongoing peer review of research flows. Such tools could be "hooked", in real time, to the underlying digital laboratory, where scientists are carrying out their research flow, and they would abstract over the complexity of the research activity and offer user-friendly dashboards.

Keywords: Open peer review · Digital science · Open Science

1 Introduction

An increasing number of researchers conduct their research adopting ICT tools for the production and processing of research products. In the last decade, research infrastructures (organizational and technological facilities supporting research activities) are investing in "e-infrastructures" that leverage ICT tools, services, guidelines and policies to support the digital practices of their community of researchers.[1] To find an analogy with traditional science, where research is often done in a laboratory, e-infrastructures are the place where researchers can define their *digital laboratories*, i.e. the subset of assets and tools that they use to conduct their research. Researchers run their digital experiments (e.g. simulations, data analysis) taking advantage of the digital

[1] European Commission, http://ec.europa.eu/programmes/horizon2020/en/h2020-section/research-infrastructures-including-e-infrastructures.

P. Manghi et al. (Eds.): IRCDL 2019, CCIS 988, pp. 195–208, 2019.
https://doi.org/10.1007/978-3-030-11226-4_16

laboratory assets (e.g. RStudio[2], Jupyter Notebook[3], Taverna workbench[4]) and generate new research data and computational products (e.g. software, R algorithms, computational workflows) that can be shared with other researchers of the same community, that can be discovered, accessed and reused and ultimately can become part of the e-infrastructure.

The role of digital laboratories is therefore twofold: on the one hand they support researchers in their advancement of science, offering the facilities needed for their daily activities; on the other hand, they foster the dissemination of research within the research community, supporting discovery, access to, sharing, and reuse of digital research products. In fact, their digital nature offers unprecedented opportunities for scientists, who can share not only scientific literature describing their findings, but also the digital results that they produced, together with the digital laboratory itself. Those features are fundamental for an effective implementation of the Open Science (OS) paradigm [1, 2]. OS is a set of practices of science, advocated by scientific/scholarly communication stakeholders (i.e., research funders[5], research and academic organisations, and researchers), according to which a research activity (intended as an activity performed to answer a research question) and all the generated products should be freely available, under terms that enable their findability, accessibility, re-use, and re-distribution [3].

If supported with adequate degrees of openness, scientists would find the conditions to repeat ("same research activity, same laboratory"), replicate ("same research activity, different laboratory"), reproduce ("same research activity, different input parameters"), or re-use ("using a product into another research activity") the results of research activities, thereby maximizing transparency and exploitation of scientific findings [4].

The ability to share research products, in combination with digital laboratories, opens the way to Open Science principles. According to these principles, science should be open not only once it is concluded, but also while it is being performed. In other words, scientists should, as much as possible, make their methodologies, thinking and findings available to enable/maximize collaboration and reuse by the community. The digital laboratory becomes therefore the core of this vision as it is the place providing the assets needed by the researchers to implement their research flow (i.e. the actual sequence of experiments required to prove the initial thesis) and at the same time the place providing the generated research products, for sharing and peer-reviewing. For example, scientists performing analysis of data using R scripts, may use a digital laboratory equipped with the software RStudio offered as-a-service by an online provider (e.g. BlueBridge e-infrastructure powered by D4Science[6]) and a repository where they can store/share their R scripts and their input and output datasets (e.g. Zenodo.org).

In the following we shall refer to the following concepts:

[2] RStudio, https://www.rstudio.com/.

[3] Jupyter Notebook, http://jupyter.org/.

[4] Taverna workbench, https://taverna.incubator.apache.org/.

[5] Examples are research funders like the European Commission [2], Wellcome Trust and funders of the cOAlition-S (https://www.scienceeurope.org/coalition-s/).

[6] BlueBridge, http://www.bluebridge-vres.eu/.

- A *research activity* is performed to answer a "research question", usually formulated as one or more hypotheses to be proved true;
- A *research flow* is made of a number of experiments, realized as sequence of steps in the context of a digital laboratory, executed by scientists driven by the ultimate intent of proving an initial scientific thesis;
- An *experiment* is a goal-driven sequence of steps set to verify a thesis, and whose result may inspire further experiments to address the target of the overarching research activity. One experiment can be constituted of several series of sequential steps executed in parallel.
- A *digital laboratory* is a pool of digital assets (e.g. on-line tools, desktop tools, methodologies, standards) used by scientists to perform the steps of an experiment and generate research products.
- A *research product* is any digital object generated during the research flow that was relevant to complete the research activity and (possibly) relevant for its interpretation once the research activity has been completed. Products are digital objects, whose human consumption depends on computer programs; they are concrete items that can be discovered, accessed, and possibly re-used under given access rights. Examples are datasets in a data repository (e.g. sea observations in the PANGAEA repository[7]), but also entries in domain databases (e.g. proteins in UNIPROT[8]), software (e.g. models implemented as R algorithms in GitHub), and of course the scientific article, reporting about the findings of a research activity.

A research activity may therefore generate a number of research products that enable scientists to draw their conclusions. Indeed, several "intermediate" products are generated at different stages, e.g. input and outputs of unsuccessful experiments, versions of the final products to be refined. A research activity can therefore be described by a research flow, i.e. a sequence of steps $S_1 \ldots S_n$, possibly grouped into experiments, carried out in the frame of a digital laboratory (see Fig. 1 left). More specifically, each step S_i of a research flow is in turn a sequence of actions enacted by humans, possibly by means of digital laboratory assets, that may require or produce (intermediate) research products. Clearly, some (or all) of the research products generated during the research flow may become, at some point in time, new assets of a digital laboratory. An example related to the field of geothermal energy science is shown on Fig. 1 (right). A researcher gets data from a GIS database and provide those data as input to the 3D GeoModeller application: those are the assets of the digital laboratory. The experiment is composed of two steps: the researcher selects one of the equations available from the GeoModeller and provide the needed input parameter for the generation of the model. The researcher then interprets the model and produces the scientific article to be published. In this (simplified) example both the generated model and the article are research products that can be shared and peer-reviewed. The configuration of the application used for generating a model could also be made available, to increase transparency and replicability. In a more complete scenario, the research flow could

[7] PANGAEA: https://www.pangaea.de/.

[8] UNIPROT: https://www.ebi.ac.uk/uniprot.

include several repetitions of the model generation, with different input parameters or with different equations, until the interpretation of the generated model would satisfy the researcher.

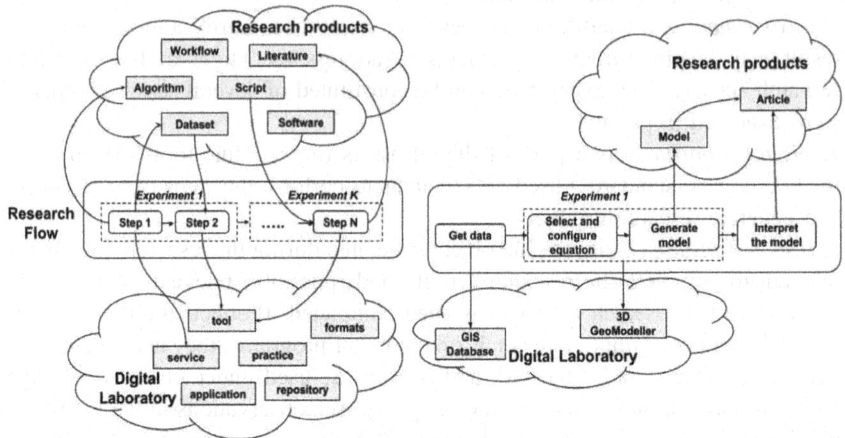

Fig. 1. The research flow in the digital era and an example on geothermal science

This article presents the foundations of a framework for the representation of research flows in support of peer review for a given discipline of science. The aim of the framework is to enable research communities to formally define research flow patterns that define which are the steps that should be peer-reviewed. Such a framework may become the scaffolding enabling the development of tools for supporting ongoing peer review of research flows. Such tools could be "hooked", in real time, to the underlying digital laboratory, where scientists are carrying out their research flow, and they would abstract over the complexity of the research activity and offer user-friendly dashboards to examine the adopted scientific process, explore the ongoing research flow, and evaluate its intermediate experiments and products.

Outline. The state of the art on current practices for the peer review of research flows is presented in Sect. 2. Section 3 describes the framework in support of peer-review of research flows. Conclusion and future work are addressed in Sect. 4.

2 Current Practices for the Peer-Review of the Research Flow

Researchers usually tend to make a clear distinction between the phase of research activities and the phase of research publishing. Research publishing is generally intended as the moment in which researchers share their findings with the broader community of all researchers, hence also the moment at which the peer review of the research flow starts, assuming that the published material somehow "represents" the whole research flow.

Traditionally, the peer review of the research flow has been delegated to scientific literature (e.g., articles, books, technical reports, PhD theses) which is still regarded as the common omni-comprehensive unit of scientific dissemination. The published material provides the means for the review of the research flow (and possibly reproducibility) by explaining and describing the different steps, the digital laboratory where they were conducted (i.e., methodology, tools, standards, etc.), and describing any product used or yielded by the research activity, thus facilitating reproducibility by a detailed, theoretically unambiguous, description of the experiments. However, a natural language description of a methodology can have different interpretations and typically does not include all the details that are needed in order to replicate the experiment or reproduce the results. In addition, it has been found [5–7] that "methodology" sections of many papers often include generic sentences, and lack the details that would be necessary to attempt the reproduction of the results. To overcome this issue, the Centre for Open Science, in collaboration with more than 3,000 journals, is testing the approach of "pre-registered reports", i.e. documents that describe the research flow in a structured and detailed form and that are submitted to the journal before the research starts [8].

To overcome the drawbacks of publishing only scientific literature, a common approach adopted today across several disciplines is that of publishing articles together with links to other digital products of the research, deposited in dedicated repositories. In the majority of cases the papers provide links to datasets, although some cutting-edge research communities are experimenting with links to computational products (e.g. software, scientific workflows), experiments and methodologies.

A growing number of data repositories and archives assign unique, persistent identifiers to the deposited datasets and apply the FAIR principles [9, 10] (data should be Findable, Accessible, Interoperable and Re-usable). Relevant examples are Zenodo and figshare (cross-discipline and allowing deposition of products of any type), DRYAD (mostly for life science), PANGAEA (earth & environmental science), Archeology Data Service (archaeology), DANS (multi-discipline, mostly humanities and social sciences). Data repositories typically implement data review processes that focus on checking the technical details of the datasets, validating their metadata and, possibly, their descriptions, without addressing the scientific value of the dataset itself. In fact, this type of data review usually is not performed by "peers", but by editors and curators of the repository, who are not necessarily researchers in the same field of the depositors, but are instead expert of data management, archiving, and data preservation.

A different approach to data peer review is adopted by data journals [11], which publish data papers, i.e. papers describing datasets in terms of content, provenance, and foreseen usage. Data journals inherited the peer-review process from traditional journals of scientific literature and apply it, with slight changes, to the data papers. The peer review of data papers is mostly focused on the review of metadata, whose completeness and clarity are considered fundamental to facilitate data re-use [12–14]. With the existing approaches, the reproducibility of a dataset (when applicable, as some datasets cannot be reproduced, such as those generated by devices for atmospheric measurements) is not considered an important aspect of data (peer) review, although reproducibility is crucial to demonstrate the correctness of data and its analysis, upon which researchers' conclusions are based.

In addition to the publishing of research data, researchers started to publish also their computational products, such as software, R algorithms, computational workflows. The publishing is typically performed by means of tools and services that are not meant for scholarly communication but that implement general patterns for collaboration and sharing of computational products. Examples are software repositories (or Version Control Systems (VCSs)) with their hosting services like Github, and language-specific repositories like CRAN (The Comprehensive R Archive Network), the Python Package Index, and CPAN. Github is currently the most popular online software repository and, thanks to the collaboration with Zenodo, DOIs can be assigned to software releases.

In order to proceed on the road of Open Science, research in information science has started to explore and conceive solutions that focus on generating research products whose purpose is sharing "experiments" rather than providing "final results". Such products are digital encodings, executable by machines to reproduce the steps of an experiment or an entire research flow. They extract from the scientific article the concepts of experiment and research flow, making them tangible, machine-processable and shareable products of science. Research in the area of scholarly communication has focused mainly on data (information) models for the representation of digital products encoding experiments, and on tools for generating (and later executing) experiment products that should include all the details of the digital laboratory used to run the experiment and needed for repeatability and reproducibility. Relevant examples of information systems for experiment publishing and reproducibility are protocols.io [15], ArrayExpress [16] and myExperiment [17].

In conclusion, literature is the most common way to make a research flow sharable, since other scientists can discover and read about somebody else's methods, protocols, and findings, but in general it does not allow a complete assessment of the research flow. Some solutions have reproducibility of science as their main objective, rather than peer review, hence they focus on the executable representation of digital objects that encode final successful experiments. Research is still peer-reviewed out of its original context (the digital laboratory) and the concepts of machine-assisted peer-review and ongoing peer-review are not being considered. It would be desirable to have tools for machine-assisted peer-review, built on the very same digital laboratory assets that were used to generated the research products. Although humans would still play a central role in the peer-review process with regards to the evaluation of novelty and impact of a research flow and its final products, such tools would support reviewers facing challenges going beyond their capabilities, like checking the quality of each record in a database, or the conformance to structural and semantic requirements [18]. The ultimate goal should be that of an ongoing peer review of the research flow. In contrast with traditional peer review models, which assess scientific results only once the research activity has been successfully completed, ongoing peer review could also be applied as a sort of monitoring and interim evaluation process. The sharing of intermediate research flow experiments and steps would open up the possibility of publishing negative results. This practice could have a twofold positive effect: on the one hand, the researcher might receive comments and advice from colleagues, on the other hand, she would help the community by suggesting to avoid the same "mistakes" [19].

3 A Framework in Support of Peer-Review of the Research Flow

3.1 Overview

The implementation of a fully-fledged methodology for the peer review of the research flow has requirements (tools and practices) that differ from those identified in Open Science for reproducibility. Reproducibility of science and its underlying principles are indeed crucial to support transparent peer review, but existing practices are not enough to fully address research flow peer review. In order to support this kind of peer review, reviewers should evaluate science by means of a user-friendly environment that transparently relies on the underlying digital laboratory assets, hides their ICT complexity, and gives those guarantees of repeatability and reproducibility recognized by the community.

Depending on the tools and technology available in a digital laboratory, scientists may generate products whose goal is not just sharing "findings" but also sharing "methodologies". Methodology products are digital objects encoding experiments or the research flow itself. As such, they are generated to model the actions performed by the scientists and enable their machine-assisted repetition. The availability of research products at various stages of the research flow (see Fig. 2) makes it possible to introduce peer review stages while the research activity is ongoing. Specifically, depending on the kind of products made available, different degrees of peer review may be reached, to support manual but also machine-supported reproducibility and consequently enforce more transparent and objective research flow peer review practices:

- Manual reproducibility: the digital laboratory generates, or supports researchers at generating:
  - Literature, defined as narrative descriptions of research activities (e.g. scientific articles, books, documentation);
  - Datasets, defined as "digital objects used as evidence of phenomena for the purpose of research or scholarship" [20];
  - Computational products (e.g. software, tools), intended as digital objects encoding business logic/algorithms to perform computational actions over data; Reviewers are provided with the products generated by a research flow, whose steps are reported in an article together with references to the digital laboratory. Reproducibility and research flow assessment strongly depends on humans, both in the way the research flow is described and in the ability of the reviewers, and in general of other researchers, to repeat the same actions.
- Machine reproducibility of experiments: the digital laboratory generates literature, datasets and computational products together with:
  - Experiments, intended as executable digital objects encoding a sequence of actions (e.g. a methodology) that make use of digital laboratory assets to deliver research products. Reviewers are provided with an experiment, inclusive of products and digital assets. Reproducibility can be objectively supported by a machine and finally evaluated, but the assessment of methodology as a whole still depends on humans.

- Machine reproducibility of research flows: the digital laboratory generates literature, datasets, computational products, experiments together with
  - Research flows, intended as digital objects encoding a flow, inclusive of experiments, intermediate, and final products, and their relationships; the research flow may be encoded as a sharable and possibly reproducible digital product. Reviewers are provided with technology to reproduce experiments and research flows. In this scenario, human judgment is supported by machines, which can provide a higher degree of transparency.

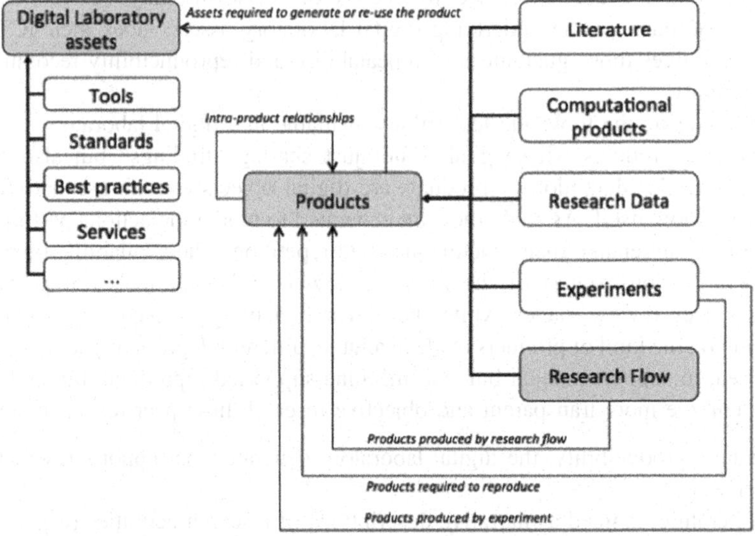

Fig. 2. Entities of the research flow

We propose a framework in support of the peer-review of the research flow. The framework is built around the notion of *research flow templates*. These are representations of the scientific processes in terms of patterns (sequences and cycles) of experiments and relative steps to be peer reviewed. Note that such templates should include only the experiments and steps that are relevant for peer-reviewing the research flow, including their inputs and outputs. In other words, research flow templates are not intended to describe the detailed experiments and steps of a research activity (as would be the case for reproducibility), but are intended to model the subset of actions that are relevant to assess the quality of the research flow.

3.2 Concepts of the Framework

In order for a research community to provide specifications for the peer-reviewable parts of its research flow and be able to build adequate tools in support of reviewers, a simple formal framework capable of describing the structure of the templates for that community should be available. Each template should reflect one particular way of performing science, capturing the steps which should be subject to peer review (a community may have more than one template). At the same time, templates help researchers to comply with certain rules and expectations when producing science. Templates express common behaviour, determine good practices, facilitate reproducibility and transparent evaluation of science. To make an analogy, the structure of a fully-fledged template should reflect the structure of a recipe for cooking. It should specify a list of all the types of products needed from the digital laboratory at each step of the research flow (the ingredients) and should provide a detailed description, possibly machine actionable, of all the steps to be executed (the mixing and the cooking) in order to obtain the research results (the cake).

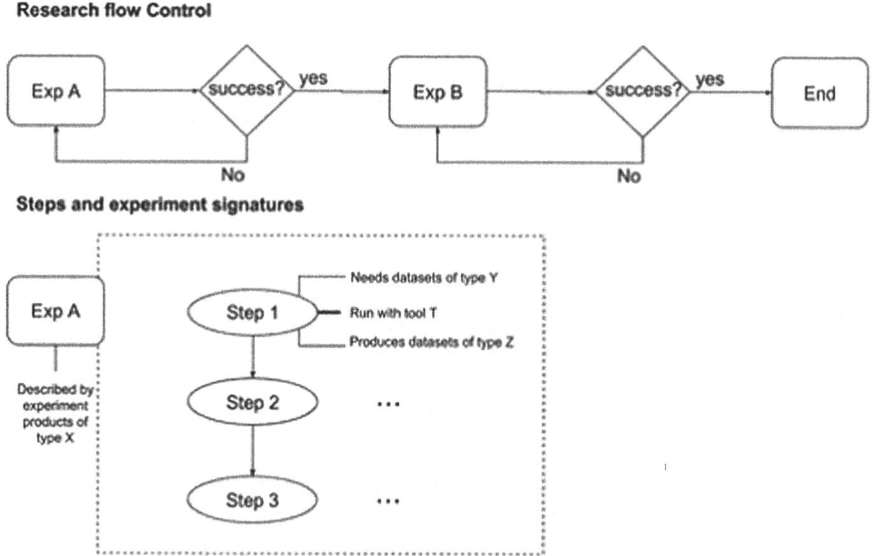

Fig. 3. Research flow templates concepts

A research flow review framework should encompass the following concepts (see Fig. 3):

- Research flow template: the model of research flow to be followed by scientists in terms of experiments, including cycles, conditions, etc. to be peer reviewed;
- Signatures of steps and experiment, intended as:
  - The types of input and output products (e.g. datasets, computational products, documentation, scientific articles);
  - Asset of the digital laboratory (which is not necessary a research product) required for the execution of the step or of the experiment (e.g. tool, service, application);
  - For experiments: the format in which the experiment will be digitally represented and shared with peers.

Referring again to the example in Fig. 1 (geothermal science research), we show in Fig. 4 a more detailed view of the elements of a possible template. The template would specify the input and output of the first step (obtaining data from a Geo database); it would then specify the input (obtained data), the output (the generated model) and the tool (the 3D GeoModeller) for the second step, which could be executed several times, each time generating a "research object" containing all these data; finally, it would specify the input (the final generated model) and the output (the paper to be published) of the last step, which obtains the research results.

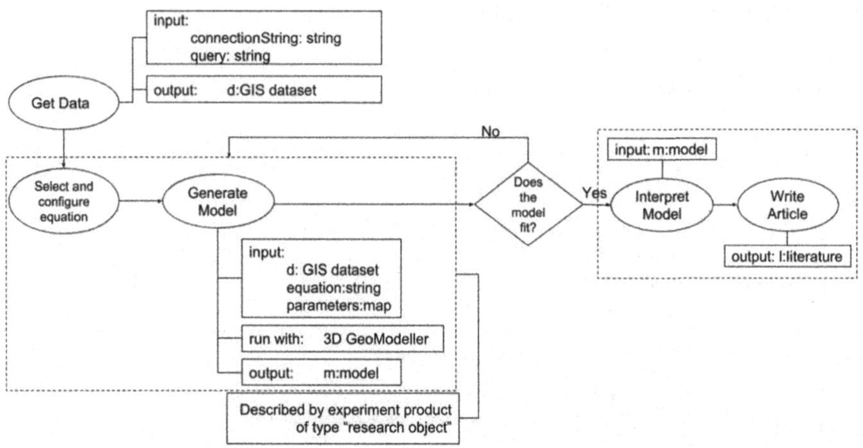

Fig. 4. A possible template for geothermal research

3.3 Building Peer-Review Tools on Top of the Framework

The framework and its templates may become the scaffolding on top of which developers can build tools to support an ongoing peer review of research flows by "real-time hooking" to the underlying digital laboratory, where scientists are carrying out their research activities. Such tools would abstract over the complexity of the research activity and offer user-friendly dashboards to examine the adopted scientific process, explore the ongoing research flow, and evaluate its intermediate experiments and relative products. In a less advanced implementation, such tools might provide scientific process and research flow to reviewers once the research activity has been terminated, inclusive of all intermediate experiments, steps and research products.

For example, consider the scientific process in Fig. 5 [21], which models one experiment repeatedly executed until the research activity is successful. At every cycle, the researcher designs (1) and collects (3) input data, instruments the digital laboratory with processing algorithms (2) and performs some computations (4) to produce output data. Finally, it publishes (5) all such products. In this model, we might assume that the only point for review is the one of "publication" (5), where input data and all the digital laboratory assets are made available. The corresponding research flow review template would model the same cycle and be made of one experiment including a single step of peer review, the one of publication mentioned above. Tools for an ongoing peer review would allow reviewers to select a given execution of the experiment in time, explore and assess input and output data, and re-execute the given step, given the related products. Of course, such tools should be equipped with functionalities to provide feedback and evaluation.

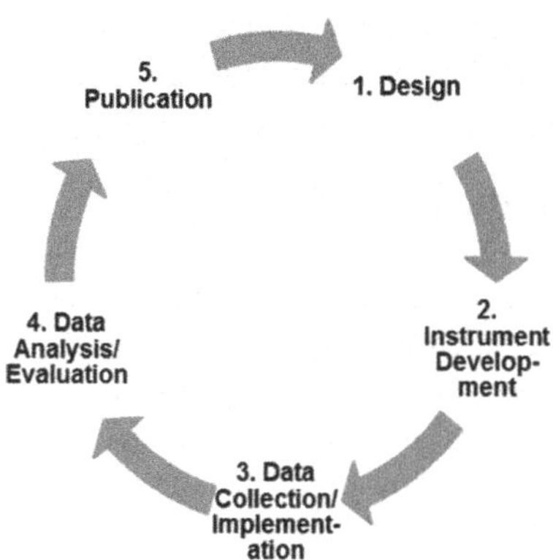

Fig. 5. Research lifecycle adapted from the research process model by Kraker & Lindstaedt

Sharing a framework of this kind allows the realization of research publishing tools and review tools that allow scientists to produce products as expected by the community and allow other scientists to access such products, for reuse, reproducibility, and review. As mentioned above, to be effective and used in practice, such tools should be:

- Integrated with digital laboratory assets used to perform science: scientists should focus on developing their science rather than publishing it; the process of creating research products and methodology products should be delegated as much as possible to machines, together with tracking the history of the actual research flow; digital laboratory assets require research publishing tools (e.g. wrappers, mediators) capable of flanking the experiment functionality they support with functionality for packaging and publishing the relative products, so that review tools can benefit from those;
- Easy to use: user-friendly enough for scientists to access machine-assisted review tools without development skills; reviewers should be able to view the actual research flow, to view its current stage of development, and to apply machine-assisted validation from end-user interfaces;
- Trustworthy: easy to use is a property that should come with guarantees of fairness, typically endorsed by the community adopting research publishing and review tools.

Implementing this vision raises serious challenges, among which a major one is the realization and maintenance of tools for publishing and review, whose cost do not easily find a donor in communities that are typically formed by scientists rather than institutions.

In addition, endorsement of communities and cultural convergence are required towards scholarly communication practices that enable to share, cite, evaluate and assign scientific reward (i.e. author credit) for all the types of research products. In particular, the research communities should understand that, together with the advantages of peer reviewing the research flow and all the research products, there would be an increased burden for the researchers and the reviewers, mitigated as much as possible by the facilities provided by the infrastructure.

4 Conclusion and Future Work

The Open Science paradigm calls for the availability, findability and accessibility of all products generated by a research activity. That practice is a prerequisite for reaching two of the main goals of the Open Science movement: reproducibility and transparent assessment of research activities. In this paper we have described the current practices for the peer review of research flows, which range from traditional peer-review via scientific literature to peer review by reproducibility of digital experiments. We have argued that current practices have reproducibility of science as their main objective and they do not fully address transparent assessment and its features like publishing negative results, supporting peer-review while the research activities are ongoing and enabling machine-assisted peer review.

Foundations of a framework for the peer-review of research flows have been presented. The goal of the framework is to be the bridge between the place where the research is conducted (i.e., the digital laboratory) and the place where the research is published (or in general, made available and accessible). The framework aims at providing the scaffolding on top of which reviewers can evaluate science by means of a user-friendly environment that transparently relies on the underlying digital laboratory assets, hides their ICT complexity, and gives guarantees of repeatability and reproducibility recognized by the community. One of the building blocks of the framework is the notion of research flow template, through which a community can model the research flow to be followed by scientists in terms of experiments, including cycles, conditions, etc. to be peer reviewed. The framework allows communities to define one or more research flow templates, each capturing the steps which should be subject to peer review for a specific type of research activity. Templates are not only useful to peers willing to evaluate a research activity, but also enforce researchers at complying with certain expectations of their community, like best practices and common behaviour.

The framework is theoretically applicable to any field of research adopting digital objects and/or producing digital research outputs. Detailed analysis on the applicability of the framework is ongoing. Specifically, the fields of geothermal energy science and archeology have been considered as representatives of non-fully digital disciplines, which may pose challenges from the modelling point of view, as not all the research assets and products may be available in a digital laboratory.

Acknowledgement. This work is partially funded by the EC project OpenUP (H2020-GARRI-2015-1, Grant Agreement: 710722). The content of this work reflects the views of the author(s). The European Commission is not responsible for any use that may be made of the information it contains.

References

1. European Commission: Validation of the results of the public consultation on Science 2.0: Science in Transition [report]. Brussels: European Commission, Directorate-General for Research and Innovation (2015). http://ec.europa.eu/research/consultations/science-2.0/science_2_0_final_report.pdf
2. European Commission's Directorate-General for Research & Innovation (RTD): Open Innovation, Open Science and Open to the World (2016). https://ec.europa.eu/digital-single-market/en/news/open-innovation-open-science-open-world-vision-europe
3. FOSTER: Open Science Definition. https://www.fosteropenscience.eu/foster-taxonomy/open-science-definition
4. Bechhofer, S., et al.: Why linked data is not enough for scientists. Future Gener. Comput. Syst. **29**(2), 99–611 (2013). https://doi.org/10.1016/j.future.2011.08.004. ISSN 0167-739X
5. Smagorinsky, P.: The method section as conceptual epicenter in constructing social science research reports. Writ. Commun. **25**, 389–411 (2008). http://journals.sagepub.com/doi/pdf/10.1177/0741088308317815
6. Teytelman, L.: We've been itching to share this! Integration of GigaScience and protocols.io is an example of how science publishing should work. Protocols.io news (2016). https://www.protocols.io/groups/protocolsio/news/weve-been-itching-to-share-this-integration-of-gigascience
7. Cotos, E., Huffman, S., Link, S.: A move/step model for methods sections: demonstrating rigour and credibility. Engl. Specif. Purp. **46**, 90–106 (2017). https://doi.org/10.1016/j.esp.2017.01.001. ISSN 0889-4906
8. Center for Open Science: Registered Reports: peer review before results are known to align scientific values and practices. https://cos.io/rr/
9. FORCE11: Guiding Principles for Findable, Accessible, Interoperable and Re-usable Data Publishing Version B1.0 (2014). https://www.force11.org/fairprinciples
10. Wilkinson, M.D., et al.: The FAIR Guiding Principles for scientific data management and stewardship. Sci. Data **3**, 160018 (2016). https://doi.org/10.1038/sdata.2016.18
11. Candela, L., Castelli, D., Manghi, P., Tani, A.: Data journals: a survey. J. Assoc. Inf. Sci. Technol. **66**, 1747–1762 (2015). https://doi.org/10.1002/asi.23358
12. Assante, M., Candela, L., Castelli, D., Tani, A.: Are scientific data repositories coping with research data publishing? Data Sci. J. **15**, 6 (2016). https://doi.org/10.5334/dsj-2016-006
13. Mayernik, M.S., Callaghan, S., Leigh, R., Tedds, J., Worley, S.: Peer review of datasets: when, why, and how. Bull. Amer. Meteor. Soc. **96**, 191–201 (2015). https://doi.org/10.1175/BAMS-D-13-00083.1
14. Carpenter, T.A.: What Constitutes Peer Review of Data: a survey of published peer review guidelines (2017). arXiv preprint arXiv:1704.02236. https://arxiv.org/pdf/1704.02236.pdf
15. Protocols.io team: How to make your protocol more reproducible, discoverable, and user-friendly (2017). http://dx.doi.org/10.17504/protocols.io.g7vbzn6
16. Tang, A.: ArrayExpress at EMBL-EBI - quality first! Repositive blog (2017). https://blog.repositive.io/arrayexpress-at-embl-ebi-quality-first/

17. De Roure, D., Goble, C., Stevens, R.: The design and realisation of the myExperiment Virtual Research Environment for social sharing of workflows. Future Gener. Comput. Syst. **25**(5), 561–567 (2009). https://doi.org/10.1016/j.future.2008.06.010
18. Shanahan, D.: A peerless review? Automating methodological and statistical review (2016). https://blogs.biomedcentral.com/bmcblog/2016/05/23/peerless-review-automating-methodological-statistical-review/
19. Di Leo, A., Risi, E., Biganzoli, L.: No pain, no gain… What we can learn from a trial reporting negative results. Ann. Oncol. **28**(4), 678–680 (2017). https://doi.org/10.1093/annonc/mdx065
20. Borgman, C.L.: Big Data, Little Data, No Data: Scholarship in the Networked World. MIT Press, Cambridge (2015)
21. Kraker, P., Bachleitner, R., et al.: Deliverable D4.1 – Practices evaluation and mapping: methods, tools and user needs (2017). http://openup-h2020.eu/wp-content/uploads/2017/01/OpenUP_D4.1_Practices-evaluation-and-mapping.-Methods-tools-and-user-needs.pdf

A Practical Workflow for an Open Scientific Lifecycle Project: EcoNAOS

Annalisa Minelli[1(✉)], Alessandro Sarretta[1], Alessandro Oggioni[2], Caterina Bergami[3], and Alessandra Pugnetti[1]

[1] CNR-ISMAR Venezia, Arsenale - Tesa 104, Castello 2737/F, 30122 Venezia, Italy
annalisa.minelli@ve.ismar.cnr.it
[2] CNR-IREA, Via Bassini, 15, 20133 Milano, Italy
[3] CNR-ISMAR Bologna, Via Gobetti 101, 40129 Bologna, Italy
http://www.ismar.cnr.it/
http://www.irea.cnr.it/

Abstract. This paper represents a review of the practical application, work done and near-future perspectives of an open scientific lifecycle model. The EcoNAOS (Ecological North Adriatic Open Science Observatory System) project is an example of the application of Open Science principles to long term marine research. For long term marine research we intend here all the marine research projects based on Long Term Ecological Data. In the paper, the structure of the lifecycle, modeled over Open Science principles, will be presented. The project develops through some fundamental steps: database correction and harmonization, metadata collection, data exploitation by publication on a web infrastructure and planning of dissemination moments. The project also foresees the setting up of a data citation and versioning model (adapted to dynamic databases) and a final guidelines production, illustrating the whole process in detail. The advancement state of these steps will be reviewed. Results achieved and expected outcomes will be explained with a particular focus on the upcoming work.

Keywords: Open science · Open data · Data citation and versioning

1 Introduction

The main aim of this paper is to describe an application of Open Science principles to marine research.

During the last years, the whole scientific community has expressed an increasing interest in Open Science. This is maybe due to the wider accessibility of scientific research products when shared using Open Access instruments [1–4]. For scientific research products we intend here a various range of outcomes (and inputs) from a research project such as, for example, scientific data, research ideas, metadata, experimental results, etc. The EcoNAOS project [5] (which stays for Ecological North Adriatic Open Science Observatory System) is based

P. Manghi et al. (Eds.): IRCDL 2019, CCIS 988, pp. 209–221, 2019.
https://doi.org/10.1007/978-3-030-11226-4_17

on the testing and application of Open Science principles in marine long term ecological research. The principles we want to put the accent on are: free access to scientific research, research reproducibility, use of all available knowledge at early stage, sharing knowledge as early as possible [6] which could lead to social and economical benefits (ideas producers are also users, enabling new working models, new social relationships, saving money and time [7,8]), other than increase transparency of research and make cooperation between researchers as easy as possible. These principles are known and accepted at international level, and more specifically by the European Union, which defines the guidelines for Open Science application in scientific research and the FAIR principles applied to research data management [9]: data must be Findable, Accessible, Interoperable and Reusable (FAIR). Long Term Ecological Research (LTER) is a branch of ecological research aiming at collecting ecological data, from decadal to centennial scale, to understand environmental changes across the globe detecting trends, preventing and solving environmental and socio-ecological problems through question and problem-driven research. This data is collected and shared, when possible, by international network (ILTER) composed by ecological sites over four continents. Sites are then grouped and managed both at continent scale (eLTER) and national scale (LTER-Italy). LTER-Italy counts 79 research sites including terrestrial, freshwater and marine ecosystems distributed throughout the country, with a marked trans-ecodomain approach.

In this work we applied Open Science principles and the EcoNAOS model to the LTER macrosite "Northern Adriatic Sea", registered into the Dynamic Ecological Information Management System - Site and dataset registry (DEIMS-SDR), created to collect information about geographical macroregions (https://data.lter-europe.net/deims/92fd6fad-99cd-4972-93bd-c491f0be1301).

1.1 EcoNAOS as a Workflow

When dealing with the usual research lifecycle, we think to a linear process involving: research project design, data collection, data analysis, data preservation and curation, presentation of results. More recently, the "shape" of this process has been evolved from linear to circular [10,11] involving a research review phase which allows the initial project to be corrected and to perform all the other phases subsequently.

The EcoNAOS project has been conceived as a spiral-shaped workflow, which represents the Open Research project lifecycle (Fig. 1). This lifeycle is composed by many different phases of sharing research products: inputs (research ideas), data, metadata, results, procedures, code, and reviews in order to establish a flux of knowledge between the project and the scientific world. In particular, an open peer review process allows the reviewers to be identified and the review accounted as research act [12].

The EcoNAOS project was funded by the RITMARE (Italian Research for the Sea) flagship project of the Italian Ministry of Education and Research (http://www.ritmare.it/) which had, among others, the aim to create an homogeneous and coordinate marine observatory system. The North Adriatic Sea

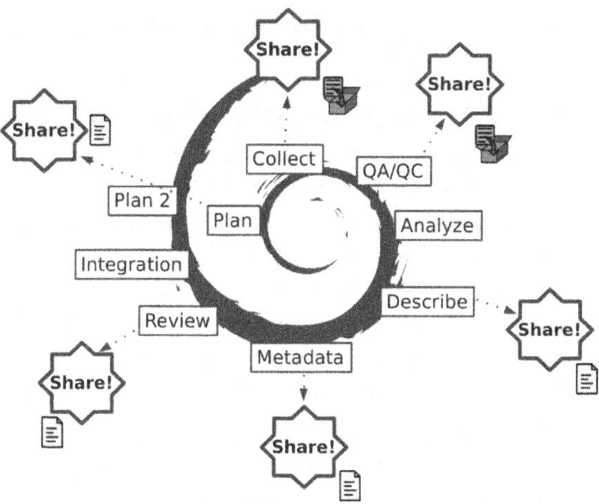

Fig. 1. The Open research project lifecycle.

(NAS) represents the perfect area for a marine observatory because of its transnational characteristics, the numerous interests involved (touristic, commercial, economical) from public and private actors and the presence of marine protected areas. Moreover, data from this zone is diverse in typology (single point observations, time series, samples collected in field or analyzed in laboratory), spatial and temporal coverage. So, the more heterogeneous data is, the more it is complex to manage. In this way, we obtain a wide range of possible situations that could occur in a marine observatory.

CRUISE	STATION	mon/day/yr	hh:mm	Long	Lat	Depth	TEMP	SAL	DENS	pH	Alkal Tot	Oxyg	Ox%
PP/1	B	04/12/1965	9:33	12.68	45.33	0.5	13.122	29.610	22.220	8.422	2.810	6.880	115.82
PP/1	B	04/12/1965	9:33	12.68	45.33	5.0	12.345	35.66	27.040	8.330	2.740	6.390	110.42
PP/1	B	04/12/1965	9:33	12.68	45.33	10.0	12.450	35.43	26.850	8.329	2.710	6.590	113.91
PP/1	B	04/12/1965	9:33	12.68	45.33	20.0	12.136	38.01	28.920	8.333	2.680	6.410	112.15
PP/1	C	04/12/1965	12:20	12.86	45.28	0.5	12.251	35.44	26.890	8.241	2.730	6.290	108.28
PP/1	C	04/12/1965	12:20	12.86	45.28	5.0	12.237	35.46	26.930	8.331	2.690	6.320	108.80
PP/1	C	04/12/1965	12:20	12.86	45.28	10.0	11.155	37.79	28.950	8.312	2.730	6.430	110.03
PP/1	C	04/12/1965	12:20	12.86	45.28	20.0	12.301	37.92	28.810	8.335	2.740	6.490	113.85
PP/2	A	04/28/1965	6:42	12.48	45.40	0.5	12.266	33.0	25.030	8.197	2.919	6.070	102.80
PP/2	A	04/28/1965	6:42	12.48	45.40	1.0	12.370	33.39	25.300	8.316	2.892	6.110	103.94
PP/2	A	04/28/1965	6:42	12.48	45.40	5.0	12.437	35.39	26.980	8.255	2.779	6.120	105.89
PP/2	A	04/28/1965	6:42	12.48	45.40	10.0	12.225	37.3	28.350	8.277	2.753	5.780	99.76
PP/2	B	04/28/1965	9:10	12.68	45.33	0.5	12.485	32.9	24.890	8.275	3.014	6.510	110.64
PP/2	B	04/28/1965	9:10	12.68	45.33	5.0	12.432	33.78	25.600	8.225	2.907	6.490	110.84
PP/2	B	04/28/1965	9:10	12.68	45.33	10.0	11.917	37.21	28.340	8.221	2.734	6.200	107.35
PP/2	B	04/28/1965	9:10	12.68	45.33	20.0	10.502	37.72	29.000	8.217	2.758	6.330	106.75

Fig. 2. Example of observations stored in the database with specification of cruise and station code, date, hour, coordinates, water depth where the observation was collected, and parameters.

1.2 LTER Marine Data in the Northern Adriatic Sea

The database on which we applied the EcoNAOS model is a collection of LTER data in the LTER_EU_IT_012 (NAS) site. Observations are both abiotic measurements and plankton (phyto- and zoo-) counting, collected during oceanographic cruises (data in a specific time range and heterogeneously distributed over a geographical zone) or by sensors (continuous data in a fixed geographical position). The time range of these observations spans from 1965 to 2015 and the first ones came from on board journals, until 1990, when data was passed in an unique spreadsheet. Now the database counts about 36000 observations of 22 parameters, intended as a separate datasets, reporting date and time of the observation, name of the sampling station (where present) and geographical coordinates. An extract of the database can be seen in Fig. 2.

The database is dynamic, because it is always growing due to new observations from cruises, sensors or laboratory analysis.

2 Implementation

The application of Open Science principles to the LTER marine database of the NAS passes through some fundamental steps:

Task 1: data harmonization since the database is heterogeneous it must be harmonized before being exploited for any analysis or being published for sharing;

Task 2: metadata collection since the database covers a time range of 50 years, methods and instruments changed over time. It is necessary to collect all available information regarding data, methods and tools in order to evaluate reliability of data for any possible purpose;

Task 3: data exploitation a first exploitation of data is accomplished through the upload of data into GET-IT (Geoinformation Enable Toolkit StarterkIT [17]), an interoperable suite software for enabling researchers to share data and metadata in a SDI (Spatial Data Infrastructure). GET-IT allows the management, sharing and visualization of observational data;

Task 4: sharing and dissemination in coherence with the Open Science framing, it is fundamental to plan sharing moments, intended here not only as publication of research inputs and outputs, but also the dissemination of new concepts and methods (e.g. by participating in meetings and conference) and the promotion of exchanges with other researchers, potentially interested into the same topic, which could pick new ideas for their work and, conversely, improve EcoNAOS project;

Task 5: data citation since our database is dynamic (e.g new observations are added by different people), data citation can not be intended in a traditional way. Anyway we could perform queries on data and cite only a portion of the database. It is therefore fundamental to set up versioning methods for data citation;

Task 6: guidelines preparation preparation of guidelines could be useful for summarizing the EcoNAOS experience, contributing to the improvement of

Openness of scientific workflows and FAIRness of research data in future research projects.

In the next paragraphs we will go deep into the work done with particular focus on tasks to address or currently in progress in order to better understand how we can face specific issues and define a fair starting point for near-future work.

2.1 Completed Tasks

Task 1: Data Harmonization. Probably due to some errors in transcribing old data from on board journals to spreadsheet and to some inconsistencies in the name of sampling stations, the database was quite heterogeneous. First of all, the names of the stations were homogenized maintaining the most recently used station codes. Then we corrected the position of the points wrongly located on land into their right position at sea by matching the sample station names. These procedures have been executed in GRASS GIS [13] and vector layers of sampling stations and 3D layer of observations have been produced. The whole procedure has been automatized by means of a Python code, released under GNU GPL v.3 license and available on GitHub at the following link: https://github.com/CNR-ISMAR/econaos/tree/master.

Task 2: Metadata Collection. With a database covering a 50 years period, methods and instruments changed over time, in terms of unit of measures, standard errors associated to observations and so on, which could lead to database inconsistency when treated as a unique element. With the aim to prevent this data inconsistency, we collected all possible metadata associated to instruments and data. We started from the historical cruises examining instruments on board of research vessels: we produced some technical reports [14] listing all the instruments, units of measures and other elements qualifying data reliability in relation to the period/method of the observation. We then examined the whole database including more recent data and, for each parameter, we listed the instruments/methods used in time. All this information is stored into the database and associated to each single observation. However, no parameter values were manipulated and recalculated due to changes in the unit of measure, in order to preserve original data following the principle to "Keep raw data raw" suggested in best practices works [15,16]. A summary of parameters and sensors is reported in Table 1. These methods/instruments have been also published in GET-IT infrastructure and described using SensorML language.

Task 3: Data Exploitation. We decided to upload a first set of data in the GET-IT platform, in order to share them in an interoperable and standard way, compliant with INSPIRE Directive (https://inspire.ec.europa.eu/about-inspire/563) and Open Geospatial Consortium - OGC (http://www.opengeospatial.org/about). GET-IT has been developed for the broader RITMARE project and it is a distributed and interoperable SDI that allows at

Table 1. Review of methods/sensors used in time for each parameter of the database.

Parameter	Nr. of samples	Temporal coverage	Current method or sensor	Unit of measure	Previous method or sensor
Transparency	7840	1965–2015	Secchi Disk	m	-
Temperature	35594	1965–2015	CTD	C	Tilting thermometer
Salinity	35639	1965–2015	CTD	PSU	Autosal salinometer; Salinometer Bisset-Berman; Mohr-Knudsen Titration
Density	28253	1965–2015	Derivation parameter	Kg/mc	-
pH	12833	1965–2011	CTD	-	Strickland and Parsons; Grasshoff 1999; Beckman Zeromatic
Alkalinity	2948	1965–2002	Titrino titration	meq/l	-
Oxygen	12176	1965–2012	CTD	cc/l	Winkler titration; Methron titration; Titrino titration
N-NH3	10401	1965–2015	Easy Chem Plus	mol/l	Strickland and Parsons; Grasshoff 1983; Grashoff 1999
N-NO2	10478	1965–2015	Easy Chem Plus	mol/l	Strickland and Parsons; Grasshoff 1983; Grashoff 1999
N-NO3	10545	1965–2015	Easy Chem Plus	mol/l	Strickland and Parsons; Grasshoff 1983; Grashoff 1999
P-PO4	10448	1965–2015	Easy Chem Plus	mol/l	Strickland and Parsons; Grasshoff 1983; Grashoff 1999
Si-SiO4	10669	1965–2015	Easy Chem Plus	mol/l	Strickland and Parsons; Grasshoff 1983; Grashoff 1999
Chlorophyll-a	11121	1965–2015	Spettrofluorimeter Holm Hansen	g/l	Spettrophotometer Perkin Elmer SCOR
Pheopygments	5960	1979–2015	Spettrofluorimeter Holm Hansen	mg/l	Spettrophotometer Perkin Elmer SCOR
Phytoplankton	2949	1977–2015	Inverted microscope	Cell./l	-
Diatoms	2949	1977–2015	Inverted microscope	Cell./l	-
Dinoflagellates	2949	1977–2015	Inverted microscope	Cell./l	-
Coccolithophores	2949	1977–2015	Inverted microscope	Cell./l	-

sharing data and instruments. Using GET-IT, we can visualize at the same time different types of spatial data referring to one or more geographical areas or create graphs of available data for specific sampling station and sensors (Fig. 3). It is possible to experience GET-IT capabilities following this link: http://demo2.get-it.it/.

Task 4: Sharing and Dissemination As showed in Fig. 1, almost all the steps of a research lifecycle can be shared or participated. At the present time we took some initiatives in order to share our work:

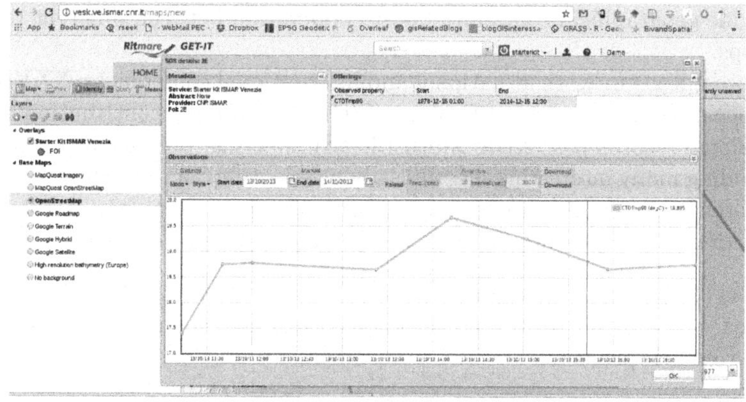

Fig. 3. A graph created by querying temperature data on "2E" sampling station.

- We published a "research idea" [5] as statement of our project in RIO journal (Research Ideas and Outcomes). We have chosen this specific journal for many reasons:
  - it is Open Access;
  - it includes a wide range of publication types that cover all the research life-cycle;
  - it implements an open peer review process where reviews are open, allowing research to be transparent and anyone from outside the process to comment;
  - reviews have a DOI, so that the review work is recognized and directly citable (e.g. [18,19]).
- We shared the code used to harmonize the database. A data sample, pseudocode, the Python code and a brief description, are available under GNU GPL v.3 license and in the release 0 of the code [20].
- We shared a subset of data by publishing in GET-IT the superficial (at the sea surface) value for each observation and for each parameter in the database. Metadata of the sensors are also shared in GET-IT, using Sensor Metadata Language (SensorML) edited by using the EDI interface [21,22], which is a powerful metadata editor, developed for RITMARE project as well. These metadata are accessible following this link: http://vesk.ve.ismar.cnr.it/sensors/.
- We organised a workshop involving other researchers from the NAS LTER_EU_IT_012 macrosite in order to present our work and to understand their feelings towards Open Science and Open Access. There is a real interest in these themes but there's still some fear in losing intellectual property of data. Anyway, researchers manifested their interest in sharing a portion of their data in order to analyze the variation of an index (TRIX, [23]) along Mediterranean Sea. This experiment is currently ongoing and it is conceived in order to show how Open Data and Open Science can speed up analyses

on wide geographical zones and boost cooperation between different research groups.
- We presented our work at national and international conferences: XXVII Conference of Italian Society of Ecology (SItE) publishing a contribution on congressional records [24]; RDA Ninth Plenary Meeting, presenting a poster and attending many interesting meetings about scientific data handling; EurOcean conference on ocean observation systems, presenting a poster and we wrote an article for a book about Responsible Research and Innovation [25].

A schema of these dissemination actions is reported in Fig. 4. There, it is possible to evidence that some general steps reported in Fig. 1 changed in reason of the specific research project.

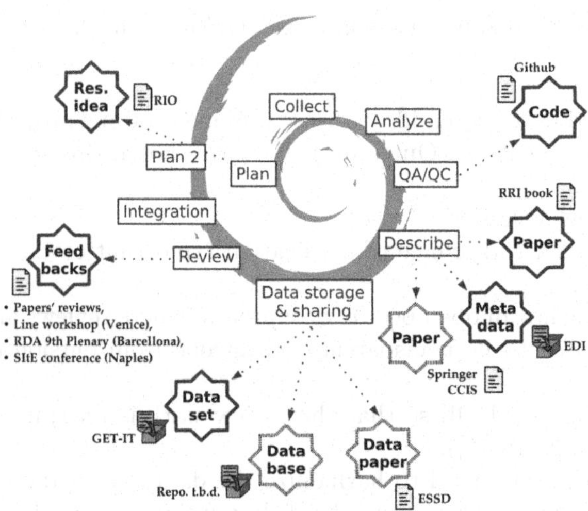

Fig. 4. The Open Research Project Lifecycle related to LTER data in the Northern Adriatic Sea macrosite. Filled-line callouts identify dissemination actions already taken, dotted-line callouts identify dissemination actions in progress.

2.2 Ongoing Works

Task 4: Sharing and Dissemination We are currently writing a datapaper and planning to release the entire database in Open Access mode. The database released will be as compliant as possible with the FAIR data principles. For this purpose, we chose Earth System Science Data, which is an Open Access journal allowing scientific data publication in repositories with a persistent identifier, with an open license (e.g. CC-BY: anyone must be free to copy, distribute, transmit, and adapt the data sets as long as he/she gives credit to the original authors), accessible over the Web, and long-term availability.

Task 5: Data Citation The study of data citation comes from library science, lately it has been extended to the more general data science.

Our database is a dynamic database since it changes as long as we collect new observations recorded by sensors and during cruises. Despite the different available technological solutions, it is relatively easy to share a standard database, conversely dynamic databases rises some new questions:

- how to make data available for citation? if the database changes, citation must change accordingly;
- how to cite a portion of a dataset and how to cite aggregated data?
- how to make a citation persistent if the original database changes?
- how to update the reference to the database, if data changed?
- what is the threshold to define a "substantial" change in the database, to the point that its reference must change accordingly?

Facing these questions is a relatively recent issue, in fact data citation itself is a quite recent theme, even if the importance of data publishing with particular attention to data reference is fairly recognized [26,27]. A review on the evolution in time of data citation is formulated by Altman and Crosas [28] and some fundamental concepts are expressed by Silvello [29].

Our database had two main characteristics: it is dynamic and contains oceanographic data.

Dynamic database citation case has been recently afforded from RDA working group on dynamic database citation which first created a set of 14 rules [30] in order to create an automated mechanism able to:

- identify and cite databases or portions of it;
- cite and retrieve data also in past versions of database;
- be interoperable.

These rules contain recommendations on how to prepare data and store queries, how to persistently identify datasets, how to retrieve portions of database in a client-server architecture and what to focus on if database infrastructure is modified. Another strength point of RDA WG on data citation rules is that their application is in continuous testing phase on real evolving databases. The monitoring of rules applications on these pilot projects will lead to rules improvement and adaptation based on specific and generic requirements. A framework for citing evolving data, by quantification of the changes in the database as long as new data are added, is formulated in [31,32]. Citation of aggregated data has been also afforded by Baker, Amsi and Uytvanck [33].

Oceanographic data citation is matter of a literature work collecting all the pilot projects on this theme [34]. Urban et al. not only identify projects but also Open Access journals which follow specific rules for database release or Open Access Servers and repositories (e.g. Earth System Science Data journal, PANGEA repository and the Woods Hole Open Access Server). The Ocean Link project [35] focuses on data discovery instead and it is a web platform which identifies "links between data centers, digital repositories, and professional societies to enhance discovery, enable collaboration, and begin to assess research contribution" on oceanographic projects. Particularly interesting is the use of semantic-based systems for data discovery. A very specific study on Long Term Oceanographic data practices is conducted by Baker and Chandler [36]. This work focuses on growth of information infrastructures that support multi-scale sampling, data repositories, and data integration, comparing two projects. The work also recognize the importance of a global information management strategy (long and short term) for any long term oceanographic research project.

Guidelines Preparation. Another task to tackle is the preparation of guidelines, which could both resume and detail our experience. In fact, the scope of these guidelines is both to facilitate (easily explain) and guide (detailing phases) researchers through an application of Open Science principles to their research projects. In general, we suppose we could categorize actions in two groups:

- acting generically on process: all the actions aimed at making project more "Open Science compliant". Examples are the release of source code, drafting of data policy, choice of journals with open peer review, etc.
- acting specifically on data: actions aimed at making data as FAIR as possible. For example operations on database structure, semantic harmonization, efforts on interoperability, etc.

Obviously the guidelines preparation can only be faced when all the other tasks are completed, in order to oversee the entire process when the application of Open Science principles is "complete".

3 Conclusions and Future Perspectives

The EcoNAOS project represents an attempt to apply Open Science principles not only to specific and sporadic research products but to a whole research project and it proposes a complete workflow from the formulation of a research idea to the review of the whole project by the scientific community. It is specifically conceived around marine science and LTER data but the application of these principles can be extended to projects in any research topic and involving any kind of data. Moreover, the projects envisages a number of moments to share ideas, material and revisions with other researchers and the scientific community: this allowed us not only to facilitate exchanges with researchers working on the same topics, but also to deepen into explicit and implicit barriers to a complete application of Open Science principles in science. Results about this theme are in an analysis phase and soon to come. EcoNAOS does not want to overturn previous researchers' habits, but since Open Science must be helpful and facilitate research, our work wants to provide an example of Open Science application at everyday research work. This model might not be exhaustive or complying with all the possible necessities, so it might be completed and adapted according to specific requirements.

After having collected above cited literature information and experiences on dynamic database citation and versioning, we plan to focus on data citation and versioning task in the near future [37–39].

For sure, the interest on deepen this argument is exploring new perspectives of data citation of complex data in format and substance. For example, for geographical data, there are not many studies involving data citation and OGC standards. From a data analysis point of view, it could be interesting to study citation methods of complex data which must be ordered, extracted and aggregated with the aim to be distributed via web following up an OGC standard request. These requests often involve not only one type of data, but multiple types of data (numeric, geographical, metadata, semantic).

Moreover, aggregated data citation is still an open research topic and there are not standard and well-defined procedures. In our specific case, since we want to redistribute data (or portions of data) following up a request from a client, the definition of a URI (Uniform Resource Identifier) is a central point. Then, once the URI is defined, the data attribution is also a central element. Another interesting point is that, while data citation science is exploring new and always growing perspectives in other fields (bibliometrics, economy, music, biology), there are still few significant experiences and applications in long term series of spatially distributed oceanographic and ecological data. Consequently, there are not standards to cite oceanographic datasets. This could represent a good starting point for a new and different research topic. Since this seems to be a wide and still open theme, we propose, for this specific task, to enlarge the discussion and to deepen in parallel the argument of oceanographic and ecological data citation.

References

1. Stevan, H., Brody, T.: Comparing the impact of open access (OA) vs. non-OA articles in the same journals. D-lib Mag. **10**(6) (2004). https://doi.org/10.1045/june2004-harnad
2. Hajjem, C., Harnad, S., Gingras, Y.: Ten-year cross-disciplinary comparison of the growth of open access and how it increases research citation impact. arXiv preprint cs/0606079 (2006)
3. Gargouri, Y., et al.: Self-selected or mandated, open access increases citation impact for higher quality research. PloS one **5**(10), 13636 (2010). https://doi.org/10.1371/journal.pone.0013636
4. McKiernan, E.C., et al.: How open science helps researchers succeed. eLife **5** (2016). https://doi.org/10.7554/elife.16800
5. Minelli, A., et al.: The project EcoNAOS: vision and practice towards an open approach in the Northern Adriatic Sea ecological observatory. Res. Ideas Outcomes **4** (2018). https://doi.org/10.3897/rio.4.e24224
6. European Commission: Open innovation, open science, open to the world - a vision for Europe. (2016) RTD-PUBLICATIONS@ec.europa.eu [ISBN 978-92-79-57346-0] 10.2777/061652

7. David, P.A.: The economic logic of "open science" and the balance between private property rights and the public domain in scientific data and information: a primer. The Role of the Public Domain in Scientific and Technical Data and Information 19–34 (2003)
8. Peters, M.A.: Open education and the open science economy. Yearb. Nat. Soc. Study Educ. **108**(2), 203–225 (2009)
9. European Commission: H2020 Programme - Guidelines on FAIR Data Management in Horizon 2020 (2016). http://ec.europa.eu/research/participants/data/ref/h2020/grants_manual/hi/oa_pilot/h2020-hi-oa-data-mgt_en.pdf
10. Pennock, M.: Digital curation: a life-cycle approach to managing and preserving usable digital information. Libr. Arch. **1**, 34–45 (2007)
11. Ingram, C.: How and why you should manage your research data: a guide for researchers. An introduction to engaging with research data management processes, JISC (2016)
12. Tennant, J.P., et al.: A multi-disciplinary perspective on emergent and future innovations in peer review. F1000Research **6**, 1151 (2017). https://doi.org/10.12688/f1000research.12037.3
13. GRASS Development Team: Geographic Resources Analysis Support System (GRASS) Software, Version 7.2. Open Source Geospatial Foundation (2017). http://grass.osgeo.org
14. Scovacricchi, T.: Technical recovery of material and methods applied in the cruises of 1965, 1966, 1978/79 as described by P. Franco (1970, 1972, 1982). Internal Report, CNR-ISMAR Venezia (Italy), (2017)
15. Borer, E.T., Seabloom, E.W., Jones, M.B., Schildhauer, M.: Some simple guidelines for effective data management. Bull. Ecol. Soc. Am. **90**(2), 205–214 (2009). https://doi.org/10.1890/0012-9623-90.2.205
16. Hart, E.M., et al.: Ten simple rules for digital data storage. PLoS Comput. Biol. **12**(10), e1005097 (2016). https://doi.org/10.1371/journal.pcbi.1005097
17. Oggioni, A., et al.: Interoperability in marine sensor networks through SWE services: the RITMARE experience, pp. 200–223 (2017) https://doi.org/10.4018/978-1-5225-0700-0.ch009
18. Marchesini, I.: Review of: the project EcoNAOS: vision and practice towards an open approach in the Northern Adriatic Sea ecological observatory. Res. Ideas Outcomes **4**, e24224 (2018). https://doi.org/10.3897/rio.4.e24224.r72863
19. Peterseil, J.: Review of: the project EcoNAOS: vision and practice towards an open approach in the Northern Adriatic Sea ecological observatory. Res. Ideas Outcomes **4**, e24224 (2018). https://doi.org/10.3897/rio.4.e24224.r72862
20. Minelli A: Data Harmonisation for EcoNAOS project (Version 0). https://doi.org/10.5281/zenodo.1416102
21. Pavesi, F., et al.: EDI - a template-driven metadata editor for research data. J. Open Res. Software **4**(1) (2016). https://doi.org/10.5334/jors.106
22. Tagliolato, P., Oggioni, A., Fugazza, C., Pepe, M., Carrara, P.: Sensor metadata blueprints and computer-aided editing for disciplined SensorML. IOP Conf. Ser. Earth Environ. Sci. **34**(1), 012036–012036 (2016). https://doi.org/10.1088/1755-1315/34/1/012036
23. Vollenweider, R.A., Giovanardi, F., Montanari, G., Rinaldi, A.: Characterization of the trophic conditions of marine coastal waters with special reference to the NW Adriatic Sea: proposal for a trophic scale, turbidity and generalized water quality index. Environ. Official J. Int. Environ. Soc. **9**(3), 329–357 (1998)

24. Minelli, A., et al.: Handling Long Term Ecological marine data: an Open Science approach. La ricerca ecologica in un mondo che cambia. Libro degli Abstract, XXVII Congresso Nazionale della Società Italiana di Ecologia (2017)
25. L'Astorina A., Di Fiore M.: Scienziati in affanno? Ricerca e Innovazione Responsabili (RRI) in teoria e nelle pratiche. 180 p. Cnr Edizioni. ISBN 978 88 8080 250 1, (2018). https://doi.org/10.26324/2018RRICNRBOOK
26. Wood, J., et al.: Riding the wave: How Europe can gain from the rising tide of scientific data. European Union (2010)
27. Ball, A., Duke, M.: How to Cite Datasets and Link to Publications. DCC How-to Guides, Edinburgh: Digital Curation Centre (2015). http://www.dcc.ac.uk/resources/how-guides
28. Altman, M., Crosas, M.: The evolution of data citation: from principles to implementation. IAssist Quarterly **37**, 62–70 (2013)
29. Silvello, G.: Theory and practice of data citation. J. Assoc. Inf. Sci. Technol. **69**(1), 6–20 (2018)
30. Rauber, A., et al.: Data citation of evolving data: recommendations of the working group on data citation (WGDC). Result of the RDA Data Citation WG **20** (2015)
31. Proll, S., Rauber, A.: Scalable data citation in dynamic, large databases: model and reference implementation. In: 2013 IEEE International Conference on Big Data. IEEE (2013)
32. Proell, S., Rauber, A.: A scalable framework for dynamic data citation of arbitrary structured data. In: 3rd International Conference on Data Management Technologies and Applications (DATA2014) (2014). https://doi.org/10.5220/0004991802230230
33. Rauber, A., Amsi, A.: Uytvanck, Dv., Pröll, S.: Identification of Reproducible Subsets for Data Citation. Sharing and Re-Use. Bulletin of IEEE Technical Committee on Digital Libraries, Special Issue on Data Citation, 6–15 (2016)
34. Urban, E., et al.: Pilot projects for publishing and citing ocean data. Eos, Trans. Am. Geophys. Union **93**(43), 425–426 (2012)
35. Narock, T., et al.: The oceanlink project. In: 2014 IEEE International Conference on Big Data (Big Data). IEEE (2014)
36. Baker, K.S., Chandler, C.L.: Enabling long-term oceanographic research: changing data practices, information management strategies and informatics. Deep Sea Res. Part II: Topical Stud. Oceanograp. **55**(18–19), 2132–2142 (2008)
37. Angelini, M., Fazzini, V., Ferro, N., Santucci, G., Silvello, G.: CLAIRE: a combinatorial visual analytics system for information retrieval evaluation. Inf. Process. Manage. **54**(6), 1077–1100 (2018)
38. Alawini, A., Davidson, S.B., Silvello, G., Tannen, V., Wu, Y.: Data citation: a new provenance challenge. IEEE Data Eng. Bull. **41**(1), 27–38 (2018)
39. Agosti, M., Ferro, N., Silvello, G.: Digital libraries: from digital resources to challenges in scientific data sharing and re-use. In: Flesca, S., Greco, S., Masciari, E., Saccà, D. (eds.) A Comprehensive Guide Through the Italian Database Research Over the Last 25 Years. SBD, vol. 31, pp. 27–41. Springer, Cham (2018). https://doi.org/10.1007/978-3-319-61893-7_2

Data Deposit in a CKAN Repository: A Dublin Core-Based Simplified Workflow

Yulia Karimova(✉), João Aguiar Castro, and Cristina Ribeiro

INESC TEC, Faculty of Engineering, University of Porto, Rua Dr. Roberto Frias, 4200-465 Porto, Portugal
ylaleo@gmail.com, joaoaguiarcastro@gmail.com, mcr@fe.up.pt

Abstract. Researchers are currently encouraged by their institutions and the funding agencies to deposit data resulting from projects. Activities related to research data management, namely organization, description, and deposit, are not obvious for researchers due to the lack of knowledge on metadata and the limited data publication experience. Institutions are looking for solutions to help researchers organize their data and make them ready for publication. We consider here the deposit process for a CKAN-powered data repository managed as part of the IT services of a large research institute. A simplified data deposit process is illustrated here by means of a set of examples where researchers describe their data and complete the publication in the repository. The process is organised around a Dublin Core-based dataset deposit form, filled by the researchers as preparation for data deposit. The contacts with researchers provided the opportunity to gather feedback about the Dublin Core metadata and the overall experience. Reflections on the ongoing process highlight a few difficulties in data description, but also show that researchers are motivated to get involved in data publication activities.

Keywords: Research data management · Metadata · Dublin Core · CKAN · Data publication

1 Introduction

Research data management (RDM) is becoming an important activity for researchers. To promote auditability of results, access, reuse, and transparency, the deposit of research data is required in the grant applications to most funding agencies [10]. Moreover, Data Management Plans (DMP) are also required, to provide detailed information about the project, indicating the context and objectives, method, tools and techniques of data collection, the form of preparation, how data will be described, preserved, and shared, as well as issues related to reuse [3,6]. Therefore, competence in RDM is considered an essential skill for good scientific practice.

It has been observed that researchers show interest in publishing data [22], thus having their work discovered, reused and cited in essential [24]. Yet,

P. Manghi et al. (Eds.): IRCDL 2019, CCIS 988, pp. 222–235, 2019.
https://doi.org/10.1007/978-3-030-11226-4_18

researchers still face several difficulties in RDM activities, such as insufficient experience, lack of knowledge on metadata standards, inadequate tools for deposit and description of the data, lack of time, and lack of perceived rewards for the RDM tasks [18–20].

In this context, many institutions are looking for solutions to help researchers publish their data, supporting them in the RDM activities and providing tools and repositories [13,17,24]. From the researchers' perspective, data description and deposit should be simple, supported by tools that ease the creation of metadata. Metadata are essential for data access, interpretation and preservation. However, metadata standards can be complex and hard to adopt by researchers [7,15].

In this work we introduce researchers to RDM through data description, in a quick and practical fashion, using Dublin Core descriptors. The assumptions are that (1) the domain-neutral nature of Dublin Core is convenient for situations where a specific assessment of metadata requirements is not feasible; and (2) it is easy for researchers to grasp the concepts behind Dublin Core descriptors.

The aim of this paper is to describe a set of data deposit examples performed by researchers, with specific attention to the difficulties that they face and ways to overcome them. The next section is an overview of issues related to the development of the data repository at INESC TEC (Institute for Systems and Computer Engineering, Technology and Science, Portugal)[1], followed by a presentation of the data deposit process on the repository in Sect. 3 and the details of the examples with the identification of difficulties in Sect. 4. Results are presented in Sect. 5, followed by the discussion of feedback by researchers in Sect. 6. Section 7 presents the conclusions and future work.

2 The Data Repository at INESC TEC

Under the TAIL project[2], we are creating RDM workflows based on the integration of different tools according to the requirements of the researchers and their groups. The complete workflow covers important stages of the data lifecycle. The description stage occurs in the Dendro[3] platform, which helps researchers prepare datasets, combining generic and domain-specific metadata elements. In the context of the TAIL project, we elaborated specific metadata models for Material Fracture, Analytical Chemistry, Biodiversity, Simulation of Vehicles, Biological Oceanography, Hydrogen Production [4] and adopted descriptors from the Data Documentation Initiative [23] for several areas in the Social Sciences. These metadata models were based on contributions by researchers concerning the contextual information required to enable data interpretation. When they are ready for publication, data are transferred to a data repository, such as B2SHARE[4] [12].

[1] https://www.inesctec.pt/en.
[2] https://www.inesctec.pt/en/projects/tail.
[3] https://github.com/feup-infolab/dendro.
[4] https://b2share.eudat.eu/.

Although we recognize the need to prepare metadata according to domain-specific requirements, this process may take some time and require an effort that researchers are not able to commit. Moreover, there are many interesting datasets from closed projects that will not reach publication stage without a more agile process for deposit. As an alternative, we designed a workflow where data are directly deposited in the data repository at INESC TEC[5]. The data repository is an instance of CKAN (Comprehensive Knowledge Archive Network)[6], an open-source data platform built as a data management system, popular with open government data around the world (e.g. UK government and European Commission), and widely supported by the developer community [1,5,24].

CKAN provides an intuitive interface and visualization tools, which make data easily accessible. Moreover, it has a flexible architecture that allows for the customization of its features. Metadata fields, for instance, can be customized with key-value pairs, so users can define new ones [1].

Research at INESC TEC covers many domains, and the work with researchers to capture metadata requirements and design metadata models is ongoing. In this simplified workflow we use Dublin Core as a domain-neutral metadata schema. This is considered as a prudent entry plan for researchers lacking RDM skills. Many data repositories are already based on Dublin Core metadata[7], some allowing the addition of new descriptors. Moreover, a standard metadata schema is convenient for search and access, accounting for the diversity of research data from different scientific domains.

CKAN has default descriptors suitable for datasets: Title, Description, Tags, License, Organization, Visibility, Source, Version, Author, Author email, Maintainer, Maintainer Email, and Group. More detail can be added with the descriptors available for each file of the dataset: Name, Description, and Format. Dates for the creation and modification of the dataset are automatically generated upon deposit, and recorded on the Created and Last Updated CKAN descriptors. Each dataset and each of its files get an ID in the process. Most descriptors are easily mapped to Dublin Core, which allows for OAI-PMH (Open Archives Initiative Protocol for Metadata Harvesting) compliance. The CKAN metadata schema is very simple, yet it can be extended according to researchers' requirements and to assure platform interoperability [24]. In the INESC TEC data repository some key-value pairs were added to enable the use of descriptors beyond the default CKAN ones.

3 Simplified Data Deposit Workflow

In the context of the TAIL project, we collaborated with several researchers from different domains on RDM issues [16]. Some contacts led to data description and then deposit at the INESC TEC repository. The process starts with the decision of researchers to share their data or to cite data in a research paper and a

[5] https://rdm.inesctec.pt/.
[6] https://ckan.org/about.
[7] https://www.re3data.org/metrics/metadataStandards.

contact with the RDM team. The RDM process proceeds with a first meeting with researchers about general RDM issues and an introduction to the INESC TEC data repository. This also serves to assess familiarity of the researchers with respect to data publication and metadata standards.

To simplify the preparation of the data, we created a dataset deposit form based on Dublin Core[8]. This form is a template for the researcher to fill in. The researcher completes the form and returns it to the curator, who validates the metadata and completes the deposit process.

We chose Dublin Core as the core of the dataset deposit form since this standard is understandable by most [9], while the use of descriptors widely used in repositories allows for basic interoperability [8] and interdisciplinary discovery [14].

The dataset deposit form contains several Dublin Core descriptors[9], Dublin Core Qualifiers[10], and CKAN descriptors. CKAN descriptors Organization, Visibility, Version, Maintainer, Maintainer email and Group are not part of the form. They are assigned by the curator in the deposit step.

Table 1. Dataset attributes and corresponding descriptors in the repository

Dataset attributes	Corresponding descriptor and vocabulary
Availability	Visibility (CKAN), DOI
Bibliometric data	-
Coverage	Coverage.Temporal (Dublin Core), Coverage.Spatial (Dublin Core)
Date	Date (Dublin Core)
Format	Format (CKAN), Format (Dublin Core), Format.Extent (Dublin Core)
License	License (CKAN), License (Dublin Core)
Minimal description	Title (CKAN), Name (CKAN), Author (CKAN), Author email (CKAN), Description (CKAN), Maintainer (CKAN), Maintainer email (CKAN), Type (Dublin Core), Language (Dublin Core), Publisher (Dublin Core), Contributor (Dublin Core)
Paper reference	Relation (Dublin Core)
Project	Organization (CKAN), Group (CKAN)
Provenance	Source (CKAN), Version (CKAN)
Subjects	Tags (CKAN)

Descriptors from several vocabularies are being used in research data repositories such as Dryad, Figshare, Zenodo or CSIRO. There is no agreed-upon vocabulary for scientific data, but a set of eleven so-called classes of metadata attributes have been identified by Assante et al. to capture the essential aspects of datasets [2]. Table 1 presents a mapping of these dataset attributes into the descriptors used in the INESC TEC repository.

8 https://tinyurl.com/ybbwvq57.
9 http://dublincore.org/documents/dcmi-terms/.
10 http://dublincore.org/documents/2000/07/11/dcmes-qualifiers/.

The Availability attributes include descriptors that help to get access to the dataset [2]. Descriptor Visibility used in our form defines whether the dataset is publicly available or privately closed, and is therefore classified as an Availability attribute. If the dataset is private only the curator has access to the dataset. This is provided to comply with embargo periods, and the availability status can be altered at any time. The INESC TEC repository also assigns DOI to datasets. The DOI descriptor also contributes to the Availability attribute and its assigned by the curator. The INESC TEC data repository does not provide bibliometric data, such as statistics about data visualization or the number of downloads. These are important features to address in future development. This fact is acknowledged in the table in the line corresponding to the Bibliometric Data attribute.

The rest of the attributes correspond to standard descriptors and can provide information such as author, title, description, format, license, spatial, temporal coverage, data creation and related publication for the dataset. In some cases, we added Dublin Core descriptors even though the corresponding CKAN descriptors are present. One example is the License descriptor from both CKAN and Dublin Core, used since the CKAN descriptor does not include the "*Creative Commons Attribution-NonCommercial-NoDerivs 2.0 Generic (CC BY-NC-ND 2.0)*" in its default license list.

The deposit process is accomplished with researchers filling the form, by themselves or with our support, and with the verification of the metadata before deposit. This "approval" step provides control over the description and enforces some required information, such as the data formats and the size of the dataset and its files. As soon as the researcher sends the first version of the form, we evaluate the metadata record taking into account the knowledge of the nature of the domain, acquired in previous meetings. When a dataset contains GPS data and the metadata record lacks information about the geographic coverage, we assume that this is a possible metadata quality limitation, and ask the researcher to fill in the corresponding descriptor. If necessary, the complementary metadata is added with our help. This approach to metadata quality [21] is based on a human assessment performed by the curator while verifying the form. Moreover, the adoption of Dublin Core as a standard to ensure interoperability and the existence of this second round of description to enrich the metadata records also contribute to metadata quality.

4 Examples of Deposited Datasets

The deposit process resulted in 21 datasets from research groups in the domains of Biomedical engineering (1 dataset), Environmental radioactivity (7 datasets), Biomedicine (3 datasets), Robotics (1 dataset), Information science (1 dataset), Natural language processing (3 datasets), Music streaming (1 dataset), and Information retrieval (4 datasets). In general we had the collaboration of one researcher from each group for the description and deposit of their data. However, in every case all the group elements were aware of the process and validated the deposits. This is a test to a deposit process for research groups at INESC TEC where RDM tasks and the contact with curators are delegated to some group members.

The size of the files in the datasets is in the range of 2 kB to 4 GB, which is the configured limit on the repository. However, there is no limit on the number of files in a dataset. Deposits took place over a period of one and a half year, with some groups that make systematic data collection contributing with several datasets. Table 2 shows the distribution of deposits in time, and their accessibility status (public—open to all; private—not accessible to all). Sharing of private datasets is not excluded, but it requires a request to the authors and possibly some agreement on the terms of use.

Table 2. Datasets deposited at the INESC TEC data repository up to June 2018

Domain	Datasets deposited in 2017				2018	
	1 trimester	2 trimester	3 trimester	4 trimester	1 trimester	2 trimester
Biomedical engineering	•					
Environmental radioactivity	•	•	•	•	•	•
Biomedicine		•			•	
Robotics					•	
Information science					•	
Natural language processing		•	•	◇		
Music streaming	•					
Information retrieval	•		◇			

• - *public datasets* ◇ - *private datasets*

We kept record of the collaboration with researchers: for each case, we wrote a short description of the dataset, issues, questions, and features of interest mentioned by the researchers. This included datasets that researchers decided not to deposit, with the arguments supporting their decisions. In the following we provide a brief description of the process in each group.

Biomedical Engineering: The goal of this group is the development of products, tools, and methods for prevention and early detection of diseases[11]. The first contact revealed a lack of knowledge in RDM. We explained the meaning of the descriptors in our form. Afterward, the researcher sent us the completed form. We changed the Title, added information about Authors, Contributors, Format, Format.Extent and Relation. The references to papers were standardized and associated to the existing DOI. After checking all this information, we proceeded with the deposit on the repository and sent the link to the researcher to verify the description. Although this group has only one deposited dataset, they promoted the institutional repository with other groups, by sharing our

[11] https://www.inesctec.pt/en/centres/c-ber.

contact, showing others how to access the deposited dataset, and telling about their RDM experience.

Environmental Radioactivity: The Environmental radioactivity research group deals with engineering problems facing the industry, by analyzing, designing, mining and implementing large information systems[12]. They had prior RDM experience, namely on metadata standards and on the use of a domain-specific data repository. We check this repository and obtained an example of a Readme.txt file with all the recommended descriptors. However, in conversation with the group it was decided to use the INESC TEC dataset deposit form because the descriptors recommended in the domain repository were considered too specialized and not suitable for their data. After the first deposit this group made regular deposits with data from ongoing campaigns, with increased description quality. This constitutes a running collaboration that has raised the interest of this group in RDM activities, leading to further collaboration in the design of a data management plan.

Biomedicine: A researcher of this domain (see footnote 11) had interest in data deposit to publicize results related to neuro-technologies. The dataset contained sensitive information, namely images of patients, and although the information was anonymized the researcher decided to keep the data as restricted access. A common requirement from researchers in this domain is to restrict dataset download to registered users under the acceptance of a specific license. Therefore, we recommended the preparation of a password-protected zipped dataset and the specification of the license in the dataset description. The researchers showed interest in having an interface with mandatory fields for prospective users, providing information on how to request access to the dataset. This request has been recorded for future implementation.

Information Science: The researcher in this domain worked in a group related to the development and promotion of innovation management practices, and was familiar with RDM activities and metadata related issues. Therefore, the data description and deposit tasks ran easily and the deposit was completed with little effort.

The ***Natural language processing*** and ***Information retrieval*** research groups are part of the Information Systems and Computer Graphics center (see footnote 12), with research related to programming languages and data processing. In the data preparation phase, we identified, in both cases, that some datasets could be made publicly available while others were private, depending on the permission status granted by the original databases.

The process in the ***Robotics***[13] and ***Music streaming***[14] domains followed the defined approach, without any specific challenge. We expect a productive collaboration with these groups, due to their strong Data Science connection, and the volumes of data generated in their projects. Datasets are expected from

[12] https://www.inesctec.pt/en/centres/csig.
[13] https://www.inesctec.pt/en/centres/liaad.
[14] https://www.inesctec.pt/en/centres/cras.

robotic solutions, autonomous navigation, a variety of sensor measurements, and also complex objective decision models. Researchers in these domains are likely to raise interesting issues for the RDM process.

5 Description Results

In retrospect, most of the researchers that we have worked with never received RDM training of any sort, not knowing, in some cases, anything about data description and data deposit. They agree on the challenging nature of the data description process. We noticed that some concepts were easily understood, but others such as metadata or descriptor required more discussion, and the support provided by the RDM team was valued. Another common difficulty was the knowledge of metadata standards to be used in their domains. Dublin Core was used as an example of a generic standard. Although they felt the need to make their data accessible to others, they did not know how to do it. Table 3 compares the number of descriptor occurrences, by descriptor, filled in by the researchers in the first description round, with the final number of occurrences after the collaboration with the curator. The final number corresponds to the metadata actually included in the deposit of the dataset.

The results show that the Title, Author and Author email descriptors were the most frequently used. The Description element is also among the most used ones, which is natural since it is a descriptor that gives flexibility to capture information that otherwise would make sense in domain-specific elements, e.g. concerning experimental configurations. The descriptor Tags was widely used by the researchers to represent the subject, with the goal of improving data findability in the repository. The descriptors Source, Contributor, and Format.Extent were the least used. The Contributor descriptor was used a few times and only for the description of external parties, while group members were identified as Author. In all cases, when the raw data belonged to other institutions or researchers, the descriptor Source was used, sometimes upon recommendation.

Moreover, the results show that in general the metadata was improved after the feedback provided by the curator, particularly with a more detailed description by increasing the number of descriptors used. The Date descriptor, which can be captured in every domain, was added fifteen times by the researchers. We looked into this and tried to understand why the date information was missing in some cases. We concluded that the descriptor meaning was too ambiguous for the researchers, who often asked if the date was for the creation of the dataset or for the start of the project. Based on this feedback we added a more precise definition and made sure the Date information was present in all metadata records by the time the datasets were deposited.

Although some descriptors have the same number of occurrences, some of them have also been corrected by the curator to improve the quality of the description. The dataset Title was edited in some circumstances, for instance from "*Capsule videos*" to a more accurate "*Red Lesion Endoscopy Dataset*" after the recommendations by the curator.

Table 3. Descriptor occurrences before and after curator mediation

Descriptor	Descriptors used by researchers	Descriptors after curator feedback
Title	21	21
Author	21	21
Author email	21	21
Description	20	21
Format	20	21
Tags	19	21
License	16	21
Coverage (Temporal)	16	17
Type	16	20
Date	15	21
Coverage (Spatial)	14	15
Language	14	16
Publisher	12	21
Relation	12	15
Source	10	10
Contributor	6	6
Format.Extent (File size)	5	21

Some difficulties felt by the researchers had an influence on their decisions. For instance, the Format.Extent descriptor was perceived as ambiguous and in many cases researchers did not provide it. In general, researchers state that they do not want to spend too much time in the description so they prioritize other descriptors. Data organization issues also emerged, as researchers wanted to deposit datasets as one zip file, so the format was described only as zip. Sometimes that made sense, but in most cases we advised them to deposit files separately. This makes the contents of the dataset more explicit and favours detailed metadata at file level, making the data easier to interpret. Thus, we edited the information in descriptor Format by replacing *.zip* with the extensions of the corresponding files, *.tiff* and *.py*, for example.

The difference between descriptors Format and Type is also a known issue. To clarify this, we used examples from the data repository. Examples of format are *.jpg, .txt, .xls* whereas type can be *Measurements*, *Events*, or *Entity Annotated News*. In cases where it was difficult to distinguish between the description of the dataset and the description of individual files in the dataset, we have explained that the dataset includes information about all the contained files, and each file can have its own specific description.

Some questions arised concerning controlled vocabularies. For example, the descriptor Language was filled inconsistently with strings such as "*Português*" or "PT". This is a case where a controlled vocabulary can help to normalize the description and facilitate the introduction of the text. In this example we could use Dublin Core Encoding Schemes (see footnote 9), namely ISO 639-2: Codes for the representation of names of languages.

Another question related to controlled vocabularies has to do with the License. By default, in CKAN values for this descriptor come from a list of licenses, as a closed controlled vocabulary. In some cases, it was necessary to add the Dublin Core descriptor License to add specific information, not on the list, e.g. "*Creative Commons Attribution-NonCommercial-NoDerivs 2.0 Generic (CC BY-NC-ND 2.0)*".

Controlled vocabularies are useful tools and could be used in specific descriptors as custom fields in INESC TEC repository. In the context of the TAIL project, we developed and implemented them on the Dendro platform in the Hydrogen Production domain. Preliminary results on the use of controlled vocabularies showed that they contribute to simplify the description process and to reduce metadata errors [11].

In general, many questions were raised in each collaboration. Researchers were curious about data citation, the overall data repository functionality, the limits on file upload size, the inclusion of sensitive data. The availability of the repository in the long run was also a concern for them. Furthermore, researchers inquired about data preservation, demonstrating a sense of awareness about this RDM dimension.

6 Feedback from Researchers

The experience of getting researchers to participate in metadata-related activities has shown that it is difficult to anticipate RDM scenarios and researchers' expectations. Although most researchers are not familiar with metadata concepts, let alone metadata standards, they show different levels of awareness, thus requiring us to adapt our approach to each domain. The data deposit process was adapted to researchers' perspectives and agendas. Each collaboration took from one to more than two months. It was important to adopt flexible strategies to gradually involve researchers. To accomplish that we systematically gathered feedback from them, and adjusted or approach to their contexts. We noticed that more experienced researchers showed greater interest, and took advantage of the collaboration to deepen their knowledge in RDM. The collaboration has branched, in some of the groups, to the definition of a data management plan, to the creation of metadata models for their domain, and to data description in the Dendro platform, along with experiences with other tools besides the repository platform.

Even considering some challenges, most researchers were willing to deposit their data, recognizing the advantages. Once the deposit was completed, we asked researchers to comment on the overall experience and its impact on their RDM awareness. To this end, an informal email was sent with several questions about the experience. Their opinions were written in Portuguese, which we freely translate here.

Some researchers confirm that their datasets were shared by others and cited in scientific articles: "*Yes, I have shared my dataset several times with other researchers and for project proposals*"; "*We have used the dataset link in our papers*", yet they point out the lack of a mechanism to show information about the downloaded datasets: "*I think our data was not reused yet (or, if they were, we are not informed)*", therefore "*It would be useful to have some idea of how many times the data was downloaded*". Currently, the repository does not provide download statistics.

Most people state that with each deposit they have gained more confidence and motivation: "*At first I found it hard, but as we go it becomes much easier and simpler*". Moreover, some of them highlight the importance of having assistance: "*The process itself is a bit time consuming. The choice of descriptors is not something for which we are oriented and the support of the curator is fundamental here*". In other words, they have improved their skills in describing data, each time the description process takes less time and fewer corrections, and researchers become more engaged and independent in RDM activities.

In most cases researchers showed their datasets to others, promoting the INESC TEC data repository at the same time - "*Yes, once or twice I have recommended the deposit of data in the repository*". They acted as intermediaries between our team and other interested parties - "*Yes, I already gave your contact to one of my postdocs, who has seen my data in the repository and showed interest in depositing another kind of data (laboratory measurements)*".

In brief, our experience provides preliminary insight on the diversity of needs, issues, and motivations to publication, but most importantly to the level of awareness researchers have to RDM and metadata at our institution. With this in mind we are adapting the data preparation and deposit phases accordingly. Notwithstanding, Dublin Core proved to be a suitable metadata standard to initiate researchers in RDM activities.

7 Conclusion

The use of the Dublin Core descriptors as the basis for metadata on the INESC TEC data repository was assumed as a first step to involve researchers in data description. This is also regarded as the starting point in RDM training activities, leading researchers to understand metadata terms and standards and familiarizing them with RDM tools. In order to further our approach and the kind of collaboration described here, we still have to address specific data description requirements to improve the overall quality of the metadata. This will probably lead to an extension of the proposed metadata form. Moreover, given the experience gathered with these examples, we have to continue our work and focus on helping researchers make their data fit for reuse.

Although the Dublin Core elements have provided satisfactory results and good feedback, they have also revealed cases where the metadata requirements, or researchers' expectations, are not quite fulfilled. For instance, after the deposit of the Information Science dataset, we kept improving the metadata record, based on more detailed description contributed by the researcher, using some elements from the Data Documentation Initiative standard.

A researcher from the biomedicine domain decided not to deposit the data unless access restrictions were implemented. This example motivated the definition of new configurations in the repository, to address the requirements of sensitive data. It also shows how researchers can provide a critical view of the repository, when considering their priorities and the features of their data.

As the deposit process in the INESC TEC repository proceeds we will gather further insight on domain-specific requirements. Future work will address those requirements, with incremental adjustments to our dataset deposit form, allowing researchers to choose from or to add more descriptors. In addition, work also proceeds on workflows with more substantial involvement of researchers and more work on the definition of metadata models. Flexible metadata tools, like the Dendro platform, are essential to accommodate domain-specific requirements prior to data deposit, leading to richer metadata but also requiring a deeper involvement of the researchers.

Acknowledgements. This work is financed by the ERDF – European Regional Development Fund through the Operational Programme for Competitiveness and Internationalisation - COMPETE 2020 Programme and by National Funds through the Portuguese funding agency, FCT - Fundação para a Ciência e a Tecnologia within project TAIL, POCI-01-0145-FEDER-016736. João Aguiar Castro is supported by research grant PD/BD/114143/2015, provided by the FCT - Fundação para a Ciência e a Tecnologia. Yulia Karimova is supported by research grant SFRH/BD/136332/2018, provided by the FCT - Fundação para a Ciência e a Tecnologia.

References

1. Amorim, R., et al.: A comparison of research data management platforms: architecture, flexible metadata and interoperability. Univers. Access Inf. Soc. **16**, 851–862 (2017). https://doi.org/10.1007/s10209-016-0475-y
2. Assante, M., et al.: Are scientific data repositories coping with research data publishing? Data Sci. J. **15**, 6 (2016). https://doi.org/10.5334/dsj-2016-006
3. Bishoff, C., Johnston, L.: Approaches to data sharing: an analysis of NSF data management plans from a Large Research University. J. Libr. Sch. Commun. **3**(2), eP1231 (2015). https://doi.org/10.7710/2162-3309.1231
4. Castro, J.A., et al.: Involving data creators in an ontology-based design process for metadata models. In: Developing Metadata Application Profiles, pp. 181–214. IGI Global (2017). https://doi.org/10.4018/978-1-5225-2221-8.ch008
5. European Commission: Accompanying the document Proposal for a Directive of the European Parliament and of the Council on the re-use of public sector information. SWD/2018/145 final - 2018/0111 (COD). Brussels (2018). https://eur-lex.europa.eu/legal-content/EN/TXT/?uri=SWD%3A2018%3A145%3AFIN
6. European Commission: Horizon 2020. Work Programme 2016 - 2017. Annex L. Conditions related to open access to research data (2017). https://ec.europa.eu/research/participants/data/ref/h2020/other/wp/2016-2017/annexes/h2020-wp1617-annex-ga_en.pdf
7. Van den Eynden, V., et al.: Managing and sharing data - best practice for researchers. UK Data Archive, pp. 1–40 (2011). ISBN 1904059783

8. Farnel, S., Shiri, A.: Metadata for research data: current practices and trends. In: International Conference on Dublin Core and Metadata Applications, pp. 74–82 (2014). http://dcpapers.dublincore.org/pubs/article/view/3714
9. Gartner, R.: Metadata becomes digital. Metadata, pp. 27–39. Springer, Cham (2016). https://doi.org/10.1007/978-3-319-40893-4_3
10. Hudson Vitale, C.R.: The current state of meta-repositories for data. In: Johnston, L.R. (ed.) Curating Research Data, Volume One: Practical Strategies for Your Digital Repository, pp. 251–261. Association of College and Research Libraries, Chicago (2017)
11. Karimova, Y.: Vocabulários controlados na descrição de dados de investigação no Dendro. Universidade do Porto, Faculdade de Engenharia (2016). http://hdl.handle.net/10216/85221
12. Karimova, Y., Castro, J.A., da Silva, J.R., Pereira, N., Ribeiro, C.: Promoting semantic annotation of research data by their creators: a use case with B2NOTE at the end of the RDM workflow. In: Garoufallou, E., Virkus, S., Siatri, R., Koutsomiha, D. (eds.) MTSR 2017. CCIS, vol. 755, pp. 112–122. Springer, Cham (2017). https://doi.org/10.1007/978-3-319-70863-8_11
13. Lee, D.J., Stvilia, B.: Practices of research data curation in institutional repositories: a qualitative view from repository staff. PLoS ONE **12**(3), 1–44 (2017). https://doi.org/10.1371/journal.pone.0173987
14. Qin, J., Ball, A., Greenberg, J.: Functional and architectural requirements for metadata: supporting discovery and management of scientific data. In: Proceedings of the DCIM International Conference on Dublin Core and Metadata Applications, pp. 62–71 (2012). http://dcpapers.dublincore.org/pubs/article/view/3660
15. Qin, J., Li, K.: How portable are the metadata standards for scientific data? A proposal for a metadata infrastructure. In: Proceedings of the International Conference on Dublin Core and Metadata Applications, pp. 25–34 (2013). http://dcpapers.dublincore.org/pubs/article/view/3670
16. Ribeiro, C., et al.: Projeto TAIL - Gestão de dados de investigação da produção ao depósito e à partilha (resultados preliminares). In: Cadernos BAD N.2, jul-dez, pp. 256–264 (2016). https://www.bad.pt/publicacoes/index.php/cadernos/article/view/1603
17. Rocha, J., Ribeiro, C., Lopes, J.C.: The Dendro research data management platform: applying ontologies to long-term preservation in a collaborative environment. In: Proceedings of the 11th International Conference on Digital Preservation, iPRES (2014)
18. Sayogo, D.S., Pardo, T.A.: Exploring the determinants of scientific data sharing: understanding the motivation to publish research data. Gov. Inf. Q. **30**, 19–31 (2013). https://doi.org/10.1016/j.giq.2012.06.011
19. Shearer, K., Furtado, F.: COAR survey of research data management: results. Confederation of OpenAccess Repositories (2017). https://www.coar-repositories.org/files/COAR-RDM-Survey-Jan-2017.pdf
20. Swan, A., Brown, S.: To share or not to share: publication and quality assurance of research data outputs. A report commissioned by the Research Information Network (2008). https://eprints.soton.ac.uk/266742/
21. Tani, A., Candela, L., Castelli, D.: Dealing with metadata quality: the legacy of digital library efforts. Inf. Process. Manag. **49**(6), 1194–1205 (2013). https://doi.org/10.1016/j.ipm.2013.05.003
22. Tenopir, C., et al.: Changes in data sharing and data reuse practices and perceptions among scientists worldwide. PLoS ONE **10**(8) (2015). https://doi.org/10.1371/journal.pone.0134826

23. Vardigan, M., Heus, P., Thomas, W.: Data documentation initiative: toward a standard tor the social sciences. Int. J. Digit. Curation **3**(1), 107–113 (2008). https://doi.org/10.2218/ijdc.v3i1.45
24. Winn, J.: Open data and the academy: an evaluation of CKAN for research data management. In: IASSIST 2013, pp. 28–31, May 2013. http://eprints.lincoln.ac.uk/9778

Information Literacy Needs Open Access or: Open Access is not Only for Researchers

Maurizio Lana(✉)

Dip. di Studi Umanistici, Università del Piemonte Orientale, Vercelli, Italy
maurizio.lana@uniupo.it

Abstract. The Open Access was initially (blandly) conceived in view not only of researchers but also of lay readers, then this perspective slowly faded out. The Information Literacy movement wants to teach citizens how to arrive at trustable information but the amount of paywalled knowledge is still big. So, their lines of development are somehow complementary: Information Literacy needs Open Access for the citizens to freely access high quality information while Open Access truly fulfils its scope when it is conceived and realized not only for the researchers (an aristocratic view which was the initial one) but for the whole society.

Keywords: Information literacy · Open access · Citizenship · Information society · Predatory journals

1 Open Access and the Researchers, and a Forgotten Promise

Today Open Access is usually meant as a matter for researchers because it is said to refer to the free access of peers to scientific literature. But an historical overview through relevant documents which are at the base of the Open Access movement shows a continual co-existence of both the researchers and the society, as the main beneficiaries of the new paradigm. An archaeology of Open Access writings could possibly start with Guédon ending words of his essay "In Oldenburg's long shadow": "Librarians can (and ought to) help create a navigable, worldwide ocean of knowledge, open to all; … a distributed intelligence civilization – a civilization open to all that are good enough (excellence), and not only to those who can afford it (elites)" [1]. An *ocean of knowledge* is what we today know as the domain of Open Access publications, but *open to all* is ambiguous: we probably mean "all" in a widely inclusive sense, while Guédon explains it in an aristocratic sense, "all who excel hence deserve it" as a reaction to the traditional, consolidated (oligarchic!) sense of "all who have the power to obtain it". What clearly appears is that the concept of future Open Access starts as a matter internal to the world of research. This was in 2001.

Subsequently in 2008 Guédon in his "Open Access and the divide between "mainstream" and "peripheral" science" never mentions the society, only one time the school and the citizens: "Likewise, the school system, at least the secondary level, could benefit from free access to the research literature, particularly in the social sciences and the humanities. Citizens would also have a chance of being better

P. Manghi et al. (Eds.): IRCDL 2019, CCIS 988, pp. 236–247, 2019.
https://doi.org/10.1007/978-3-030-11226-4_19

informed" [2]. Similarly goes in the 2016 paper of Guédon and Jensen, "Crystals of Knowledge Production" [3] which is a discussion about Open Science and humanities: the word *research* recurs 34 times, the word *society* 1 time ("open access gives value for researchers and their institutions, for companies, and for society as a whole"), the word *citizens* 0 times.

Suber in 2003 in his overview of Open Access [4] has one phrase about the relation between Open Access and citizens: "Citizens: OA gives them access to peer-reviewed research (most of which is unavailable in public libraries) and gives them access to the research for which they have already paid through their taxes. It also helps them indirectly by helping the researchers, physicians, manufacturers, technologists, and others who make use of cutting-edge research for their benefit". Apart from the description of what is Open Access and its reasons, the passage essentially says: "Open Access helps citizens because it really helps researchers working for their benefit". The citizens are not active, involved in the personal acquisition of new knowledge, rather they are passive receivers of what others do for them. More interesting is what Suber writes in 2012 in his "Open Access" book: "OA allows us to provide access to everyone who cares to have access, without patronizing guesswork about who really wants it, who really deserves it, and who would really benefit from it. … The idea is to stop thinking of knowledge as a commodity to meter out to deserving customers, and to start thinking of it as a public good, especially when it is given away by its authors, funded with public money, or both" [5] which is probably one the most thorough statement one can find about the strong interconnection between Open Access and citizens. He also introduces the concept of "lay reader", the non-professional reader who has nevertheless a personal interest in the scientific knowledge (this is similar but not identical to thinking in terms of society and citizens).

This overview can end with documents and declarations by institutions and public bodies. The Budapest Open Access Initiative document [6] in 2002 describes the Open Access speaking of "world-wide electronic distribution of the peer-reviewed journal literature and completely free and unrestricted access to it by all scientists, scholars, teachers, students, and other curious minds" and of "free availability [of scientific literature] on the public internet, permitting any users to read … the full texts of these articles". The world of scientist and scholars is well present but it is complemented by "other curious minds" and by the fact that the promise of free reading is for "any users". The subscribers of the Berlin Declaration [7] say in 2003 "our mission of disseminating knowledge is only half complete if the information is not made widely and readily available to society" and the word "society" is clear and explicit. And the preamble of the Italian "Dichiarazione di Messina" signed in 2004 mentions both the "importanza fondamentale che la diffusione universale delle conoscenze scientifiche riveste nella crescita economica e culturale della società" and the "esigenza avvertita in seno alle comunità accademiche internazionali e negli Atenei italiani di individuare forme alternative di diffusione della comunicazione scientifica che garantiscano la più ampia disseminazione e il più alto impatto scientifico dei prodotti culturali creati al loro interno". The presence of the "crescita economica e culturale della società" in the first statement is balanced by the presence of "il più alto impatto scientifico dei prodotti culturali creati al loro interno" where the scientific impact is a matter internal to the scientific/academic world.

One of the most recent assertions of the access for the citizens as a component of Open Access is present (and bounding) in the Horizon 2020 programme Manual: *"Why Have Open Access To Publications And Data In Horizon 2020? […]*

Broader access to scientific publications and data helps to

- *build on previous research results (improved quality of results)*
- *encourage collaboration and avoid duplication of effort (greater efficiency)*
- *speed up innovation (faster progress to market means faster growth)*
- *involve citizens and society (improved transparency of the scientific process)."* [8].

Here we see the presence of society and citizens - but properly speaking they are mentioned as *controllers* who thanks to the transparency of the process may keep an eye over its development and management and not as *learners* as it was in other texts among those we mentioned above.

If we come to the current scientific debate about Open Access, some recurrent subtopics appear – among which the relation between Open Access and society is not of primary relevance. Apparently, the biggest subtopic – hence the biggest discussion issue – is the relation between Open Access and impact factor: 'does publishing in Open Access produce better impact score than publishing in toll access?'. Piwowar et al. [9] declare in 2018 "our results show that the percentage of the literature available as OA is growing, and that articles diffused through this form are generally more cited than closed access articles". And seven years ago it was the same, suffice to cite the work of Lewis [10] who among many publications of the previous years about this question mentions a supporting metanalysis by A. Swan [11]. Another relevant subtopic is: 'which are the implications of Open Access publishing face to the evaluation of research?' and we can see for example Turbanti [12], Michetti et al. [13] The latter states "sia le norme dettate dall'ANVUR (Agenzia Nazionale di Valutazione del sistema Universitario e della Ricerca) circa la valutazione della qualità della ricerca scientifica, sia le regole definite dalle procedure di Abilitazione Scientifica Nazionale spesso spingono gli autori verso la scelta di sedi editoriali che pubblicano in modalità classica". Other issues are the relation between Open Access and Open Data [14], the feasibility of various economic approaches to Open Access [15], and so on.

The relation of Open Access with society and the citizens is only marginally present in the current scientific debate about Open Access and this somehow configures a forgotten promise. The data speak for themselves: in Google Scholar the search for `"open access" citizens` gives around 461.000 matches; the search for `"open access" research` gives around 4.230.000 matches – the ratio is 1:9. If we focus on the year 2018, the results are respectively around 15.800 and around 47.000 with a ratio of around 1:3[1] what shows that recently the *citizens* occupy a growing space in debate about Open Access, even if still smaller than the one occupied by the *research.*

---

[1] At the date of 15 November 2018.

2 Information Literacy: What Is It? Some Definitions

A domain near to Open Access where there is great attention to the access to information is that of Information Literacy. Information Literacy was conceived in the times of print, in 1974, when P. Zurkowski wrote an internal report for the National Commission on Libraries and Information Science, Washington, DC. The title was quite bureaucratic: "The Information Service Environment Relationships and Priorities. Related Paper No. 5" [16] but already in the abstract the focus was pragmatic and evident: "the top priority of the National Commission on Libraries and Information Science should be directed toward establishing a major national program to achieve universal information literacy by 1984". So, a first relevant point is that Information Literacy is not in itself a product or an expression of the digital world. The key passages of Zurkowski reasoning, in views of the argument we are developing, are these:

> "We experience an overabundance of information whenever available information exceeds our capacity to evaluate it. … The infrastructure supporting our information service environment transcends traditional libraries, publishers and schools. It embraces the totality of explicit physical means, formal and informal, for communicating concepts and ideas. … People trained in the application of information resources to their work can be called information literate. They have learned techniques and skills for utilizing the wide range of information tools as well as primary sources. The individuals in the remaining portion of the population, while literate in the sense that they can read and write, do not have a measure for the value of the information, do not have an ability to mold information to their needs, and realistically must be considered to be information illiterates … The effort must be done to give *to all the information illiterates* the same capabilities of the one sixth of already literate US population … [the national program of information literacy] would involve the coordination of funding of a massive effort to train all citizens in the use of information tools now available as well as those in the development on testing states. The pattern of growth in this field is well established and should be built upon to expand the overall capability of all of US. Citizens".

In the last decade particularly in the Anglo-American world many definitions of Information Literacy considering the digital world and Internet were developed, by Jisc, CILIP, SCONUL, ACRL, NHS Education Scotland, all variously based onto "the 5 competencies":

- define a specific need for information
- find the appropriate sources
- do the search
- evaluate the results
- use the results

These definitions evolved in recent times when the world faced the phenomena of fake news diffusion in digital social environments. The most striking one in this new perspective is that of CILIP, the professional association of UK librarians: "Information literacy is the ability to think critically and make balanced judgements about any information we find and use. It empowers us as citizens to reach and express informed views and to engage fully with society" [17] because it abandons the previous descriptive/operative approach and simply affirms a need: "ability to think critically". CILIP definition explicitly states that (valuable, correct) information is needed by citizens engaging with the society but it contains a problematic aspect as Testoni recently wrote: "[CILIP definition] rischia di sussumere il nucleo concettuale dell'Information literacy in quello, troppo ampio e vago, di "pensiero critico"" [18].

On the same subject of what is Information Literacy there is abundant literature from Unesco and European institutions. From Unesco we can mention the report by F. W. Horton, "Overview of information literacy resources worldwide" [19], who in 2008 has also been the author of the big manual "Understanding Information Literacy: A Primer" [20]. On the Europe side, the European Council in the "Council conclusions of 30 May 2016 on developing media literacy and critical thinking through education and training" [21] focuses on the invitation to the member States "to encourage sufficient attention to be paid to developing media literacy and critical thinking in education and training at all levels, including through citizenship and media education" and the report of the European Commission on "Promoting media and information literacy in libraries" [22] discusses if "media and information literacy programmes in public libraries can be called effective in general".

2.1 Information Literacy According to the *Manifesto per l'Information Literacy* of AIB

AIB, the Italian associations of librarians recently published its *Manifesto per l'Information Literacy* [23]. Information Literacy is there described in reference to two external definitions: the UNESCO/IFLA Media Information Literacy definition

> "Media and Information Literacy consists of the knowledge, the attitudes, and the sum of the skills needed to know when and what information is needed; where and how to obtain that information; how to evaluate it critically and organise it once it is found; and how to use it in an ethical way. The concept extends beyond communication and information technologies to encompass learning, critical thinking, and interpretative skills across and beyond professional and educational boundaries" [24]

and the AGID[2] Information literacy definition

> "l'insieme di abilità, competenze, conoscenze e attitudini che portano il singolo a maturare nel tempo, durante tutto l'arco della vita, un rapporto complesso e diversificato con le fonti informative: i documenti e le informazioni in essi contenuti. … In sintesi la competenza informativa prevede la capacità di riconoscere un bisogno informativo, ricercare, valutare, utilizzare le informazioni in modo consapevole per creare nuova conoscenza." [25]

while at the same time declaring the need for "una definizione operativa e agile di IL, complementare a quelle prodotte da IFLA e AGID, che rifletta le peculiarità dello scenario italiano e europeo". So, at definitions level things are a little blurred. But on the relation of Information Literacy with citizenship in the Information Society the statements are unambiguous: "l'Information Literacy è un diritto di base per i cittadini"[3]; "l'Information Literacy fa parte di una costellazione più ampia che include

[2] AGID is the Italian State agency "Agenzia per l'Italia Digitale".

[3] The reference is to the statement "Information Literacy …is a basic human right in a digital world and promotes social inclusion of all nations" which is part of the IFLA Alexandria Proclamation on Information Literacy and Lifelong Learning of 2005, https://www.ifla.org/publications/beacons-of-the-information-society-the-alexandria-proclamation-on-information-literacy.

competenze necessarie per esercitare i propri diritti civili politici economici sociali e culturali; acquisire e applicare nuove competenze, arricchire la propria identità ed espressione culturale, partecipare al processo decisionale ed alla vita di una società civile attiva e impegnata"[4].

The most relevant concepts of the Manifesto are the awareness that people are not only consumers of information (hence the need to draw a road which should bring to sound and trustable information) but also producers of information in the social media world, and the intersection of printed sources in the physical world with digital sources. Accordingly, the Manifesto gives methodological indications to help people to avoid the pitfalls. In fact in the Manifesto is present a disguised sequence of steps for moving from more general to more specific information resources. We say disguised because the Manifesto contains in its second half 17 themes/focuses which are, it is explicitly said, "listed in casual, not structured order". But they really are related to one another and the relations, when brought to evidence, change the random list into a rich set of conceptual nets. One of these "conceptual nets" is precisely the one describing a methodological approach to the research of information inside the available, different types of resources. The steps mentioned in the Manifesto are:

"utilizzare i motori di ricerca
utilizzare Wikipedia
utilizzare le fonti aperte
utilizzare fonti specialistiche
conoscere le fonti informative appropriate per la propria area disciplinare" [23].

They contain a mismatch between "fonti aperte [open access sources]" and "fonti specialistiche [specialized sources]" as if the open access sources couldn't be specialized or vice-versa. Another problematic aspect of these definitions is that what are called open access *sources* are Google Books, Internet Archive, Gutenberg Project, Treccani Encyclopedia, Europeana, Internet Culturale, which *in a context where the ultimate scope are specific documents containing the requested information* can hardly be called sources given that also the found, relevant documents are sources. It is more appropriate to call "resources" these collections of documents and to leave the name of "sources" to the documents they give access to.

So, the steps of the research for information could be more properly redefined in this general form:

1. using generalist search engines - Google search, Google Books, etc.
2. using encyclopedias – Wikipedia, Treccani, …
3. using multidisciplinary resources/specialized search engines - Google Scholar, Scopus, WoS, DoAJ, etc.

[4] The reference is to "exercise their civil, political, economic, social and cultural rights; be economically active, productive and innovative; learn and apply new skills; enrich cultural identity and expression; take part in decision-making and participate in an active and engaged civil society", in the Lyon Declaration on Access to Information and Development of 2014, https://www.lyondeclaration.org/.

4. using specialized resources, like publishers' websites, SIGs, databases, etc.
5. using resources specifically focused onto the disciplinary domain of interest, like scientific journals.

The first two steps are probably more relevant if the interested person is completely new of the field she wants to investigate and therefore needs to build her own vocabulary of things and concepts. Fact is that in the subsequent three steps (using specialized search engines, using specialized resources, using resources specifically focused onto the disciplinary domain of interest) it is more than probable that the reader (lay or professional) comes across toll access resources, mainly but not only scientific journals. If the intention of giving to all of the citizen the ability to access relevant, trustable information on every field is at the core of Information Literacy, *then this intention crashes against the paywall of scientific journals.*

3 Citizens Need Free Access to Scientific Knowledge

On one side, that all citizens must have full access to the whole corpus of scientific knowledge is a concept bridging Information Literacy and Open Access, without forcing the meaning of both movements: Information Literacy needs a content explaining/showing the usefulness of the literacy itself and Open Access needs a broad scope not simply a focused one. On the other side, one basic argument against Open Access is precisely that full knowledge open to all is not really needed or, one could rephrase, society doesn't need it. Things are more complex, though. Open Access needs a broad scope because if it is meant only for researchers – which is the dominant trend of today – some mechanism internal to the research domain surely can be found to give all the researchers the access to scientific literature; but that would mean that Open is open only to those who deserve it, that knowledge is open to the knowledge workers and not to the others – somehow a coming back to the positions of Guédon in 2001 [1]. The true change of paradigm happens instead when we recognize that knowledge must be practically, not only in principle, open to all, and knowledge *really becomes* open to all. There are two main aspects of it: the use of existing knowledge and the production of new knowledge.

Use of Existing Knowledge. Present times and the present society are usually described as an Information Society because information is abundant, flows everywhere and being out of this flow means being out of the life blood of every activity (we all know that on the management and use of information are based the biggest corporations of the present world). So, being able to access, understand and (re)use information is obviously a major aim and issue for the citizens of this type of society. The above-mentioned new version of the Information Literacy definition published by CILIP [18], notwithstanding the doubts it can raise, precisely tries to map this situation where managing information in the widest sense is vital for every aspect of citizens' life. Simple words like "managing information in the widest sense is vital" hide one of the biggest problem of IL, that is not simply explaining/teaching how specific pieces of information must be correctly analyzed, rather teaching how to autonomously find the sources of trustable information and how to evaluate them when technical competence is needed.[5] Or – to express the matter in other words – IL is not simply (must not be reduced to) a type of training to the use of 'intellectual devices'[6]: it is instead a literacy (!) which is learnt over the years as the already cited "Promoting media and information literacy in libraries" states: "Ultimately, information literate people are those who have learned how to learn".

Usually when speaking of what could be the interest for citizens in Open Access first of all one thinks of medical information[7]. Medical information means which therapies are really, and most, effective – and this has implications in relation to the expenses paid by the institutions running the medical system and by the citizens who pay to obtain the therapies; but this also puts in evidence which hospitals are better in caring specific illnesses. All this in turn has implications for the perspectives and expectancy of life of people and for the costs the public institutions will have to pay, or not, for the present and future health of those people - at least in the European welfare. The intersection with the theme of Open Data is also clear: clever readers of Open Data released by transparent administrations can understand in depth many aspects of the management of health which today are fairly obscured.

But the perspectives are really much wider. Let's see an example. An article studying the pros and cons of open space arrangement in offices, versus cubicles or private rooms, was recently published in the "Occupational & Environmental Medicine" journal [26]. It would be of interest for all of the workers facing a rearrangement of their workspaces to know the results of these and similar researches. "Occupational & Environmental Medicine" is an Open Access journal; but most probably the vast public who could be interested in such an article does not know that these studies exist, that some of them can be freely accessed, that they can be used to make choices with a high impact on the individual lives: *and this ignorance is a problem of Information Literacy*. FOSTER Plus European project [27], for example, specifically tackles this problem with its module "Integrating Open Science in Information Literacy education" but once more its aim are the researchers, not the society or the citizens: FOSTER aim is "to contribute to a real and lasting shift in the behaviour of European researchers to ensure that Open Science (OS) becomes the norm".

On the problematic side, in various situations, people don't want to share data in open access because they think that they could in the future, in today unforeseeable

[5] For example, competence in statistics is needed when medical data are under scrutiny: how the data are collected, with which criteria, what do they describe, what do they imply. Hence for example: US medical data describing the outcome of a therapy for an illness can be directly meant to describe the outcome for EU patients?

[6] We can think of a variety of places (physical and digital) and activities like courses, workshops, MOOCs undoubtedly useful.

[7] Health literacy is the most frequently mentioned literacy in the titles of European institutions publications.

ways, take profit – economic, intellectual, etc. – from the data they actually produced and feel as 'their own'[8]. But this about Open Data is a much wider discourse.

Production of New Knowledge. The high complexity of today's world has us all thinking that the production of knowledge is reserved to those who (already) knows. Undoubtedly there are real reasons to think so, but this way of thinking implies an idea of knowledge as repetition, an idea of science as walled garden. The idea of trusting those who already proved trustable. And the situation of paywall around a big part of the knowledge excludes those who work and don't study *hence (apparently) have no need to intellectually progress their life*. But real (radical) innovation requires at least that also new persons can 'enter the domain' that is that they can access the knowledge body actually available. The core of the concept lies in the word "new", new persons: that is outsiders, those who are not already part of the research domain be it academic or private. Take for example a student who has finished her/his degree programmes: as soon as s/he goes out of the academia s/he loses the legal access to the paywalled scientific publications. But probably that is the moment when s/he is more intellectually productive in an innovative way. The assumption of Information Literacy in 1974 that an improved ability of all of the citizens and workers to access sources of information of assured quality and exploit them in their activities is beneficial for the whole country and its economy could be rephrased. We could say that the human capital and the cultural capital must be preserved and fostered, and this happens if people of every type – not only scientists and scholars – have continuous, abundant, free access to authoritative sources of information and knowledge.

In line with these reflections Catalani [28] commenting the conference "Sfide e alleanze tra Biblioteche e Wikipedia", held in 2017 at the Biblioteca Nazionale Centrale di Firenze, wrote: "Progetti del genere [Wikimedia, Wikisource, Wikidata] consentono di centrare diversi obiettivi: la valorizzazione del patrimonio bibliografico, il miglioramento della qualità dell'informazione sulle piattaforme Wikimedia, il trasferimento delle conoscenze a beneficio dell'intera società civile in un'ottica di terza missione, il coinvolgimento degli studenti nel processo di costruzione del sapere a seguito dell'acquisizione di abilità di media literacy." The presence of "trasferimento delle conoscenze a beneficio dell'intera società civile" is of primary relevance, obviously.[9]

The Need for Literacy The main, obvious objection to the above paragraphs is that "it is not easy", "one needs to be an expert", "to do so a lot of education is necessary".

---

[8] Every researcher feels that the data s/he produced are their own – be it only until the data are used for a publication, what has a strict relation with the concept of intellectual property and authorship. One could think that data are not fully comparable to an original creative intellectual product because they would be a property of things which comes to evidence. Nevertheless, data are the product of a "question" asked by the researcher on the basis of her/his original creative intellectual construct describing the state of things s/he is studying, so an approach to data as intellectual property is legitimate.

[9] Crowdsourcing scientific activities (like collaborative transcription of ancient manuscripts; tagging of historical pictures; and so on) is not relevant in this respect, as no one of the participants will write a *scientific paper* on the texts they transcribed. Someone else, a scholar, will do that, taking profit of the work of the transcribers.

Yes, it is true – see e.g. what Lopes et al. [29], and many others, wrote[10]. And here is the point where Open Access and Information Literacy connect to each other: the flow of information is complex and to intercept it, to take profit of it, the usual literacy is not sufficient. An Information Literacy is needed. In 1974 Paul Zurkowski understood this need more clearly than today when apparently the dominating idea is that using the devices corresponds to thus being informationally and digitally literate. The phenomenon of predatory journals (publication of unevaluated research articles on pay-to-publish journals) is one of the holes on the dark side of research, which shows that (more) Information Literacy is necessary also on the part of reputed scholars and scientists, as it seems if they contribute to those journals. The first organized description expression of the problem probably was the so called "Beall list" (https://beallslist.weebly.com/) and the last one at the moment of writing of this paper was the article published by to investigative journalists, Langhans and Krause, on the Süddeutsche Zeitung [30] showing that unfortunately many serious scholars publish on predatory journals. The article specifically investigated these practices in the German research context but nothing allows to think that for any other country the situation would be much different. One of the focal points of the matter was expressed by a post signed by Gerd Antes, scientific director of the Cochrane Germany Foundation, commenting the Süddeutsche Zeitung article and published in the Cochrane community blog [31][11]. He wrote that "the technical revolutions [brought by the digital world] that have taken place allow every lay individual to put together a professional-looking journal on the Internet, in which scientists from reputable institutions may then publish their findings, without even realizing what they are getting into". If it is sufficient for a journal to be "professional looking" for a scholar to judge it suitable to publish there, then a lot of education into Information Literacy is necessary also for those who could be deemed already fully literate.

4 Once More, Digital Libraries

The most radical difference between the times of Zurkowski and ours is the digital world: while information continues to be abundant in the physical world (mainly in the form of print) its part present in the digital world is much more manageable and easily reachable but requires new perspectives, new abilities, new competence. In fact, it is today that the ideas of Zurkowski become really capable to change the reality. Antes comments instead that "this development [the spread of predatory journals] is one of the systematically overlooked, undesirable side effects of the digit[al]ization movement" as if being still at the times of Oldenburg could be better. We on the contrary

[10] The "terza missione" of the University, as it is called in Italy, that is "la valorizzazione e il trasferimento delle conoscenze verso il contesto socio-economico" doesn't escape the approach where the focus is on the transmission of knowledge, not on the education which allows people to individually and autonomously build knowledge.

[11] The Cochrane collaboration is a no-profit initiative for producing high-quality, relevant, accessible systematic reviews of scientific literature so allowing to make health decisions through high-quality information. They work mainly with scientific journals.

think that the problems we face are those of our time - it means that there will be a lot of work for librarians to do, to bring not only to Open Access but also to Information Literacy scholars and scientists, students and citizens. And for the scientific information and knowledge the digital libraries digital continue to have a role to play.

References

1. Guédon, J.-C.: In Oldenburg's Long Shadow: Librarians, Research Scientists, Publishers, and the Control of Scientific Publishing. Association of Research Libraries, Washington, D.C. (2001)
2. Guédon, J.-C.: Open Access: Contro Gli Oligopoli Nel Sapere. Edizioni Ets, Pisa (2009)
3. Guédon, J.-C., Jensen, T.W.: Crystals of knowledge production. An intercontinental conversation about open science and the humanities. Nordic Perspectives on Open Science **1**, 1 (2015)
4. Suber, P.: Open access overview. Exploring Open Access Pract. J. **1**(1), 14 (2009)
5. Suber, P.: Open Access. MIT Press, Cambridge (2012)
6. Budapest Open Access Initiative| Read the Budapest Open Access Initiative. https://www.budapestopenaccessinitiative.org/read
7. Berlin Declaration. https://openaccess.mpg.de/Berlin-Declaration
8. European Commission: Open access - H2020 Online Manual. http://ec.europa.eu/research/participants/docs/h2020-funding-guide/cross-cutting-issues/open-access-data-management/open-access_en.htm
9. Piwowar, H., et al.: The state of OA: a large-scale analysis of the prevalence and impact of open access articles. Peer J. **6**, 1–23 (2018)
10. Lewis, D.W.: The inevitability of open access. College Res. Libr. **73**, 493–506 (2012)
11. Swan, A.: The Open Access citation advantage: Studies and results to date. https://eprints.soton.ac.uk/268516/
12. Turbanti, S.: L'editoria scientifica e la valutazione/Scientific publishing and research assessment. Il capitale culturale. Studies on the Value of Cultural Heritage, pp. 59–69 (2018)
13. Michetti, E., Lovascio, C., Morici, S.: L'accesso aperto alla letteratura scientifica: un'analisi multilivello/Open access to scientific literature: a multilevel analysis. Il Capitale Culturale. Studies on the Value of Cultural Heritage, pp. 71–93 (2018)
14. Mueller-Langer, F., Andreoli-Versbach, P.: Open access to research data: strategic delay and the ambiguous welfare effects of mandatory data disclosure. Inf. Econ. Policy **42**, 20–34 (2018)
15. Siler, K., Haustein, S., Smith, E., Larivière, V., Alperin, J.P.: Authorial and institutional stratification in open access publishing: the case of global health research. PeerJ. **6**, e4269 (2018)
16. Zurkowski, P.G.: The Information Service Environment Relationships and Priorities. Related Paper No. 5. (1974)
17. CILIP: CILIP Definition of Information Literacy 2018 (2018). https://infolit.org.uk/ILdefinitionCILIP2018.pdf
18. Testoni, L.: Una nuova definizione di Information literacy. Alcune riflessioni Vedianche **28**, 29–31 (2018)
19. Horton, F.W.: Overview of information literacy resources worldwide. UNESCO (2014)
20. Horton, F.W.: Understanding information literacy: a primer. UNESCO (2008)

21. Council conclusions of 30 May 2016 on developing media literacy and critical thinking through education and training. Official Journal of the European Union C212, 5–8 (2016). https://eur-lex.europa.eu/legal-content/EN/TXT/?uri=uriserv:OJ.C_.2016.212.01.0005.01.ENG&toc=OJ:C:2016:212:FULL
22. Huysmans, F.: Research for CULT Committee - Promoting media and information literacy in libraries: in-depth analysis. European Parliament, Directorate-General for Internal Policies, Brussels (2016). http://www.europarl.europa.eu/RegData/etudes/IDAN/2017/573454/IPOL_IDA(2017)573454_EN.pdf
23. AIB: Manifesto per l'Information Literacy. http://www.aib.it/struttura/commissioni-e-gruppi/gruppo-literacy/ilmanifesto/
24. IFLA: IFLA Media and Information Literacy Recommendations. https://www.ifla.org/publications/ifla-media-and-information-literacy-recommendations
25. Agenzia per l'Italia Digitale: Programma nazionale per la cultura, la formazione e le competenze digitali. LINEE GUIDA. Presidenza del Consiglio dei Ministri (2014)
26. Lindberg, C.M., et al.: Effects of office workstation type on physical activity and stress. Occup. Environ. Med. **75**, 689–695 (2018)
27. FOSTER. https://www.fosteropenscience.eu/
28. Catalani, L.: Spread open knowledge to create new one. Report of the conference "Challenges and Alliances between Libraries and Wikipedia" (Central National Library of Florence, November 10th 2017). Bibliothecae. it. 7, 391–404 (2018)
29. Lopes, C.A., Antunes, M., Sanches, T.: Contributos da literacia da informação para a ciência aberta. La contribución de la alfabetización informacional a la ciencia abierta **12**, 59–67 (2018)
30. Langhans, K., Krause, T.: Tausende Forscher publizieren in Pseudo-Journalen (2018). https://www.sueddeutsche.de/wissen/wissenschaft-tausende-forscher-publizieren-in-pseudo-journalen-1.4061005
31. Antes, G.: Predatory Journals and Predatory Publishers – Challenges within the Publishing Sector (2018). https://community.cochrane.org/news/predatory-journals-and-predatory-publishers-challenges-within-publishing-sector

The OpenUP Pilot on Research Data Sharing, Validation and Dissemination in Social Sciences

Daniela Luzi(✉), Roberta Ruggieri, and Lucio Pisacane

Institute for Research on Population and Social Policies, National Research Council, Rome, Italy
d.luzi@irpps.cnr.it

Abstract. The paper presents the results of a pilot carried out within the European project OpenUp (Opening up new methods, indicators and tools for peer review, dissemination of research results and impact measurement). Aim of the pilot is to investigate the applicability of peer review and/or Open Peer Review (OPR) to datasets in disciplines related to Social sciences. Main emphasis is given to the characteristic and features of data sharing and validation in this heterogeneous scientific field, thus providing the basis for the selection of the community chosen for the pilot. Indications emerging from the analysis of the interviews carried out in the pilot can drive the adoption of data quality assessment, and hence peer review, as well as provide some principles that can incentivize other scientific communities to share their research data.

Keywords: Data quality · Open data · Open dataset review and validation · Open Peer Review (OPR) · Social sciences

1 Introduction

The study presented is part of OpenUP [1] (OPENing UP new methods, indicators and tools for peer review, dissemination of research results and impact measurement), a European funded project that addresses the currently transforming science landscape on innovative peer review, dissemination and impact measuring. The project test the achieved results in a set of seven pilots [2, 3]. They are related to the three project's pillars and are applied to specific research areas and communities: arts and humanities, social sciences, energy and life sciences.

The results presented in this paper are related to the pilot study that investigated the applicability of peer review and/or OPR to datasets in Social sciences. The pilot aims at identifying strong and weak elements in the process of dataset review and validation and intends to outline best practices that facilitate transparency of the process as well as data dissemination, reliability and reuse.

In particular the paper reviews data sharing and evaluation practices in Social sciences, on which the selection of the pilot community is based, and reports on the interviews with the management team of the selected community. Lessons learned that

P. Manghi et al. (Eds.): IRCDL 2019, CCIS 988, pp. 248–258, 2019.
https://doi.org/10.1007/978-3-030-11226-4_20

can help identifying requisites and best practices for OPR of research data are reported in the conclusions.

2 Methods

To reconstruct the context of data sharing and evaluation in Social sciences, a landscape scan was performed to identify relevant literature, guidelines and scientific communities' practices. This first phase provided the basis for the selection of potential communities to be involved in the pilot, representative for this heterogeneous scientific field, as well as the identification of specific characteristics and problematic issues. For these reasons the landscape scans focused on surveys related to the researchers' motivation and constraints towards data sharing and on desk research enabled the identification of types of research data, dataset providers and modes of validating and sharing/publishing datasets in Social sciences.

After considering the involvement of different research communities in Social sciences, a collaboration was formalized with the Human Mortality Database (HMD). HMD is an open database that provides detailed, consistent and high quality data to researchers, students, journalists, policy analysts, and others interested in the history of human longevity and its prospects for the future (https://www.mortality.org/). HMD constitutes a good example of a well-known source of information providing open access to data in the scientific community of demographers. Moreover, the collaborative organization of HMD, as well as the high number and variety of data users worldwide, represented a good premise to get further insights into data managing practices and reuse.

The second phase of the analysis was devoted to the development of an interview schema that aimed at exploring the following HMD features: origin, motivations and organizational features of the scientific community, data quality assessment process, opinion on Open access of data. A further step of the project concerned the development of a users' survey carried out in collaboration with HMD to get insights into users' perspectives and feedback on data reuse. The results of the HMD survey are not included in this paper and will be presented in further publications. The interviews with the selected community were conducted on the 31st of January and 1st of February 2018 at the Max Planck Institute for Demographic Research in Rostock, Germany. They were performed according to interviewees' role in HMD, and for the selection of interviewees we also considered gender balance. The two directors, two researchers in their role of country responsible (in charge of analysing data for specific countries) were interviewed. These interviews covered the majority of HMD staff (4 out of 7). The summary content presented in this paper was revised, commented and approved by the interviewees.

The paper presents the results of the landscape scans related to the main characteristics of data management and validation in Social sciences. Moreover, a summary of the interviews is provided highlighting in particular scientific motivations for data sharing, organizational features as well as the quality assessment process as important success factors for data publishing.

3 Data Sharing and Evaluation Practices in Social Sciences

Similar to peer review of publications, data peer review is a quality assessment process of a dataset performed by experts in the field. Data quality assessment is a complex process that has to consider the different phases of the data lifecycle, starting from the development of a Data Management Plan (DMP) at the initial stage of a scientific project to the publication of its results. Data publication (some authors speak about Publication with capital letter, [4, 5]) that undergoes a peer review process validating data quality is currently performed in data journals and data repositories. However, analyses by Candela et al. [6], and Carpenter [7] show that there is room for improvement, as peer review activities in data journals vary widely and are mostly focused on metadata rather than data themselves, aiming at assessing the documentation and metadata description that facilitates data reuse. Assante et al. [8], in the analysis of generalist repositories (Zenodo, Dryad, Figshare etc.), also come to the conclusion that different criteria and quality control mechanisms are implemented based on various policies and/or guidelines. Best practices of data validation can be taken from the publication in trusted data repositories [9], in which the data quality control can be considered a form of review by experts in the field carried out in a pre-publication phase. This form of pre-publication review is then confirmed by the use of the dataset by data consumers in the post-publication phase through formal citations and/or statistics of use (see Fig. 1).

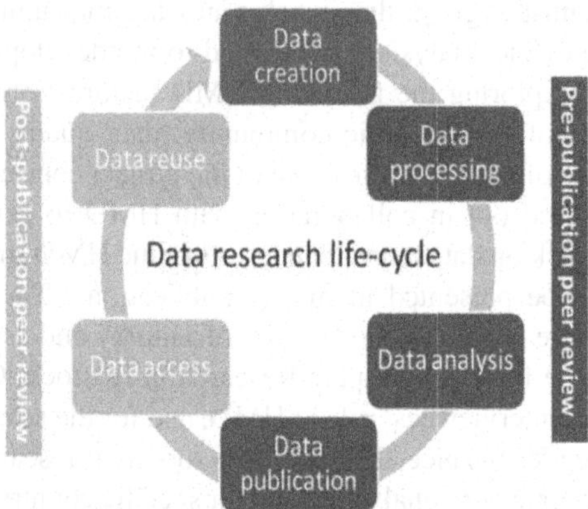

Fig. 1. Pre and post-publication peer review within the data research life-cycle

3.1 Researchers' Motivation and Constraints

Several surveys have investigated researchers' attitudes to analyse barriers and facilitators towards data sharing. General surveys allow us to compare social scientists' attitudes with other disciplines. Tenopir et al. [10] found that social scientists have a lower propensity to share the data they produce compared to the STEM researchers. These results have been confirmed in other surveys [11, 12]. This may depend on the nature of data, especially when qualitative data are involved, privacy and confidential issues, lack of technical standards and easy-to use platforms. Social scientists share the same concerns as scientists in other disciplines, such as not being recognised for making the data available, misuse of data, costs and time-consuming activities required.

Concerning peer review, Kratz and Strasser's [13] survey shows that researchers of different disciplinary fields are still unsure on how data peer review should work and in which context it should occur, even if they expect that data in repositories are subject to validation. The OpenUP survey [14] indicates that social scientists together with ICT researchers are the ones that are less satisfied with the traditional peer review process of publications.

3.2 Types of Dataset Providers

A specific characteristic in this field is that a significant portion of data is produced for purposes other than research [15]. These are data created by governmental bodies that have to comply with transparency regulations (such as the UK Freedom of information act) and make data they collect publicly available. Examples of these data comprise census figures, cohort and longitudinal studies, cross national surveys, economic indicators, etc. Among governmental bodies it is worth mentioning the data produced by national statistical offices that apply standard procedures to collect and process data, provide detailed supplementary documentation to describe the dataset, and also guarantee long-term preservation. These data collection constitutes trustworthy information, on which many other studies are based representing an important data source not only for social scientists.

While these sources of information can be compared to the big data produced by STEM, long-tail data are produced by social scientists to investigate local phenomena in small collaborative groups, often within interdisciplinary projects or individually. They are usually facing privacy issues that make the dataset sharing more complex.

3.3 Modes of Sharing/Publishing Datasets

In Social sciences, data publication model is mostly related to dataset submission in a data repository. In fact, there is only one data journal covering Humanities and Social sciences: "Research Data Journal (RDJ)" [16]. It was created by DANS [17] in 2016 with the aim to increase the visibility of data stored in the archive and to provide more extensive and detailed documentation. This journal conforms to well-established data journals in other disciplines such as Earth System Science Data, Geoscience Data Journal, and Scientific Data, it assigns a DOI to the article and provides the related DOI assigned to the dataset stored. On the other hand, DANS archive does not provide a standard description to cite the article. Currently eleven data papers have been published and three papers refer to the field of Social sciences.

Considering trusted data repositories, their main feature is that of data centres that act at national level as main information sources in this field. Worth mentioning are the UK Data Archive [18], GESIS [19] and DANS. The majority of these national centralized data centres are also part of two consortia, CESSDA [20] at a European level and ICPSR [21] at international level. These consortia provide a single access to international data and also develop and coordinate initiatives on standards, protocols and best practices to support data management and dissemination. Most of them provide access to data produced by governmental bodies and by research groups.

3.4 Modes of Validating Datasets

The above-mentioned data repositories are certified by the Data Seal of Approval [22] that has identified 16 requirements based on 5 criteria: data availability on the Internet, accessibility (clear rights and licenses), usability (format), reliability and identification of dataset through a persistent identifier. Note that these also correspond to the criteria used to evaluate the data themselves, similar to the FAIR principles. Given that data validation represents an iterative process that encompasses the entire research lifecycle, these trusted repositories provide guidelines on how to develop a data management plan at the very beginning of a research to assure data quality. Moreover, they require data producers to establish copyright and appropriate licenses, to use proper data formats and metadata schemas to facilitate access and reuse.

Trusted data repositories provide guidelines and/or template for a correct data ingestion according to the metadata schema of DDI [23], a standard supported by the Social sciences community that facilitate data replication and/or reproduction. They assure long-term data preservation and curation, develop data discovery tools (such as landing pages; [24]), suggest users a data citation format that acknowledge data provenance. Moreover, there are different initiatives to increase data re-use and make it traceable. The suggestion of a data citation format represents an important means to support data citations that are an indirect appraisal of the quality of the dataset at the post-publication phase. Some trusted repositories have adopted tools to track data use. For instance, DANS provides data users with a validation template to rank data set available in EASY: users can provide the rating (up to five stars) to data quality, quality of documentation, completeness of the data, consistency, structure and usefulness of the file format [25].

4 Interviews with the Human Mortality Database Management Team

The scientific community that manages the Human Mortality Database (HMD) was selected for the pilot as it fulfilled the requirements set up in the OpenUP methodology, and not least, for their willingness to an active collaboration on the analysis. The Human Mortality Database documents the longevity revolution of the modern era and facilitates research into its causes and consequences providing open data on human mortality. HMD was launched in 2002 as a result of a collaborative project that involved researchers of the Department of Demography at the University of California Berkeley (UCB) and the Max Planck Institute for Demographic Research (MPIDR). The following paragraphs summarise the key points of the interviews carried out with the two directors and two country specialists (CSs). As previously mentioned, its content was revised and approved by the interviewees.

4.1 Origin, Motivations and Organisational Features

Two previous relevant experiences guided the development of the database: the Kannisto-Thatcher Database on Old Age Mortality (KTD) at the MPIDR and the Berkeley Mortality Database (BMD), founded by John Wilmoth at UCB. Both experiences were concerned with what was at that time an emerging phenomenon of low mortality at young and adult ages, falling mortality at old ages, and greater survival to an advanced age, leading to a potential increase in the number of people exposed to degenerative diseases, which are difficult to treat or prevent. To understand this phenomenon, it was necessary to analyse and model longevity and survival of humans with a special emphasis on advanced (frontier) age over a long period of time. This research needed reliable data at international level providing long-term and continuous series without gaps, running up to the highest ages, providing fine details according to age, time, and cohort dimensions, ensuring sufficient quality and comparability across time and populations. HMD was therefore developed to answer this scientific question providing a methodology based on the previous mentioned experiences as well as freely available high-quality data [26].

The two HMD directors explained that "*the collaboration was originally, (and still is), based on a small, very well-established group of internationally based demographers who were willing to serve the scientific community interested in demographic studies*". The workload is equally distributed among the team that comprises CSs who have high-level competences on demographic development of a set of specific countries and are responsible for collecting and analysing data from the related national statistical offices. Other tasks comprise the development of computer codes, which are also made freely available to the end user who wants to reproduce the analysis, as well as the management of the website. Strong collaboration pertains the data quality process performed before data are publicly available, which constitutes a form of internal pre-publishing peer review process. During the interview the two directors agreed that "*trust among the team and scientific curiosity are the drivers of this successful cooperation*", that only recently was formalized by a Memorandum of understanding.

4.2 Goals and Main Features of the Database

The main goal of HMD is to support research on human mortality and longevity providing open data on 39 countries and some sub-areas and sub-populations with series starting as early as 1751 (i.e. Sweden) and covering more than 100 years for 16 populations. Birth and death counts are generally based on data from national vital registration systems, while data on population are based on the national census and estimates between censuses. However, differences may exist among countries in the periodicity of census, methods and definition used as well as in data format. Moreover, some countries have experienced changes in their territorial boundaries, have suffered substantial loss during war periods and/or faced substantial consistent migration over the period covered by HMD. For these reasons, as underlined by the two directors, HMD has developed a methodology to produce detailed death counts and population estimates, to correct mortality estimates at old ages, and to build high quality life tables (as described in detail in the Methods protocol). "*All HMD data are prepared using this standard methodology. This assures comparability in time and across countries"*. The two County specialists explained, that *"when special methods are needed to accommodate issues in data availability, this is documented in the country-specific documentation as well as reported in summary tables"* [27]. Country-specific details related to the data quality and statistical system in each country are therefore documented in the country-specific Background and Documentation file accessible from each country webpage. The application of these thorough procedures, *"the punctual explanation of the estimations and refinements of data sources make this database different from other sources providing mortality rates"*. These procedures guarantee a uniform analysis of raw data, facilitating the comparability across time and space, while the detailed documentation and the availability of source data allow end user to reproduce the analysis. The HMD team has also developed software code that guide them in the evaluation of data quality as well as software packages that facilitate end user to import and working with HMD data. These tools are freely available to end users along with technical reports explaining how to use these scripts [28]. This is another value-added feature of HMD.

4.3 The HMD Data Quality Assessment Process

The HMD team has developed a set of procedural steps to ensure data quality. This important topic was addressed in the interviews with the two directors and particularly explored in the interviews with the CSs. An activity diagram that reconstructed the workflow of the activities performed before data publication was presented to the CSs

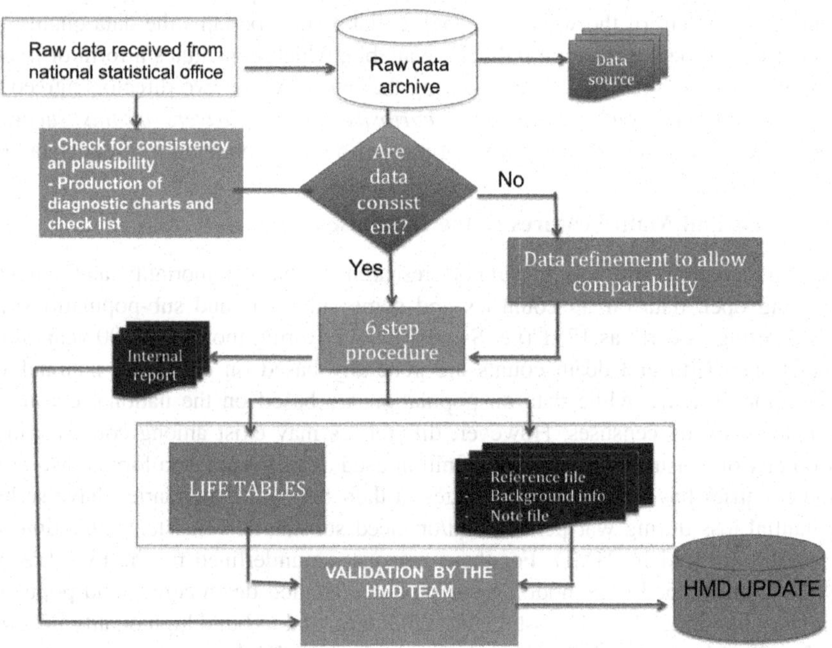

Fig. 2. Data quality assessment process

and discussed to have further insights on the procedures adopted to assess data quality. This intended to explore whether collaborative activities resembling a peer review process could be tracked in HMD data quality assessment. A high-level description resulting from the interviews is provided in Fig. 2.

During the interviews the CSs explained that each country or area is assigned to an individual researcher, a CS, who maintains a close relationship with a local expert generally at national statistical offices, and has an extensive knowledge of the population dynamics as well as how data are collected at national level. A CS is responsible for the first quality checks that evaluate consistency and plausibility of input data, prepares pre-calculation file (Lexis files) and analyses the results on the basis of a pre-defined data quality checklist and diagnostic charts that help him/her to explore unusual fluctuation and/or any other issues in data sources. The results of this analysis are shared within the HMD community via an internal report and are the basis for the application of the six-step procedure to produce the complete data series (exposures to risk, death rates, life expectancy and other life tables). Before data are published, the HMD team perform an additional phase of validation. These activities are crucial especially when a new country has to be included in HMD. However, they constitute a routine procedure every time data are updated. *"In cases of unexpected changes in national statistical systems or in regimes of national statistical registration, the updating procedures are non-trivial"*.

All steps in the computing of data analysis are documented in detail and made available to end users in the different files (*Background and documentation*, *Data source* and *Explanatory Notes*). According to the CSs interviewed, this is the distinctive feature of HMD: "*Data refinements and harmonization that allows comparison across countries are documented in detail so that researchers in this field are aware of possible problems in the data and know how these issues have been solved*".

4.4 Opinion on Open Access of Data and Peer Review

HMD management team declared that open access and open data in particular are very important for the development of demographic studies. Although they have no official statements on open policy, since its beginning, HMD provided open access data, based on a user agreement indicating that the data in the HMD are provided free of charge to all individuals who request access to the database [29]. Moreover, users are required to cite the database in their publications, following the citation guidelines provided by HMD [30]. Citations tracked through Google scholar are also reported in the website, and further steps to improve their collection are going to be planned in the next future.

When asked about long preservation of data, it emerged that the two HMD directors are dependent on funds. At the moment MPIDR support their activities *("MPIDR researchers are allowed to spend half of their work time on HMD")*, while the UCB team has to provide its own funds. A clear commitment of the organisation would therefore be very important and would also mean a clear recognition of their activities. Between the lines, it emerged that publication of scientific papers are generally considered more important than managing a database. In their opinion, *"the analysis of data, their quality check is not only a service for the community of reference but is a researcher activity in itself."* The majority of the interviewees has heard about open review of journals but has little knowledge on all its traits. If they see a similarity with peer review of data, this is associated in particular with transparency as a means of reconstructing the methods and procedures used for the data analysis.

5 Lessons Learned

Some important indications emerged from the analysis of the interviews that can drive the adoption of data quality assessment, and hence peer review, as well as some principles that can incentivize other scientific communities to share their research data. As stated by the HMD interviewees "*the guiding principles to create an open access database were: comparability, flexibility, accessibility and reproducibility*". *Comparability* was reached using a uniform, scientific methodology to calculate the various statistics of the 39 countries included in the database. *Flexibility* was achieved in the analysis of results using a uniform set of procedures for each population, but at the same time giving significant attention to each population in terms of its history and socio-political development. This is also reflected in the available formats of output data series. This is achieved thanks to the experiences and knowledge CSs, that is persons in charge of collecting data from a specific number of countries, who interact with statistical offices, check data consistency and provide population statistics together with a country report that explains specificity and motivation of analysis. *Accessibility* was guaranteed from the beginning by free of charge access of data, as well as by the provision of data in an open, no-proprietary format. *Reproducibility* is provided by the reconstruction of the data lifecycle that includes the availability of raw data, the method applied, the related results as well as the explanatory documentation. One of the main successful features of HMD is its transparent way of data managing and sharing that has two central phases of data validation. The first one is carried out by the CSs, who analyse the raw data according to a common predefined checklist that verifies consistency and plausibility of data. The second one is carried out in a collaborative way within the HMD team that validate the statistics before their publication, each time the database is updated.

Moreover, another successful component of HMD was its collaborative approach that is based on a strong scientific interest in the field as well as on the trust among the involved community that only recently has formally signed a Memorandum of understanding. The interviews also highlighted some indications that confirm some concerns already mentioned by other surveys. Interviewees stressed the importance of having a strong commitment of the organization in supporting the development of data infrastructures. This pertains different aspects: a long-term financial support (beyond the project duration), a policy endorsement on open data as well as a formal recognition of scientists for the efforts in data curation and quality assurance.

Implementation of other pilots should be further promoted in different sub-disciplines of Social sciences to get a deeper insight into sharing and evaluation practices of research data, focusing in particular on the procedures that document data validation and scientific assessment. It is necessary to promote transparency in the process of data evaluation, similar to the one adopted by HMD, so to facilitate the reproducibility of the research.

Acknowledgments. This study is part of the Horizon 2020 OpenUP project. Grant agreement no. 710722. The authors acknowledge the support and the collaborative efforts of the Human Mortality Database management team, namely Magali Barbieri (University of California, Berkeley and INED, Paris), Vladimir Shkolnikov (Max Planck Institute for Demographic Research (MPIDR) and Dmitri A. Jdanov, Head of the Laboratory of Demographic Data at MPIDR. A great thanks goes to our CNR colleague Cristiana Crescimbene for the valuable technical support during the OpenUP Pilot.

References

1. OpenUP. http://openup-h2020.eu/. Accessed 31 July 2018
2. Vignoli, M.: Project OpenUP-Deliverable D6.2 – Interim Use Case Evaluation Report, 30 November 2017. http://openup-h2020.eu/wp-content/uploads/2017/01/OpenUP_D6.2_Interim-Use-Case-Evaluation-Report.pdf
3. Blümel, C., et al.: Project OpenUP-Deliverable D6.3 – Final Use Case Evaluation Report, 14 September 2018. http://openup-h2020.eu/wp-content/uploads/2018/09/OpenUP_D6.3_Final-Use-Case-Evaluation-Report.pdf
4. Lawrence, B., Jones, C., Matthews, B., Pepler, S., Callaghan, S.: Citation and peer review of data: moving towards formal data publication. Int. J. Digital Curation **6**(2), 4–37 (2011). https://doi.org/10.2218/ijdc.v6i2.205
5. Mayernik, M.S., Callaghan, S., Leigh, R., Tedds, J., Worley, S.: Peer review of datasets: when, why, and how. Bull. Am. Meteorol. Soc. **96**(2), 191–201 (2015). https://doi.org/10.1175/BAMS-D-13-00083.1
6. Candela, L., Castelli, D., Manghi, P., Tani, A.: Data journals: a survey. J. Assoc. Inf. Sci. Technol. **66**(9), 1747–1762 (2015). https://doi.org/10.1002/asi.23358
7. Carpenter, T.A.: What Constitutes Peer Review of Data: A Survey of Published Peer Review Guidelines, April 2017. http://arxiv.org/abs/1704.02236
8. Assante, M., Candela, L., Castelli, D., Tani, A.: Are scientific data repositories coping with research data publishing? Data Sci. J. **15**, 1–24 (2016). https://doi.org/10.5334/dsj-2016-006
9. Callaghan, S., et al.: Guidelines on recommending data repositories as partners in publishing research data. Int. J. Digital Curation **9**(1), 152–163 (2014). https://doi.org/10.2218/ijdc.v9i1.309
10. Tenopir, C., et al.: Data sharing by scientists: practices and perceptions. PLoS One **6**(6), e21101 (2011). https://doi.org/10.1371/journal.pone.0021101
11. Kim, Y., Adler, M.: Social scientists' data sharing behaviours: investigating the roles of individual motivations, institutional pressures, and data repositories. Int. J. Inf. Manage. **35**, 408–418 (2015). https://doi.org/10.1016/j.ijinfomgt.2015.04.007
12. Faniel, I.M., Kriesberg, A., Yakel, E.: Social scientists' satisfaction with data reuse. J. Assoc. Inf. Sci. Technol. **67**(6), 1404–1416 (2015). https://doi.org/10.1002/asi.23480
13. Kratz, J.E., Strasser, C.: Researcher perspectives on publication and peer review of data. PLoS ONE **10**(2), e0117619 (2015). https://doi.org/10.1371/journal.pone.0117619
14. Stančiauskas, V., Banelytė, V.: OpenUP survey on researchers' current perceptions and practices in peer review, impact measurement and dissemination of research results survey, 19 April 2017. https://doi.org/10.5281/zenodo.556157
15. Borgman, C.L.: Scholarship in the Digital Age: Information, Infrastructure, and the Internet. MIT Press, Cambridge (2007)
16. Research Data Journal. https://brill.com/view/journals/rdj/rdj-overview.xml. Accessed 19 Sept 2018

17. DANS - Data Archiving and Network Services. https://dans.knaw.nl/en. Accessed 19 Sept 2018
18. UK Data Archive. http://www.data-archive.ac.uk/. Accessed 19 Sept 2018
19. GESIS - Gesellschaft Sozialwissenschaftlicher Infrastruktureinrichtungen. https://www.gesis.org/en/home/. Accessed 19 Sept 2018
20. CESSDA - Consortium of European Social Science Data Archives. https://www.cessda.eu/. Accessed 19 Sept 2018
21. ICPSR - Interuniversity Consortium for Political and Social Research. https://www.icpsr.umich.edu/icpsrweb/. Accessed 19 Sept 2018
22. Data Seal of Approval. https://www.datasealofapproval.org/en/. Accessed 19 Sept 2018
23. DDI - Data Documentation Initiative. http://www.dcc.ac.uk/resources/metadata-standards/ddi-data-documentation-initiative. Accessed 19 Sept 2018
24. Callaghan, S.: Data without peer: examples of data peer review in the earth sciences. D-Lib Mag. **21**(1/2), 9 (2015). https://doi.org/10.1045/january2015-callaghan
25. Data review in Easy. http://datareviews.dans.knaw.nl/. Accessed 19 Sept 2018
26. Barbieri, M., Wilmoth, J.R., Shkolnikov, V.M., et al.: Data resource profile: the human mortality database (HMD). Int. J. Epidemiol. **44**(5), 1549–1556 (2015). https://doi.org/10.1093/ije/dyv105
27. Special methods used for selected population. https://www.mortality.org/Public/Docs/SpecialMethods.pdf. Accessed 19 Sept 2018
28. Max Planck Institute for Demographic Research Technical reports. https://www.demogr.mpg.de/en/projects_publications/publications_1904/mpidr_technical_reports/all.htm. Accessed 19 Sept 2018
29. User Agreement. https://www.mortality.org/Public/UserAgreement.php. Accessed 19 Sept 2018
30. Citation guidelines. https://www.mortality.org/Public/CitationGuidelines.php. Accessed 19 Sept 2018

Crowdsourcing Peer Review: As We May Do

Michael Soprano([✉]) and Stefano Mizzaro

Department of Mathematics, Computer Science, and Physics, University of Udine, Udine, Italy
michael.soprano@outlook.com, mizzaro@uniud.it

Abstract. This paper describes Readersourcing 2.0, an ecosystem providing an implementation of the Readersourcing approach proposed by Mizzaro [10]. Readersourcing is proposed as an alternative to the standard peer review activity that aims to exploit the otherwise lost opinions of readers. Readersourcing 2.0 implements two different models based on the so-called codetermination algorithms. We describe the requirements, present the overall architecture, and show how the end-user can interact with the system. Readersourcing 2.0 will be used in the future to study also other topics, like the idea of shepherding the users to achieve a better quality of the reviews and the differences between a review activity carried out with a single-blind or a double-blind approach.

Keywords: Scholarly publishing · Peer review · Crowdsourcing

1 Introduction

The main mechanism to spread scientific knowledge is the *scholarly publishing* process, which is based on the *peer review* activity; a scientific article written by some authors is judged and rated by colleagues of the same degree of competence.

Although peer review is a reasonable and well established a priori mechanism to ensure the quality of scientific publications, it is not free from problems, and indeed it is characterized by various issues related to the process itself and the malicious behaviour of some stakeholders. Just to cite an example, in some cases reviewers cannot correctly evaluate a publication, e.g., when the paper reports data from an experiment which is long and complex and, therefore, not replicable by the reviewer itself; thus, an act of faith (that the author is honest) is sometimes required [4].

Also taking into account several of the issues and flaws of peer review that are widely analyzed in the literature, Mizzaro [10] conjectures that reviewers of scientific publications can be seen as a scarce resource which is being exhausted. To support such a thesis Mizzaro describes in detail ten different factors that contribute to it. As a solution, he proposes to take advantage of readers' opinions by outsourcing the peer review activity to their community and calls this approach *Readersourcing*, as a portmanteau for "crowdsourcing" and "readers".

P. Manghi et al. (Eds.): IRCDL 2019, CCIS 988, pp. 259–273, 2019.
https://doi.org/10.1007/978-3-030-11226-4_21

Although this might seem a radical solution, it is important to remark that: (i) similar approaches, suggesting variants and changes to peer review including collaborative reviews and/or a more distributed peer review practice, have already been proposed in the past [2,3,8]; and (ii) the usage of crowdsourcing in scholarly publishing is being proposed and analyzed for even more radical approaches, for example to outsource some steps of writing of scientific publications [15].

A crucial aspect of Readersourcing that must necessarily be addressed consists in providing a mechanism for which being a "good" reviewer is gratifying, in order to encourage readers to express adequate ratings (i.e., ratings which are truthful and unbiased). As a related issue, some stakeholder of the scholarly publishing process can have a malicious behaviour. This is reported from multiple sources and it can be caused by different factors. In this paper we do not provide an exhaustive description of all those behaviours and their causes, but we mention some examples. In particular, there is a recent article published on The Economist [16] according to which there are more and more journals where peer review activity is not performed, in contrast with what stated by their publishers. This leads scholars to inflate the list of their publications with articles that, probably, would not pass peer review. There are several discussions related to this phenomenon. One of the main causes (although it is not the only one) is the change of the business model that allows publishers to get a profit. In recent years those publishers have gone from monetization through the resale of subscriptions to readers to a payment request of a publication fee to the authors of articles. These articles can subsequently be read without any payment according to the open access model. This model, therefore, promotes the dissemination of knowledge but, at the same time, risks corrupting it. The article of The Economist [16] goes on by describing different malicious behaviours adopted by publishers of at least questionable periodicals to appear respectable and trustworthy when in the reality it is not like that at all. All this is also caused by the institutions of the scientific world which seem to worry less about where the financed research is published. We remark that we are not stating the existence of connections between the lack of reviewers and the malicious behaviour of some stakeholders; rather, these issues provide two different motivations to our work.

One of the possible solutions to deal with the above mentioned issues could be to rely on readers. As hypothesized by other researchers, it can be assumed that readers are a resource of which there is no shortage: they are many more than the reviewers, so if their opinions can be gathered they might allow to rate publications quality. This approach is not free from problems itself (e.g., lobbies, lazy readers [9]); although these need to be taken into consideration we do not have the space in this paper to discuss them.

In this paper we present our implementation of a system which is called *Readersourcing 2.0* that has two main goals: (i) to implement different models in order to take advantage of readers' ratings, as well as making easy to add more of them in the future, and (ii) to allow readers to express their ratings in a way that does not require too much effort, with just a few clicks or keystrokes. This paper is structured as it follows: Sect. 2 describes what a generic Readersourcing model should to able to do and compute, and how it should do that; then, two of those models are presented. Section 3 presents Readersourcing 2.0 implementation; we list its requirements, sketch its architecture, and briefly present the technologies actually used for its development. Moreover, we describe it from the point of view of a reader by showing and commenting its user interface and interaction capabilities. Section 4 concludes the paper.

2 Models

To outsource the peer review activity of publications to their readers a model of some kind can be useful. Every publication is characterized by one or more numerical ratings, each one provided by a reader. These ratings are the input data of such a model. From these data the model should define a way to measure the overall quality of a publication as well as the reputation of a reader as an assessor; moreover, from these measures it should be possible to derive the reputation of a scholar as an author. In other terms, the main issue to deal with consists in how the ratings that the assessed entity (i.e., a publication) receives should be aggregated into indexes of quality and, from these indexes, how to compute indexes of reputation for the assessors (i.e., the readers) and, eventually, indexes of how much an author is "skilled" (i.e., a measure of his ability to publish papers which are positively rated by their readers). In the following, we hypothesize to compute a single index for each of these measures.

This aggregation must be carried out by taking into consideration the fact that not all ratings are equal and that each of them has an intrinsic adequacy (i.e., a measure of how much truthful and unbiased they are) that characterizes it; in other words, it has to be possible to distinguish adequate from inadequate ratings and, then, good from bad assessors and, again, skilled from unskilled authors. Models that are able to do this are based on *co-determination algorithms*. In these algorithms the quality of the assessed entities is used to estimate the corresponding reputation/skill of the assessors/authors. Every time a new rating is given, these quantities are updated.

There is a further aspect to consider: what scale of values readers should use to express their ratings? continuous or discrete values? which interval of values should be used? Inevitably, this choice has an impact on the chosen co-determination algorithm. Medo and Rushton Wakeling [7] study the performance of different co-determination algorithms with ratings characterized by continuous or discrete values. From their analysis emerges as the best alternative the use of a scale characterized by an interval of values sufficiently "detailed" (e.g., 0–100) as it leads, in general, to the best performance for the co-determination process. Such a scale, in a real application, can be easily implemented and used by means of a slider component in the user interface.

A key point of the above characterization is that it allows to exploit the Readersourcing approach as a pre-publication replacement or as a post-publication addition to the standard peer review activity.

We now briefly describe two models based on co-determination algorithms.

2.1 The Readersourcing Model

The first model that we describe is the *Readersourcing Model* (RSM) proposed by Mizzaro [10] on the basis of a previous work [9]. In RSM, three different entities are identified: publications, authors, and readers. Each of them is characterized by a rating; articles scores aim to measure their quality and authors/readers scores measure their skill/reputation. A generic user of a system based on this model can assume both the roles of an author and a reader. As a reader of publications, the user is asked to give a numerical rating to those he read. As an author of a publication, a user is characterized by a score computed on the basis of the ratings given by readers. More generally, scores are dynamic and they change depending on user behaviour. For example, if an author with a low score publishes an article positively judged by readers, that score increases. If a reader expresses an inadequate rating (i.e., a rating which is judged as untruthful and/or biased because "distant" from other ratings) about an article, his score decreases, and so on.

Each entity characterized by a score also has an associated steadiness value (of the score itself). For example, publications read and rated by many readers will have high steadiness, while those of new authors and readers will have low steadiness. Steadiness affects the update of the scores because a high (low) value of it leads to faster (slower) changes of the scores themselves. As time passes, authors add new publications while readers read and rate them with numerical ratings. Those actions lead to an update of scores and steadiness values. High values of the scores represent, depending on the entity to which they refer, quality publications or skilled/good authors and readers, while steadiness values provide an estimate of how much that scores are reliable and stable.

2.2 The TrueReview Model

A second model is the *TrueReview Model* (TRM) proposed by De Alfaro and Faella [5]. They identify issues similar to those identified by Mizzaro [10] and they define an incentive system for the readers of publications to ensure that those publications will receive adequate reviews and precise evaluations.

There is a key difference that characterizes TRM with respect to RSM; the former does not computes a quality score for publications, while the latter does that. TRM, indeed, computes only a score for readers and leaves complete freedom about how to aggregate into a single index the ratings received by a single publication. However, the basic reader action does not change; readers are asked to give a single numerical rating to the publications they read.

The incentive scheme proposed by De Alfaro and Faella [5] aims to reward a reader every time that he provides a rating which is *informative* and *accurate*. Therefore, every given rating contributes with a certain "bonus" to reader's reputation which is computed on the basis of those two parameters. The aggregation of all these bonuses gives the reader's reputation itself and the one with the highest reputation is the "best" reviewer. Then, those reviewers should be ranked by their reputation and publicly shown in order to establish a healthy competition by pushing "bad" reviewers to improve themselves.

In order to compute the bonus for a given rating, the *informativeness* provides an incentive to select publications whose current evaluation is most different from what the future consensus will be, so it depends on the *previous* and the *future* ratings of the paper, but not on the one given by the reader under consideration. Thus, once the reader rates a certain publication, informativeness plays no further role and the bonus depends entirely on *accuracy loss*. The accuracy loss is computed by comparing the current rating provided by the reader under consideration with future ratings only. This eliminates any incentive to give a rating similar to those already expressed in the past by other reviewers which, probably, would end up going against the true beliefs of the reader itself.

In other words, this incentive scheme based on the concepts of informativeness and accuracy aims to reward reviewers who provide new information which is then presented to other reviewers in a compelling manner.

3 Readersourcing 2.0

In Sect. 1 we have outlined the motivations and the models which are the basis for the idea of outsourcing the peer review activity of scientific publications to their readers to improve the quality of the scholarly publishing process. We have implemented a system that actually allows to take advantage of this approach which is called *Readersourcing 2.0* and is now described.

3.1 Requirements

There are four main requirements that Readersourcing 2.0 has to satisfy:

- **R1**: provide to the reader a way to rate a publication by expressing a numerical rating in a seamless and effortless way;
- **R2**: allow readers to review publications in a way which is independent from the used device or software;
- **R3**: be able to aggregate the ratings received by a publication according to both RSM and TRM and show the computed scores to the users;
- **R4**: be general, extensible, and easily adaptable to other models besides RSM and TRM.

R1 is imperative: if the rating activity is not seamless and fast, readers will simply not rate the papers they read; the system must not require too much effort to the reader, which has to be able to express the rating with just a few clicks or keystrokes and without the need to open more windows, new browser tabs or even an external software. R1 is related to R2, which depends on how scholarly publishing is carried out. Usually, scientific articles are collected into journals that are made available to the scholars community through some publishing systems. So, the digital library of a publishing company consists in a large collection of files mainly encoded in PDF format. This might not be the best solution, but it is a sort of de facto standard. When a reader wants to read a publication, he will look for one of those PDF files available on such publishing systems. Once he finds the wanted one, it is opened inside a browser (tab) and then the reader itself has the choice to read it there or to download and store it somewhere on his filesystem, or even on an external device. This is the pivotal point; the reader must be able to easily rate the publication directly from the browser or from some sort of a reference stored *inside* the downloaded file.

A rating component located on the user interface of the client browser will suffice to satisfy R1: the user will simply select a rating for the publication and click a button. However, that cannot satisfy all the use cases, and R2 must be taken into consideration. Indeed, a reader could just close the browser and read the publication by using other software (PDF viewers) or even other devices (e.g., tablets). These considerations justify the previously introduced "file-oriented" approach. Our proposed solution consists in the following steps: (i) the publication chosen by the reader is downloaded locally to Readersourcing 2.0 server, (ii) the corresponding PDF file is annotated with a link that, once clicked, will take the reader to an ad-hoc rating page. After that, the system makes the paper available for the download.

3.2 Architecture

Readersourcing 2.0 is an ecosystem composed of more than one application. Indeed, there must be one application that acts as a server to gather all the ratings given by readers and one that acts as a client to allow readers to effectively rate publications. There is one additional component since the task of editing files encoded in PDF format is carried out by an ad hoc software library exploited by the server side application. An overview of Readersourcing 2.0 architecture is shown in Fig. 1; in the following we briefly describe these three components.

RS_Server [13] is the server-side application which has the task to collect and aggregate the ratings given by readers and to use RSM and TRM to compute quality scores for readers and publications. RS_Server must be deployed on a machine along with an instance of RS_PDF, otherwise it can not work properly. Then, there are up to n different browsers, with the corresponding end-users, which communicate with the server: each of them has an instance of *RS_Rate*, which is the true client. Both RS_PDF and RS_Rate are described in the following. This setup means that every interaction between readers and server is carried out through clients installed on readers' browsers and these clients have to handle the registration and authentication of readers, the rating action and the download action of link-annotated publications.

During the design phase of RS_Server some strategies have been adopted to ensure its extensibility and generality, to meet the R4 requirement proposed in Sect. 3.1. This means that: (i) it is straightforward to add new models, (ii) each model shares the same input data format, and (iii) if a model needs to save values locally to the RS_Server (i.e., in its database), there is a standard procedure to allow that.

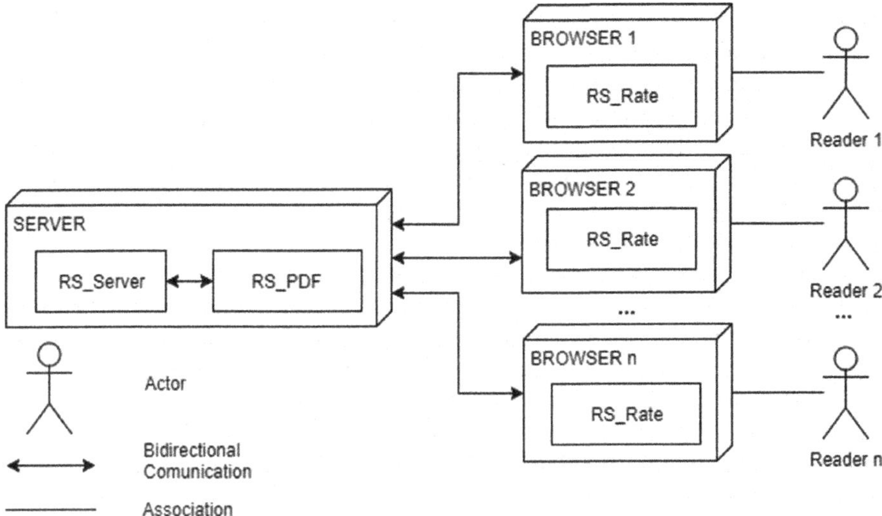

Fig. 1. Architecture of Readersourcing 2.0.

RS_PDF [11] is the software library which is exploited by RS_Server to actually edit the PDF files to add the URL required when a reader requests to save for later the publication that he is reading, as outlined in Sect. 3.1. It is a software characterized by a command line interface and this means that RS_Server can use it directly since they are deployed one along the other, without using complex communication channels and paradigms.

RS_Rate [12] is an extension for *Google Chrome*[1] and the client that readers actually use to rate publications; this means that every interaction with RS_Server is carried out through this client. We intend to generalize RS_Rate by providing an implementation for each of the major browsers (i.e., Firefox and Safari); moreover, we intend to provide an implementation of a fully fledged web application and a mobile application for each of the major operating systems (i.e., iOS and Android).

3.3 Implementation and Technologies

RS_Server is developed in Ruby on Rails,[2] which is a framework that allows to build applications strongly based on the Model-View-Controller (MVC) architectural pattern.

RS_Server is a Web Service (Server API-Only, according to Rails terminology) based on a communication paradigm composed of RESTful (REpresentational

[1] https://www.google.com/chrome/.
[2] https://rubyonrails.org/.

State Transfer) interfaces and on the exchange of messages encoded in JSON format through the transport layer provided by the HTTP protocol.

The technology used to develop RS_PDF is the Kotlin object-oriented programming language, whose main feature is to be fully compatible with the Java Virtual Machine. This feature is of great importance because it allows a developer to exploit code contained in any other software published in jar format and, more generally, to import any Java class, interacting with them through the syntax of Kotlin itself.

We have chosen Kotlin because it has many modern features (it has been created just three years ago) and it is supported rather intensively; furthermore, there are openings to other platforms that have greatly expanded its use possibilities. The most important reason, however, is that the underlying tool used to actually edit files encoded in PDF format is PDFBox,[3] which is a software library developed with Java and proposed as a complete toolkit to edit files in that specific format. So, RS_PDF is a wrapper for PDFBox that adds the needed links inside the PDFs requested by readers.

RS_Rate is an extension for Google Chrome; those extensions are developed using standard web technologies such as HTML, CSS and Javascript. Therefore, they are simple "collections" of files packaged in a CRX archive. This particular format is nothing more than a modified version of a ZIP archive with the addition of some special headers exploited by Google Chrome.

As for the Javascript component, RS_Rate does not actually use the "pure" language but instead uses the jQuery library, to simplify the selection, manipulation, management of events and the animation of DOM elements in HTML pages, as well as the implementation of AJAX features, that are widely used by RS_Rate to improve the user experience during its use.

3.4 User Interface

In this section we describe Readersourcing 2.0 user interface and we provide some details about how a reader could interact with it. A technical documentation on the design details of the components of the system can be seen in [14].

Accordingly to the R1 requirement proposed in Sect. 3.1, which states that a reader should be able to seamlessly rate a publication with a low effort and a few clicks or keystrokes, we have chosen to characterize our client (Google Chrome extension) as a popup which appears in the page that the user is browsing, when he clicks its toolbar button.

Figure 2 shows a section of a Google Chrome instance with our client active as a popup for a publication. This is the typical situation of a reader visiting a publisher's web site to access the PDF of a paper he is interested in. The figure also shows the first page that a reader looks at when he interacts with the client itself, which is used to take him to the login page, which is shown in Fig. 3a, or to the sign up page. From the login page a reader who has forgotten his password can reach the password recovery page (not shown), very similar to the login one.

[3] https://pdfbox.apache.org/.

Fig. 2. RS_Rate as an Google Chrome extension characterized by a popup action.

If a reader has still to sign up to Readersourcing 2.0 he can reach, from the page shown in Fig. 2, the one shown in Fig. 3b and fill in the sign up form. Once he completes those standard sign up and login operations, he will finally find himself into the rating page, which is shown in Fig. 3c, where the operations outlined in Sect. 3.1 can take place.

Regarding the requirement R1 outlined in Sect. 3.1, in the central section of the rating page a reader can use the slider to choose a rating value in a 0–100 interval, as suggested by Medo and Rushton Wakeling [7]. Once he selects the desired rating, he only needs to click the green *Rate* button and that will be all; with just three clicks and a slide action he can submit his rating. Furthermore, he can also click the options button and, if preferred, check an option to anonymize the rating he is about to provide. We remark that the reader has to be logged in to express an anonymous rating to prevent spamming, which in this case would be a very dangerous phenomenon. When such a rating is processed, the information regarding its reader will not be exploited (apart from avoiding the reader to rate the same publication multiple times).

Regarding the requirement R2 outlined in Sect. 3.1, if the reader wants to provide his rating at a later time rather than directly rate the publication, he can instead click the *Save for later* button and take advantage of the editing procedure of publications that stores a reference (an URL link) inside the PDF file that he is looking at. As soon as such an editing procedure is completed (usually just a few seconds), the *Save for later* button becomes a *Download* button, as shown in Fig. 3d. The reader can finally download the link-annotated publication by clicking on it. Furthermore, he can also use the refresh button (on the right of the *Download* button) to, as it says, refresh the link-annotated publication. This means that a new copy of the publication file will be downloaded, annotated, and made available to the reader. This feature is useful since a publication could be updated at a later time by its author.

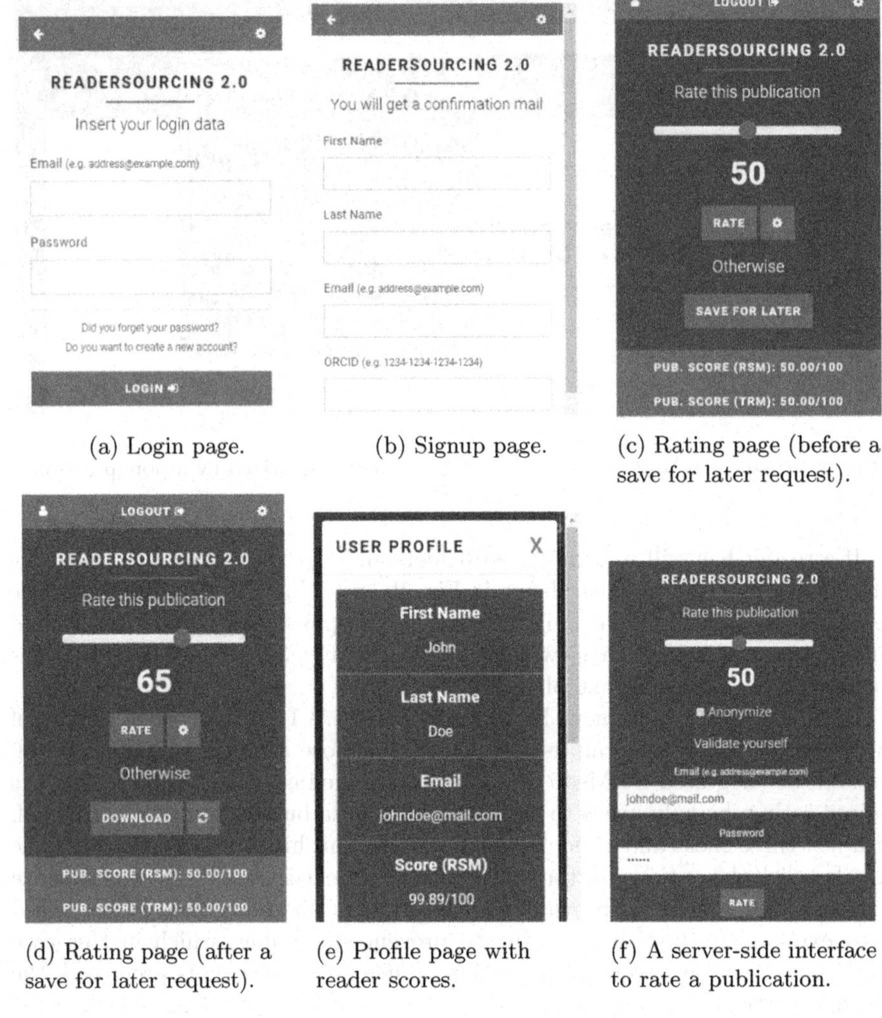

(a) Login page.

(b) Signup page.

(c) Rating page (before a save for later request).

(d) Rating page (after a save for later request).

(e) Profile page with reader scores.

(f) A server-side interface to rate a publication.

Fig. 3. The user interface of RS_Rate.

As soon as the link-annotated publication is downloaded, the reader will find a PDF containing a new final page with the URL. In Fig. 4 an example of such link-annotated publication can be seen; in that case, the reader has chosen to open it with his favourite PDF reader.

Once the reader clicks on the reference which, as outlined in Sect. 3.1, is a special link to RS_Server, he will be taken to the server-side application itself, which will show to him an interface that allows him to express his rating in a way that is independent from the browser extension used to actually store the reference. Therefore, if he sends his link-annotated publication to a tablet-like device, for example, he will take advantage of the built-in browser to express

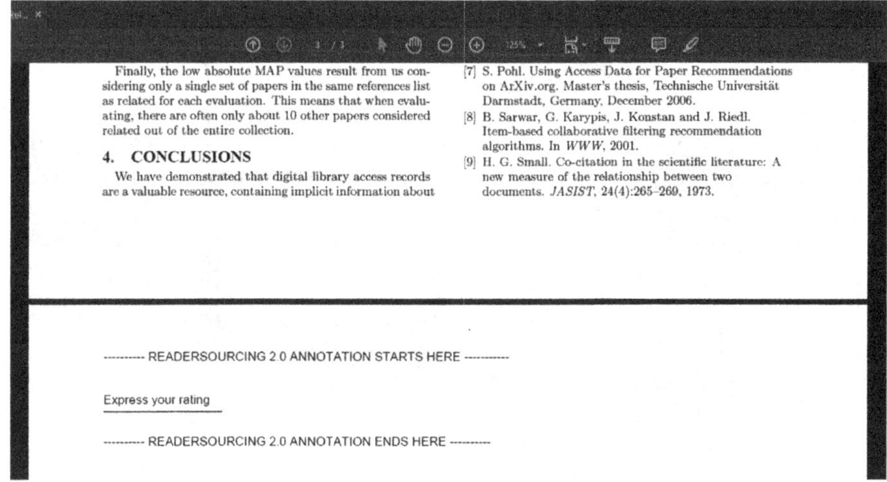

Finally, the low absolute MAP values result from us considering only a single set of papers in the same references list as related for each evaluation. This means that when evaluating, there are often only about 10 other papers considered related out of the entire collection.

4. CONCLUSIONS

We have demonstrated that digital library access records are a valuable resource, containing implicit information about

[7] S. Pohl. Using Access Data for Paper Recommendations on ArXiv.org. Master's thesis, Technische Universität Darmstadt, Germany, December 2006.
[8] B. Sarwar, G. Karypis, J. Konstan and J. Riedl. Item-based collaborative filtering recommendation algorithms. In *WWW*, 2001.
[9] H. G. Small. Co-citation in the scientific literature: A new measure of the relationship between two documents. *JASIST*, 24(4):265–269, 1973.

---------- READERSOURCING 2.0 ANNOTATION STARTS HERE ----------

Express your rating

---------- READERSOURCING 2.0 ANNOTATION ENDS HERE ----------

Fig. 4. A link-annotated publication.

his rating. Figure 3f shows the interface that the reader sees after a click on the stored reference. The reader is required to authenticate himself again as a form of security since, otherwise, the stored reference could be used by anyone who gets a copy of the link-annotated publication.

Regarding the requirement R3, every time a reader rates a publication every score is updated according to both RSM and TRM, and each reader can see the result through RS_Rate. In the bottom section of the rating page the score of the current publication can be seen (one for each model), as shown in Figs. 3c and d. To see his score as a reader (once again, one for each model), a user must click the profile button on the upper right corner. Once he does that, he will see the interface shown in Fig. 3e. From there, he could also edit his password since that interface acts as a profile page.

An overview of Readersourcing 2.0 capabilities is shown in Fig. 5. Let us suppose that there are four readers which are using RS_Rate to rate a publication P1, namely RD1, RD2, RD3 and RD4. Both RD1, RD2 and RD3 exploit the *Save for later* functionality of RS_Rate itself to express their rating at a later time. By doing this, they receive a link-annotated version of P1, namely P1+Link. After some time, RD1 chooses to open P1+Link with his favourite PDF reader. RD2, instead, chooses to send it to his iPad, while RD3 simply opens it with his instance of Google Chrome. When they click on the URL added by RS_Server, they are taken to the special page provided by RS_Server where they provide their rating. On the contrary, RD4 simply chooses to give his rating as soon as he finishes to read P1 directly through the interface of RS_Rate.

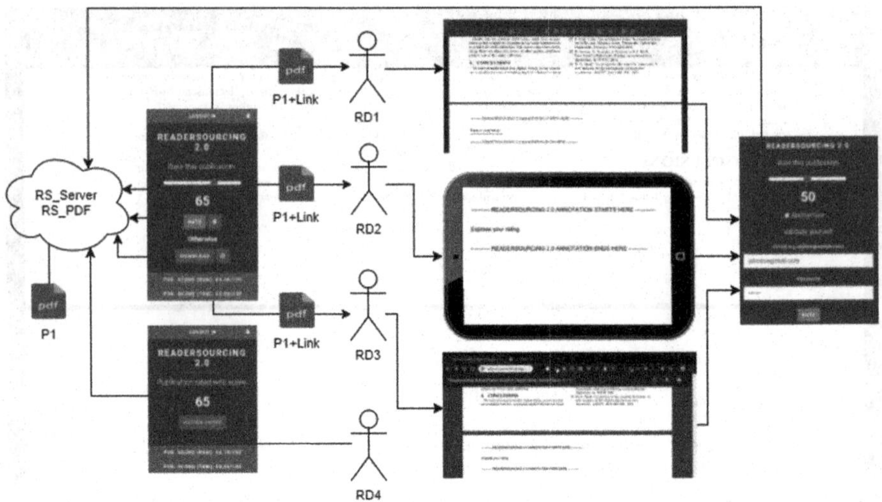

Fig. 5. Readers's interaction modalities with the Readersourcing 2.0 ecosystem

4 Conclusions and Future Work

Readersourcing 2.0 is still an early prototype and it must be considered as work in progress. During the next months we will keep improving it and what we have shown in the previous section about its appearance could still change. However, the overall architecture and the core functionalities will hardly be changed.

As one obvious future development from an architectural standpoint, we plan to take into account the other common browsers besides Google Chrome, and implement browser extensions for them. As a second step we also plan to implement some stand alone app for various architectures, to build a more complete ecosystem that allows the users to choose their preferred interaction modalities.

Once a more stable version is built it will be used to gather fresh data in terms of ratings of publications which will be analyzed and validated and, moreover, it will be used to study some specific topics that we briefly outline in the following. The results of those analysis will be published in a future work.

4.1 Review Quality

One of the biggest criticisms of an approach based on *Crowdsourcing* is that often the so called "workers" performing a tasks tend to do it hastily and approximately, without attention/motivation. Since the Readersourcing approach is nothing more than a particular type of Crowdsourcing, it is reasonable to analyze the question. In particular, to encourage reviewers to express quality ratings, in addition to the co-determination algorithms proposed by Mizzaro [9] and De Alfaro and Faella [5], there are techniques independent from the application domain that can be used.

One of such technique is studied by Dow et al. [6]. They focus on the benefits of user *shepherding*, namely guiding users through self-evaluation practices of the work carried out within the assigned task or through the evaluation of the work itself by external feedback. They compare two scenarios, one with shepherding and one without, and they analyze specific aspects of such practices (when to show feedback, how much detailed it should be, who should provide it, etc.) Once done that, they describe how self-assessment and evaluation carried out through external feedback lead workers to obtain different benefits and, in general, a higher quality outcome for the assigned task.

Finally, they ask themselves if workers are able to become shepherds for the remaining ones, suggesting that the more "expert" ones can assume that role. In the light of these results, it may be useful to add to our Readersourcing 2.0 ecosystem a self-assessment page of the rating that a reader has just expressed to obtain a higher quality of process.

Another well known technique to increase review quality is to establish awards and other forms of public recognition. We plan to evaluate this technique within a community of expert readers to see if it can improve the results obtained by our Readersourcing 2.0 ecosystem.

4.2 Single Blind vs. Double Blind Review

One of the various issues to be addressed in the context of a peer review process (even when it is outsourced to the readers of the publications) consists in showing (*single-blind review*) or not (*double-blind review*) the name of the author and his affiliation during the review phase of the publication. Tomkins et al. [17] analyze this question in two different scenarios.

In the first scenario, the reviewers are divided into two groups, one for the single-blind approach and one for the double-blind approach. Subsequently, each of them is asked to consider a set of publications and to state, one by one, if they intend to carry out the review, if they would consider the possibility or if they are not interested.

In the second scenario, the reviewers are asked to proceed with the review activity by giving a rating to each publication. The results of the experiments lead Tomkins et al. [17] to state that although many of the possible bias described by the detractors of the single-blind approach do not lead to statistically significant effects, the choice to show or not the names of the authors of a publication and their affiliation has effects on the behavior of the reviewers.

In particular, those who have access to such information tend to recommend acceptance of the publications of the most "famous" authors (both personally and in relation to their affiliation) compared to those who perform the review with the double-blind approach. According to Tomkins et al. [17], therefore, this is an aspect that must be taken into account during the definition of a peer review process. Since our process is an outsourced form of the standard peer review process itself, this is an interesting question to study.

4.3 Legal Issues

Regarding any legal issues related to the editing of proprietary PDF content, we hypothesize that it depends on where the PDF content has been published. There are many publishing systems and/or repositories where an author can distribute his papers under a Creative Commons license of his choice. Such a form of licensing allows to "remix, transform and build upon the material for any purpose" [1]; therefore, it should be possible to edit such PDF contents freely. However, there are publishers which have their own publishing and copyright licenses that must be studied on a case-by-case basis; therefore, the right approach within our system could be to allow the use of the "save for later" functionality of Readersourcing 2.0 outlined in Sect. 3.4 only within publishing systems which are safe from a legal viewpoint. This topic needs further investigation.

References

1. CC Attribution 4.0 International Public License (2010). https://creativecommons.org/licenses/by/4.0/legalcode
2. OpenReview (2016). https://openreview.net/
3. Akst, J.: I Hate Your Paper: many say the peer review system is broken. Here's how some journals are trying to fix it. Sci. **24**, 36 (2010). http://www.the-scientist.com/2010/8/1/36/1/
4. Arms, W.Y.: What are the alternatives to peer review? Quality control in scholarly publishing on the web. JEP **8**(1) (2002). https://doi.org/10.3998/3336451.0008.103
5. De Alfaro, L., Faella, M.: TrueReview: a platform for post-publication peer review. CoRR (2016). http://arxiv.org/abs/1608.07878
6. Dow, S., Kulkarni, A., Klemmer, S., Hartmann, B.: Shepherding the crowd yields better work. In: Proceedings of ACM 2012 CSCW, pp. 1013–1022. ACM (2012)
7. Medo, M., Rushton Wakeling, J.: The effect of discrete vs. continuous-valued ratings on reputation and ranking systems. EPL **91**(4), 48004 (2010). http://stacks.iop.org/0295-5075/91/i=4/a=48004
8. Meyer, B.: Fixing the process of computer science refereeing, October 2010. https://cacm.acm.org/blogs/blog-cacm/100030-fixing-the-process-of-computer-science-refereeing/fulltext
9. Mizzaro, S.: Quality control in scholarly publishing: a new proposal. JASIST **54**(11), 989–1005 (2003). https://doi.org/10.1002/asi.22668
10. Mizzaro, S.: Readersourcing - a manifesto. JASIST **63**(8), 1666–1672 (2012). https://onlinelibrary.wiley.com/doi/abs/10.1002/asi.22668
11. Soprano, M., Mizzaro, S.: Readersourcing 2.0: RS_PDF, October 2018. https://doi.org/10.5281/zenodo.1442597
12. Soprano, M., Mizzaro, S.: Readersourcing 2.0: RS_Rate, October 2018. https://doi.org/10.5281/zenodo.1442599
13. Soprano, M., Mizzaro, S.: Readersourcing 2.0: RS_Server, October 2018. https://doi.org/10.5281/zenodo.1442630
14. Soprano, M., Mizzaro, S.: Readersourcing 2.0: technical documentation, October 2018. https://doi.org/10.5281/zenodo.1443371
15. Sun, Y., et al.: Crowdsourcing information extraction for biomedical systematic reviews. CoRR abs/1609.01017 (2016)

16. The Economist: Some science journals that claim to peer review papers do not do so (2018). https://www.economist.com/science-and-technology/2018/06/23/some-science-journals-that-claim-to-peer-review-papers-do-not-do-so
17. Tomkins, A., Zhang, M., Heavlin, W.D.: Reviewer bias in single- versus double-blind peer review. PNAS **114**(48), 12708–12713 (2017). http://www.pnas.org/content/114/48/12708

Hands-On Data Publishing with Researchers: Five Experiments with Metadata in Multiple Domains

Joana Rodrigues(✉), João Aguiar Castro, João Rocha da Silva, and Cristina Ribeiro

Faculty of Engineering of the University of Porto, INESC TEC,
Rua Dr. Roberto Frias, 4200-465 Porto, Portugal
joanasousarodrigues.14@gmail.com, joaoaguiarcastro@gmail.com,
joaorosilva@gmail.com, mcr@fe.up.pt

Abstract. The current requirements for open data in the EU are increasing the awareness of researchers with respect to data management and data publication. Metadata is essential in research data management, namely on data discovery and reuse. Current practices tend to either leave metadata definition to researchers, or to assign their creation to curators. The former typically results in ad-hoc descriptors, while the latter follows standards but lacks specificity. In this exploratory study, we adopt a researcher-curator collaborative approach in five data publication cases, involving researchers in data description and discussing the use of both generic and domain-oriented metadata. The study shows that researchers working on familiar datasets can contribute effectively to the definition of metadata models, in addition to the actual metadata creation. The cases also provide preliminary evidence of cross-disciplinary descriptor use. Moreover, the interaction with curators highlights the advantages of data management, making researchers more open to participate in the corresponding tasks.

Keywords: Research data management · Data publication · Metadata · Dendro

1 Introduction

Current research is characterized by an unprecedented growth in the volume of data being produced, as powerful computational capabilities are available to even small research groups—the so-called long-tail of science [6]. Usually, small groups or individual researchers have very limited resources to ensure long-term availability of their data. As such, they need adequate research data management (RDM) practices supported by practical tools, so that the datasets they produce can be made available to others. This is especially important as more research funding agencies adhere to the European Commission's Guidelines on FAIR Data

P. Manghi et al. (Eds.): IRCDL 2019, CCIS 988, pp. 274–288, 2019.
https://doi.org/10.1007/978-3-030-11226-4_22

Management in Horizon 2020, which advocate for a set of principles to make data Findable, Accessible, Interoperable and Reusable [10].

Data publishing involves peer review, unique identification and semantic enrichment of datasets. Published data raises awareness of new research claims or findings, promotes reuse, and brings scholarly credit to data authors [15]. Research data are slowly becoming first-class research objects on par with traditional publications, but a solid data citation culture is required for this to become the norm [13].

Data reuse depends on the quality of the metadata associated to a dataset, because that is often the only information available for researchers to interpret the data and decide on their quality and relevance to their work. Also, the production of metadata for research datasets requires the involvement of data creators, as domains are diverse and specific knowledge of the domain is required.

Researchers in the long-tail may commit to data organisation and description, but will probably lack the expertise to create FAIR data and metadata and to publish them in the most suitable repository. On the other hand, data curators working on their own will probably not be able to provide the rich contextual information that enables reuse. This exploratory study focuses on practical aspects of research data publication, namely the importance of the collaboration between researchers and data curators. The process used here assumes that data creators have the assistance of a curator to formalize the knowledge of the data production context and to assist in data publishing.

The study follows five research groups in the description and publication of datasets, and considers in more depth the choice of metadata elements. It is supported on Dendro[1], a data organisation and description platform that enables the combination of generic descriptors with those tailored for the research domains. Data are then published in a data repository—in this experiment, the B2SHARE service of the EUDAT infrastructure.

The five cases correspond to different domains. Social sciences are present with a case in Family Psychology and another in Information and Innovation Management. For science and technology there is a case of named entity recognition in Portuguese, one of automatic detection of hate speech in text, and of one machine vision with a multi-camera system.

The paper is organized as follows. Section 2 provides an overview of the requirements and issues concerning the adoption of metadata standards for research data, while Sect. 3 presents related work. The study configuration is described in Sect. 4, continued in Sect. 5 with the details of the five cases. The results of the data description experiments are explored in Sect. 6 and discussed in Sect. 7.

[1] https://github.com/feup-infolab/dendro.

2 Requirements for Research Metadata

The specialization of researchers makes them natural providers of domain-specific metadata, even more so in the long-tail of science [11]. As data creators, they have unique knowledge of the data production context, including domain-specific concepts and configurations used in the production of the data. Conversely, while the skills of data curators may ensure the correctness of the metadata from a formal point of view, a metadata record produced solely by an institutional data curator may not be comprehensive enough. Curators are not domain experts, and thus may not anticipate what a researcher needs to know about the dataset to reuse it. Thus, the collaboration between the data creator and the curator has the potential to generate both correct and comprehensive metadata records.

Under the Research Data Alliance initiative[2], the Metadata Standards Catalog Working Group is working in a Metadata Directory[3] listing available metadata standards by domain, such as the Data Documentation Initiative (DDI)[4] for data description in the Social and Behavioral Sciences and the Darwin Core[5] for Biodiversity data. Moreover, the Directory also includes general standards that can be broadly applied to the scientific context, such as Dublin Core[6] for generic descriptive metadata, CERIF[7] for recording research activity and PROV[8] for data quality and reliability purposes.

Metadata elements are building blocks for a comprehensive data record. Together with identity and subject descriptors, information captured in metadata elements for aspects such as the temporal, geospatial and scientific context is essential to promote data reuse [9]. An analysis of nine scientific standards, considering domain, objective and architecture, showed that the ability to add new elements or modules to address domain-specific needs is a common requirement [18]. However, features such as simplicity and sufficiency are likely to be appreciated by researchers when describing their data, and should also be considered in the development of metadata models.

3 Related Work

The relevance of RDM is visible in the growing body of studies in this area, some with a focus on researchers' perspectives and practices regarding data organization and sharing, while others have a closer look at researchers' metadata practices.

---

2 https://www.rd-alliance.org/.
3 http://rd-alliance.github.io/metadata-directory/standards/.
4 http://www.ddialliance.org/.
5 http://rs.tdwg.org/dwc/index.htm/.
6 http://dublincore.org/.
7 http://www.eurocris.org/cerif/main-features-cerif/.
8 http://www.w3.org/2001/sw/wiki/PROV/.

A multinational survey of data sharing and reuse found that researchers are willing to share data and reuse data created by others, despite barriers slowing data sharing that may be overcome with user-friendly tools [14]. Interviews with researchers also show that journal requirements and normative pressure at the discipline level, together with the perceived benefits at the individual level, have positive effects in data sharing behaviors. On the other hand, realizing the effort involved in data sharing has a significant negative impact [7].

A study regarding barriers to data reuse suggests that the ease of access and the interoperability are important initial conditions for successful reuse. Also, while some lack of data documentation can be overcome by more experienced researchers, it is still an obstacle to data reuse [19]. Another study in the field of evolutionary biology looked into data organization and concluded that all participants used some kind of metadata or a personally created organization scheme [16], but are mostly unfamiliar with data documentation with reuse in mind [2].

Data descriptions produced by researchers were found to be more focused on the details rather than in general features when compared to those made by information specialists. This highlights the difference between descriptions meant for personal archives and those meant for data repositories, which tend to have reuse in mind [17].

Studies on the relation of researchers with RDM and metadata provide evidence of the need to bridge the gap between researchers and data curators, while guidelines and tools to support metadata and RDM are being created. A good example of a metadata tool developed with researchers in mind is a framework to record minimal information for data reuse in the geobiology domain, resulting from stakeholder engagement [8].

4 Methodology

For this exploratory study we collected five cases by challenging researchers at the University of Porto (U.Porto) to publish datasets from their projects, either recently finished or soon to be completed. These datasets were likely to lose their publication opportunity soon, due to the re-assignment of researchers to other projects. After an introduction to some of the benefits of having their data published, such as the association of a DOI, researchers demonstrated motivation to describe and make their data available to others. Our approach explores a set of techniques consistent with participatory research methods [4], namely by combining casual meetings, interviews, content analysis and data description. The flexibility to combine these techniques is essential in this case not only due to the busy schedules of the participants, but also because there are many domain-specific cultures and different points of intervention to account for in RDM [5].

Figure 1 shows the data publication workflow, which includes the description process. Although intended as a systematic one, the techniques applied in the cases varied according to the availability of researchers and also their level of awareness of RDM. The process includes contacts with researchers to select key concepts and identify metadata requirements, a description phase where the selected metadata elements are used, and ends with data deposit in a repository.

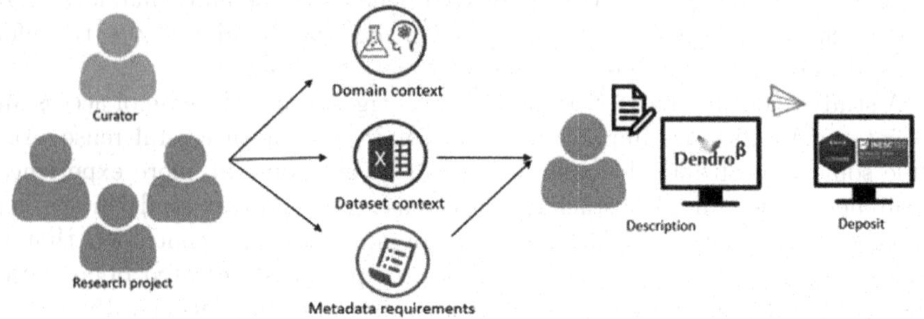

Fig. 1. Data publication process

In each case, we have conducted casual meetings with elements from the project teams to reach an agreement on the activities required to prepare data for publication. To assess the domain, the dataset and the metadata requirements, we conducted interviews or content analysis sessions—at least one in each case. The choice of method was determined by the availability of the researchers: while interviews take time from the researchers' agendas, content analysis can be performed by the curator without the researcher. In this case papers and other technical documents are used to provide the context, and the resulting metadata model requires the validation of the researchers.

After assessing the metadata requirements in the five cases, we decided to include a selection of DDI elements in the set of descriptors available in Dendro, the ontology-based platform used for the data description activities [12]. In Dendro, descriptors are drawn from generic standards such as Dublin Core, existing domain-specific ontologies, or other ontologies that built in collaboration with researchers, such as Hydrogen Generation, Vehicle Simulation, and Gravimetry, introduced as a result of previous partnership [1].

Most of the DDI elements used were already part of the DDI-RDF Discovery vocabulary[9], so we could load that ontology directly into Dendro. Those that were not in DDI-RDF Discovery were captured as a separate ontology, also loaded into the platform.

Dendro integrates with several data repositories and platforms (e.g. DSpace, figshare, CKAN, EUDAT's B2SHARE) [12]. This is used in the final step of the process, where a package containing the dataset and its metadata is submitted to the B2SHARE repository[10] and in some cases also to the institutional CKAN-powered research data repository at INESC TEC[11].

[9] http://rdf-vocabulary.ddialliance.org/discovery.html.
[10] https://b2share.eudat.eu/.
[11] https://rdm.inesctec.pt.

This process allows researchers to create domain-specific metadata records that will be used in the data repositories to find and access the datasets, and also by other researchers to estimate their value. The use of multiple ontologies addresses metadata limitations often associated with generalist repositories that are meant to cover several research communities [3].

All data description sessions were performed in Dendro except one, where the researcher could not participate in person. In this case the curator team described the dataset, which was then validated by the researcher.

5 The Five Data Publication Cases

The workflow described above was applied to five projects in different research domains: two in social sciences (Psychology and Innovation), three in science and technology (Hate Speech, Multi-Cam, and NER).

5.1 Family Psychology (Psychology)

The goals of the underlying project are to understand how the dynamics between work and family are linked to the exercise of parenting, the parent-child relationship and the child's socioemotional development, and to examine how the relationship between teachers and children intersects with the parental roles for the socioemotional development of children in dual-earner families[12].

The research team is collecting observational data from families with pre-school children and explores them combining a cross-sectional study design with a longitudinal design. The raw data is organized in a database where subsets are then selected by researchers to work on a specific perspective or a certain reality.

A dataset containing processed data concerning children's emotions regulation, parents' work-family conflict and psychological availability, represented as descriptive statistics and organised in a table, was selected by the researchers to be published in B2SHARE[13].

5.2 Automatic Detection of Hate Speech in Text (Hate Speech)

The goal of the Hate Speech project is to study the Internet and social networks, in particular for detecting hate speech posted online. The researcher annotated a dataset in Portuguese and built a classification system for types of hate speech using a hierarchical structure. The project aims to deliver tools for automatic detection of aggressive communications. Contributions include the definition of hate concepts, namely hate speech subtypes[14].

The data was collected from Twitter, and manually annotated. The dataset contains 5,668 messages from 1,156 distinct users, and handles 85 classes of hate

[12] https://www.fpce.up.pt/reconciliar/index_eng.html.

[13] DOI: https://doi.org/10.23728/b2share.7b3c66dfa4df4a7f9ba04fbc30cfb8bc.

[14] http://hdl.handle.net/10216/106028.

speech. The data types in the dataset are tweets and class taxonomies. Data were published in B2SHARE[15] and also in the institutional INESC TEC data repository[16].

5.3 Multi-camera System for Automatic Positioning (Multi-Cam)

Taking into account the rapid evolution of multimedia platforms, this project explored the use of technological resources and applications in sports. The research focuses on the location of a ball in a 3D space field, as part of the application of computer vision to indoor team sports[17]. Several techniques for camera calibration and 3D reconstruction methods were studied and tested, resulting in the use of a limited number of conventional cameras. The published dataset[18] contains camera calibration data resulting from an acquisition protocol that considered all stages of camera calibration and different static and dynamic ball scenarios.

5.4 Named Entity Recognition (NER)

This project addresses the task of named entity recognition (NER), in the field of Natural Language Processing, and explores entity detection as an enabler for more complex tasks[19], such as relation extraction or entity-oriented search, as applied for instance in the ANT search engine[20].

The project evaluated existing NER tools to select the best approach and configuration for the Portuguese language, more specifically for institutional content. Results include a richer entity-oriented search experience with new information, as well as a better ranking scheme based on the additional context available to the search engine. The project also created several detailed manuals with systematic analyses of available tools. The dataset was published in the B2SHARE repository[21] and in the INESC TEC repository[22].

5.5 Information and Innovation Management (Innovation)

This project takes an information management perspective on research and development, innovation and entrepreneurship, applying it to the knowledge transfer and the innovation process in the University of Porto. The data from an exploratory study allow the identification of internal and external agents, resources, the relations between actors and institutions, processes and flows,

---

15 DOI: https://doi.org/10.23728/b2share.9005efe2d6be4293b63c3cffd4cf193e.
16 https://rdm.inesctec.pt/dataset/cs-2017-008.
17 http://hdl.handle.net/10216/88168.
18 DOI: https://doi.org/10.23728/b2share.b89c998e26674e8eba8b263c8b4f3a2e.
19 https://www.linguateca.pt/aval_conjunta/HAREM/harem_ing.html.
20 http://ant.fe.up.pt/.
21 DOI: https://doi.org/10.23728/b2share.93f011314ce24391a4c317779ccf8068.
22 https://rdm.inesctec.pt/dataset/cs-2017-005.

and the main inputs and outputs. The project created a model of innovation indicators in an academic context and fitted it to the University of Porto[23].

The published dataset contains innovation indicators of several Portuguese institutions, used to support the development of the model. Data from this case is published in B2SHARE[24] and in INESC TEC[25].

6 Data Description Experiment Results

Overall, researchers were satisfied with the selection of generic metadata elements. Some went beyond that and produced a more comprehensive metadata record using descriptors from their scientific context, such as temporal and spatial coverage and data collection procedures.

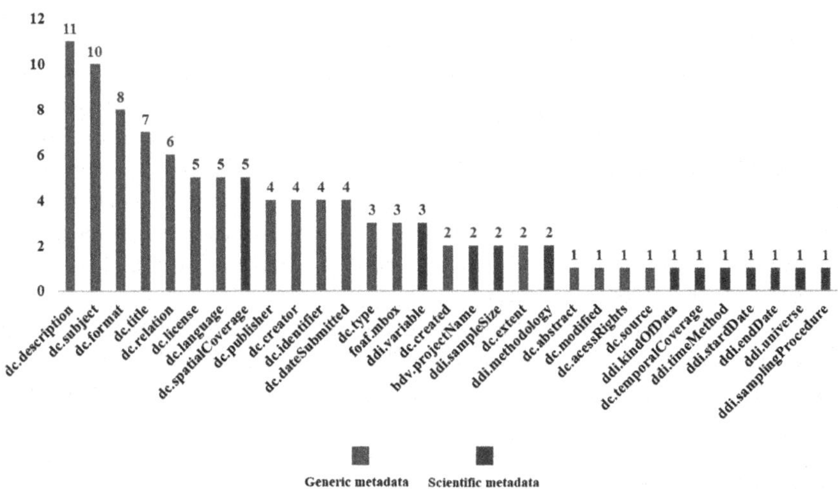

Fig. 2. Descriptors used by researchers

In the Psychology case, two researchers participated in the data description session with a data curator, who made recommendations on the use of DDI elements, specific for the Social Sciences. The researchers were autonomous in the selection of descriptors in Dendro, talking to each other and progressing without the data curator intervention. They have selected metadata elements for temporal context, namely `timeMethod` and `temporalCoverage`, and methodological information, e.g. `kindOfData`. In addition to these descriptors they used more generic descriptors such as the point of contact (`mailbox`).

---

[23] http://hdl.handle.net/10216/113262.

[24] DOI: https://doi.org/10.23728/b2share.7d60f3262d2e49e7a118911077d99eff.

[25] https://rdm.inesctec.pt/dataset/ii-2018-001.

The Hate Speech case was the only one in which the researcher was not directly involved in the description, communicating to the curators a preference for a generic and clear one. The result, based on content analysis, was proposed by the data curator and validated by the researcher. Selected descriptors were `description`, `subject` and `title`, as well as `format`, `dateCreated`, `spatialCoverage` and `relation`. The `mailbox` descriptor was used for the email contact of the researcher.

The Multi-Cam case has the largest data volume, and there was more concern with their organization and structure. The researcher who collected the data was no longer associated to the group, and two members of the team described the data in separate sessions, providing a complementary validation. They chose mostly generic descriptors, namely `creator`, `description`, `title`, `language`, `subject`, `format`, `relation`, and `type`. Spatial and temporal coverage elements were also filled in. As in other cases, a descriptor for the contact with the project researcher (`mailbox`) was included.

The NER case has concentrated on Dublin Core descriptors: 19 of the 21 selected descriptors were from this vocabulary. The researcher considered that they were sufficient to give a correct description of their dataset. They include temporal context descriptors such as `temporalCoverage`, `dateCreated`, `dateModified` and `dateSubmitted`. In addition, administrative descriptors were selected, such as `creator` and `publisher` and content descriptors such as `title`, `description` and `subject`. It is interesting to note that the researcher selected the DDI descriptor `methodology`, considering it a basic descriptor. The same happened with descriptor `mailbox`.

Finally, the researcher in the Innovation case has training in Information Science and some previous knowledge of RDM, so the mediation of the data curator was limited to a brief presentation of the activity goals and of the RDM tools to support data publication. The researcher selected generic descriptors (Dublin Core) to contextualize the dataset, including `creator`, `publisher`, `title`, `subject`, `format`. Dublin Core elements for scientific context were also used, such as `spatialCoverage`, and `temporalCoverage`. In addition to these, the researcher also selected DDI descriptors for a more specialized description: `sampleSize`, `universe`, `methodology`, `startDate` and `EndDate`. The name of the project (`projectName`) and the contact of the researcher (`mailbox`) were also chosen in this case.

Figure 2 has the distribution of descritors used in the five cases. Overall, we noticed a repeated use of the `format` descriptor (8 times). This shows that researchers consider it important to refer to the format in which the data are made available, as it can condition their visualization and reuse by others and even by themselves. Note that descriptors can be repeated; 4 occurrences of `format` are from the NER case.

After the datasets were deposited in B2SHARE, we kept track of user interactions. Table 1 shows the number of downloads and annotations made for each of the datasets exported to B2SHARE, from the date of the deposit (between December 2017 and January 2018) until October 4, 2018. As each dataset

Table 1. User interactions with datasets in B2SHARE

Case	Downloads	Annotations
Psychology	**14**	**1 comment**
dataset - table 1.docx	4	"Very interesting dataset. The description in the initial interface caused me interest, however when I opened the file I was in need of seeing more information ... maybe it was a short dataset. However the description we see in the file "(Re) conciliar.txt" informs us about extremely important details and also gives us the indication of the name of the project, which allows to research more about it. It is good to have tools like B2NOTE to share opinions between data producers and users."
(Re)conciliar.json	1	
(Re)conciliar.rdf	5	
(Re)conciliar.txt	3	
(Re)conciliar.zip	1	
Hate Speech	**10**	**0**
annotator_classes.csv	2	
dataset_dummy_classes.csv	1	
graph_hierarchical_classes.csv	1	
Portuguese Hate Speech Twitter Dataset.json	2	
Portuguese Hate Speech Twitter Dataset.rdf	2	
Portuguese Hate Speech Twitter Dataset.txt	2	
Portuguese Hate Speech Twitter Dataset.zip	0	
README.txt	0	
Multi-Cam	**8**	**0**
Multicamera System for Automatic Positioning of Objects in Game Sports.json	3	
Multicamera System for Automatic Positioning of Objects in Game Sports.rdf	0	
Multicamera System for Automatic Positioning of Objects in Game Sports.txt	2	
Multicamera System for Automatic Positioning of Objects in Game Sports.zip	3	
NER	**3**	**2 comments**
HAREM NER Models for OpenNLP, Stanford CoreNLP, spaCy, NLTK.json	0	"The information associated with each file is quite limited. there are many descriptors that could be shown for all datasets, for example the license, and for all files, for example the format." "I would like to find usage examples for the pre-trained models for each of the NER tools."
HAREM NER Models for OpenNLP, Stanford CoreNLP, spaCy, NLTK.rdf	0	
HAREM NER Models for OpenNLP, Stanford CoreNLP, spaCy, NLTK.zip	3	
nltk.zip	0	
open-nlp.zip	0	
spacy.zip	0	
stanford-corenlp_Copy_created_1510592294091.zip	0	
stanford-corenlp.zip	0	
Innovation	**4**	**2 comments**
dataset.xlsx	2	User 1) "Dataset of enormous importance, I would like to see more work developed in this area. Congratulations on the investment in these issues, surely these data will serve many other researchers who want to invest in this area. Certainly I will reuse your work for future investigations. I will recommend this work to colleagues in the field of information management, in particular innovation indicators in the academic context. I'm happy to be able to talk to Fabio more "informally" through tools like B2Note." User 2) "Some pages, used as drafts, could be removed as they don't contain much. Also, referencing cells between pages (opposed to copy/paste) could help with automated parsing."
U.InovAcelerator.json	0	
U.InovAcelerator.rdf	0	
U.InovAcelerator.txt	1	
U.InovAcelerator.zip	1	

consists of several files (*.zip, *.txt, *.rdf, *.json), the interactions are also provided at the file level.

A total of 39 downloads are recorded for the five cases. Only Psychology had downloads in all the files associated with the dataset, and was also the case with the highest number of downloads. The opposite happened with the NER case, with only 3 downloads of a single file. The remaining cases had a similar number of downloads, which were distributed by the various files.

As for the annotations, 5 were recorded, all in the comment format. These comments were made through B2NOTE, a EUDAT service. This service provides an environment where any interested party (authors, researchers and others) can improve the description using comments, keywords or tags.

A user remarked that the Psychology data were interesting, but noted that they expected to have more data in the dataset. The usefulness of the complementary metadata in the *.txt file was also noted, namely the name of the project.

In the NER case, two comments were made by the same user. The first is about the limited information associated with each file. The user added that descriptors such as "format" and "license" should be part of the metadata of all datasets. The second comment was more specific and had to do with the user expectations regarding the dataset.

Finally, the Innovation case has two comments by different users. The first highlights the importance of that dataset, as an incentive for more studies in this area, along with the intention to reuse and promote it. The other comment is a recommendation on how to improve the organization of the data.

7 Discussion

Regardless of their fields of expertise, researchers involved in this study have developed a sense of awareness and motivation towards RDM. After the first interactions they revealed curiosity in the data publishing process, and noticed that data management skills could contribute to improve their work environments and career opportunities. Our contacts in the five projects in the experiment were junior researchers. This is not surprising, given that they are closer to data production and also, as they are still developing their research routines, more open to introduce RDM practices in their schedules. We expect senior researchers to be attracted by the advantages of data publication as well. In further work, we look forward to include them in activities related to metadata quality and data reuse.

The Psychology researchers had no data description experience but, after some conversations, became familiar with the proposed task quite easily. In this case the researchers considered DDI convenient for their data. The importance of metadata elements that use terminology used in their routines was visible. The Innovation case was the one in which the researcher worked more autonomously, due to previous training in the area of metadata and data management. The case of NER generated the most debate between data curators and researchers.

Researchers in this project were already aware of the importance of the management of research data and, therefore, they had clear ideas on the descriptors they wanted to use prior to the data description session. Furthermore, they anticipated the potential for data reuse in their community, motivating them to make a detailed description.

Overall, the cases that seem to produce metadata records with more scientific elements are those that either have relied on the effective participation of data curators or already had a domain-specific vocabulary such as DDI.

A common feeling with researchers is that the RDM activity within their projects can have positive effects on data quality, allowing them to record details about the data collection process even prior to considering data reuse. Nevertheless, discussing metadata with researchers is never a trivial task, primarily because the boundaries between data and metadata are not always clear cut. This reinforces the importance of communicating through practical metaphors they can relate to their practice, namely those from the traditional publication workflow. Since most repositories use Dublin Core elements, those are also easier to understand by average repository users. This may have resonated in the systematic selection of Dublin Core metadata elements in the descriptions.

The systematic use of temporal and geospatial elements, like `timeMethod`, `endDate`, `startDate`, `temporalCoverage` and `spatialCoverage`, as a whole, reveals that researchers are inclined to register the temporal and spatial dimensions of their projects. Such elements locate the data in space and time, which is important for discovery and for reuse.

We observed that the `methodology` descriptor is easy to understand by researchers and suitable to describe the data collection approach independently of the research domain, if more specific descriptors are not available. Yet, only two researchers have filled in the `methodology` element. A possible solution is to consider this descriptor as a core element for generic RDM data description platforms and repositories. This will change the common practice of including methodological aspects in the more generic `description`.

8 Conclusions and Future Work

The main goal of this line of work is to raise awareness of the importance of RDM among researchers, across research domains and data types. The hypothesis here is that concrete tasks are required to illustrate the difficulties and the rewards in RDM. In the five cases presented, researchers participated in the whole process, from the selection of the metadata models, through the description up to deposit and publication. The interactions summarized in Table 1—especially the comments—show the importance of the domain-specific metadata. In the Psychology case, for instance, the end user mentioned the importance of the metadata to interpret a dataset that seemed limited at first, with respect to their expectations. Also, in the case of NER, one user said that they hoped to find more metadata, a clear indication that the metadata is relevant to the interpretation of the data.

A selection of complete cases such as those explored in this study can act as a motivator for other researchers, at our institution and elsewhere. We often observe that people ask for practical examples of data publication, especially in related domains, and also take pride in having their case included as an example. There is also a pressing need for more data to reach the publication stage so RDM can become an established practice at institutional level.

With this study we aim to provide more insight on the collaborative approach between researchers and curators. However, such an approach requires an evaluation, which depends on more data publishing cases and more evidence of end user feedback regarding the use of metadata in dataset dissemination and reuse.

Some researchers are already quite aware of the importance of good RDM practices. In the case of Family Psychology, the researchers included the publication of their data in B2SHARE in the project reports. They consider that this publication is a valuable result of the project.

Besides the 5 cases described here, more data publication scenarios are being explored using this method. With a larger number of cases, more generic observations are expected. But not all people are easily engaged: some of our tentative contacts declare that there is no need to describe data, given that colleagues from the same area will have no difficulty in understanding them.

Data description experiments are a learning process for both data curators and researchers, and are valuable to build trust between them as RDM stakeholders. As data curators, lacking in disciplinary expertise, we had to rely on the descriptions that were provided by domain experts. Even so, the question remains whether there is potential for the selection of more domain-specific descriptors.

The combination of efforts between researchers and data curators is expected to result in higher-quality metadata, but more work and considerably more time are required to evaluate this approach to data description. Testing for reuse is particularly challenging. According to participants in the Psychology case, to anticipate reuse scenarios is a difficult exercise. Moreover, reuse experiments depend on observations over an extended period of time.

Although RDM is increasingly present in the daily work of researchers, it is still necessary to raise awareness of these issues and to promote initiatives to make data repositories grow. Training actions are a good strategy, provided that researchers are involved as active participants, dealing with RDM in their own domains, solving their problems and contributing to the data management process. These initiatives are essential for researchers to become proactive in data management and to take more advantage of the collaboration with data curators.

Acknowledgements. This work is financed by the ERDF - European Regional Development Fund through the Operational Programme for Competitiveness and Internationalisation - COMPETE 2020 Programme and by National Funds through the Portuguese funding agency, FCT - Fundação para a Ciência e a Tecnologia within project TAIL, POCI-01-0145-FEDER-016736. João Aguiar Castro is supported by research grant PD/BD/114143/2015, provided by the FCT - Fundação para a Ciência e a Tecnologia.

References

1. Castro, J.A., et al.: Involving data creators in an ontology-based design process for metadata models. In: Developing Metadata Application Profiles, pp. 181–213 (2017). https://doi.org/10.4018/978-1-5225-2221-8.ch008
2. Akers, K.G., Doty, J.: Disciplinary differences in faculty research data management practices and perspectives. Int. J. Digit. Curation **8**(2), 5–26 (2013). https://doi.org/10.2218/ijdc.v8i2.263. ISSN 1746–8256
3. Assante, M., et al.: Are scientific data repositories coping with research data publishing? Data Sci. J. **15** (2016). https://doi.org/10.5334/dsj-2016-006
4. Bergold, J., Thomas, S.: Participatory research methods: a methodological approach in motion. Forum Qual. Soc. Res. **13**(1) (2012). https://doi.org/10.17169/fqs-13.1.1801
5. Cox, A.M., Pinfield, S., Smith, J.: Moving a brick building: UK libraries coping with research data management as a "wicked" problem. J. Librarianship Inf. Sci. **48**(1), 3–17 (2016). https://doi.org/10.1177/0961000614533717
6. Heidorn, P.B.: Shedding light on the dark data in the long tail of science. Libr. Trends **57**(2), 280–299 (2008). https://doi.org/10.1353/lib.0.0036. ISSN 1559–0682
7. Kim, Y.: Institutional and individual influences on scientists' data sharing behaviors. The School of Information Studies - Dissertations Paper 85 3.1, p. 304 (2013). https://doi.org/10.1002/meet.14505001093
8. Palmer, C.L., et al.: Site-based data curation based on hot spring geobiology. Plos One **12**(3), e0172090 (2017). https://doi.org/10.1371/journal.pone.0172090
9. Qin, J., Ball, A., Greenberg, J.: Functional and architectural requirements for metadata: supporting discovery and management of scientific data. In: Proceedings of the International Conference on Dublin Core and Metadata Applications, pp. 62–71 (2012)
10. European Commission: Directorate-General for Research and Innovation. Guidelines on FAIR Data Management in Horizon 2020 (2016)
11. Rice, R., Haywood, J.: Research data management initiatives at University of Edinburgh. Int. J. Digit. Curation **6**(2), 232–244 (2011)
12. da Silva, J.R., Ribeiro, C., Lopes, J.C.: Ranking Dublin Core descriptor lists from user interactions: a case study with Dublin Core Terms using the Dendro platform. Int. J. Digit. Libr. (2018). https://doi.org/10.1007/s00799-018-0238-x. ISSN 1432-300
13. Silvello, G.: Theory and practice of data citation. J. Assoc. Inf. Sci. Technol. **69**(1), 6–20 (2018). https://doi.org/10.1002/asi.23917
14. Tenopir, C., et al.: Changes in data sharing and data reuse practices and perceptions among scientists worldwide. PLos ONE **10**(8), 15 (2015). https://doi.org/10.5061/dryad.1ph92
15. Thanos, C.: Research data reusability: conceptual foundations, barriers and enabling technologies. Publications **5**(1), 16 (2017). https://doi.org/10.3390/publications5010002
16. White, H.C.: Considering personal organization: metadata practices of scientists. J. Libr. Metadata **10**(2–3), 156–172 (2010). https://doi.org/10.1080/19386389.2010.506396
17. White, H.C.: Descriptive metadata for scientific data repositories: a comparison of information scientist and scientist organizing behaviors. J. Libr. Metadata **14**(1), 24–51 (2014). https://doi.org/10.1080/19386389.2014.891896

18. Willis, C., Greenberg, J., White, H.: Analysis and synthesis of metadata goals for scientific data. J. Am. Soc. Inf. Sci. Technol. **63**(8), 1505–1520 (2012). https://doi.org/10.1002/asi.22683
19. Yoon, A.: Red flags in data: learning from failed data reuse experiences. Proc. Assoc. Inf. Sci. Technol. **53**(1), 1–6 (2016). https://doi.org/10.1002/pra2.2016.14505301126. ISSN 23739231

Data Mining

Towards a Process Mining Approach to Grammar Induction for Digital Libraries

Syntax Checking and Style Analysis

Stefano Ferilli(✉) and Sergio Angelastro

Dipartimento di Informatica, Università di Bari, Bari, Italy
{stefano.ferilli,sergio.angelastro}@uniba.it

Abstract. Since most content in Digital Libraries and Archives is text, there is an interest in the application of Natural Language Processing (NLP) to extract valuable information from it in order to support various kinds of user activities. Most NLP techniques exploit linguistic resources that are language-specific, costly and error prone to produce manually, which motivates research for automatic ways to build them.

This paper extends the BLA-BLA tool for learning linguistic resources, adding a Grammar Induction feature based on the advanced process mining and management system WoMan. Experimental results are encouraging, envisaging interesting applications to Digital Libraries and motivating further research aimed at extracting an explicit grammar from the learned models.

Keywords: Natural Language Processing · Grammar Induction · Process Mining and Management

1 Introduction

One of the most relevant peculiarities and opportunities provided by Digital Libraries (DLs for short) and Archives, with respect to their physical counterparts, is the possibility of automatically accessing and processing their content by computers for several purposes. Some examples are: indexing aimed at faster and better information retrieval; topic extraction aimed at document organization or content understanding and summarization; content analysis aimed at supporting scholars in their research; etc.

Since most of DL content is in the form of text, Natural Language Processing (NLP) techniques play an important role. Such techniques may tackle problems at several levels of complexity. From the lowest to the highest we have:

Language Identification identifies the language in which a text is written;
Stopword Removal removes uninformative terms from a text;
Normalization reduces to standardized form inflected forms of words;
Part-of-Speech Tagging associates terms to their grammatical function;
Parsing returns the syntactic structure of sentences;

P. Manghi et al. (Eds.): IRCDL 2019, CCIS 988, pp. 291–303, 2019.
https://doi.org/10.1007/978-3-030-11226-4_23

Understanding captures some kind of semantic information from the text.

While for some tasks (e.g., indexing and retrieval) the lexical level is sufficient, more advanced processing requires higher-level tasks to be carried out.

In turn, NLP techniques are often based on the use of linguistic resources: e.g., Language Identification often exploits n-gram distribution, Stopword Removal exploits lists of frequent terms, Normalization exploits lists of suffixes, Part-of-Speech (PoS for short) Tagging exploits suffixes and/or grammatical rules, Parsing uses grammars, Word Sense Disambiguation uses conceptual taxonomies or ontologies. The quality of such resources may dramatically affect the quality, or even determine the feasibility, of the NLP steps. However, developing these resources is a critical, costly, time-consuming and error prone task, because it is typically carried out manually by linguistic experts. To make things worse, each language requires its own set of resources. Most works in the literature are concerned with English [1,6,7,17,22], probably due to its having a structure which is easier than other languages and to its importance as the standard information interchange language worldwide. Little exists for a few other important languages [20], and almost nothing for the vast majority of minor languages. As a result, automatic processing techniques cannot be applied to documents in these languages, leading to the risk that entire cultures might be lost.

This situation motivated the development of (semi-)automatic techniques to learn the resources and other useful linguistic information from a (representative) set of texts in a given language. Our effort in this direction resulted in *BLA-BLA* (Broad-spectrum Language Analysis-Based Learning Application), a tool aimed at covering a wide spectrum of NLP tasks, including several techniques that allow to learn in a fully automatic way linguistic resources for language identification [12], stopword removal and term normalization [11,13] and concept extraction [18,21]. The learned resources may be used by NLP systems, and/or be taken as a basis for linguistic studies and/or further manual refinements. Most of the techniques in BLA-BLA are incremental, meaning that whenever more texts become available for the language, it is easy to run again the technique and obtain updated resources. This is a very important feature that is generally unavailable in other approaches in the literature.

This paper investigates the possibility of extending BLA-BLA with Grammar Induction and Checking features. In particular, we propose the use of an advanced Process Mining approach [16] called WoMan. As the first step in such an investigation, here we aim at assessing whether grammar models learned by WoMan are effective in recognizing the syntactic correctness of sentences in a given language. Experiments show that they are. Possible applications to document collections (libraries or archives) include an assessment of their overall linguistic quality, or an analysis of linguistic style variability therein.

This paper is organized as follows. After discussing some background and related work in the next section, Sect. 3 introduces the WoMan framework for process mining and management and Sect. 4 casts the linguistic problem into a process mining task. Then, Sect. 5 evaluates the proposed approach before concluding the paper.

2 Background and Related Work

Grammar Induction is a language acquisition problem. According to Gold's formalization [15], given a target language L from a set $\mathbf{L}$ of possible languages, a learner $\mathbf{C}$ is shown a sequence $[s_i]$ of positive examples ($\forall i : s_i \in L$) and after each example s_n it must maintain a hypothesis $L(\mathbf{C},[s_0, \ldots, s_n]) \in \mathbf{L}$ for L. Any $s \in L$ will be sooner or later present in the sequence (no guarantees on the order or frequency of examples). The hypothesis is *eventually correct* if $\exists k$ s.t. $\forall j > k : L(\mathbf{C}, [s_0, \ldots, s_k]) = L$. So, positive-only and incremental learning approaches are inherent this formalization. In general, a Grammar Induction algorithm should be able to discover an underlying grammar from examples, to be used to parse new sentences and to assess their grammaticality.

Approaches proposed in the literature can be divided into *supervised* and *unsupervised*. The former process sentences annotated with their constituent tree structure (e.g., the treebanks corpus [19]), which requires significant expert effort. In the latter, only words are annotated (manually or automatically) with their PoS tag. Unsupervised approaches typically exploit *phrase structure* or *dependency grammar* representations, and are further classified in *structural search*, aimed at discovering a suitable grammar structure that compactly describes the data, and *parameter search*, aimed at finding a set of optimal parameters for a fixed-structure grammar, such that the result best explains the language.

As regards Structural search approaches, [23] proposed a Bayesian model merging framework to find the structure of a probabilistic grammar. Possible uses include the discovery of an Hidden Markov Model (HMM) topology or the set of context-free production for a stochastic context-free grammar. The approach performs incremental merging operations on model substructures attempting to maximize the Bayesian posterior probability of the overall model. An objective evaluation of the model is missing. [7] presents a Context Distribution Clustering (CDC) algorithm that induces clusters of tag sequences based on the context in which they appear. A criterion based on *Mutual Information* between the left and right context of a sequence, is exploited to filter out non-constituent clusters. The algorithm is incorporated in a Minimum Description Length framework, whereby it chooses the clusters so that the resulting constituents have the shortest description length. However it is computationally expensive since it requires large amounts of memory.

As regards parameter search approaches, [1] proposed an inside-outside algorithm to induce Probabilistic Context-Free Grammars (PCFGs)[1], that generalizes the forward-backward algorithm for regular grammars with HMMs. The fixed model consists of productions in Chomsky Normal Form (CNF) (fully binary branching derivations). Given a sequence of words $W = w_p \ldots w_q$ in an example, the aim is to re-estimate production probabilities computing the inside probability $\beta(p, q)$ of generating W from a non-terminal X, and the outside probability $\alpha(p, q)$ of generating X and the words outside W in the example

[1] A PCFG is a context-free grammar with probabilities attached to productions.

from the start symbol. [6] extends the approach in [1] by introducing grammar constraints, which guide the search process avoiding the grammatically incompatible generation of non-terminals (e.g., a determiner from an adjective or a verb from a pronoun), and presents a set of experiments in inducing probabilistic dependency grammars.

The evaluation of a learned grammar is based on the comparison of either grammars or trees. Given a gold standard of correct parses, performance can be evaluated as the percentage of correct parses that the algorithm produces.

3 Process Mining and the WoMan Framework

This work aims at checking whether Process Mining approaches may be effective for dealing with the syntactic level of natural language. So, let us quickly recall some basic concepts of Process Mining. A *process* consists of actions performed by agents (humans or artifacts). A *workflow* is a formal specification of how these actions can be composed (using sequential, parallel, conditional, or iterative schemes) to result in valid processes. A *case* is a particular execution of activities compliant to a given workflow. It can be described in terms of *events* associated to the performed activities. Case *traces* consist of lists of events associated to time points. A *task* is a generic piece of work, defined to be executed for many cases of the same type. An *activity* is the actual execution of a task. Process Mining tasks of interest to this work are *Process Discovery*, aimed at learning a process model from sample cases, and *Conformance Checking*, aimed at checking whether a (new) case is compliant to a given process model.

In particular, inspired by the successful application of approaches based on HMMs to Grammar Induction in the literature, and by previous indications, obtained in other domains, that the Process Mining system WoMan may outperform HMMs in some cases, we propose the adoption of WoMan for our purposes. Also, while Process Mining and Management techniques in the literature have been typically motivated by and exploited in business and industrial domains, Woman proved able to support a wide variety of application domains (including Ambient Intelligence, and even Chess) [14].

The WoMan framework [9] introduced some important novelties in the process mining and management landscape. Experiments proved that it is able to handle efficiently and effectively very complex processes, thanks to its powerful representation formalism and process handling operators. In the following, we briefly and intuitively recall its fundamental notions.

WoMan takes as input trace elements consisting of 6-tuples $\langle T, E, W, P, A, O\rangle$, where T is the event timestamp, E is the type of the event (one of 'begin_process', 'end_process', 'begin_activity', 'end_activity', or 'context_description'), W is the name of the reference workflow, P is the case identifier, A is the name of the activity (or a list of contextual information for $A = \mathit{context\_description}$), and O is the progressive number of occurrence of that activity in that case.

WoMan models are expressed using two elements:

tasks: the kinds of activities that are allowed in the process;
transitions: the allowed connections between activities.

plus pre-/post-conditions (that specify what must be true for executing a given task or transition) in the form of First-Order Logic rules based on contextual and control flow information, possibly involving several steps of execution.

The core of the model, carrying the information about the flow of activities during process execution, is the set of transitions. A transition $t : I \Rightarrow O$, where I and O are multisets of tasks, is enabled if all input tasks in I are active; it occurs when, after stopping (in any order) the concurrent execution of all tasks in I, the concurrent execution of all output tasks in O is started (again, in any order). Any task or transition t is associated to the multiset C_t of training cases in which it occurred (indeed, a task or transition may occur several times in the same case, if loops or duplicate tasks are present in the model). It allows us to compute the probability of occurrence of t in a model learned from n training cases as the relative frequency $|C_t|/n$. As shown in [9,10], this representation formalism is more powerful than Petri or Workflow Nets [24], that are the current standard in Process Mining. It can smoothly express complex models involving invisible or duplicate tasks, which are problematic for those formalisms.

WoMan's supervision module, **WEST** (Workflow Enactment Supervisor and Trainer), takes the case events as long as they are available, and returns information about their compliance with the currently available model for the process they refer to. The output for each event can be 'ok', 'error' (e.g., when closing activities that had never begun, or terminating the process while activities are still running), or a set of warnings denoting different kinds of deviations from the model (e.g., unexpected task or transition, preconditions not fulfilled, unexpected resource running a given activity, etc.).

The learning module, **WIND** (Workflow INDucer), allows one to learn or refine a process model according to a case. The refinement may affect the structure and/or the probabilities. Differently from all previous approaches in the literature, it is *fully incremental*: not only can it refine an existing model according to new cases whenever they become available, it can even start learning from an empty model and a single case, while others need a (large) number of cases to draw significant statistics before learning starts. To learn conditions in form of logic theories, WIND relies on the incremental learning system InTheLex [8]. Indeed, InTheLEx is endowed with a positive only-learning feature [2], which allows it to deal with the positive-only learning approach typical of both Process Mining and Grammar Induction.

4 Grammar Induction as a Process Discovery Task

Following mainstream literature, we adopt the unsupervised setting for Grammar Induction. So, sentences in the training corpus are annotated with the sequence of PoS tags associated to their constituent tokens (words, values, punctuation). In our approach, a grammar corresponds to a process model; a sentence in natural language (actually, the sequence of PoS tags associated to the words in the sentence) is a case; a task is a PoS tag, and an activity is an occurrence of the tag in a sentence. Under this perspective, process discovery corresponds to grammar induction, and syntactic checking to conformance checking. Just as in Grammar Induction, process discovery typically adopts a positive-only learning approach (i.e., only correct sentences/process execution are included in the training corpus).

As regards the set of PoS tags to be used, several options are available in the literature. In the following, we will consider CoNLL-U, a revised version of the CoNLL-X format [5]. It represents a text in natural language as a plain text file, where three types of lines are available: comment lines (starting with #), blank lines (to separate sentences), and word lines (containing token annotations). Each word line reports 10 fields: word index *ID*; the word form or symbol *FORM* with its lemma or stem *LEMMA*; both universal (*UPOS*) and language specific (*XPOS*) PoS tag; the list of morphological features in *FEATS*; head *HEAD* of the current word (a value of *ID*) with its type of universal dependency relation *DEPREL*, and the list *DEPS* of head-deprel pairs forming the dependency graph; last, any other annotation in *MISC*. For instance, Table 1 shows the lines for sentence “Evacuata la Tate Gallery.”, having ID *isst_tanl-3*.

Table 1. Example of a sentence in CoNLL-U format

<table>
<tr><th>ID</th><th>FORM</th><th>LEMMA</th><th>UPOS</th><th>XPOS</th><th>FEATS</th><th>HEAD</th><th>DEPREL</th><th>DEPS</th><th>MISC</th></tr>
<tr><td colspan="10">#sent_id = isst_tanl-3</td></tr>
<tr><td colspan="10">#text = “Evatuata la Tate Gallery.”</td></tr>
<tr><td>1</td><td>Evacuata</td><td>Evacuare</td><td>VERB</td><td>V</td><td>Gender=Fem|
Number=Sing|
Tense=Past|
VerbForm=Part</td><td>3</td><td>acl</td><td>-</td><td>-</td></tr>
<tr><td>2</td><td>la</td><td>il</td><td>DET</td><td>RD</td><td>Definite=Def|
Gender=Fem|
Number=Sing|
PronType=Art</td><td>3</td><td>det</td><td>-</td><td>-</td></tr>
<tr><td>3</td><td>Tate</td><td>Tate</td><td>PROPN</td><td>SP</td><td>-</td><td>0</td><td>root</td><td>-</td><td></td></tr>
<tr><td>4</td><td>Gallery</td><td>Gallery</td><td>PROPN</td><td>SP</td><td>-</td><td>3</td><td>flat:name</td><td>-</td><td>-</td></tr>
<tr><td>5</td><td>.</td><td>.</td><td>PUNCT</td><td>FS</td><td>-</td><td>3</td><td>punct</td><td>-</td><td>-</td></tr>
</table>

So, the sequence of PoS tags that make up a sentence in the CONLL-U file is transformed into a case trace in WoMan, where:

- the process name expresses the language of the sentence;
- the sentence id (*#sent_id*) is the case identifier;
- each word line determines an activity with the *UPOS* PoS tag (or combination *UPOS-XPOS*, for a more detailed model) as the activity name, and generates a pair of *begin_of_activity* and *end_of_activity* events;
- the features (*FEATS*) can be used as the context of the activity, and reported as a list of FOL predicates in a *context_description* event;
- *begin_of_process* and *end_of_process* events enclose the case.

For instance, using *UPOS* only for the activities, the sentence in Table 1 would generate the following trace in WoMan format:

```
entry(1,begin_of_process,ita_grammar_single,'isst_tanl-3',start,0).
entry(2,context_description,ita_grammar_single,'isst_tanl-3',
   [gender_fem(timestamp),number_sing(timestamp),
   tense_past(timestamp),verbform_part(timestamp)],1,none).
entry(2,begin_of_activity,ita_grammar_single,'isst_tanl-3',verb,1).
entry(3,end_of_activity,ita_grammar_single,'isst_tanl-3',verb,1).
entry(4,context_description,ita_grammar_single,'isst_tanl-3',
   [definite_def(timestamp),gender_fem(timestamp),
   number_sing(timestamp),prontype_art(timestamp)],1,none).
entry(4,begin_of_activity,ita_grammar_single,'isst_tanl-3',det,1).
entry(5,end_of_activity,ita_grammar_single,'isst_tanl-3',det,1).
entry(6,begin_of_activity,ita_grammar_single,'isst_tanl-3',propn,1).
entry(7,end_of_activity,ita_grammar_single,'isst_tanl-3',propn,1).
entry(8,begin_of_activity,ita_grammar_single,'isst_tanl-3',propn,2).
entry(9,end_of_activity,ita_grammar_single,'isst_tanl-3',propn,2).
entry(10,begin_of_activity,ita_grammar_single,'isst_tanl-3',punct,1).
entry(11,end_of_activity,ita_grammar_single,'isst_tanl-3',punct,1).
entry(12,end_of_process,ita_grammar_single,'isst_tanl-3',stop,1).
```

As regards the learned process model, the set of tasks is the same as the set of activities encountered in the training sentences. Using the *UPOS* tagset, that accounts for most natural languages, the model will include at most 17 tasks, which is a fair number for state-of-the-art Process Mining systems [10]. Using the *UPOS-XPOS* option, even if only a portion of all possible combinations is actually encountered in practice, the number of tasks significantly increases, going beyond the capabilities of many Process Mining systems in the literature but still being within reach for WoMan. Transitions correspond to pairs of adjacent PoS tags allowed in a sentence (e.g., [*det*] ⇒ [*pnoun*] means that a definite article may be followed by a proper noun). Note that process models representing grammars will not include any concurrency (sentences are just plain sequences of words), which means that the full power of WoMan in handling concurrency is not used in this domain, but also makes the comparison to HMMs more fair. However, such models will involve loops (including nested and short ones), optional and duplicate tasks, which are among the main sources of complexity in process mining and some of the strengths of WoMan. In particular, duplicate tasks are relevant, because different occurrences of the same PoS tag in a sentence represent distinct components of the discourse and cannot be handled by the same element of the model.

5 Experiments

Based on the proposed mapping between grammars and processes, we ran experiments aimed at checking whether WoMan is able to learn grammar models from sample sentences and whether the learned models can be used effectively for assessing grammatical correctness of new sentences. All experiments were run on a laptop endowed with a 2.8 GHz Intel Core i7-7700HQ Quad-Core (6M Cache) processor and 16 GB RAM, running on Kubuntu Linux 17.10. Our experiments concerned the Italian language, both because less resources are available for it in the NLP literature (but its grammar is well-known and studied in the linguistic area of research), and because its syntax is quite complex compared to English, and thus it can stress more the proposed approach.

5.1 Datasets Description

In our experiments we used two standard, publicly available datasets used for two EvalITA shared tasks:

UD_Italian-ISDT from EvalITA-2014 [3], obtained by conversion from ISDT (Italian Stanford Dependency Treebank), includes Wikipedia, News and Newspapers articles, Legal texts and Various genres and sentences. Since these are more formal and controlled texts, we expect to learn more reliable grammars from them.

PoSTWITA-UD from EvalITA-2016 [4], an Italian tweets collection. Since tweets often use fancy or odd sentences, it is expected to be more tricky than the other one.

Both datasets are annotated in Universal Dependencies (that can be exploited for the training of NLP systems), and are provided in CoNLL-U format and randomly split in three subsets (training, development and test). Since our approach does not need to tune any parameter, we will ignore the development subset in our experiments.

Table 2. Datasets statistics

Dataset	Corpus + Event log							
	Training set				Test set			
	#sent	#token	#event	#act	#sent	#token	#event	#act
UD_Italian-ISDT	13121	257616	784078	294397	482	9680	29632	11153
PoSTWITA-UD	5638	99441	266854	103553	674	12668	31910	12109

Table 2 reports some statistics about the datasets, for each considered subset thereof. For the linguistic perspective, it reports the number of sentences *#sent* (i.e., cases in a process perspective) and the overall number of tokens[2] *#token*. For the process perspective, it reports the number of events *#event* and the number of activities *#act* (i.e., instances of PoS tags associated to tokens or other symbols) generated by the translation into WoMan traces.

Both have several thousand training sentences, but **PoSTWITA-UD** has less than half than **UD_Italian-ISDT**, which is relevant because the former is expected to use a more tricky grammar than the latter, and thus to be more

[2] A token is a string with an assigned and thus identified meaning. Punctuation symbols are not tokens.

complex to learn. However, the former has a larger test set than the latter. The number of tokens/activities/events (which are somehow interrelated) are in the order of hundred thousands, which means the process discovery problem is not trivial.

5.2 Model Training

As a first step, we ran WoMan's Process Discovery feature to build a model for the Italian grammar from the training set(s). The learned models also included logic theories for pre- and post-conditions of tasks, as learned by InTheLEx. Table 3 shows some statistics about the models. As regards WoMan, for each *type* of tasks adopted (UPOS or UPOS-XPOS), it reports the number of tasks (*#task*) and transitions (*#trans*) in the learned model, and the average time per sentence (*time*) needed to learn the model (in seconds). The number of tasks and transitions is consistent among the two datasets for the two task types. The Twitter dataset has slightly less tasks, denoting a simpler lexicon, but slightly more transitions, denoting a more complex grammar. Nevertheless, the average time to process each sentence is the same, and is really low, allowing the use of the system for real applications. As regards Inthelex, again for each *type* of tasks adopted (UPOS or UPOS-XPOS), Table 3 reports the number of rules (*#rules*), and the average time per example (*time*) needed to learn them, for pre- and post-conditions of tasks. It also reports, for reference, the number of examples, which is the same as the number of activities in Table 2 (because WoMan generates one example of pre-condition and one example of post-condition for each activity). Again, the complexity of the theories (number of rules) is consistent between the two datasets, and the time needed to learn them is very low.

Table 3. Model statistics

Dataset	WoMan				Inthelex				
	Type	#task	#trans	time	#ex	Pre-Conds		Post-Conds	
						#rules	time	#rules	time
UD_Italian-ISDT	UPOS	17	273	0,04	294397	24	0,02	19	0,02
	UPOS-XPOS	51	905	0,04		66	0,01	43	0,03
PoSTWITA-UD	UPOS	17	307	0,04	103553	21	0,01	17	0,02
	UPOS-XPOS	45	1082	0,04		56	0,01	49	0,03

5.3 Model Evaluation and Possible Uses in DLs

Model evaluation consisted in a grammatical checking of new sentences with respect to a learned grammar. In Process Mining terms, this corresponds to a *Conformance Checking* task of new event traces with respect to a process model.

The learned models were evaluated in two different ways. First, for each dataset and task setting (UPOS or UPOS-XPOS), we ran classical 10-fold cross validation on the training set. This allowed us to understand how good WoMan was to learn the grammar underlying a given collection. Then, we tested the grammar learned on the entire training set of **UD_Italian-ISDT** on the sentences in the test sets. Sentences in the test set of **PoSTWITA-UD** were tested on the grammar learned from **UD_Italian-ISDT**. We did so because the former is a set of tweets, that are expected to use odd sentence structures, while the latter is a set of more controlled sentences, which are expected to use a correct grammar. So, testing the former on the latter may provide an indication of how bad a grammar tweets use, and of how good the system is in rejecting sentences with wrong syntax.

Table 4 reports the experimental results, evaluated according to: *Accuracy*, computed as the average portion of sentences identified as correct (i.e., the conformance checking never raised 'unexpected task or transition' warnings); *Support*, defined as percentage of training cases having the same structure as the sentence being tested; and *Runtime* (in minutes) spent to run the test procedure.

10-fold cross-validation results show that WoMan is extremely effective in learning the grammar underlying a given collection. In a DL, this would allow the librarians to understand whether the grammar style adopted by new texts added to the collection are consistent with the previous content, or to check user comments before publishing them if a discussion section is provided for. These figures also suggest the possibility of using a further feature of WoMan, which is process prediction [14], to automatically classify the linguistic style of new incoming texts from a pre-defined set of syntactic models. Average support for **UD_Italian-ISDT** is 20%, i.e., each test sentence has the same syntactic structure as 1/5 of the training sentences. For **PoSTWITA-UD** this number is more than doubled, indicating much less variability in writing style, as expected. In a DL, this would allow the librarian to determine how rich is the grammatical structure of the collection.

In the evaluation based on test sets, figures for **UD_Italian-ISDT** basically confirm the results of the cross-validation, reaching an even better performance (100%) for the UPOS setting. As regards **PoSTWITA-UD**, accuracy drops significantly, as expected due to the very different and informal syntax used in tweets with respect to more formal texts. In particular, it is still high for the UPOS setting, albeit almost 10% less than for the 10-fold cross-validation, but it drops to less than a half the value for UPOS-XPOS, as expected due to the fact that the more tasks available, the more complex the model, the more cases are needed to fully learn it. Support is about 10%, indicating much more style variability in the test set. In a DL, this would allow the librarian to distinguish the literary level of a text, or to distinguish texts by their type of content (e.g., novels vs. articles).

Runtime is still low, considering that several hundred sentences are processed in each test phase, ensuring scalability of the framework. Interestingly, again, runtime is higher to process the separate test set than the test sets obtained in the cross-validation.

Table 4. Performance statistic

	Measures	ISDT training		PoSTWITA training	
		UPOS	UPOS+XPOS	UPOS	UPOS+XPOS
Train and test	Accuracy	100%	99%	91%	43%
	Support	19%	19%	13%	12%
	Test runtime (min)	2.57	2.24	3.5	4.79
10-fold cross validation	Accuracy	99%	99%	99%	97%
	Support	20%	20%	42%	43%
	Runtime per fold (min)	1.5	2.4	2.99	4.77

6 Conclusions and Future Work

Since most content in Digital Libraries is in the form of text, there is an interest towards the application of Natural Language Processing (NLP) techniques that can extract valuable information from it in order to support various kinds of user activities. Most NLP techniques exploit linguistic resources that are language-specific, costly and error prone to produce manually, which motivates research for automatic ways to build them. Carrying on previous work on the BLA-BLA tool for learning several kinds of linguistic resources, this paper focuses on Grammar Induction. In particular, it investigates the ability of advanced process mining and management techniques to automatically learn, from a set of texts in a given language, effective models to check grammatical correctness of sentences in that language. In particular, it works on WoMan, a declarative process mining system that proved able to learn effective models in several application domains.

Experimental results show that the approach is effective for grammar checking and allows interesting analysis of the collections in a DL. Other possible applications to DLs can be also immediately envisaged, such as classification of the linguistic style in the form of process prediction, and will be further investigated. Future work will aim at extracting an explicit grammar from the learned models. This should be feasible, since WoMan models already learn grammatical rules made up of just single PoS tags, and so more complex rules might be obtained by suitable combinations thereof.

References

1. Baker, J.K.: Trainable grammars for speech recognition. J. Acoust. Soc. Am. **65**(S1), S132–S132 (1979)
2. Bombini, G., Di Mauro, N., Esposito, F., Ferilli, S.: Incremental learning from positive examples. In: Atti del (2009)
3. Bosco, C., Dell'Orletta, F., Montemagni, S., Sanguinetti, M., Simi, M.: The Evalita 2014 dependency parsing task. In: EVALITA 2014 Evaluation of NLP and Speech Tools for Italian, pp. 1–8. Pisa University Press (2014)

4. Bosco, C., Fabio, T., Andrea, B., Mazzei, A.: Overview of the Evalita 2016 part of speech on Twitter for Italian task. In: CEUR Workshop Proceedings, vol. 1749, pp. 1–7 (2016)
5. Buchholz, S., Marsi, E.: CoNLL-X shared task on multilingual dependency parsing. In: Proceedings of the Tenth Conference on Computational Natural Language Learning, pp. 149–164. Association for Computational Linguistics (2006)
6. Carroll, G., Charniak, E.: Two experiments on learning probabilistic dependency grammars from corpora. Department of Computer Science, Univ. (1992)
7. Clark, A.: Unsupervised induction of stochastic context-free grammars using distributional clustering. In: Proceedings of the Workshop on Computational Natural Language Learning, vol. 7, p. 13. Association for Computational Linguistics (2001)
8. Esposito, F., Semeraro, G., Fanizzi, N., Ferilli, S.: Multistrategy theory revision: induction and abduction in INTHELEX. Mach. Learn. **38**(1–2), 133–156 (2000)
9. Ferilli, S.: WoMan: logic-based workflow learning and management. IEEE Trans. Syst. Man Cybern. Syst. **44**, 744–756 (2014)
10. Ferilli, S., Esposito, F.: A logic framework for incremental learning of process models. Fundam. Inform. **128**, 413–443 (2013)
11. Ferilli, S., Esposito, F., Grieco, D.: Automatic learning of linguistic resources for stopword removal and stemming from text. Proc. Comput. Sci. **38**, 116–123 (2014)
12. Ferilli, S., Esposito, F., Redavid, D.: Language identification as process prediction using WoMan. In: Proceedings of the 12th Italian Research Conference on Digital Library Management Systems (IRCDL-2016), p. 12 (2016)
13. Ferilli, S., Grieco, D., Esposito, F.: Automatic learning of linguistic resources for stopword removal and stemming from text. In: Agosti, M., Ferro, N. (eds.) Proceedings of the 10th Italian Research Conference on Digital Library Management Systems (IRCDL-2014), p. 12 (2014)
14. Ferilli, S., Esposito, F., Redavid, D., Angelastro, S.: Predicting process behavior in WoMan. In: Adorni, G., Cagnoni, S., Gori, M., Maratea, M. (eds.) AI*IA 2016. LNCS, vol. 10037, pp. 308–320. Springer, Cham (2016). https://doi.org/10.1007/978-3-319-49130-1_23
15. Gold, E.M., et al.: Language identification in the limit. Inf. Contr. **10**(5), 447–474 (1967)
16. IEEE Task Force on Process Mining: Process mining manifesto. In: BPM Workshops, LNBIP, vol. 99, pp. 169–194 (2012)
17. Lari, K., Young, S.J.: The estimation of stochastic context-free grammars using the inside-outside algorithm. Comput. Speech Lang. **4**(1), 35–56 (1990)
18. Leuzzi, F., Ferilli, S., Rotella, F.: ConNeKTion: a tool for handling conceptual graphs automatically extracted from text. In: Catarci, T., Ferro, N., Poggi, A. (eds.) IRCDL 2013. CCIS, vol. 385. Springer, Heidelberg (2013). Publications/ircdl2013.pdf
19. Marcus, M., et al.: The Penn Treebank: annotating predicate argument structure. In: Proceedings of the Workshop on Human Language Technology, HLT 1994, pp. 114–119. Association for Computational Linguistics, Stroudsburg (1994). https://doi.org/10.3115/1075812.1075835
20. Naseem, T., et al.: Using universal linguistic knowledge to guide grammar induction. In: Proceedings of the 2010 Conference on Empirical Methods in NLP, pp. 1234–1244. Association for Computational Linguistics (2010)
21. Rotella, F., Leuzzi, F., Ferilli, S.: Learning and exploiting concept networks with conNeKTion. Appl. Intell. **42**, 87–111 (2015)

22. Spitkovsky, V.I., Alshawi, H., Jurafsky, D.: Three dependency-and-boundary models for grammar induction. In: Proceedings of the 2012 Joint Conference on Empirical Methods in NLP and Computational Natural Language Learning, pp. 688–698. Association for Computational Linguistics (2012)
23. Stolcke, A., Omohundro, S.: Inducing probabilistic grammars by Bayesian model merging. In: Carrasco, R.C., Oncina, J. (eds.) ICGI 1994. LNCS, vol. 862, pp. 106–118. Springer, Heidelberg (1994). https://doi.org/10.1007/3-540-58473-0_141
24. Weijters, A., van der Aalst, W.: Rediscovering workflow models from event-based data. In: Proceedings of the 11th Dutch-Belgian Conference of Machine Learning (Benelearn 2001), pp. 93–100 (2001)

Keyphrase Extraction via an Attentive Model

Marco Passon(✉), Massimo Comuzzo(✉), Giuseppe Serra(✉), and Carlo Tasso(✉)

Artificial Intelligence Laboratory, University of Udine, Udine, Italy
{passon.marco,comuzzo.massimo}@spes.uniud.it,
{giuseppe.serra,carlo.tasso}@uniud.it

Abstract. Keyphrase extraction is a task of crucial importance for digital libraries. When performing automatically a task of this, the context in which a specific word is located seems to hold a substantial role. To exploit this context, in this paper we propose an architecture based on an Attentive Model: a neural network designed to focus on the most relevant parts of data. A preliminary experimental evaluation on the widely used INSPEC dataset confirms the validity of the approach and shows our approach achieves higher performance than the state of the art.

1 Introduction

The continuous growth of textual digital libraries, in terms of both importance and size, urgently requires advanced and effective tools to extract automatically, for each document, the most relevant content. To achieve this goal, the Natural Language Processing Community exploits the concept of "Keyphrases" (KPs), which are phrases that "capture the main topics discussed on a given document" [33].

Extracting KPs from a document can be done manually, employing human judges, or automatically; in the latter case we talk about Automatic Keyphrase Extraction (AKE), a task whose importance has been growing for the last two decades [13]. In fact, the ability to extract automatically keyphrases from documents will make it possible to build more effective information retrieval systems or to summarize [37] or cluster [12] textual documents. Other fields worth mentioning where AKE can be applied are social network analysis [26] and user modeling [27].

Classic AKE approaches rely on Machine Learning algorithms. More specifically, supervised techniques have been used for this task: Naive Bayes [34], C4.5 decision trees [33], Multilayer Perceptrons [3,20], Support Vector Machines [20], Logistic Regression [3,11], and Bagging [16]. Relevant works that investigated the unsupervised extraction of Keyphrases used a language model approach [32] or a graph-based ranking algorithm [23]. However, these approaches achieved lower performance than the one obtained in the supervised case.

M. Passon and M. Comuzzo—Equally contributed.

P. Manghi et al. (Eds.): IRCDL 2019, CCIS 988, pp. 304–314, 2019.
https://doi.org/10.1007/978-3-030-11226-4_24

Due to this difference in performance, in the last years research focus shifted towards the *features* exploited by supervised algorithms. The kind of knowledge encoded in the model can be used to discriminate between different families of approaches: *statistical knowledge* (number of appearances of KPs in the document, TF-IDF, number of sentences containing KPs, etc.), *positional knowledge* (first position of the KP in the document, position of the last occurrence, appearance in the title or in specific sections, etc.), *linguistic knowledge* (part-of-speech tags of the KP [16], anaphoras pointing to the KP [3], etc.), *external knowledge* (presence of the KP as a page on Wikipedia [7] or in specialized domain ontologies [20], etc.). Despite being a subject on several studies, AKE is still an open problem in the NLP field: in fact, even the best techniques for this task reach at best an average performance F1-Score around 50% [16,18].

Although Deep Learning techniques have been recently established as state-of-the-art approaches in many NLP tasks (i.e. sentiment classification, machine translation, etc.), to the best of our knowledge, only a few Deep Learning models addressed the AKE task. Zhang et al. [36] proposed a deep Recurrent Neural Network (RNN) model that combines keywords and context information to be exploited in the AKE task in Twitter domain. In particular, their model consists of a RNN model with two hidden layers: the first captures the keyword information, the second extracts the keyphrases according to the keyword information. Meng et al. [22] addressed the challenge of generating keyphrases that are not present in the text, investigating Encoder-Decoder Neural architecture [31]: the underlying idea is to compress the text content into an hidden representation using an encoder and generate the corresponding keyphrases with a decoder. Basaldella et al. [2] proposed an architecture for AKE based on Bidirectional Long Short-Term Memory (BLSTM) RNN, which is able to exploit both previous and future context of a specific word, differently from simple RNNs that can exploit only the previous context.

In parallel with these initiatives, the class of Attentive Models [31,35] started gaining more and more interest in NLP community, because they have been successfully applied in various text understanding tasks, like neural machine translation from a language to another [1,21,31], abstracting text [25] and sentence summarization [30]. To our knowledge, however, these Models have not been employed in AKE tasks.

In this paper, we investigate the usage of Attentive models in the Keyphrase Extraction domain. The rationale behind this choice is that Attentive Models provide weights that indicate the relevance of a word with respect to its context [1,35] and thus can help in extracting keyphrases. Preliminary experimental results on the widely used INSPEC dataset [16] confirm our hypothesis and show that our approach outperforms the competitors.

2 Keyphrase Extraction Approach

We aim at developing a system that, given a text document, is able to automatically extract its keyphrases. Our solution consists of a neural network architecture that combines Recurrent Neural models with an Attentive component. The

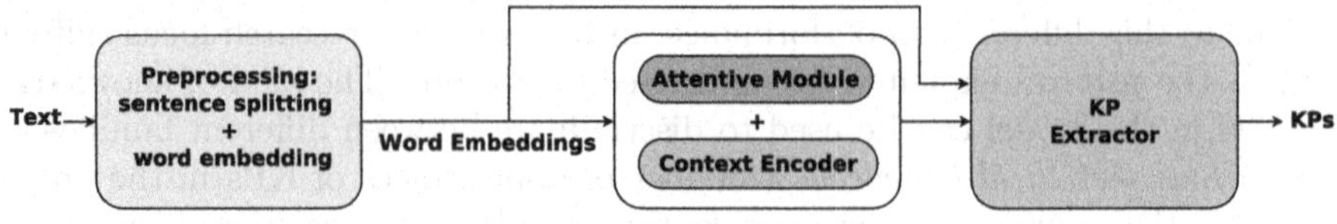

Fig. 1. Overview of the proposed approach.

proposed model takes as input a text and returns as prediction an annotated text (see Fig. 1).

First, text is split into sentences, and then tokenized in words using the library NLTK [4]. Each word is then mapped into a continuous vector representation, called word embedding, that according to recent studies [6,24] represents the semantics of words better than the "one hot" encoding word representation. For our work we used Stanford's GloVe Embeddings [29], since the common datasets adopted for AKE task are rather small, making it difficult to build custom embeddings.

However, when dealing with the keyphrase extraction, words cannot be treated with the same importance (for example, a stop word is less important than a noun, adjectives and adverbs enrich a speech but add almost nothing to the core meaning of it, etc.).

To encode this core feature, we propose to integrate in our pipeline an attentive neural component. In fact, attention models are inspired by human attention mechanisms, that do not use all the available information at a given time, but select the most pertinent piece of information, leaving out the parts considered irrelevant [8,17].

The goal of our *Attentive Model* is to associate to each word of the text an attentive value, i.e. a weight representing the attention level of the word: this information is then exploited in the subsequent processing phase and we claim it can have a significant role for a more effective and precise identification of KPs. To compute such attentive values, the Attentive Module needs, for each word w in the text, (i) the corresponding word embedding and (ii) the so called context, that is a representation of the semantics of the words appearing in the text before and after the word w. The context is computed by a specific module, the *Context Encoder*, which exploits a BLSTM network capable of producing a non-linear combination of the word embeddings belonging to the previous and future surroundings of w.

Finally, to extract keyphrases, the *Extractor module* combines word embeddings and the attentive values (concatenating their results) by means of a BLSTM neural model which is able to analyze word embeddings and their sequential features and to effectively deal with the variable lengths of sentences. For each word, the output consists of three possible classes: `NO_KP` for words that are not keyphrases, `BEGIN_KP` for words corresponding to the first token of a keyphrase, `INSIDE_KP` for a token, other than the first one, belonging to a keyphrase (see Fig. 2 for more details).

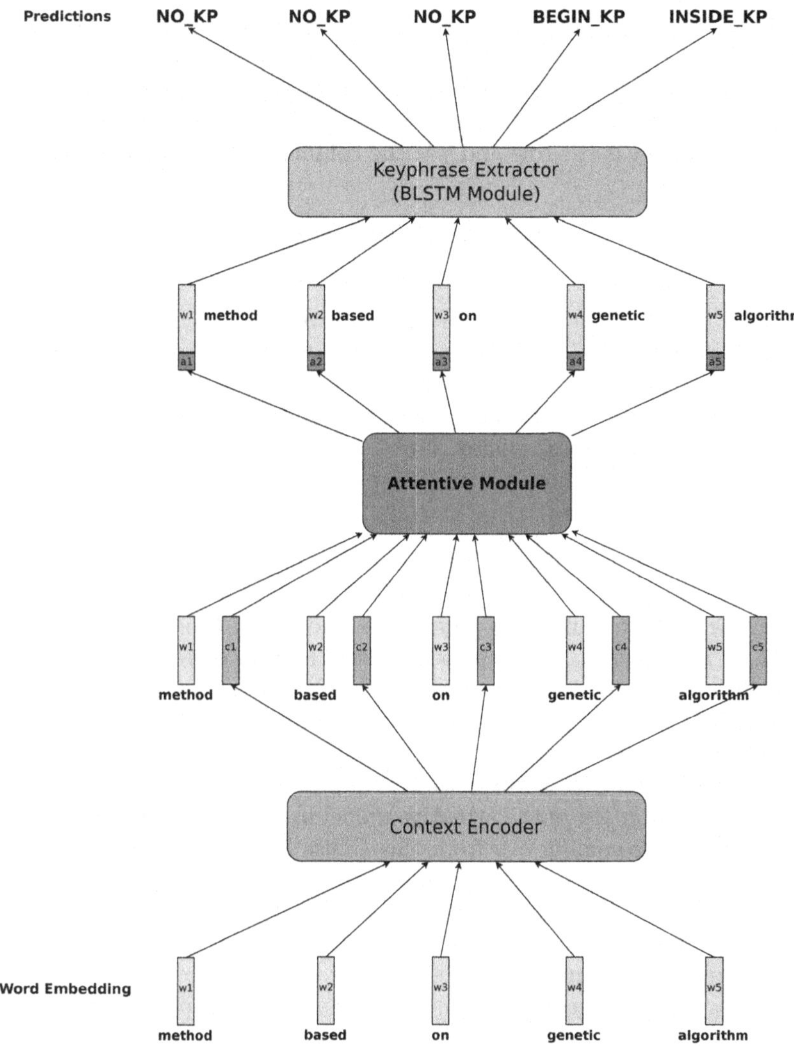

Fig. 2. Detailed schematization of our solution.

2.1 Attentive Module and Context Encoder

To extract the importance of a word in a given sentence we propose to use an attentive model. Our attentive model exploits the semantic representation of each word (the word embeddings) and the context in which the word is located. The main idea is to identify words that are more related to the context. In our architecture the context is defined as the output results of a BLSTM that takes in input the word embeddings of the text.

Let S be the matrix formed by the word embeddings $w_1, w_2, \ldots, w_s$ and C the matrix formed by the context vectors $c_1, c_2, \ldots, c_s$ (see Fig. 2). The size of each context vector is equal to size of the word embedding vector. Therefore, S and C are both $s \times d$ matrices, where d is the dimension of the word embeddings.

Our attentive model first performs the matrix multiplication between C and the transpose of S, resulting in a new matrix M. More formally, each element of M, $m_{i,j}$ (where i is the row and j is the column) is computed as follows:

$$m_{i,j} = \sum_{k=1}^{d} (C_{i,k} \cdot S_{j,k}) \tag{1}$$

In other words, each element of $m_{i,j}$ is given by the sum, for each word embedding dimension k, of the product between the element in the context matrix $C_{i,k}$ and the element in the word embedding matrix $S_{j,k}$.

Then, we compute the normalization of the matrix M using a softmax layer (that behaves almost like a argmax, but is differentiable) as follows:

$$m_{i,j} = \frac{e^{m_{i,j}}}{\sum\limits_{k=1}^{s} e^{m_{i,k}}} \tag{2}$$

Every item of M is now the range of 0 and 1 and the sum of each row is equal to 1. The element $m_{i,j}$ represents the attention score of the word w_j in the classification context of the word w_i. Through matrix multiplication between the matrices M and S we compute the matrix A, where each row represents the output of the attentive model.

The attentive output is then used as input in a Dense layer in order to manage the contribution of the attentive model in the final word representation. The output vectors coming out from this Dense layer are finally concatenated with the initial embeddings and fed into the classifier BLSTM.

Figure 3 illustrates a single iteration of the attentive model that we just outlined. Specifically, we represented the case where the importance of the single words is computed against the context vector $c3$ and saved into the vector $a3$ (in our case, this represents the third row of A). It is important to point out that there are as many context vectors as there are word embeddings and each context vector is different from the others, thus each subsequent iteration will use a different context vector and will consequently compute a different vector of weights.

2.2 Bidirectional Long Short-Term Memory (BLSTM)

Differently from feedforward neural networks, where the inputs are independent of each other, Recurrent Neural Networks (RNNs) keep an internal state that allows them to process sequences of inputs, with each input related to each other, thus granting the persistence of the information. RNNs are often employed in NLP tasks where the context is an important component needed to compute the predictions.

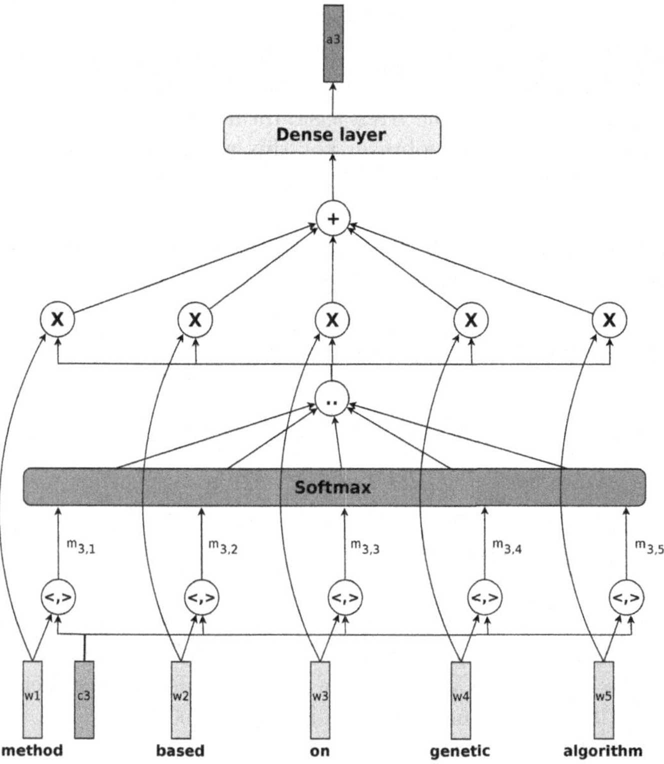

Fig. 3. Outline of a single iteration of the attentive layer.

As Recurrent Neural Network, we adopt the Long Short-Term Memory (LSTM) architecture [15], a common and effective solution employed to reduce the *vanishing gradient* problem [14] that typically affect plain RNNs. In particular an LSTM is defined as follows [9]:

$$f_t = \sigma(W_{xf}x_t + W_{hf}h_{t-1} + W_{cf}c_{t-1} + b_f) \tag{3}$$

$$i_t = \sigma(W_{xi}x_t + W_{hi}h_{t-1} + W_{ci}c_{t-1} + b_i) \tag{4}$$

$$c_t = f_t c_{t-1} + i_t \tanh(W_{xc}x_t + W_{hc}h_{t-1} + b_c) \tag{5}$$

$$o_t = \sigma(W_{xo}x_t + W_{ho}h_{t-1} + W_{co}c_t + b_o) \tag{6}$$

$$h_t = o_t \tanh(c_t) \tag{7}$$

where σ is the logistic sigmoid function, i, f, o, and c are the input gate, forget gate, output gate and cell activation vectors, and all b are learned biases.

The first step (Eq. 3) deletes the information coming from the previous element in the input sequence. Next (Eqs. 4 and 5) comes the decision of what information is going to be stored in the cell's state, replacing the one previously forgot: this is done having an input gate i deciding the values to update and then creating a candidate value c. In the last step (Eqs. 6 and 7) the output is computed: the cell's state passes through a sigmoid layer σ and finally through the tanh function in order to push the values between -1 and 1.

This kind of architecture, however, contemplates only previous information, but in our case, dealing with the AKE task, future information can support the identification of a possible keyphrase. For this reason a variant of the LSTM architecture is used, namely the Bidirectional LSTM architecture [10], that allows us to employ both past and future information. In a BLSTM the output y_t is obtained combining the forward hidden sequence $\overrightarrow{h_t}$ and the backward hidden sequence $\overleftarrow{h_t}$. A BLSTM is then defined as follows:

$$\overrightarrow{h_t} = H(W_{x\overrightarrow{h}}x_t + W_{\overrightarrow{h}\overrightarrow{h}}\overrightarrow{h}_{t-1} + b_{\overrightarrow{h}}) \tag{8}$$

$$\overleftarrow{h_t} = H(W_{x\overleftarrow{h}}x_t + W_{\overleftarrow{h}\overleftarrow{h}}\overleftarrow{h}_{t-1} + b_{\overleftarrow{h}}) \tag{9}$$

$$y_t = W_{\overrightarrow{h}y}\overrightarrow{h}_t + W_{\overleftarrow{h}y}\overleftarrow{h}_t + b_y \tag{10}$$

3 Experimental Results

In order to validate our solution, we used the well-known INSPEC dataset [16], which consists by 2000 abstract papers written in English extracted from journal papers from the disciplines Computer and Control, Information Technology. The dataset is split in: 1000 documents as training set, 500 documents as validation set, 500 documents as test set.

To write the implementation of our approach we used Pytorch [28]. The GPU employed in our experiments is a GeForce GTX 660 Ti. We train our network aiming at minimizing the Crossentropy Loss and the training is done using the Root Square Mean Propagation optimization algorithm [19]. The data is loaded into the network in batches, where each batch has a size of 32 input items. The experiments have been run with different configurations of the network's parameters, finally obtaining the best results with a size of 30 neurons for the Attentive Model, 150 neurons for the BLSTM used for classification, 150 neurons for its hidden dense layer and a value of 0.5 for the Dropout layer before the final Dense layer. The Pytorch framework does not implement a early-stopping mechanism; for this reason, we empirically set the number of epochs to 14.

Table 1. Performance obtained varying the dimension of the attentive layer.

Embedding	Attentive Dim.	Precision	Recall	F1-score	MAP	F1@5	F1@10
Glove-200 (Baseline)	-	0.326	0.643	0.432	0.356	0.286	0.353
Glove-200	10	0.291	0.624	0.397	0.327	0.271	0.326
Glove-200	20	0.348	0.654	0.455	0.370	0.297	0.371
Glove-200	30	**0.373**	**0.658**	**0.476**	**0.388**	**0.313**	**0.394**
Glove-200	40	0.321	0.648	0.429	0.356	0.287	0.350

The first of our experiments aimed at reproducing Basaldella et al. [2] results (an approach based on word embeddings and BLSTM) in order to create a solid baseline against which we can compare the results obtained by our approach based on an attentive module. Baseline results presented in Table 1 are slightly better than the original ones [2], because here we adopted a different value of the dropout layer.

Table 1 also presents performance varying the dimension of the attentive module: the size of the Dense layer that allows us to weight the attention effect. Note that a small attentive layer does not bring any benefit, on the contrary the performances are lower compared to the baseline where no attentive module is present. The reason behind this behavior may be the attentive layer focusing on a part of information that is too small and leaving other important parts out. Further increasing the dimension of the attentive module causes an improvement to the performances achieving the best score (in all metrics) with an attentive layer of dimension 30. An additional increase of the attentive layer makes it focus on a part of information that is too big, actually not focusing on anything in particular thus not making use of the attention mechanism. In fact, performance are similar to the ones obtained without attentive model.

Finally, we compare our results with state-of-the-art systems, which rely on supervised and unsupervised machine learning techniques (see Table 2). The first system is the one proposed in [2] that uses a BiLSTM architecture (our baseline); the second technique proposed an approach based on Encoder-Decoder Neural architecture [22]; the next three are works presented in [16] that use three different techniques, respectively: n-grams, Noun Phrases (NP) chunking and patterns; the last one [5] relies on a topical representation of a document, making use of graphs to extract keywords. Note, our proposed approach achieves state of the art performance under every measure considered. It is worth noting that we perform better than the results presented in [2] and [22], two recent works that make use of Deep Learning techniques.

Table 2. Comparison results on INSPEC dataset

Method	Precision	Recall	F1-score	F1@5	F1@10
Proposed approach	*0.373*	*0.658*	*0.476*	*0.313*	*0.394*
BiLSTM [2]	0.340	0.578	0.428	-	-
KP Generation [22]	-	-	-	0.278	0.342
n-grams with tag [16]	0.252	0.517	0.339	-	-
NP Chunking with tag [16]	0.297	0.372	0.330	-	-
Pattern with tag [16]	0.217	0.399	0.281	-	-
TopicRank [5]	0.348	0.404	0.352	-	-

4 Conclusion

In this work, we proposed a network that uses an Attentive Model as its core in order to perform automatic keyphrase extraction. The approach has been validated on the well-known INSPEC dataset and the experiments have been performed varying the size of the attentive model. Comparison evaluation shows that our approach outperforms competitive works on all metrics. As future works we intend testing the proposed architecture on other Keyphrase datasets and we will investigate advanced attentive architectures, such as Tree and Graph Attention models that can deal with complex text representation.

Acknowledgements. This project was partially supported by the FVG P.O.R. FESR 2014-2020 fund, project "Design of a Digital Assistant based on machine learning and natural language".

References

1. Bahdanau, D., Cho, K., Bengio, Y.: Neural machine translation by jointly learning to align and translate. arXiv preprint arXiv:1409.0473 (2014)
2. Basaldella, M., Antolli, E., Serra, G., Tasso, C.: Bidirectional LSTM recurrent neural network for keyphrase extraction. In: Italian Research Conference on Digital Libraries, pp. 180–187 (2018)
3. Basaldella, M., Chiaradia, G., Tasso, C.: Evaluating anaphora and coreference resolution to improve automatic keyphrase extraction. In: Proceedings of International Conference on Computational Linguistics, pp. 804–814 (2016)
4. Bird, S., Klein, E., Loper, E.: Natural Language Processing with Python. OReilly Media Inc., Sebastopol (2009)
5. Bougouin, A., Boudin, F., Daille, B.: TopicRank: graph-based topic ranking for keyphrase extraction. In: Proceedings of International Joint Conference on Natural Language Processing, pp. 543–551 (2013)
6. Collobert, R., Weston, J., Bottou, L., Karlen, M., Kavukcuoglu, K., Kuksa, P.: Natural language processing (almost) from scratch. J. Mach. Learn. Res. **12**, 2498–2537 (2011)
7. Degl'Innocenti, D., De Nart, D., Tasso, C.: A new multi-lingual knowledge-base approach to keyphrase extraction for the Italian language. In: Proceedings of International Conference on Knowledge Discovery and Information Retrieval, pp. 78–85 (2014)
8. Desimone, R., Duncan, J.: Neural mechanisms of selective visual attention. Ann. Rev. Neurosci. **18**(1), 193–222 (1995)
9. Gers, F.A., Schraudolph, N.N., Schmidhuber, J.: Learning precise timing with LSTM recurrent networks. J. Mach. Learn. Res. **3**, 115–143 (2002)
10. Graves, A., Schmidhuber, J.: Framewise phoneme classification with bidirectional LSTM and other neural network architectures. Neural Netw. **18**(5–6), 602–610 (2005)
11. Haddoud, M., Abdeddaïm, S.: Accurate keyphrase extraction by discriminating overlapping phrases. J. Inf. Sci. **40**(4), 488–500 (2014)
12. Hammouda, K.M., Matute, D.N., Kamel, M.S.: CorePhrase: keyphrase extraction for document clustering. In: Perner, P., Imiya, A. (eds.) MLDM 2005. LNCS (LNAI), vol. 3587, pp. 265–274. Springer, Heidelberg (2005). https://doi.org/10.1007/11510888_26

13. Hasan, K.S., Ng, V.: Automatic keyphrase extraction: a survey of the state of the art. In: Proceedings of the 52nd Annual Meeting of the Association for Computational Linguistics, (Volume 1: Long Papers), vol. 1, pp. 1262–1273 (2014)
14. Hochreiter, S., Bengio, Y., Frasconi, P., Schmidhuber, J., et al.: Gradient flow in recurrent nets: the difficulty of learning long-term dependencies (2001)
15. Hochreiter, S., Schmidhuber, J.: Long short-term memory. Neural Comput. **9**(8), 1735–1780 (1997)
16. Hulth, A.: Improved automatic keyword extraction given more linguistic knowledge. In: Proceedings of the 2003 Conference on Empirical Methods in Natural Language Processing, pp. 216–223 (2003)
17. Itti, L., Koch, C., Niebur, E.: A model of saliency-based visual attention for rapid scene analysis. IEEE Trans. Patt. Anal. Mach. Intell. **20**(11), 1254–1259 (1998)
18. Kim, S.N., Medelyan, O., Kan, M.Y., Baldwin, T.: SemEval-2010 task 5: automatic keyphrase extraction from scientific articles. In: Proceedings of the 5th International Workshop on Semantic Evaluation, pp. 21–26 (2010)
19. Kingma, D.P., Ba, J.: Adam: a method for stochastic optimization. arXiv preprint arXiv:1412.6980 (2014)
20. Lopez, P., Romary, L.: HUMB: automatic key term extraction from scientific articles in GROBID. In: Proceedings of the 5th International Workshop on Semantic Evaluation, pp. 248–251 (2010)
21. Luong, M.T., Pham, H., Manning, C.D.: Effective approaches to attention-based neural machine translation. arXiv preprint arXiv:1508.04025 (2015)
22. Meng, R., Zhao, S., Han, S., He, D., Brusilovsky, P., Chi, Y.: Deep keyphrase generation. arXiv preprint arXiv:1704.06879 (2017)
23. Mihalcea, R., Tarau, P.: TextRank: bringing order into texts. In: Proceedings of the 2004 Conference on Empirical Methods in Natural Language Processing (2004)
24. Mikolov, T., Sutskever, I., Chen, K., Corrado, G.S., Dean, J.: Distributed representations of words and phrases and their compositionality. In: Advances in Neural Information Processing Systems, pp. 3111–3119 (2013)
25. Nallapati, R., Zhou, B., Gulcehre, C., Xiang, B., et al.: Abstractive text summarization using sequence-to-sequence RNNs and beyond. arXiv preprint arXiv:1602.06023 (2016)
26. De Nart, D., Degl'Innocenti, D., Basaldella, M., Agosti, M., Tasso, C.: A content-based approach to social network analysis: a case study on research communities. In: Calvanese, D., De De Nart, D., Tasso, C. (eds.) IRCDL 2015. CCIS, vol. 612, pp. 142–154. Springer, Cham (2016). https://doi.org/10.1007/978-3-319-41938-1_15
27. De Nart, D., Degl'Innocenti, D., Pavan, A., Basaldella, M., Tasso, C.: Modelling the user modelling community (and other communities as well). In: Ricci, F., Bontcheva, K., Conlan, O., Lawless, S. (eds.) UMAP 2015. LNCS, vol. 9146, pp. 357–363. Springer, Cham (2015). https://doi.org/10.1007/978-3-319-20267-9_31
28. Paszke, A., et al.: Automatic differentiation in PyTorch (2017)
29. Pennington, J., Socher, R., Manning, C.: GloVe: global vectors for word representation. In: Proceedings of the 2014 Conference on Empirical Methods in Natural Language Processing (EMNLP), pp. 1532–1543 (2014)
30. Rush, A.M., Chopra, S., Weston, J.: A neural attention model for abstractive sentence summarization. arXiv preprint arXiv:1509.00685 (2015)
31. Sutskever, I., Vinyals, O., Le, Q.V.: Sequence to sequence learning with neural networks. In: Advances in Neural Information Processing Systems, pp. 3104–3112 (2014)

32. Tomokiyo, T., Hurst, M.: A language model approach to keyphrase extraction. In: Proceedings of the ACL 2003 Workshop on Multiword Expressions: Analysis, Acquisition and Treatment, vol. 18, pp. 33–40 (2003)
33. Turney, P.D.: Learning algorithms for keyphrase extraction. Inf. Retrieval **2**(4), 303–336 (2000)
34. Witten, I.H., Paynter, G.W., Frank, E., Gutwin, C., Nevill-Manning, C.G.: KEA: practical automatic keyphrase extraction. In: Proceedings of ACM Conference on Digital Libraries (1999)
35. Xu, K., et al.: Show, attend and tell: neural image caption generation with visual attention. In: International Conference on Machine Learning, pp. 2048–2057 (2015)
36. Zhang, Q., Wang, Y., Gong, Y., Huang, X.: Keyphrase extraction using deep recurrent neural networks on Twitter. In: Proceedings of the 2016 Conference on Empirical Methods in Natural Language Processing, pp. 836–845 (2016)
37. Zhang, Y., Zincir-Heywood, N., Milios, E.: World wide web site summarization. Web Intell. Agent Syst. Int. J. **2**(1), 39–53 (2004)

Semantically Aware Text Categorisation for Metadata Annotation

Giulio Carducci[2(✉)], Marco Leontino[1], Daniele P. Radicioni[1], Guido Bonino[2], Enrico Pasini[2], and Paolo Tripodi[2]

[1] Dipartimento di Informatica, Università degli Studi di Torino, Turin, Italy
{marco.leontino,daniele.radicioni}@unito.it

[2] Dipartimento di Filosofia, Università degli Studi di Torino, Turin, Italy
giulio.carducci@protonmail.com, {guido.bonino,enrico.pasini, paolo.tripodi}@unito.it

Abstract. In this paper we illustrate a system aimed at solving a long-standing and challenging problem: acquiring a classifier to automatically annotate bibliographic records by starting from a huge set of unbalanced and unlabelled data. We illustrate the main features of the dataset, the learning algorithm adopted, and how it was used to discriminate philosophical documents from documents of other disciplines. One strength of our approach lies in the novel combination of a standard learning approach with a semantic one: the results of the acquired classifier are improved by accessing a semantic network containing conceptual information. We illustrate the experimentation by describing the construction rationale of training and test set, we report and discuss the obtained results and conclude by drawing future work.

Keywords: Text categorization · Lexical resources · Semantics · NLP · Language models

1 Introduction

To date natural language processing (NLP) resources and techniques are being used in many tasks, such as conversational agents applications [22], question answering [13], automatic summarization [15], keywords extraction [24], text categorisation [17]. In this paper we propose a system to automatically annotate metadata related to scholarly records; in particular, we show how lexical resources can be paired to standard categorisation algorithms to obtain accurate categorisation results.

This work is carried out in the frame of a broader philosophical research project aimed at investigating a set of UK doctoral theses collected by the Electronic Theses Online Service (EThOS).[1] Although we presently consider only the EThOS dataset, a huge amount of such documents have been collected within

[1] https://ethos.bl.uk.

P. Manghi et al. (Eds.): IRCDL 2019, CCIS 988, pp. 315–330, 2019.
https://doi.org/10.1007/978-3-030-11226-4_25

the project activities from different sources and countries, such as US, Canada, Italy, and other PhD theses are currently being searched to collect further data. Of course, many issues arise when trying to apply a uniform data model to such heterogeneous data; data is noisy, with partly missing information (e.g., abstracts are mostly missing until more recent years), and so on. Amongst the most basic issues, we single out a problem of text categorisation. In fact, when searching for philosophical theses in the EThOS dataset (i.e., those with 'Philosophy' in the `dc:subject` field) not all retrieved records are actually related to Philosophy, but rather to cognate disciplines such as Sociology, Religion, Psychology, and so forth. Additionally, in some cases the subject field is empty, or it contains numbers, or different sorts of noisy information. The thesis subject may be of little relevance in this setting because in UK there is no clear and univocal administrative classification of PhD titles according to disciplines. We presently focus on the problem of categorising such records in order to further refine the information provided by the `dc:subject` field, and to individuate philosophical theses. Although the task at hand is a binary classification problem, it is not that simple in that *(i)* in many cases the thesis disciplines are distinct though not well separated; *(ii)* the abstract may be lacking (thus very little information is available), and *(iii)* no labelled data is available to train some learning algorithm.

Although the methodology described in the paper has been developed to cope with a specific problem, the proposed solution is general; the whole system basically implements an attempt at integrating domain specific knowledge (acquired by training a learning system) and general knowledge (embodied in the BabelNet semantic network). Specifically, we show that the output of a state-of-the-art algorithm (Random Forest [14], an ensemble learning technique building on decision trees) trained on a specific dataset can be refined through a search over a semantic network grasping general conceptual knowledge. The obtained results significantly improve on those provided by the two software modules separately. Also, the system enjoys the nice property of providing a concise explanation illustrating why a thesis should be considered as properly philosophical, based uniquely on the information available in the thesis title.

The paper is structured as follows: in Sect. 2 we briefly survey the related work on text categorisation; we then describe the EThOS dataset and provide some descriptive statistics to qualify it (Sect. 3). The System is then illustrated in full detail (Sect. 4). In Sect. 5 we present and discuss the results of the evaluation of the system—which was tested on a dataset handcrafted by two human experts—and conclude by pointing out present weaknesses and future work (Sect. 6).

2 Related Work

Classification of textual documents is a task that draws particular interest in the field of natural language processing and is characterised by numerous challenges such as the high dimensionality and sparsity of the data, unbalanced classes, the lack of enough annotated samples and the time and effort required to manually inspect large datasets.

During the years, many techniques have been proposed that address one or more of the mentioned challenges trying to reduce their negative impact. Traditional approaches usually feature machine learning algorithms such as decision trees, random forests [3,8], support vector machines (SVM) [2,16], Naïve Bayes [5,25]. Some hybrid approaches have been proposed that combine the result of the classification with other types of information. Wang integrates the classification of documents and the knowledge acquired from Chinese digital archives into a concept network, enhancing the metadata of documents and their organisation in digital libraries [32]. Similarly, Ferilli *et al.* build a semantic network from the text, where concepts are connected by a set of relationships, consisting in verbs from the input documents [9]. The resulting taxonomy can be used to perform some semantic reasoning or understand the content of the documents, although it needs some refinement. Nigam *et al.* address the problem of scarcity of annotated data by combining the Expectation-Maximization (EM) and a Naïve Bayes classifier [29]. They show how the classification error can be significantly reduced by an appropriate weighing of the documents and modelling of the classes. Gabrilovich *et al.* propose a classifier that is able to match documents with Wikipedia articles, then integrate the concepts extracted from such articles into the features of the original document, thus enriching its semantic representation [11].

Textual data is often represented using bag-of-words (BoW) techniques, in which a given document is mapped onto a high-dimensional vector space [30]. The resulting vector can then be used to train a linear classifier, for example Linear Regression or SVM. There is also a significant volume of research in literature on the use of Random Forests; Cutler *et al.* show that Random Forests outperform linear methods for three ecology-related tasks [7]; Akinyelu and Adewumi achieve an high accuracy on classification of phishing emails using a combination of meticulously defined features [1], while Xu *et al.* optimise the classification accuracy by weighing the input features of the individual trees and excluding the ones that negatively affect the performance of the classifier [34].

A rather novel language modeling technique consists in word embeddings, that is, dense vector representation of words, that have the property of carrying semantic information about words and their context. Word embeddings gained increasing interest in the latest years and are normally employed in a deep learning context as in [18,19]: documents are transformed using a pre-trained dictionary and are processed by the neural network which ultimately outputs a class label.

3 Dataset and Gold Standard

The EThOS initiative is aimed at sharing information about UK Doctoral theses and at "making the full texts openly available for researchers".[2] The dataset used

[2] http://ethostoolkit.cranfield.ac.uk.

in this work consists of a *corpus* of PhD theses whose publication dates range from the second half of the Twentieth Century to the most recent years. Such *corpus* has been kindly made available by the staff of the EThOS service of the British Library, and consists in nearly half a million bibliographic records (namely 475, 383); records with empty abstract are 57.6% (overall 273, 665), while the abstract is present in 42.4% of such theses (that is, 201, 718). The corpus implements the following metadating schema:

- `uketdterms:ethosid`: the identifier of the record within the EThOS digital library;
- `dc:title`: the title of the thesis;
- `dc:creator`: the PhD student who authored the thesis;
- `uketdterms:institution`: the name of the University;
- `dc:publisher`: may differ from institution in some cases;
- `dcterms:issued`: year of publication;
- `dcterms:abstract`: abstract of the thesis (when available);
- `dc:type`: always "Thesis or Dissertation";
- `uketdterms:qualificationname`: "Thesis", sometimes followed by area of study and University;
- `uketdterms:qualificationlevel`: "Thesis","Doctoral" or similar;
- `dc:identifier`: pointer to the resourse in EThOS digital library;
- `dc:source`: pointer to the original location of the resourse (e.g., institutional website);
- `dc:subjectxsi`: empty for all records;
- `dc:subject`: synthetic description of the area of study.

Table 1. Statistics about the textual content of the dataset. The values reported are computed on subject, title, and (if present) abstract of the record.

Measure	With abstract	Without abstract	Whole dataset
Words	64, 946, 071	3, 480, 858	68, 426, 929
Words after preprocessing	37, 875, 285	2, 548, 988	40, 424, 273
Unique words	1, 496, 488	258, 045	1, 610, 896
Unique words after preprocessing	435, 825	124, 650	476, 769
Average words per record	321.96	12.72	143.94
Average words per record after preprocessing	187.76	9.31	85.03

The above schema employs three different vocabularies to define the metadata of a document. Dublin Core Metadata Element Set (`dc`) and its extension DCMI Metadata Terms (`dcterms`) are both defined in the Dublin Core Schema [33], which features a number of attributes that can be used to describe a digital or physical resource within a collection (e.g., a book in a library), while the uketd_dc namespace (`uketdterms`) is defined on top of `dcterms` and describes the core set of metadata for UK theses that are part of the EThOS dataset.[3]

Some descriptive statistics about the textual content of the records are reported in Table 1 that details total words, total unique words and average number of words per element, before and after preprocessing of the text. Such figures are computed also on the two subsets individuated based on the distinction between empty/valued abstract. We considered three fields: `dc:subject`, `dc:title` and `dcterms:abstract`, when available. We note that the presence *vs.* absence of the abstract is a key aspect for a record; in fact, records containing abstract information account for almost 95% of the total word count.

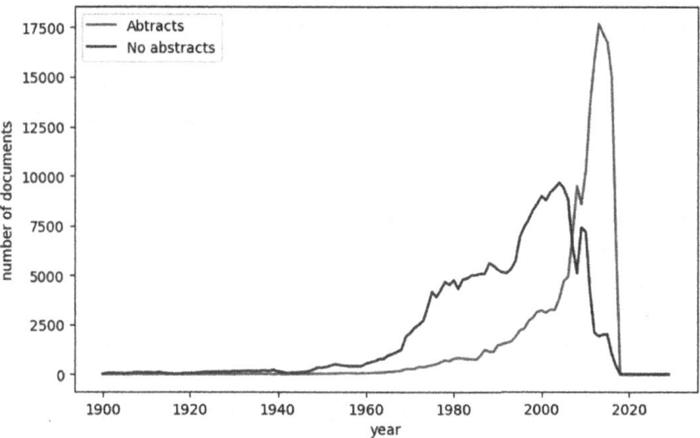

Fig. 1. Distribution of the number of theses by year of publication in the dataset. The corpus with abstracts counts less elements and they are distributed in a shorter and more recent time period.

We note that the preprocessing phase has higher impact on the elements containing abstract information (where we observe 42% reduction of the available words after the preprocessing step) with respect to the second one (27% decrease). This is because titles and subjects tend to be shorter and more synthetic, sometimes consisting only in a list of keywords or concepts, in contrast with abstracts that are more exhaustive and written in fully fledged natural language. This tendency is in fact evident in Table 1; the average number of words increases by a factor of 25 when the abstract is present. Finally, in Fig. 1 we plotted the distribution of the number of theses per year of publication. The graph is computed separately for the two subsets of data (with-without abstract information), and clearly shows that the records with abstract are more recent

[3] Full account of the EThOS UKETD_DC application profile can be found at the URL http://ethostoolkit.cranfield.ac.uk/tiki-index.php?page=Metadata.

and concentrated in a smaller time span. Both distributions have their peak after year 2000, and drop right before 2020, in accord with intuition.

4 The System

The goal of our work is to identify as many philosophy theses as possible: as mentioned, the problem at hand is that of individuating the theses that are actually related to philosophy, by discarding all records related to similar though distinct disciplines. The original dataset is not annotated and so it does not contain any explicit information that we could use to pursue our goal. We had two options: *(i)* to apply an unsupervised learning technique on the structured data, such as clustering or topic modelling, in order to single out philosophy samples among the multitude of subjects; or *(ii)* to automatically annotate the data (i.e., an educated guess), and subsequently to use such annotated data to train a supervised learning algorithm. We chose the second option, and set up a binary classification framework where a record from the dataset is classified as either philosophical or non-philosophical. We hypothesised that a supervised model would have fit our use case way better that an unsupervised one. In fact, we can train the algorithm by providing specific examples of the two classes, which will result in a better-defined decision boundary.

In the following we first describe the data employed and how we built a training set (based on a educated guess) and a test set (annotated by human experts). We then illustrate the training of a binary classifier (hereafter Random Forest Module), and elaborate on the learnt features. Finally, we introduce the Semantic Module, devised to refine the predictions of the Random Forest Module.

4.1 Building the Training Set and the Test Set

The first step was devised to build the training and the test set based on an educated guess. This bootstrapping technique is a key aspect of the whole approach, as it allowed us to adopt supervised machine learning algorithms. In many settings, in fact, a first raw, automatic categorisation can be attempted in order to overcome the limitation due to the lack of labelled data. Given the huge number of documents in the *corpus*, we did not consider the option of manually annotating the data in order to select a significant sample. We instead employed a text-based extraction method to search for relevant documents in the dataset by using a regular expression. We searched in the field `dc:subject` of each document and selected all samples matching the keyword *philosophy*, or a meaningful part of it (i.e., the substring *philosop*). We consider such documents as positive examples, while we consider all the other ones as negative examples. Of course this strategy is not completely fault-free, in fact it is possible that a given document is philosophical even though there is no *philosophy* specified in the subject (e.g., *Kant's reasoning*).

Table 2. Statistics of the dataset, partitioned into philosophical and non-philosophical records based on the educated guess.

Corpus	Philosophy	Not Philosophy	Total
With abstracts	1,495	200,223	201,718
Without abstracts	1,982	271,683	273,665
Whole dataset	3,477	471,906	475,383

Table 2 illustrates how the records in the dataset have been classified, based on this simple partitioning rule. We observe that only 3,477 records (that is 0.73% of the whole dataset), were initially recognised as pertaining to philosophy theses, while the remaining 471,906 are negative examples from all other fields of study.

Building the Training Set. We then left out 500 randomly chosen records from the positive examples and as many records from the negative examples that were used at a later time in order to build a test set. The final training set is thus composed of 2,977 positive and 471,406 negative examples. Not all negative examples were actually used to train the classifier: the training set has been built by randomly selecting a number of negative samples that outnumbers its positive counterpart by a factor of 10, thereby resulting in 29,770 records. Some descriptive statistics of the training set are reported in Table 3.

Table 3. Basic statistics about the textual content of the training set. The values reported are computed only on title.

Measure	Value
Total words	371,478
Total words after preprocessing	249,266
Total unique words	53,338
Total unique words after preprocessing	34,549
Average words per document	11.41
Average words per document after preprocessing	7.65

Building the Test Set. To create the test set we randomly selected 500 documents from each of the two groups, thus creating a new set of 1,000 samples. Such samples were manually annotated by two domain experts. Interestingly enough, even though they had access to the whole record (different from our system, that only sported the `dc:title` field), in some cases (around 20 out of thousand records) the domain experts could not make a clear decision. All such ambiguous cases were left out from the test set. We did not record the inter-annotator agreement, since only the records where the annotators agreed were retained.[4] The final test set was built by adding further randomly chosen records that were annotated by the experts, finally obtaining a balanced set of 500 philosophical records and 500 non-philosophical records.

4.2 The Random Forest Module

We then trained the classifier to acquire a model for the categorisation problem at hand.[5] In order to train the classifier we considered only the terms in the `dc:title` field, which is available in all records of the dataset and that in almost all cases suffices also to human experts to classify the record. A preprocessing step was devised, in order to filter out stopwords and to normalise the text elements (please refer to Table 2 reporting the statistics of the dataset after the preprocessing step). We chose not to use abstracts to train the model, since they are not available for most records; nor we used such information at testing time, even if available. By doing so, we adopted a conservative stance, and we are aware that some helpful information is not used, thereby resulting in a lower bound to the performance of the categorisation system. The applied preprocessing steps are:

1. **Conversion to lowercase** "Today I baked 3 apple pies!" → "today i baked 3 apple pies!".
2. **Stop-words removal**[6] "today i baked 3 apple pies!" → "today baked 3 apple pies!".
3. **Punctuation removal** "today baked 3 apple pies!" → "today baked 3 apple pies".
4. **Numbers removal** "today baked 3 apple pies" → "today baked apple pies".
5. **Stemming**[7] "today baked apple pies" → "today bake apple pie".
6. **Short document removal** documents with $n_{tokens} < 3$ are removed.

After preprocessing, we transformed the documents into vectors using a bag-of-words approach that maps each of them to the vector space with the tf-idf transformation. Tf-idf computes the frequency of terms in a document, weighed by the number of documents (within a given collection) that contain such term. This procedure favours important and more discriminative terms rather than common ones. The resulting dictionary vector (containing all meaningful terms in the collection) has been truncated to 60,000 features, based on the frequency of the terms in the corpus, so to discard highly uncommon ones.

---

[4] The final test set is available within the bundle containing the implementation of the described system [4].

[5] An off-the shelf implementation of the Random Forest algorithm was used, as provided by the scikit-learn framework, http://scikit-learn.org/stable/.

[6] We used the list of English stop-words from the NLTK package available at the URL https://gist.github.com/sebleier/554280.

[7] Stemming was done using the WordNet Lemmatizer, also available within the NLTK library, https://github.com/nltk/nltk/blob/develop/nltk/stem/wordnet.py.

The estimator that we employed to acquire a binary classifier is Random Forest [14]. This is an ensemble method that trains a set of decision trees by using random subsets of input features, and assigns to a given sample the class that is predicted more often among the different classifiers. This choice is motivated by the fact that Random Forest can handle a large number of features and provides a measure of their importance; this may be of particular interest to examine the intermediate stages of the computation. The output of the classifier includes the set of terms that are most probably predictive for a sample to be positive or negative for a given class label. However, several algorithms could be used in principle in this step, by plugging a different learner into the overall system.

Table 4. Configuration parameters used for the Random Forest classifier. Namely, 50 decision trees were trained, each of them assigning either a class label 0 or 1 to a given vector. The final class label will be the most frequent one. Other parameters are kept as their default value.

Parameter	Value
Number of estimators	50
Max features	0.6
Random state	none
Max depth	none

We preprocessed each document in the training set and extracted the corresponding vector representation along with its label (which was computed based on the educated guess, as illustrated above). Given the binary categorisation setting, labels did encode only two classes: 'philosophy' and 'non-philosophy'. The training set was fed to the estimator, to extract significant patterns in the data and to learn how to exploit them to individuate philosophy theses. Table 4 shows some relevant configuration parameters.

Figure 2 reports the 30 most important features, along with a relevance score, ranging over [0,1]. The score of a feature is computed for a single tree of the forest as the total decrease of node impurity brought by that feature, and is averaged among all trees. We also report the standard deviation of their values. We observe that the majority of such terms is highly predictive of a philosophical context, even though among the most relevant learnt features also terms proper to the Religion class are present (e.g., 'theology', 'church', 'religious', 'biblical').[8]

For this reason we further investigated the score acquired for the features, with particular focus to philosophy-related ones:[9] in Fig. 3 we show 30 salient

[8] It is worth noting that the human experts adopted a rather inclusive attitude with respect to religious studies, based on their previous acquaintance with an analogous dataset of US PhD dissertations, in which a significant number of 'religious' dissertations have been defended in philosophy departments.

[9] We obtained a list of some relevant philosophical concepts from the upper levels of the Taxonomy of Philosophy by David Chalmers, http://consc.net/taxonomy.html.

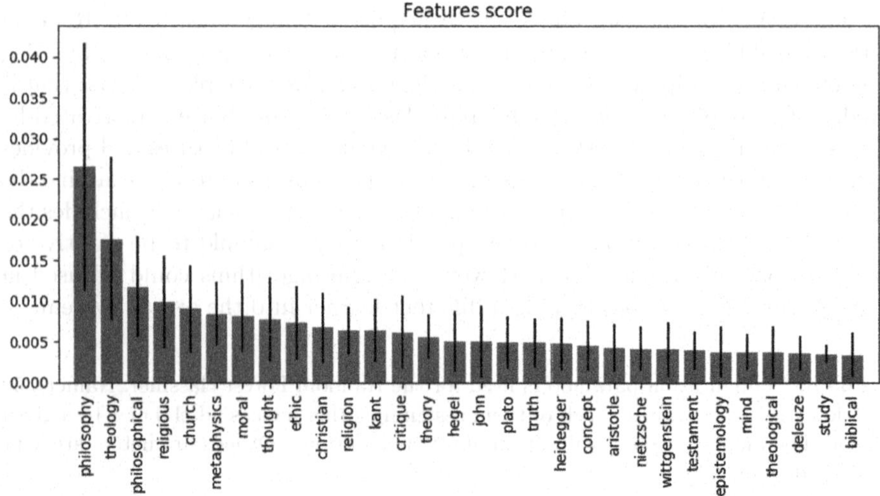

Fig. 2. The top 30 most discriminating features of the classifier: red bars report the average relevance score among the trees, and black bars report the standard deviation.

philosophical terms, whose score is lower than that learnt for the term 'biblical', which is the rightmost feature portrayed in Fig. 2. Such scores were likely to negatively affect the recall of the Random Forest Module, which acquired inaccurate weights, probably due to the scarcity of philosophical training data and to the noise present in the educated guess. This is why we devised the other module that—independent of the information in the training set—relies on the knowledge available in BabelNet, as described in the following.

4.3 The Semantic Module

The semantic module performs some basic Information Extraction tasks, accessing the lexical conceptual resource of BabelNet [28]. BabelNet is a multilingual semantic network resulting from the integration of WordNet and Wikipedia; it builds on the constructive rationale of WordNet—that is, it relies on sets of synonyms, the Babel synsets—which is extended through the encyclopedic structure of Wikipedia. In particular, the nodes in the network represent concepts and entities (that is, persons, organisations and locations), and the edges intervening between each two nodes represent semantic relations (such as *IsA*, *PartOf*, *etc.*). Although further lexical resource exist containing different sorts of knowledge (such as, e.g., WordNet [27], ConceptNet [23], COVER [20,26], or a hybrid approach proposed by [12,21]), we chose to adopt BabelNet in that it ensures a broad coverage to concepts and entities as well, that in the present domain are particularly relevant. The semantic module aims at searching the terms present in the theses title, to individuate the underlying concept and then at checking whether they are either philosophical concepts (that is, linked to 'philosophy' in

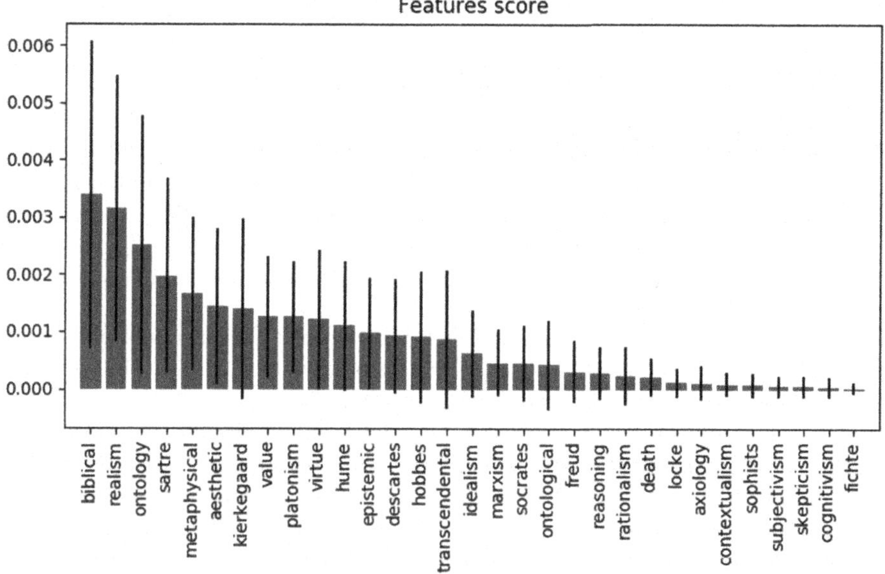

Fig. 3. Score of 30 additional philosophy-related terms compared to the word 'biblical'.

the BabelNet taxonomy) or philosophers. It performs three steps: named entities recognition (NER), multiwords expressions (MWEs) extraction, and BabelNet search, that are illustrated in the following.

NER. At first, named entities are extracted;[10] out of all recognised entities, only persons are retained.

MWEs extraction. We first perform Part-Of-Speech (POS) tagging[11] of each record title, and we then select both individual NOUNs and multi-word expressions. MWEs are extracted based on few patterns: NOUN+NOUN (e.g., matching expressions such as 'belief revision', or 'quantum theory'); ADJ+NOUN (e.g., matching 'analytic philosophy'); and NOUN+PP+NOUN ('philosophy of mind'). Such lexical elements are enriched with their conceptual counterpart in the subsequent step.

BabelNet search. The previously extracted terms are then searched in BabelNet, and their corresponding synsets (that is, sets of synonyms along with their meaning identifiers) retrieved. At this stage of the computation, we discard the MWEs that are not present in BabelNet, thus implementing a semantic filtering for the terms individuated through the patterns described above. For each sense_t or entity_t associated to each extracted term t we inspect if it corresponds to philosophy (bn:00061984n) or philosopher (bn:00061979n), and whether it is linked to either concept. In doing so, we basically explore

[10] We presently employ the Stanford Named Entity Recognizer [10].

[11] We presently employ the Stanford POS Tagger [31].

the relations *IsA* and *Occupation*, and we retain any sense_t and entity_t such that
- [sense_t,entity_t] *IsA* philosophy/philosopher; or
- [sense_t,entity_t] *Occupation* philosopher.

Building the PHILO-ENTITIES array. Such elements are added to the description of the record for the thesis being classified, in the philosophical-entities set. We note that thanks to the linking of BabelNet synsets with external triple stores (such as Wikidata), such triples can be exploited to perform further analysis of the record, and of the entities herein contained.

The decision rule of the semantic module is very simple: if the array of philosophical entities associated to this record is not empty, we label it as a philosophical one; we label it as a non-philosophical one, otherwise.

The set of PHILO-ENTITIES can be used to build simple yet informative explanations of why a given record has been categorised as a philosophical one. This approach, based on simple templates such as the system described in [6] will be extended to build explanations also for non-philosophical records in next future. Let us consider, as an example, a record whose title is "Dialectic in the philosophy of Ernst Bloch"; this record has been marked as philosophical by human annotators. While processing this record, the Semantic Module detects the concepts philosophy (bn:00061984n) and dialectic (bn:00026827n) as associated to the concept philosophy, as well as the Named Entity Ernst Bloch (bn:03382194n) as a person whose occupation is that of philosopher.

The semantic module is executed when the first module (implementing the Random Forest-based classifier) returns 0, that is when the record is not recognised as a philosophical one in the first stage of the computation.

5 Evaluation

We evaluated the system on a test set composed of 1,000 records, annotated by human experts, and built as described in Sect. 4.1. All modules of our system were run with only title information in input[12]. In the experimentation we recorded (*i*) the results of the Random Forest Module alone (which is a state-of-the-art algorithm, thus working as our baseline); (*ii*) the results of the Semantic Module alone; and (*iii*) the results of both modules, where the latter module is executed only in case a record is predicted to be non-philosophical by the former one. The results are presented in Table 5.

Discussion. The system obtained encouraging results. First of all, as earlier mentioned, the dataset was strongly unbalanced, with a vast majority of records that were non-philosophical (please refer to Table 2), but with many records coming from closely related research fields. Namely, out of the overall 475K records, those concerned with philosophy were less than 3.5K, thus in the order of 0.7%. Yet, to conduct a thorough experimentation we restricted to considering only

[12] The implemented system is delivered through the Zenodo platform [4].

Table 5. Categorisation results obtained on the test set by experimenting with the Random Forest Module, with the Semantic Module, and with their combination.

	RF	SEM	RF+SEM
Precision	**0.8227**	0.8269	0.7944
Recall	0.5660	0.6400	**0.7880**
F1	0.6706	0.7215	**0.7912**
Accuracy	0.7220	0.7530	**0.7920**

title information, thus often exploiting only a fraction of the available information. To consider in how far this limitation can be harmful to categorisation, let us consider that the human experts in some cases were not able to decide (or to decide consistently) the class of the considered records: when available, they had the opportunity to inspect the abstract and any other field of the record. Additionally, the assumption underlying the Semantic Module was rather fragile: just looking for people's occupation and for concepts hypernyms is a crude way to determine whether philosophy (or any other discipline) is mentioned. It was necessary to avoid more noisy relations in BabelNet (such as *SemanticallyRelated*), that allow retrieving many more entities connected to the concept at hand, but in less controlled fashion.

We observe that the Random Forest Module obtains a high precision, at the expense of a poor recall, caused by a significant number of false negatives, as expected by inspecting the feature weights. The attempt at correcting this behaviour has been at the base of the design of the semantic module; specifically, we strove to reduce the number of false negatives, meantime limiting the growth of the false positives. The key of the improvement in the recall (over 22%) obtained by the whole system with respect to the Random Forest Module is thus easily explained: the whole system incurs in false negatives in less than half cases, with a reduced increase of false positives.

Provided that the explanatory features of the system were not object of the present experimentation, nonetheless we briefly report on this point, too, as about a preliminary test. An explanation is built only when a record is associated to either some philosopher(s) or to philosophical concept(s): it is thus presently conceived simply as a listing of the elements collected in the PHILO-ENTITIES array. The system generated overall 496 explanations: in 394 cases this correctly happened for a philosophical record (thus in 78.8% of cases), whilst in 102 cases an explanation was wrongly built for non-philosophical records. Interestingly enough, when both modules agree on recognising a record as a philosophical one, the PHILO-ENTITIES array contains on average 1.78 elements; when the Random Forest Module predicts 'non-philosophical' label and Semantic Module (correctly) overwrites this prediction, the PHILO-ENTITIES array contains on average 1.57 elements. Thus less information is available also to the Semantic Module, which can be interpreted as a recognition that records misclassified by the Random Forest Module are objectively more difficult. However, further investigation is required to properly interpret this datum, and to select further semantic relations in BabelNet.

6 Conclusions

In this paper we have presented a system for categorising bibliographic records, to automatically characterise the metadata about the subject of the record. The research question underlying this work was basically how to integrate domain specific knowledge (acquired by training a learning system) and general knowledge (embodied in the BabelNet semantic network). As we pointed out, the difficulty of the present task was caused by the unfavourable bootstrapping conditions.

We have described the EThOS dataset, and illustrated the methodology adopted: based on the educated guess, we tentatively classified all records. After partitioning the data between training and test set, we trained a Random Forest learner to acquire a classifier for the training set. On the other side, we developed the Semantic Module, which is charged to extract concepts and entities from the title field of the records, exploiting the BabelNet semantic network. The evaluation revealed that the system integrating both modules works better than the individual software modules: we obtained interesting results. Future work will include improving the explanation, exploring additional semantic relations, and considering further knowledge bases.

Acknowledgments. The authors wish to thank the EThOS staff for their prompt and kind support. Giulio Carducci and Marco Leontino have been supported by the REPOSUM project, BONG_CRT_17_01 funded by Fondazione CRT.

References

1. Akinyelu, A.A., Adewumi, A.O.: Classification of phishing email using random forest machine learning technique. J. Appl. Math. **2014** (2014). Hindawi
2. Begum, N., Fattah, M., Ren, F.: Automatic text summarization using support vector machine. Int. J. Innov. Comput. Inf. Control **5**, 1987–1996 (2009)
3. Breiman, L.: Random forests. Mach. Learn. **45**(1), 5–32 (2001)
4. Carducci, G., Leontino, M., Radicioni, D.P.: Semantically Aware Text Categorisation for Metadata Annotation: Implementation and Test Files (2018). https://doi.org/10.5281/zenodo.1446128
5. Chen, J., Huang, H., Tian, S., Qu, Y.: Feature selection for text classification with naïve bayes. Expert Syst. Appl. **36**(3), 5432–5435 (2009)
6. Colla, D., Mensa, E., Radicioni, D.P., Lieto, A.: Tell me why: computational explanation of conceptual similarity judgments. In: Medina, J., et al. (eds.) IPMU 2018. CCIS, vol. 853, pp. 74–85. Springer, Cham (2018). https://doi.org/10.1007/978-3-319-91473-2_7
7. Cutler, D.R., et al.: Random forests for classification in ecology. Ecology **88**(11), 2783–92 (2007)

8. Amasyalı, M.F., Diri, B.: Automatic turkish text categorization in terms of author, genre and gender. In: Kop, C., Fliedl, G., Mayr, H.C., Métais, E. (eds.) NLDB 2006. LNCS, vol. 3999, pp. 221–226. Springer, Heidelberg (2006). https://doi.org/10.1007/11765448_22
9. Ferilli, S., Leuzzi, F., Rotella, F.: Cooperating techniques for extracting conceptual taxonomies from text. In: Appice, A., Ceci, M., Loglisci, C., Manco, G. (eds.) Proceedings of the Workshop on Mining Complex Patterns at AI*IA XIIth Conference (2011)
10. Finkel, J.R., Grenager, T., Manning, C.: Incorporating non-local information into information extraction systems by gibbs sampling. In: Proceedings of the 43rd Annual Meeting on Association for Computational Linguistics, pp. 363–370. Association for Computational Linguistics (2005)
11. Gabrilovich, E., Markovitch, S.: Overcoming the brittleness bottleneck using wikipedia: enhancing text categorization with encyclopedic knowledge. In: Proceedings of the 21st National Conference on Artificial Intelligence. AAAI 2006, vol. 2, pp. 1301–1306. AAAI Press (2006)
12. Ghignone, L., Lieto, A., Radicioni, D.P.: Typicality-based inference by plugging conceptual spaces into ontologies. In: Proceedings of the AIC. CEUR (2013)
13. Harabagiu, S., Moldovan, D.: Question answering. In: Mitkov, R. (ed.) The Oxford Handbook of Computational Linguistics. Oxford University Press, New York (2003)
14. Ho, T.K.: Random decision forests. In: Proceedings of the Third International Conference on Document Analysis and Recognition (Volume 1). ICDAR 1995, vol. 1, pp. 278–282. IEEE Computer Society, Washington, DC (1995)
15. Hovy, E.: Text summarization. In: Mitkov, R. (ed.) The Oxford Handbook of Computational Linguistics, 2nd edn. Oxford University Press, New York (2003)
16. Joachims, T.: Text categorization with support vector machines: learning with many relevant features. In: Nédellec, C., Rouveirol, C. (eds.) ECML 1998. LNCS, vol. 1398, pp. 137–142. Springer, Heidelberg (1998). https://doi.org/10.1007/BFb0026683
17. Johnson, R., Zhang, T.: Semi-supervised convolutional neural networks for text categorization via region embedding. In: Advances in Neural Information Processing Systems, pp. 919–927 (2015)
18. Joulin, A., Grave, E., Bojanowski, P., Mikolov, T.: Bag of tricks for efficient text classification. In: Proceedings of the 15th Conference of the European Chapter of the Association for Computational Linguistics, Short Papers, vol. 2, pp. 427–431. Association for Computational Linguistics (2017)
19. Lai, S., Xu, L., Liu, K., Zhao, J.: Recurrent convolutional neural networks for text classification. In: Proceedings of the Twenty-Ninth AAAI Conference on Artificial Intelligence, pp. 2267–2273. AAAI 2015. AAAI Press (2015)
20. Lieto, A., Mensa, E., Radicioni, D.P.: A resource-driven approach for anchoring linguistic resources to conceptual spaces. In: Adorni, G., Cagnoni, S., Gori, M., Maratea, M. (eds.) AI*IA 2016. LNCS (LNAI), vol. 10037, pp. 435–449. Springer, Cham (2016). https://doi.org/10.1007/978-3-319-49130-1_32
21. Lieto, A., Radicioni, D.P., Rho, V.: Dual peccs: a cognitive system for conceptual representation and categorization. J. Exp. Theoret. Artif. Intell. **29**(2), 433–452 (2017). https://doi.org/10.1080/0952813X.2016.1198934
22. Lison, P., Kennington, C.: Opendial: a toolkit for developing spoken dialogue systems with probabilistic rules. In: Proceedings of ACL-2016 System Demonstrations, pp. 67–72 (2016)

23. Liu, H., Singh, P.: Conceptnet-a practical commonsense reasoning tool-kit. BT Technol. J. **22**(4), 211–226 (2004)
24. Marujo, L., Ribeiro, R., de Matos, D.M., Neto, J.P., Gershman, A., Carbonell, J.: Key phrase extraction of lightly filtered broadcast news. In: Sojka, P., Horák, A., Kopeček, I., Pala, K. (eds.) TSD 2012. LNCS (LNAI), vol. 7499, pp. 290–297. Springer, Heidelberg (2012). https://doi.org/10.1007/978-3-642-32790-2_35
25. McCallum, A., Nigam, K.: A comparison of event models for naive bayes text classification. In: IN AAAI-98 Workshop on Learning for Text Categorization, pp. 41–48. AAAI Press (1998)
26. Mensa, E., Radicioni, D.P., Lieto, A.: COVER: a linguistic resource combining common sense and lexicographic information. Lang. Resour. Eval. **52**(4), 921–948 (2018)
27. Miller, G.A.: WordNet: a lexical database for english. Commun. ACM **38**(11), 39–41 (1995)
28. Navigli, R., Ponzetto, S.P.: BabelNet: building a very large multilingual semantic network. In: Proceedings of the 48th ACL, pp. 216–225. ACL (2010)
29. Nigam, K., McCallum, A.K., Thrun, S., Mitchell, T.: Text classification from labeled and unlabeled documents using EM. Mach. Learn. **39**(2–3), 103–134 (2000)
30. Harris, Z.S.: Distributional structure. Word **10**, 146–162 (1954)
31. Toutanova, K., Manning, C.D.: Enriching the knowledge sources used in a maximum entropy part-of-speech tagger. In: Proceedings of the 2000 Joint SIGDAT Conference on Empirical Methods in Natural Language Processing and Very Large Corpora: Held in Conjunction with the 38th Annual Meeting of the Association for Computational Linguistics, vol. 13. pp. 63–70. Association for Computational Linguistics (2000)
32. Wang, J.: A knowledge network constructed by integrating classification, thesaurus, and metadata in digital library. Int. Inf. Libr. Rev. **35**(2–4), 383–397 (2003)
33. Weibel, S.: The dublin core: a simple content description model for electronic resources. Bull. Am. Soc. Inf. Sci. Technol. **24**(1), 9–11 (1997)
34. Xu, B., Guo, X., Ye, Y., Cheng, J.: An improved random forest classifier for text categorization. JCP **7**(12), 2913–2920 (2012)

Collecting and Controlling Distributed Research Information by Linking to External Authority Data - A Case Study

Atif Latif(✉), Timo Borst, and Klaus Tochtermann

ZBW - Leibniz Information Center for Economics, Kiel, Germany
{A.Latif,T.Borst,K.Tochtermann}@zbw.eu

Abstract. With respect to the world wide web, scientific information has become distributed and often redundantly held on different server locations. The vision of a current research information system (CRIS) as an environment for constant monitoring and tracking of a researcher's output has become vivid, but still fighting with issues like legacy information and institutional repository structures to be established yet. We therefore suggest to gather those scattered research information through identifying its authors by means of authority data already associated with them. We introduce author pages as a proof-of-concept application collecting research information not only from a local source such as an institutional repository, but also from other external bibliographic sources.

Keywords: Digital library · Research information · Authority data · Linked open data

1 Introduction

Platforms for digital libraries have become the gateway for the dissemination and provision of scientific publications. However, recent advancements in Open Access and Open Science require digital libraries to transform their publication centered model. At current state of affairs, digital libraries are striving for the acquisition and management of supplementary digital science artifacts such as datasets, software and learning resources. Many of these artifacts are managed by open access repositories that foster the integration with a digital library setup [1]. Open access repositories provide users with barrier free access to scientific resources and already play a significant role in the dissemination of scientific results and the increase of author visibility. However, apart from providing freely available resources, these repositories are not well connected with respect to their metadata.

Basically, we see two challenges for traditional information systems relying on biographical information. The first challenge is that we are facing a landscape of distributed research information residing on different server locations, preventing

P. Manghi et al. (Eds.): IRCDL 2019, CCIS 988, pp. 331–339, 2019.
https://doi.org/10.1007/978-3-030-11226-4_26

us from scanning the current information space at a glance. Search engines had been introduced to handle this issue, but they are still quite weak in *identifying* information in terms of authorship or provenance. This leads us to the second challenge: with information often being redundantly published and distributed, it becomes uncontrolled in the sense that it is often unclear which person in fact is accountable for a piece of scientific information. We therefore suggest to tackle these two challenges by linking distributed research information to external authority data that is preferably exposed as linked open data (LOD). Through this study, we want to emphasize that a well linked and connected open access repository can provide users with author related information that promote persons in their role as contributors.

From long, libraries have used authority control files for the unique identification and better organization of bibliographic data. Authority control uses a unique heading or a numeric identifier to identify entities such as persons, subjects or affiliations. It has helped libraries to make bibliographic information less ambiguous and better findable. For instance, the Integrated Authority File (German: Gemeinsame Normdatei, also known as: Universal Authority File) or GND is an authority file particularly used for the organization and cataloging of names, subject terms and corporate bodies.

The program of LOD, on the other hand, stresses the significance of open and machine readable structured data for the purpose of unique identification, open data publishing and cross-linkage of (related) digital resources. Throughout the last decade, it has yielded a bunch of open, structured and interlinked heterogeneous datasets [2]. Moreover, it has inspired various national and international libraries to provide their catalog data [3] and authority control files as LOD. These authority data files were subsequently reused and interlinked by popular LOD hubs like DBPedia, Wikidata or FreeBase. In summary, both developments with respect to authority data and LOD converge to solve the problem of identification and reliable linking of resources across different domains.

2 Related Work

The work of this paper touches several aspects that are subject to ongoing research in information practice and computer science. [4,5] provide an overview of the whole topic, while [6] addresses the topic of authority data for persons from the classic viewpoint of cataloging as a more formal and context independent endeavour. [7] focuses more on potential usage application scenarios where authority data can unfold its full potential. Apart from the decision which descriptive information to be included in an authority record, there are several models for maintaining authority data: from a library-centered approach to automatic clustering to a more community-based effort, giving researchers the opportunity to claim their (suggested) publications [8–10]. With respect to identifiers for researchers and related systems for current research information (CRIS), [11] address the need to integrate internal names with external identifiers, while [12] focus more on additional and proprietary data to be managed by CRIS, neglecting the fact that those systems presuppose a certain data infrastructure that must be established yet. [13] identifies the opportunities for authority resp. library data serving as a backbone for the Semantic Web. Pages with scholar profiles already had been introduced approximately ten years ago by libraries [14], search engines [8] and publishers [10], but with a focus on global visibility and access, rather than local and contextual linking [15]. In that sense, there are efforts to conduct author identification already during the early stage of publishing by assigning a temporary ORCID key to a metadata field inside a DSpace system, so that a local researcher profile can be generated and associated with the publication(s) [16].

3 Motivation

At our institution, we run an open access repository named EconStor [17]. Currently it comprises more than 150k publications from Economics, most of them being working papers. EconStor has contributions from more than 100k authors, with more than 1000 persons contributing more than 20, and 27 persons contributing more than 100 publications (cf. Fig. 1).

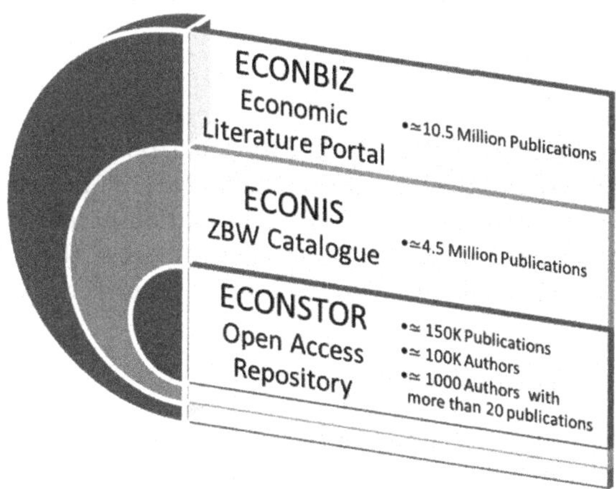

Fig. 1. Distribution of bibliographic databases in EconBiz subject portal

Although EconStor items are mainly crawled by search engines (in particular Google Scholar), the repository provides its own interface with jump off pages, web statistics and a local search engine. To promote its content even better, but also to normalize, to cluster and to enrich it, we decided to introduce author pages into the application, which reflect both a researcher's local output in EconStor and his or her contextual scholarly record that is compiled from our subject portal EconBiz.

Before we step into the details of our data processing, we want to point out that this work is primarily not concerned with the classic topic of disambiguating persons, e.g. by their publications, citations or co-author networks. Rather, we take a pragmatic attitude towards this issue by identifying those authors which are already associated with an identifier as part of a larger identifier system and maintenance workflow. In the following, we particularly make use of the GND identifier for persons provided by the German National Library, and the handle URLs of EconStor publications.

4 Datasets

Given below are the details of the datasets and authority data which we use in our work.

4.1 EconStor

For the purpose of our analysis and showcase application, we used a EconStor dataset dump from April 2016 that is made available as LOD since 2014 [1]. As of April 2016, the data set consists of **111107** publications with which **218185** author names are associated.

4.2 ECONIS

ECONIS is the catalogue of the German National Library of Economics being completely integrated into the EconBiz search portal [18]. It includes title records for indexed literature and subject specific information procured by the German National Library of Economics. ECONIS contains more than five million title records, most of them manually linked to a GND identifier.

4.3 Integrated Authority File (GND)

According to the German National Library (DNB), the GND is a dataset for describing and identifying persons, corporate bodies, conferences and events, geographic information, topics and works [19]. Centrally provided by the DNB, the data is constantly maintained by several other national and university libraries, requiring a mandate to introduce or to update central information on e.g. a new researcher. By cataloging EconStor authors, they will be associated with a GND identifier according to the general cataloging rules. As a national contribution, the GND dataset is integrated into the VIAF authority file.

4.4 Wikidata

Since its launch in 2012, Wikidata has become one of the major connecting data hubs and has been created to support roughly 300 Wikimedia projects. Despite of interlinking all Wikipedia pages to the relevant items, it also connects more than

1500 sources of (national) authority data files. The biographical information aggregated and linked by Wikidata is taken from different sources, in the first place maintained and updated by editors, if not by the communities or the authors themselves (in contrast to GND, which is maintained only by dedicated supporting library staff). Hence, it may prove to be both the most up-to-date and accurate source despite a certain likelihood to provide wrong or even manipulated data. Linking to Wikidata resp. to other connected identifier systems is a means for associating names with persons. Currently, in total Wikidata has more than 4.29 million persons listed as items, from which more than 509K persons have GND identifier and more than 25K persons are listed as economists (according to Wikidata property p106:occupation) with approximately 11743 represented with GND identifier. This distribution is shown in the scattered Venn diagram (Fig. 2).

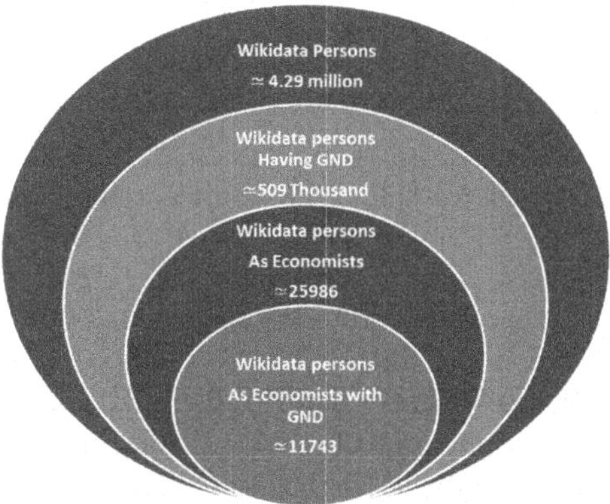

Fig. 2. Wikidata person items (May 2018)

5 Study and Showcase Application

Given below are the details of a multi-stage approach which we employed for linking the EconStor authors with external identifiers. It is important to note that the approach is specific with respect to the local data sources (ECONIS, EconStor) and identifiers it processes. On the other hand, it might serve as an example for globalizing and contextualizing those data sources by means of commonly used identifier systems such as handles or data hubs like Wikidata. An illustration of this multi-stage approach is given in Fig. 3.

5.1 Locating the GND-ID of the Authors from ECONIS Database

To conduct this step, we first transformed the recent ECONIS database from native PICA into JSON format for better processing. We then used a Perl script to search for all EconStor publications whose authors are assigned with a GND identifier, listing them in a data table. The script returns the Handle URL of

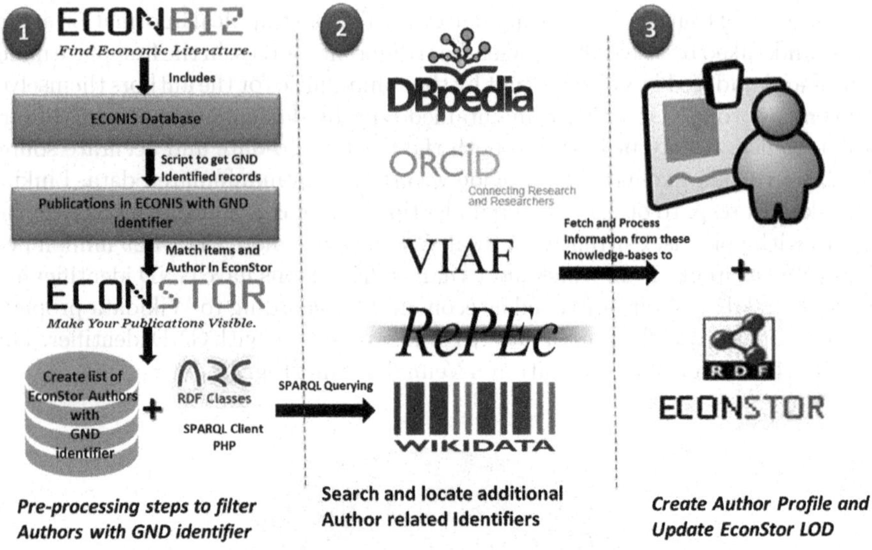

Fig. 3. Multistage approach for linking EconStor authors with external identifiers

the publications (with the unique Handle prefix 10419 indicating an EconStor publication) together with the author names including their GND identifiers, plus some other metadata elements. The Handle URL is critical here, as it is the only means for mapping publications between EconStor and ECONIS databases.

In a following step, we matched the Handle URLs from the results with EconStor publications to retrieve the EconStor publication id and its corresponding author(s). Afterwards, we reconciled the names of authors from EconStor with the listed GND authors, so that the EconStor authors become assigned a GND-ID (at this stage, outside of the repository application). Thus we were able to answer the following basic questions:

How many EconStor names are already associated with a GND-ID (according to our catalog)?

We found that 114185 out of 218185 EconStor names have valid GND identifiers according to ECONIS records. In distinct numbers, 25461 GND identified authors contributed to 69588 EconStor publications, which already is a good percentage (37%), but still quite incomplete with respect to a total of 111107 publications. Hence we considered introducing author pages at least for the most active researchers in terms of publishing.

Are the most publishing EconStor authors already provided with a GND-ID in ECONIS?

For determining the most publishing authors, we set the number of publication threshold to 25. We found that there are 1121 authors contributing at least 25 publications to our EconStor repository. By applying the same condition to our analysis, we found that 750 out of those most publishing 1121 authors are already associated with a GND-ID (67%), so this looked like a good basis to us.

5.2 Search and Locate Additional Author Related Identifiers via Wikidata

The next step of our multistage approach is to query, search and connect with additional external identifier systems apart from GND. The primary reason for this is to find out the coverage of different identifier systems, and to prove our preference for GND. In our context, the most common additional identifier systems are:

- VIAF as the international authority dataset provided by OCLC,
- RePEc author service as the largest identifier inventory for researchers in economics,
- ORCID as being promoted by the publishing industry, and
- Wikidata as a community endeavour and central data hub aggregating all the aforementioned identifier systems.

We looked up EconStor distinct author names by the following listed SPARQL query to the endpoint provided by Wikidata (to be more precise, we setup a local endpoint by ourselves). As a result, with reference to the baseline of 25461 GND identified EconStor authors, we got 1780 matches to Wikidata items, including 1775 matches to VIAF items, including 465 matches to RePEc items, and including another 44 matches to ORCID identifiers. Overall, approximately 7% of total 25461 distinct EconStor authors are associated with a different identifier system than GND, cf. Fig. 4. By analysing the results again, we found a critical mass of the prominent EconStor authors (more than 25 publications) who have additional external identifiers along with bibliographical and biographical information (most of them from Wikidata and VIAF). This is adequate enough to build a proof of concept application for author profiles which is accessible at: http://beta.econbiz.de/atif/.

Listing 1.1. SPARQL query at Wikidata endpoint to lookup external identifiers for a GND identified author

```
SELECT ?WikidataID ?viafID ?RePEcID ?ORCID WHERE {
 # WIKIDATA-ID of EconStor author "Dennis Snower" over GND
  ?WikidataID wdt:P227 "124825109".
   # request for VIAF ID
  OPTIONAL { ?WikidataID wdt:P214 ?viafID. }
    # request for RePEc ID
  OPTIONAL { ?WikidataID wdt:P2428 ?RePEcID. }
    # request for ORCID ID
  OPTIONAL { ?WikidataID wdt:P496 ?ORCID. }
  }
```

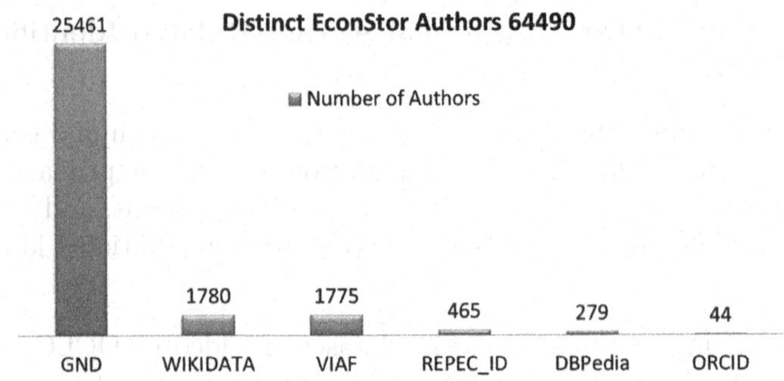

Fig. 4. Number of external identifiers linked with EconStor authors

5.3 Proof of Concept Application

To showcase the initial idea of a scholar's profile page in this proof of concept application, users are provided with an index page where all of the prominent authors are listed with their name and the hyperlink to the corresponding author page. When a user clicks on the link, the profile page is generated on the fly with biographical information queried and collected from external identifier systems. In addition, bibliographical information is compiled from publication lists both from the local repository (EconStor) and our subject portal as external bibliographic data source (EconBiz). An automatically generated author profile page of "Dennis J. Snower" is accessible at: https://tinyurl.com/yc9xd4d8.

6 Conclusion and Future Work

We demonstrated how to collect and reconcile distributed research information by means of automatic interlinking between different biographical sources. The approach relies fundamentally on the identification of persons by linking their names to identifier systems, which originally has been an intellectual or manual cataloging workflow. Hence, the approach does support neither the identification of an author nor the de-duplication of his or her works, but the controlled aggregation across different sources by means of intermediary datahubs. In this respect, we emphasized on the use of sources for authority data such as GND file, and showcased how Wikidata can be used as a connecting hub to find author related information. We are of the view that our study of author data linking service can be a reference enabler for the Digital Libraries to contribute for the digitization of science cause. As future work, we would like to expand the publication list of author by including other external sources, and secondly we would like to investigate the opportunities for enriching Wikidata both by editorial means and by bots, the latter to bypass rather static and cumbersome library workflows.

References

1. Latif, A., Borst, T., Tochtermann, K.: Exposing data from an open access repository for economics as linked data. D-Lib Mag. (2014). http://www.dlib.org/dlib/september14/latif/09latif.html
2. The Linked Open Data Cloud. https://lod-cloud.net/
3. Yoose, B., Perkins, J.: The LOD landscape in libraries and beyond. J. Libr. Metadata **13**(2–3), 197–211 (2013)
4. Rotenberg, E., Kushmerick, A.: The author challenge: identification of self in the scholarly literature. Cat. Classif. Q. **49**(6), 503–520 (2011). https://doi.org/10.1080/01639374.2011.606405
5. Gasparyan, A.Y., Nurmashev, B., Yessirkepov, M., Endovitskiy, D.A., Voronov, A.A., Kitas, G.D.: Researcher and author profiles: opportunities, advantages, and limitations. J. Korean Med. Sci. **32**(11), 1749–1756 (2017). https://doi.org/10.3346/jkms.2017.32.11.1749
6. Tillett, B.: Authority control: state of the art and new perspectives. In: Tillett, B., Taylor, A.G. (eds.) Authority Control in Organizing and Accessing Information. Definition and International Experience, pp. 1–48. Taylor & Francis, Oxford (2004)
7. Gorman, M.: Authority control in the context of bibliographic control in the electronic environment. Cat. Classif. Q. **38**(3–4), 11–22 (2004). https://doi.org/10.1300/J104v38n03_03
8. Google Scholar. https://scholar.google.de/
9. RePEc Author Service. https://authors.repec.org/
10. ORCID. https://orcid.org/
11. Jörg, B., Höllrigl, T., Sicilia, M.A.: Entities and identities in research information systems. In: EuroCRIS (2012). http://dspacecris.eurocris.org/handle/11366/102
12. Nabavi, M., Jeffery, K., Jamali, H.R.: Added value in the context of research information systems. Data Technol. Appl. **50**(3), 325–339 (2016). https://doi.org/10.1108/PROG-10-2015-0067
13. Neubert, J., Tochtermann, K.: Linked library data: offering a backbone for the semantic web. In: Lukose, D., Ahmad, A.R., Suliman, A. (eds.) KTW 2011. CCIS, vol. 295, pp. 37–45. Springer, Heidelberg (2012). https://doi.org/10.1007/978-3-642-32826-8_4
14. WorldCat Identities. https://www.worldcat.org/identities/
15. Latif, A., Afzal, M.T., Helic, D., Tochtermann, K., Maurer, H.A.: Discovery and construction of authors' profile from linked data (A case study for open digital journal). In: Proceedings of the Linked Data on the Web Workshop (LDOW2010), Raleigh, North Carolina, USA, 27 April 2010. CEUR Workshop Proceedings (2010). ISSN 1613-0073
16. Bollini, A.: ORCID Integration (2016). https://wiki.duraspace.org/display/DSPACECRIS/ORCID+Integration
17. https://www.econstor.eu/
18. http://www.econis.eu/
19. http://www.dnb.de/EN/Standardisierung/GND/gnd.html

Interactive Text Analysis and Information Extraction

Tasos Giannakopoulos, Yannis Foufoulas(✉), Harry Dimitropoulos, and Natalia Manola

University of Athens, Greece and Athena Research Center, Athens, Greece
johnfouf@di.uoa.gr

Abstract. A lot of work that has been done in the text mining field concerns the extraction of useful information from the full-text of publications. Such information may be links to projects, acknowledgements to communities, citations to software entities or datasets and more. Each category of entities, according to its special characteristics, requires different approaches. Thus it is not possible to build a generic mining platform that could text mine various publications to extract such info. Most of the time, a field expert is needed to supervise the mining procedure, decide the mining rules with the developer, and finally validate the results. This is an iterative procedure that requires a lot of communication among the experts and the developers, and thus is very time-consuming. In this paper, we present an interactive mining platform. Its purpose is to allow the experts to define the mining procedure, set/update the rules, validate the results, while the actual text mining code is produced automatically. This significantly reduces the communication among the developers and the experts and moreover allows the experts to experiment themselves using a user-friendly graphical interface.

1 Introduction

Text mining of scientific publications is a very important task as it offers the tools for extracting useful information from their content that is of interest not only to researchers and research communities, but also to funders, publishers, policy-makers, etc. This information 'enriches' publications and allows the interlinking of relevant content; a process critical for allowing researchers to discover, share and re-use scientific results in context, and research administrators to assess research impact and investment in a transparent and efficient way.

In OpenAIRE[1], we tackle the problem of linking publications to projects and/or communities that are members of OpenAIRE. By initiating bilateral collaborations with national funding agencies, research and infrastructure initiatives, OpenAIRE is able to serve them with the OpenAIRE mining services and research impact suite of services. OpenAIRE mining services can automatically infer links from publication full-texts to datasets, projects, software, and

[1] https://www.openaire.eu/.

P. Manghi et al. (Eds.): IRCDL 2019, CCIS 988, pp. 340–350, 2019.
https://doi.org/10.1007/978-3-030-11226-4_27

research initiatives. Today such services are manually configured, based on a model of the concepts to be discovered by mining and a set of mining rules. This is a difficult text mining task because each new community/funder requires a different approach, so we actually need to customize the mining rules and run an almost new mining algorithm for every new funder/community.

Currently, an information extraction algorithm is developed following the steps below:

- Communicate with a field expert and exchange some information or data
- Produce an initial version of the algorithm
- Run the current algorithm version on a large 'test' corpus of publication full-texts
- Send the results to the expert for validation
- Update the algorithm using the experts' feedback.

The last three steps are in fact an iterative procedure. The algorithm is finalised when the quality of its results is satisfying. Since, each mining task is unique and the produced algorithm differs, this may be a time consuming method with a lot of communication between experts and developers.

In this paper, we provide the experts with an interactive mining platform which allows them to set up their mining rules, validate the intermediate results and update the rules accordingly. This platform covers the following requirements:

- It is user friendly, since its users are not developers
- It provides the users with enough configuration tools to produce their mining profiles
- It creates and runs automatically the mining algorithms on sample data selected by the user
- It supports reproducibility of the mining algorithms.

The rest of the paper is organised as follows: First, we describe the configuration tools and how users are able to produce and tune a mining algorithm. Then, we present the user interface of the platform. We explain how users can evaluate a produced mining algorithm using sample datasets and we present the reproducibility features of the platform. Finally, we discuss in brief the future work.

2 Configuration Tools

A complete set of configuration tools are available, so that users are able to produce and update their algorithms. These tools are divided in three main categories:

- Preprocessing tools
- Processing tools
- Evaluation tools.

Preprocessing tools are all the tools that a data miner uses during the preprocessing phase of a text mining procedure. Such tools are stemmers, tockenizers, normalizers, etc. During this step the user uploads the concepts that are to be mined. Each concept consists of a string (i.e., its name) and a set of n-grams/phrases that usually are used when an author mentions this concept.

Processing tools include the main tools that a user utilises during the extraction phase. The algorithm runs a scrolling window over the text searching for matches. The user defines the length of this window. S/he also selects positive and negative weighted phrases. These phrases influence the confidence level of a match. Finally, the user selects the matching policy: when higher recall rates are prefered then the matching policy is more soft; otherwise the policy is strict.

Evaluation tools include the tools that are required to calculate the precision of an algorithm. Users are able to run their algorithms on predefined datasets or define and upload their own datasets. Moreover, during a run they have access to a preview where the matching areas, the positive/negative phrases, and the actual matches are highlighted. This makes the validation/update process easier since users are able to tune the algorithm rules and view online the results of their updates, thus facilitating rapid algorithm development.

3 User Interface

The user interface and its usability is very important since it provides the users with all the available tools to create the algorithm. In this section, we go through the portal and show how a user can produce algorithms, experiment himself, set his rules, etc.

Users are landed in the home page of the interactive mining platform which is shown in Fig. 1. Here, the user is able to see the saved profiles or create new profiles. Some example profiles are already available so that users may use them to familiarize themselves with the platform.

Figures 2 and 3 illustrate how the user uploads/edits his mining concepts. After selecting/creating a mining profile, users are able to configure their algorithm. The first step regards the addition/deletion of mining concepts. Users can either use the online form to edit their concepts or drag and drop a tabular file. For each concept users upload an identifying string and some phrases/n-grams that the authors often use to refer to this concept.

Figure 4 presents the main configuration and experiment page of the portal. When the concepts are ready, users are able to configure their mining rules. They can define their mining strategy (choose between high recall or high precision), add positive/negative phrases/keywords, tune the preprocessing steps, and modify the length of the mining area size (i.e., the length of the text area before and after a match that the algorithm uses as context to decide if a match is a true positive or not).

Positive phrases are phrases or keywords that are very likely to be found in the vicinity of a match. Different weights can be used to specify the relative importance of the different phrases. Negative phrases are phrases that when

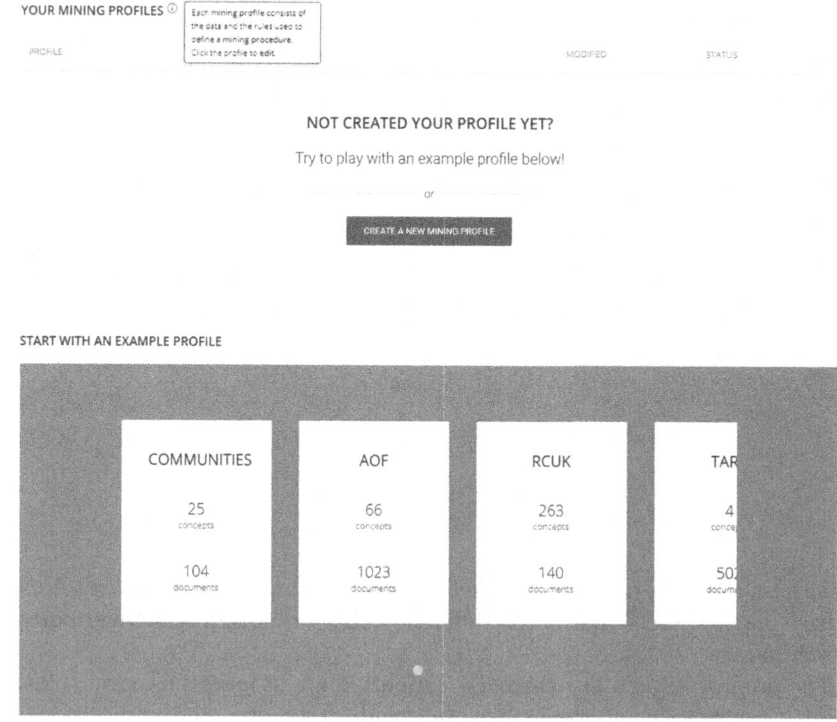

Fig. 1. Home page of the interactive mining platform

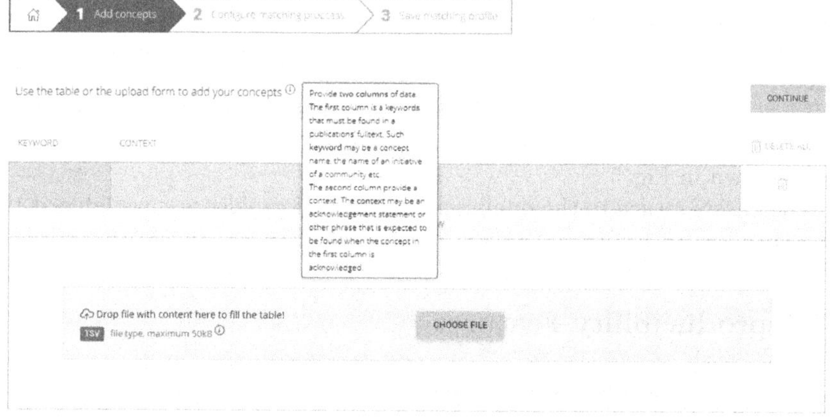

Fig. 2. Upload concepts

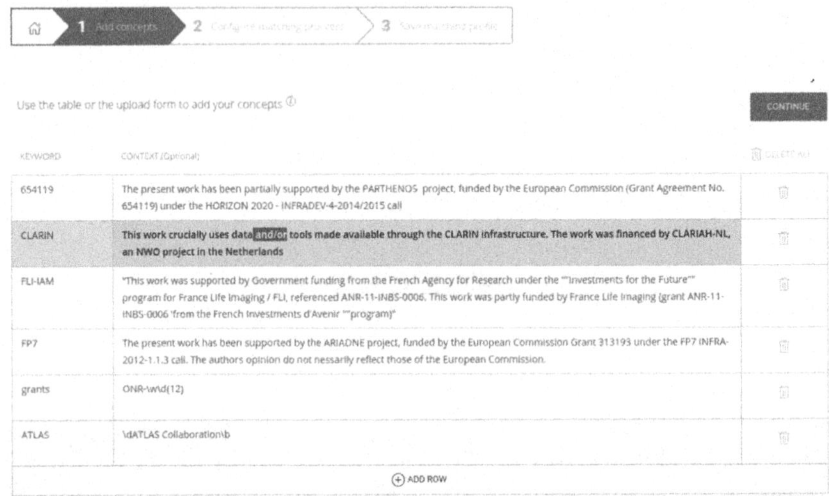

Fig. 3. Edit concepts

found near a match increase the likelihood of it being a true negative. As with positive phrases, users can specify different weights to assign relative importance to each phrase.

The preprocessing steps currently supported are stopword removal (removes common words such as articles like ‘an’, ‘and’, ‘the’, etc., and prepositions like ‘after’, ‘to’, etc.), punctuation removal, normalization (converting text to lower case), and word stemming (the process by which variant forms of a word are reduced to a common form, for example: connection, connections, connective, connected and connecting, are reduced to the stem ‘connect’).

Moreover, users can test online their mining rules against the selected datasets. The mining results are presented using annotated and highlighted text. The users edit their rules and run experiments repeatedly until they get valid results.

When users are satisfied with their mining rules they can continue to the last step of the mining configuration. Users can save their configuration for future use, as shown in Fig. 5.

When users return to the mining platform their profiles are available at their home page for further modifications and testing (Fig. 6).

4 Reproducibility Features

Since the purpose of the platform is to allow users to build and update their own mining algorithms, reproducibility features are highly important. Users should be able to revisit their algorithms, update their rules, and continue their experiments. To support this, a database file is stored for each user of the platform.

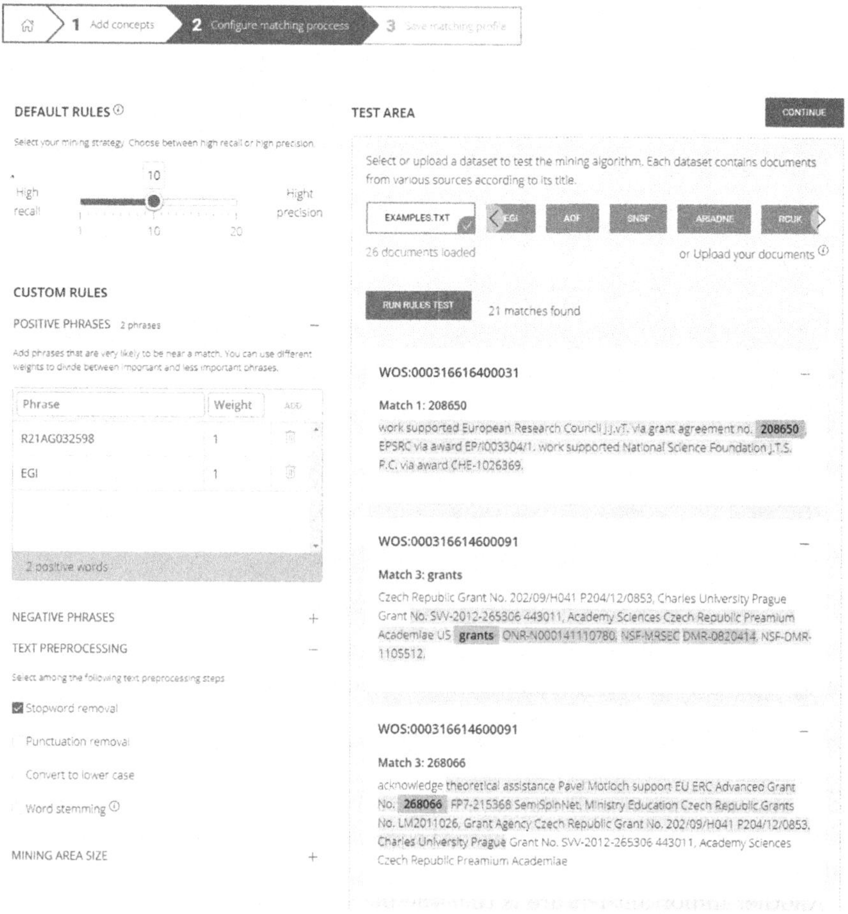

Fig. 4. Configuration Page. The page is split into two main horizontal sections. The left section is where users define their mining rules and choose between high recall or high precision with a slider. Here they can add or edit their positive and negative phrases/keywords, define the preprocessing steps to be used, and advanced users can also define the length of the text mining area size. The right section is the test area where mining results are presented using annotated and highlighted text, allowing users to tune their rules and run experiments repeatedly until they get valid results.

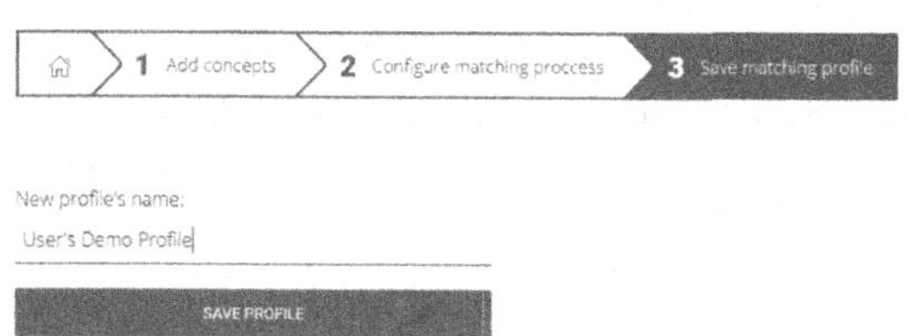

Fig. 5. Save a mining profile

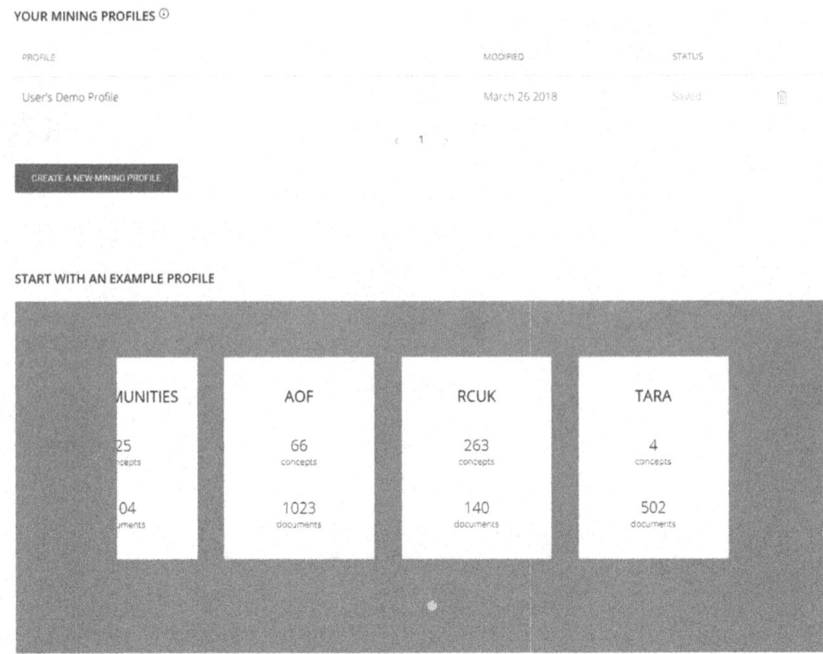

Fig. 6. When users revisit the mining platform their profiles are available at their home page for further modifications and testing.

This database contains all the saved algorithms per user. This list is shown to the users when they are connected to the portal. Users are able to select a profile and update it.

Another important feature is that the platform also maintains the history of the saved changes. So, users may visit a previous version of their algorithm. This is a very important feature that allows users to compare different versions.

5 Implementation Details

The mining platform is implemented using Python's Tornado Server[2]. Tornado is a Python web framework and asynchronous networking library using non-blocking network I/O. Its front end is implemented in Angular 4[3] and communicates with the back-end via a REST API.

The back-end is implemented on top of madIS [2], a powerful extension of a relational DBMS with user-defined data processing functionality. MadIS is built on top of the SQLite API[4].

[2] https://www.tornadoweb.org/en/stable/.
[3] https://angular.io.
[4] https://www.sqlite.org/.

MadIS allows the creation of user-defined functions (UDFs) in Python and it uses them in the same way as its native SQL functions. Both Python and SQLite are executed in the same process, greatly reducing the communication cost between them. This is a major architectural element and has a positive impact on joint performance.

MadIS is highly scalable, easily handling 10s of Gigabytes of data on a single machine. This benefit transparently carries over to distributed systems (e.g., Hadoop [3], Exareme [4]) which can use madIS in each node.

In madIS, queries are expressed in madQL: a SQL-based declarative language extended with additional syntax and user-defined functions (UDFs).[5] One of the goals of madIS is to eliminate the effort of creating and using UDFs by making them first-class citizens in the query language itself. To allow easy UDF editing with a text editor, madIS loads the UDF source code from the file system. Whenever a UDF's source code changes, madIS automatically reloads the UDF definition. This allows rapid UDF development iterations, which are common in data exploration and experimentation.

MadIS supports three types of UDFs:

- Row functions: Programmable row functions work in a similar way as standard SQL row functions such as abs(), lower() and upper().
- Aggregate functions: Programmable aggregate functions work in a similar way as standard SQL aggregate functions such as sum(), min() and max().
- Virtual table functions: These are actually functions that take parameters and output table like data. They can be used in the SQL syntax wherever a regular table would be placed.

All UDFs are written in Python and can use pre-existing Python libraries (NumPy[6], SciPy[7], etc.), thus inheriting features that are commonly used by data scientists [1].

The expressiveness and the performance of madIS allow developers to implement fast data analysis and complex text mining tasks [5–8]. The above were compelling reasons for choosing it as our processing engine.

The following is an example of an automatically produced query that text mines publications to extract links to research projects funded by the EC's seventh framework programme (FP7). The query preprocesses the text converting it to lower case and extracting its keywords, then joins the extracted keywords with the grants list and finally searches the context for positive words/phrases using pattern matching.

---

[5] MadIS, as well as the vast majority of other UDF systems, expects "functions" to be proper mathematical functions, i.e., to yield the same output for the same input, however, this property is not possible to ascertain automatically since the UDF language (Python) is unconstrained.

[6] http://www.numpy.org.

[7] https://www.scipy.org.

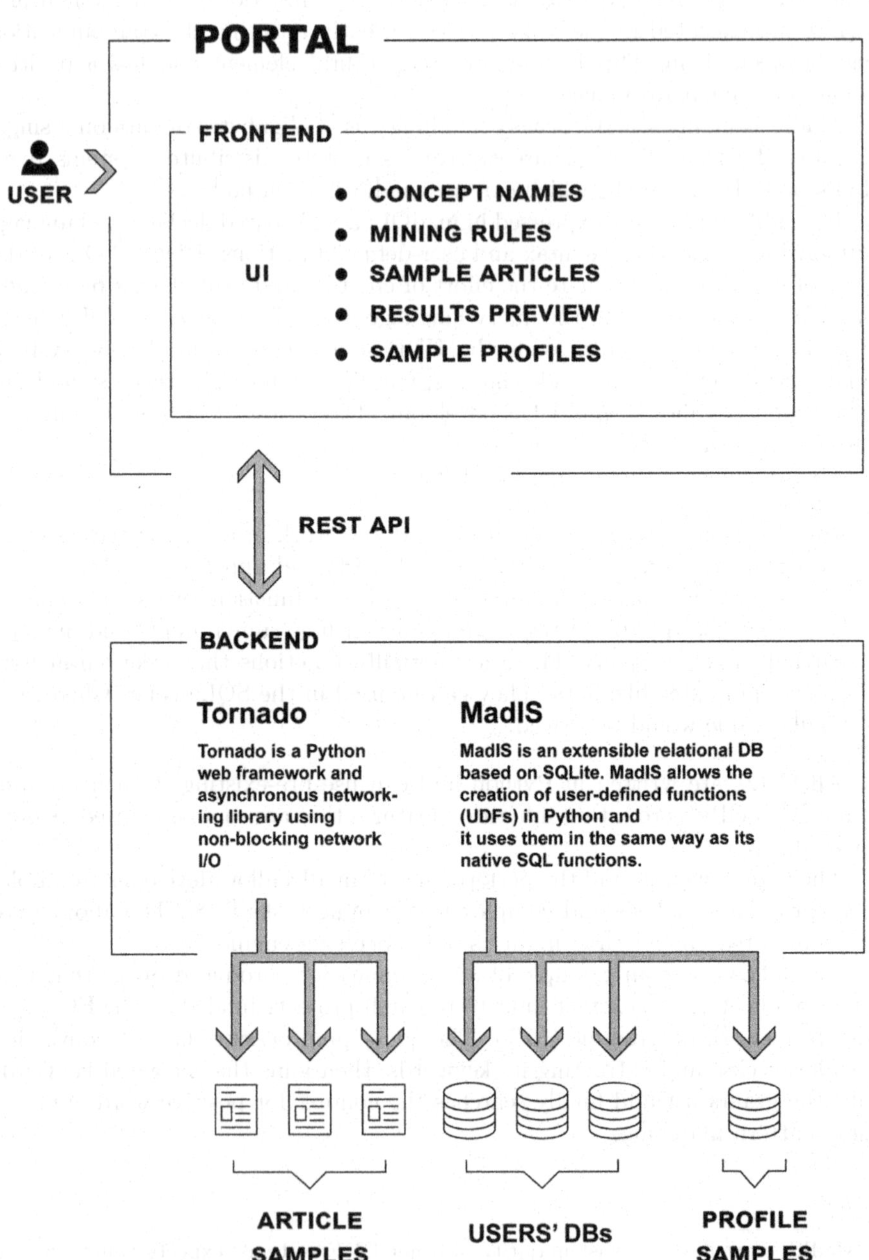

Fig. 7. Architecture of the platform

```
select docid, id, mining_category, mining_concept from (
    select * from (
        select
            document_id,
            textwindow(keywords(lower(document_text)), 20, 1, 20)
        from input_corpus
        ), concepts_list
        where mining_category = "FP7" and
              mining_concept=document_text_term and
              regexpr("fp7|support|grant|contract|funded|
                       european commission|acknowledge",text_window)
) group by document_id, mining_concept_id;
```

The user sets the parameters using the User Interface. These parameters are sent to the back-end where they are translated into an SQL query with the appropriate UDFs. All the processing is expressed within a single query. The query is run and stored for future use.

The architecture of the presented platform is shown in Fig. 7. The front-end includes the User Interface of the Platform and offers the necessary tools to the users. The back-end includes the Tornado Web Server and the processing engine (madIS). The storage layer contains the sample datasets, the sample mining profiles that are offered as examples, and one database file per user. The algorithms and other properties of each user are stored in this database.

6 Future Work

The future work mainly concentrates on utilization of machine learning techniques to make recommendations. Such recommendations are based on user's feedback. The platform could suggest both mining configurations according to already saved algorithms, and test datasets using topic modelling techniques.

Another useful functionality regards sharing of mining algorithms. A user may share his algorithm with the community so that an other user may validate it or even update it. History of all updates will be stored to support reproducibility.

Acknowledgements. This work is funded by the European Commission under H2020 projects OpenAIRE-Connect (grant number: 731011) and OpenAIRE-Advance (grant number: 777541).

References

1. Agrawal, R., Shim, K.: Developing tightly-coupled data mining applications on a relational database system. In: KDD (1996)
2. madIS, Lefteris Stamatogiannakis, Mei Li Triantafillidi, Yannis Foufoulas. http://www.github.com/magdik/madIS. Accessed 4 Oct 2018
3. Shvachko, K., Kuang, H., Radia, S., Chansler, R.: The hadoop distributed file system. In: 26th Symposium on Mass Storage Systems and Technologies (MSST) (2010)
4. Chronis, Y.: A relational approach to complex dataflows. In: EDBT/ICDT Workshops (2016)
5. Giannakopoulos, T., Foufoulas, I., Stamatogiannakis, E., Dimitropoulos, H., Manola, N., Ioannidis, Y.: Discovering and visualizing interdisciplinary content classes in scientific publications. D-Lib Mag. **20**(11), 4 (2014)

6. Giannakopoulos, T., Foufoulas, I., Stamatogiannakis, E., Dimitropoulos, H., Manola, N., Ioannidis, Y.: Visual-based classification of figures from scientific literature. In: Proceedings of the 24th International Conference on World Wide Web, pp. 1059–1060. ACM, May 2015
7. Giannakopoulos, T., Stamatogiannakis, E., Foufoulas, I., Dimitropoulos, H., Manola, N., Ioannidis, Y.: Content visualization of scientific corpora using an extensible relational database implementation. In: Bolikowski, Ł., Casarosa, V., Goodale, P., Houssos, N., Manghi, P., Schirrwagen, J. (eds.) TPDL 2013. CCIS, vol. 416, pp. 101–112. Springer, Cham (2014). https://doi.org/10.1007/978-3-319-08425-1_10
8. Foufoulas, Y., Stamatogiannakis, L., Dimitropoulos, H., Ioannidis, Y.: High-pass text filtering for citation matching. In: Kamps, J., Tsakonas, G., Manolopoulos, Y., Iliadis, L., Karydis, I. (eds.) TPDL 2017. LNCS, vol. 10450, pp. 355–366. Springer, Cham (2017). https://doi.org/10.1007/978-3-319-67008-9_28

Author Index

Printed in the United States
By Bookmasters